THE BRITISH WAY IN WARFARE 1688–2000

TITLES OF RELATED INTEREST

British diplomacy and foreign policy 1782–1865: the national interest
John C. Clarke

Crises in the British state 1880–1930
edited by Mary Langan and Bill Schwarz

The decline of British economic power since 1870
M. W. Kirby

European armies and the conduct of war
Hew Strachan

Evangelicalism in modern Britain: a history from the 1730s to the 1980s
David Bebbington

Fire-power: British army weapons and theories of war 1904–1945
Shelford Bidwell and Dominick Graham

In defence of naval supremacy: financial limitation, technological innovation and British naval policy
Jon Tetsuro Sumida

The making of the Second World War
Anthony P. Adamthwaite

Military effectiveness:
volume 1, *the First World War*
volume 2, *the interwar period*
volume 3, *the Second World War*
edited by Alan R. Millett and Williamson Murray

Modern England
R.K. Webb

The naval war in the Mediterranean 1914–1918
Paul G. Halpern

The origins of the Second World War reconsidered: the A. J. P. Taylor debate after twenty-five years
edited by Gordon Martel

Town and countryside: the English landowner in the national economy 1660–1860
edited by C. W. Chalkin and J. R. Wordie

The war years: a global history of the Second World War
Loyd Lee

Warfare in the twentieth century: theory and practice
edited by Colin J. McInnes and G. D. Sheffield

THE BRITISH WAY IN WARFARE 1688–2000

David French
University College, London

London
UNWIN HYMAN
Boston   Sydney   Wellington

© David French 1990

This book is copyright under the Berne Convention. No reproduction without permission. All rights reserved.

Published by the Academic Division of

Unwin Hyman Ltd
15/17 Broadwick Street, London W1V 1FP, UK

Unwin Hyman Inc.,
955 Massachusetts Avenue, Cambridge, Mass. 02139, USA

Allen & Unwin (Australia) Ltd,
8 Napier Street, North Sydney, NSW 2060, Australia

Allen & Unwin (New Zealand) Ltd in association with the
Port Nicholson Press Ltd,
Compusales Building, 75 Ghuznee Street, Wellington 1, New Zealand

First published in 1990

British Library Cataloguing in Publication Data

French, David *1954–*
 The British way in warfare, 1688–2000.
 1. Great Britain. Defence. Policies of government, history
 I. Title
 355.033541

 ISBN 0-04-445789-8
 ISBN 0-04-445791-X pbk

Library of Congress Cataloging in Publication Data

Available from the Library of Congress

Typeset in 10/12 point Garamond
Printed in Great Britain by The University Press, Cambridge

Contents

		Page	
	Acknowledgements		ix
	Introduction		xi
1	The Emergence of a Great Power, 1688–1714		1
2	War for Empire, 1714–63		32
3	The American War of Independence, 1763–83		62
4	The French Revolutionary and Napoleonic Wars		88
5	The Era of the 'Pax Britannica', *c* 1815–80		119
6	The Rise and Fall of the 'Blue Water' Policy		146
7	Deterrence and Dependence, 1917–42		175
8	The End of Empire, 1942–82		202
	Conclusion: From Thatcher to the Millennium		225
	Notes		240
	Guide to Further Reading		245
	Index		253

Acknowledgements

This book could not have been written without the help and encouragement of many people. Paul Kennedy suggested the subject to me many years ago and has since provided much unobtrusive encouragement. Brian Bond, Michael Dockrill, Brian Holden Reid and the members of the military history seminar at the Institute of Historical Research, University of London, have provided help and intellectual stimulation over more than fifteen years. I am grateful to Jeremy Black, John Darwin, Martin Daunton, Michael Handel, Julian Hoppit, Barry Hunt, Bill Mihiel, Keith Neilson, Reinhard Rummel, Alan and Caroline Russell, the Library of Congress and the Library of University College, London, who all assisted me in numerous ways. I am especially grateful to the Woodrow Wilson International Centre, Washington, DC, for giving me a Fellowship in 1988/9 to complete this book. Charles Blitzer, Sam Wells Jr and Rob Litwak and their colleagues went out of their way to provide perfect working conditions. Parts of this book have been given as papers before audiences at the Woodrow Wilson International Centre, the National War College, Fort McNair, Washington and the Royal Military College of Canada, Kingston, Ontario. I am most grateful to the participants for their comments. I alone am responsible for any errors of fact or judgement.

This publication was prepared (in part) under a grant from the Woodrow Wilson International Centre for Scholars, Washington, DC. The statements and views expressed herein are those of the author and are not necessarily those of the Wilson Centre.

This book is dedicated to the memory of my mother, Lillian Esther French and to Stephen Thomas Russell in the hope that he will grow up never to know the reality of war.

David French *London/Washington DC*

Introduction

In 1988 Sir John Nott, who had been Secretary of State for Defence from 1981 to 1983, compared the Ministry of Defence, and by implication current British defence policy, to 'a huge supertanker: well captained, well engineered, well crewed and with its systems being continuously updated, with no one ever asking where the hell it's going'.[1] It might seem presumptuous that a historian should attempt to answer the question implied in Sir John's criticism, where is British defence policy going and where ought it to go? It might seem paradoxical, or even irrelevant, that he should try to do so by writing a history of British defence policy beginning in 1688. My justification for attempting this task is my conviction that it is impossible to understand the choices facing today's defence policy-makers without some knowledge of the history of British defence policy over the last three hundred years.

It is necessary to explain the significance and meaning of the phrase 'defence policy'. Over the last three centuries British defence policy had to meet three criteria if it was to succeed. It had to provide an adequate measure of physical security for the home islands and for British interests overseas. It had to achieve those objectives at an acceptable cost. Policies which placed a ruinously high social, economic, or financial cost on British resources would have been counter-productive. They would have consumed the human and economic assets they were supposed to protect. And thirdly, although the limits of what was socially, economically and financially acceptable expanded in wartime, there were some barriers beyond which no prudent government could go in either peace or war. It required decades to create effective armies and navies. Their development would have been hopelessly hindered if, every time the political complexion of the government changed, so did the prevailing notions of a viable defence policy. Defence policies had to be acceptable to the politically dominant groups in British society. The study of British defence policy therefore involves an examination of the way in which Britain marshalled its human, economic and political resources to protect its security interests.

The book begins in 1688 because in that year Britain was successfully invaded for the last time. It also marked the start of a generation of warfare, which came to an end in 1714, during which Britain joined that select group of states which were recognized by their neighbours as being great powers. She retained that status until the second half of the twentieth century. Three things distinguished great powers from their lesser neighbours. They were secure against the attacks of single lesser powers, although they did have something to fear from other great powers or combinations of great powers. Their security interests extended beyond their own frontiers and went beyond mere territorial defence to embrace the maintenance of a continental or even a global balance. And they were able to project their military power beyond their own frontiers so they could wage offensive and defensive operations and assist their allies. Other members of this group, with their approximate entry and exit dates were France (1495–1940), Austria (1495–1918), Spain (1495–1808), the Ottoman Empire (1495–1699), the Netherlands (1609–1713), Sweden (1617–1721), Russia (1721 to date), Prussia/Germany (1740–1945), Italy (1863–1943), Japan (1905–45), China (1949 to date) and USA (1898 to date).

Between 1688 and 1945 Britain participated in twelve wars in which she was pitted against one or more great powers. They are listed in Table I.1. A series of paradigms has been developed to explain the course of British defence policy since 1688. They can be divided into two categories: those which have been used to analyse the policies adopted by the British in their relations with their continental neighbours in peacetime and those which have been employed to analyse the ways in which the British conducted their great power wars. For the sake of convenience the first will be referred to as 'peacetime' paradigms and the second as 'wartime' paradigms.

The most commonly employed peacetime paradigm has suggested that British security rested on a stable balance of power in Europe. Britain only intervened directly in continental affairs when the balance of power was in jeopardy because of the danger that one power or a coalition of powers was about to go to war to

Table I.1 Britain's Great Power Wars since 1688

1689–97	Nine Years' War in alliance with Spain, Austria and Holland against France
1702–13	War of the Spanish Succession in alliance with Austria and Holland against France and Spain
1718–20	War of the Quadruple Alliance in alliance with France, Holland and Austria against Spain
1726–9	Anglo-Spanish War
1739–48	War of Jenkins's Ear/War of the Austrian Succession in alliance with Austria against France and Spain
1756–63	Seven Years' War in alliance with Prussia against France and Spain
1775–83	American War of Independence against the Thirteen Colonies, France and Spain
1793–1802	French Revolutionary Wars in alliance with Spain, Austria, Russia and Prussia against France
1803–15	Napoleonic Wars in alliance with Spain, Austria, Russia and Prussia against France
1854–6	Crimean War in alliance with France against Russia
1914–18	First World War in alliance with Russia, France, Italy, Japan and USA against Germany and Austria
1939–45	Second World War in alliance with France, USA and Russia against Germany, Italy and Japan

impose their hegemony on their neighbours. At other times Britain remained aloof from entangling European alliances so she could devote resources to expanding her interests outside Europe. Quincy Wright argued that the pursuit of the balance of power became part of the doctrine of British foreign policy in the late seventeenth and early eighteenth centuries and was formerly recognized as the basis of the Peace of Utrecht. Neutrality at all other times was advantageous to Britain because 'To be able to remain neutral is to hold the balance of power'.[2] David Thomson characterized the exponents of this policy in the nineteenth century as 'A succession of great foreign ministers...[who]... developed a characteristically free-handed British foreign policy'.[3]

Between 1688 and 1850 Britain could do this because she was an island and because the British people were prepared to spend money to make the Royal Navy the most powerful fleet in European waters. The Hundred Years' War had cured the British of any desire to acquire continental territory. Instead they sought wealth in overseas trade and empire. However, after c. 1850 the spread of the industrial revolution to Britain's continental neighbours and the United States, and the impact of industrial technology on naval power, eroded the security which Britain's island geography had once conferred upon her. By the beginning of the twentieth century Britain's relative power had so declined that she could no longer remain aloof and hold the balance of power. In 1904 she was forced to take the side of one of the continental alliances and since then she has not been able to create such a stable balance that she could afford to remain aloof from continental entanglements.

The analysis of the wartime paradigms must begin with an examination of the works of the German military philosopher Carl von Clausewitz, the author of *On War*. Clausewitz did not write a systematic analysis of the way in which Britain conducted her wars but because his book transcended the experiences of any one nation, it deserves to be the starting-point of any study of British policy. Clausewitz argued that war was an act of force exerted by one state on another to compel the latter to submit to the former's will. It was not an autonomous activity but 'a continuation of political activity by other means'.[4] In theory there was no logical limit to the force which belligerents might deploy against each other. But in practice 'real war' never quite reached this 'absolute' state, although he believed that it had come close to it during the Napoleonic Wars. The degree of violence employed by belligerents was constrained by several factors. 'Friction', a product of physical fatigue, misleading or inadequate intelligence concerning the enemy, poor judgement, bad luck and the technological limitations under which all armed forces laboured, conspired 'to lower the general level of performance, so that one always falls short of the intended goal'.[5] The manifold problems associated with mobilizing armed forces and engaging allies made it impossible for states to bring all of their resources to bear against their enemies simultaneously. And the degree of force which belligerents exerted was conditioned by their political purpose. Each 'would act on the principle of using no greater force, and setting himself no greater military aim, than would be sufficient for the achievement of his political purpose'.[6] Many wars, particularly in the eighteenth century, ended before one side or the other had suffered total political collapse. The cost of inflicting such an outcome upon the enemy, even if it were practical, far outweighed the political aims for which his opponent had gone to war. If the objective for which a state was fighting was limited, a strategy designed to induce the enemy to negotiate peace terms by disrupting his alliances or wearing down his resources by occupying one or more of his provinces was more cost-effective than one designed to produce his complete military and political collapse.

In the late nineteenth and early twentieth centuries two writers attempted to use Clausewitz's insights to analyse British practices. They were the American Captain A. T. Mahan, author of *The Influence of Sea Power upon History* (1889) and *The Influence of Sea Power upon the French Revolution and Empire, 1793–1812* (1893) and the Englishman Sir Julian Corbett, author of *Some Principles of Maritime Strategy*, (1911). Each took a particular strand of Clausewitz's ideas and used it as the starting-point to develop a maritime paradigm of Britain's wartime policy. Although Mahan wanted to determine the significance of sea-power upon the course of history and the prosperity of nations, much of his work examined the basis of Britain's naval predominance between 1660 and 1815. He suggested that 'It was not by attempting great military operations on land but by controlling the sea, and through the sea the world outside Europe,' that the two Pitts 'ensured the triumph of their country'.[7] Britain rarely committed her own troops to major operations on the continent, preferring instead to use the income generated by her burgeoning colonial trade to subsidize her allies. 'The system of subsidies, which began nearly half a century before in the wars of Marlborough and received its most extensive development half a century later in the Napoleonic wars, maintained the efforts of her allies, which would have been crippled, if not paralysed without them'.[8]

Mahan was determined to discover a series of decisive naval battles which altered the course of history. He imposed Clausewitz's analysis of Napoleonic warfare on to Britain's eighteenth-century wars without understanding the importance of the distinction Clausewitz made between limited and unlimited war. In the words of one of his critics, he 'did not grasp the fact that it [eighteenth-century warfare] was limited, not only because of technology and manpower, but also because of shifting limited objectives as well'.[9] Corbett did understand that distinction and developed it constructively. He wrote his book to illustrate the profound differences between 'the British or Maritime School – that is our own traditional School' and the 'German or Continental School of Strategy'.[10] He suggested that Britain could fight a series of limited wars in the eighteenth century because the Royal Navy was sufficiently powerful to ensure that her enemies could never transform them into unlimited wars by invading the home islands. He had a shrewd appreciation of the practical limitations of sea-power. The British had employed their fleet not to seek the complete overthrow of their enemies but to emerge from the war with some material advantages 'which were usually colonial or overseas territory'.[11]

Neither Mahan nor Corbett argued that Britain had ever waged purely maritime wars. They accepted that Britain had required an army for home defence because, given the vagaries of winds and tides, the fleet could not be certain of intercepting small expeditions sent against Britain. The land forces in Britain had to be sufficiently strong to compel an enemy to come in such large numbers that they would be sure to be intercepted at sea. They agreed that when Britain had employed troops outside Britain they had been most effective when they had been used in an amphibious role to raid the enemy's coastline and compel him to withdraw forces which might otherwise have been used to fight Britain's continental allies, to cripple the enemy's fleet by destroying his naval bases, or to capture his overseas colonies.

In a seminal lecture which he gave to the Royal United Services Institute for Defence Studies in 1931 Captain (Sir) Basil Liddell Hart tried to synthesize their ideas into what he later called the 'British way in warfare'. He argued that since the sixteenth century continental military expeditions had played only a minor role in British policy. Instead Britain had relied upon her fleet to cripple her continental enemies. By disrupting their colonial trade and capturing their colonies, Britain had not only denied her enemies the means to pay for their war effort, but she had also augmented her own resources.

> Our historic practice, as we have seen, was based on economic pressure exercised through sea-power. This naval body had two arms; one financial, which embraced the subsidizing and military provisioning of allies; the other military, which embraced seaborne expeditions against the enemy's vulnerable extremities.[12]

He could only lament the fact that during the First World War the British had abandoned this 'British way in warfare' and sent a continental-scale army to France because policy-makers had been seduced by the mistaken notion that their proper objective was to destroy the German army.

The notion that there was a peculiarly 'British way in warfare' is now deeply rooted in the literature of British defence policy. A concise contemporary exposition was provided by Christopher Layne who wrote in 1979 that

> Prior to approximately 1900, British grand strategy was based on the protection of her overseas Empire and on avoiding committing major British forces to do battle on the Continent of Europe. With respect to Europe, Britain sought to use her naval superiority to blockade continental enemies and to conduct raids against the enemy's homeland and overseas possessions. While Britain, in numerous past wars, had utilized her financial strength to organize and subsidize the armies of her European allies, she had never sent a major portion of her own army to fight on the Continent. Even the armies of Britain's two most renowned generals, Marlborough and Wellington, were primarily composed of European, rather than British, troops.[13]

But even in the eighteenth century Whig politicians could be found who accepted that Britain had to fight her enemies with armies sent to the continent. More recently Correlli Barnett, without proposing a comprehensive alternative paradigm, has suggested that the notion of the 'British way in warfare' was strategically flawed: 'The navy can and has assured British survival; but is only of limited value as an instrument of national policy in Europe or in the interior of any other continent'. When Britain tried to limit her war effort to naval forces and small expeditions, she was usually unsuccessful. Expeditions sent to the West Indies usually 'failed to collect anything but yellow fever'. The wars against Louis XIV, Napoleon, the Kaiser and Hitler were fought to prevent France and then Germany establishing their hegemony in Europe. Since Britain's enemies were self-sufficient land powers, they could not be defeated by depriving them of their colonies. He wrote that 'Only when expeditionary forces have been transformed into a field army on the Continent "for the duration", able and willing to fight major battles against European opponents, has British intervention been decisive'.[14]

An alternative paradigm to the 'British way in warfare' has been suggested by G. S. Graham, Michael Howard and Paul Kennedy. For want of a better title it can be labelled the 'mixed' paradigm. They accepted the navalists' arguments concerning the link between sea-power, the acquisition of colonies and national wealth, but they denied that Britain alone, even when she had a powerful navy and army, could expect to defeat a continental great power, or even safeguard her own security. Graham suggested that the American War of Independence demonstrated that 'Without allied support on the continent to divert French energies, the Royal Navy was not strong enough to ensure continuous control even in the Channel. Unless buttressed by effective alliances on the Continent, command of the sea was a delusive concept'.[15] Britain's victories against France in the eighteenth century and Germany in the twentieth century were won by powerful British naval and land forces operating in conjunction with continental allies.

> Without Frederick the Great on the continent, Britain would never have won so handsome an empire in 1763, and in similar fashion the Second British Empire of 1815 owed more than can be calculated to British allies who in the final years of the war against Napoleon prepared the way for Waterloo as the indispensable sequel to Trafalgar.[16]

Kennedy suggested that Mahan ignored a number of non-naval factors which were of considerable importance in enabling Britain to defeat France between 1688 and 1815. In all but one of the six wars she fought against France, French power was drained not just by the Royal Navy but by Britain's continental allies. Britain did not just support her allies with gold but she also dispatched her own troops to fight in their support. According to Howard

> a commitment of support to a Continental ally in the nearest available theatre, on the largest scale that contemporary resources could afford, so far from being alien

to traditional British strategy, was absolutely central to it. The flexibility provided by sea power certainly made possible other activities as well: colonial conquest, trade war, help to allies in Central Europe, minor amphibious operations, but these were ancillary to the great decisions by land, and they continued to be so throughout the two world wars. Secondly, when we did have recourse to a purely maritime strategy, it was always as a result, not of free choice or atavistic wisdom, but of *force majeure*. It was a strategy of necessity rather than of choice, of survival rather than of victory.[17]

These paradigms can be reduced to a number of propositions which are capable of being tested. Politicians expressed their strategic preferences by their willingness to enter into alliances and to spend money on one service at the expense of the other. If the peacetime paradigm accurately reflected British practice, British statesmen should have pursued a policy of diplomatic isolation between each war, they should have been more reluctant than their continental colleagues to enter into alliances with their neighbours and in peacetime the Royal Navy should have absorbed the lion's share of the defence estimates. If the 'British way in warfare' paradigm of Britain's wartime practice was correct, policy-makers relied upon the navy, and it should have continued to absorb the lion's share of defence spending. The army should have remained a Cinderella service which performed two functions. It should have maintained a sufficiently large force at home to ensure that if an enemy did attempt an invasion he would have to concentrate such a large number of warships and transports that the Royal Navy would have ample opportunity to intercept him before he landed. The army should have operated in conjunction with the fleet to raid the enemy's coast or to capture enemy colonies. The British should rarely have committed large armies to the European mainland and when they did so their commitment should have been confined to foreign mercenaries rather than subject, i.e. British, troops and to subsidies granted to foreign princes. But if the mixed paradigm reflected British wartime practices, policy-makers should have consistently balanced the needs of the army and the navy and allotted approximately equal financial resources to them. They may have dispatched some troops to occupy the enemy's colonies or to raid his coast and they may have spent some funds subsidizing European partners, but they should also have sent the largest possible landforce to Europe to operate in conjunction with their allies.

In examining the development of British defence policy since 1688 this book will attempt to test these propositions. One way in which it will do so is by examining the way in which Parliament voted to divide the money it was willing to spend on defence between sea services and land services. From the outset, the reader must be aware that the figures given here need to be treated with caution. For the period before 1868 the figures have been taken from those compiled by a senior Treasury clerk, H. W. Chisolm and published in *Parliamentary Papers* 1868/9, vol. xxxv. For the period after 1869 they have been taken from B. R. Mitchell and P. Deane's *An Abstract of British Historical Statistics*[18] and, for the period of the two twentieth-century world wars, from *Parliamentary Papers*.

Certain adjustments to these figures have been made of which the reader should be aware. Until the Act of Union the Irish Exchequer funded that part of the army stationed in Ireland and the cost of the Irish establishment has been included in calculating the proportion of defence spending devoted to land services before 1801. In calculating the proportion of defence spending devoted to sea services in the eighteenth century it would be unrealistic to take account only of the monies granted annually by Parliament to meet the navy estimates. To a large extent the eighteenth-century navy ran on tick. Until the 1820s Parliament permitted the navy to amass a considerable debt by allowing it to issue its own bills and the value of this debt has been included in calculating total spending on the navy. A second way in which this book will attempt to test the validity of the paradigms under investigation is by analysing the way in which the policy-making elite tried to deploy Britain's landforces. It is assumed that each government had three options. It could retain troops at home, it could deploy them on the continent of Europe, or it could commit them to overseas theatres outside Europe. Evidence for the way in which policy-makers wished to deploy troops was drawn from the annual army votes recorded in the *Journals of the House of Commons* for the period 1688–1815. For the two world wars it was taken from the orders of battle prepared by the Official Historians. The data used was based upon establishments voted by Parliament before 1815 and numbers of divisions after 1914. For reasons which will be alluded to in this book, the number of soldiers actually deployed on the ground often fell short of these theoretical maximums. The figures given here often represent the aspirations of policy-makers rather than their achievements.

1 The Emergence of a Great Power, 1688–1714

Almost from the moment he became king in 1661 Louis XIV wished to expand France's borders. By acquiring territory in north-west Italy, western Germany and the Netherlands he hoped to add glory to his reputation and to be able to erect a barrier of fortresses around France to protect her from invasion. His ambitions provoked a series of protracted wars which continued intermittently until almost the end of his reign in 1715. The English were drawn into this struggle in November 1688 when the *Stadholder* of the United Provinces, William III, invaded England. William came because he had been invited by a group of Protestant nobles who feared that James II meant to Catholicize England, because he wanted to safeguard the inheritance of his wife, James's daughter Mary, and because he wanted to use English resources in his struggle against Louis.

European observers in the 1680s recognized the existence of five great powers, France, Spain, the Holy Roman Empire ruled by the Austrian Habsburgs, Sweden and the United Provinces. The England of James II was numbered amongst the powers of the second rank, together with states like Portugal, Bavaria and Savoy. They only had sufficient power to play an independent role intermittently. States acquired their position in this hierarchy because of their size, location, population, natural resources and the ability of their governments to mobilize their wealth and use it to raise powerful armed forces. On all of those counts Louis XIV's France was Europe's predominant great power in 1688. England was to emerge as a great power during the generation of almost continuous war against France which she fought between 1689 and 1714.

The Glorious Revolution reversed thirty years of pro-French policy in England. Earlier in the century England had fought three wars against Holland but they were intended to destroy Dutch shipping and trade, not to alter the political configuration of the continent. Before 1688 England had demonstrated that she was a considerable naval power but her military interventions on the continent in the seventeenth century had been brief and sporadic and her armed forces were not supported by the complex infrastructure of barracks, fortifications and dockyards that other powers, notably France, had developed, to enable them regularly to project their naval and military power beyond their own borders. But after 1688 England for the first time began to display a sustained interest in determining the political configuration of the continent and to develop the logistical potential that enabled her to rival her great power neighbours. This transformation was due to three factors: William was a Dutchman and a statesman with a European-wide vision; the English were ambitious to further their trade; but, most important of all, it was due to the determination of most Englishmen to maintain England as a Protestant state.

Under William the English did not seek to crush France, merely to curb her power. Rather than trying to annihilate their enemy's armed forces in battle and to occupy his capital, the English tried to achieve their aims by a process of attrition. To the twentieth-century observer that might suggest that they sought to wreck their enemies' economies by blockade and to exhaust their manpower in a series of great battles. Such concepts were anachronistic in the late seventeenth-century. Wars had a comparatively small impact on the fundamentally agrarian economies of Europe where the harvest remained the most important economic event. A naval blockade might be able to disrupt a nation's overseas trade and exacerbate local famines by interrupting the movement of food around the coast, but it could not reduce a nation as rich as France to starvation. The enlistment in wartime of considerable numbers of underemployed farm labourers had only a small disruptive impact on levels of agricultural production.

In the face of the immense problems and costs involved in raising, equipping and maintaining armies and navies, late seventeenth century rulers were reluctant to hazard them in battle unless they were nearly certain of victory. The path to success in war lay through bankrupting the enemy's treasury. Rather than attempt the impossible and starve their enemies into submission or kill so many of their troops that their armies disintegrated, the English tried to force their enemies to consume their resources on land and at sea faster than they could replace them. This strategy was facilitated by the fact that all belligerents accepted that war should impinge as little as possible on the civil economy. Once a state's supply of specie were exhausted, once it had reached the narrow limits within which the money supply could safely be inflated and once its opportunities to borrow had run dry, it had no option other than to make peace. If it chose to continue fighting beyond that point it risked wrecking the things it was trying to protect, the political and economic fabric of its society. England's objective was to reduce her enemies to the point at which they were so short of money that their armies were melting away because their troops were unpaid and their ships and crews were rotting at their moorings because there was no money to victual or repair them. When they were reduced to that position they could either continue the war and face total collapse or they could negotiate peace before calamity overtook them. As long as the English were ready to offer them even half reasonable terms, they chose the second course.

Between 1688 and 1714 William and his successors and their subjects fought the French for three reasons. The Glorious Revolution marked the point at which England began to exhibit a continuous interest in the preservation of a balance of power in Europe. William contributed to this by trying to preserve the liberty of the European states threatened by French aggrandizement because he believed that the Protestant religion would not be safe in a state system dominated by Catholic France. The treaty by which England acceded to the Grand Alliance of 1701 contained no mention of the need to preserve a European 'balance', but it did warn of the danger that if Spain and France were united under one throne they might be sufficiently powerful to dominate the whole of Europe. William's subjects were quicker to discern that the easiest way to check French aggrandizement was by creating a force to balance it. In 1697 the Commons thanked William for giving England 'the honour ... of holding the Balance of Europe'. In 1713 the government claimed for itself 'the same principle ... [which is] to preserve the equilibrium in Europe'.[1] But there remained three questions. What exactly was the balance of power (because few of the men who used the phrase so glibly bothered to define it with any rigour); how to determine if it was threatened; and how should Britain act to maintain it? They were to beset policy-makers for a long time after 1714.

Whatever the precise answers to these questions, the fact that the pursuit of the balance of power was a major policy goal limited the way in which the English used their armed forces to secure their objectives. The need to secure a more stable balance implied that they were seeking to reduce their enemies' power, not that they were trying to destroy them completely. Had Britain, as she may be called after the Union between England and Scotland in 1707, achieved the total overthrow of Bourbon France between 1689 and 1714, she would only have succeeded in creating another set of problems. Other powers would have become as suspicious of an over-mighty Britain as they had been of an over-mighty France. Britain might have found herself the victim of a hostile coalition determined to reduce her power in much the same way that she had helped to create two coalitions to check Louis's ambitions.

The second reason why the English fought France was to further their overseas trade. In the century after 1660 economic thinkers believed that wealth and state power were synonymous. A favourable balance of trade was welcomed because it increased England's stocks of precious metals and her ability to pay for her wars. In 1651, 1660 and 1662 Parliament passed Navigation Acts in an effort to undermine the role of the Dutch as the world's carrier, to foster England's merchant marine and increase the basis of England's naval power. Henceforth England's trade with her colonies could only be carried in English-owned ships manned by English sailors. Colonies were coveted because they provided a secure source of raw materials and foodstuffs which did not drain precious specie out of the English economy. After 1660 the French began to replace the Dutch in the minds of English merchants as their major competitors. In 1674 a group of London cloth merchants, incensed that French tariff policies discriminated against the export of English cloth, drew up the *Scheme of Trade*. Its statistics were almost pure invention. They purported to show that England was suffering from an annual deficit of nearly £1,000,000 on direct trade with France. For the rest of the seventeenth century and into the next, the *Scheme* was one of the staples of anti-French polemicists who never tired of pointing to the connection between France's burgeoning overseas trade and her naval and military power. Ministers could never be deaf to the interests of overseas merchants for they produced income which could readily be taxed. But the emphasis which the English placed on trade again served to limit the ways in which they used their military power. It meant that victory or defeat could be calculated according to the number and profitability of the colonies or ships lost or won.

The third reason why the English fought France made her an exception to the generalization that after the Thirty Years' War religious rancour was no longer a motivating force in the European great power system. In 1688 William and his wife Mary, the daughter of James II, were invited to invade England because a significant part of the English political nation feared that James II was determined to impose Catholicism on his Protestant subjects. James fled to France where the Catholic Louis XIV, whose revocation of the Edict of Nantes in 1685 had caused consternation amongst Protestant Englishmen, promised support to regain him his throne. Louis's refusal to recognize the legitimacy of the new English monarchy and the armed support which he gave to the Jacobite cause, was one reason for the enmity in Anglo-French relations which marked this period. Although French support for Jacobitism waned after Louis's death in 1715 it did not disappear. It re-emerged, albeit in an attenuated form during the War of the Austrian Succession, and at times other states, notably Sweden and Spain, were willing to support the Jacobites. An outright French victory in any one of the wars which she waged against Britain down to 1763 would have threatened the Protestant succession. It was the need to preserve the Protestant regime which, more than anything else, persuaded Englishmen who might otherwise have been reluctant to become involved in expensive European wars that they had little choice in the matter.

The use of the phrase 'the English' in the preceding paragraphs is a convenient shorthand for those monarchs, courtiers, politicians, soldiers, sailors, diplomats and members of the political nation outside Whitehall and Westminster, who had some say in the making of defence policy or who aspired to have some influence over how it was made. All late Stuart and Hanoverian monarchs, with the possible exception of Queen Mary, were determined to rule as well as to reign. None could do so without the assistance of trusted ministers and all discovered that the structure of British domestic politics placed considerable limitations on their freedom to wage war when and how they chose. The ability of a number of competing elites, each of which was represented in Parliament, to influence the development of defence policy was the reason why that policy was apparently so inconsistent. No particular political or professional faction was ever able to exercise exclusive control over policy-making for more than a brief period. William III had a freer hand than any of his successors. Before 1688 England had not been a great power and few English politicians had sufficient experience of European affairs to assist the king. He relied upon Dutch and Huguenot advisers. But the war meant that for eight years William was almost an absentee king, and it gave some English ministers a practical education in statecraft and strategy.

After 1688 no monarch could make policy without some thought as to what the reaction would be in Parliament and the wider political nation. The discussion of defence policy could not be confined to choosing between strictly naval and military options because it almost always involved matters of political patronage and domestic politics. Late Stuart and Hanoverian England was governed by a small, cohesive territorial oligarchy and their clients. The aristocracy was not a closed caste but intermarriage, a common educational experience, shared political ideals, the ownership of a considerable proportion of the national wealth and, before about 1780, the paucity of new creations made it seem so. Only the aristocracy proper had the right to a seat in the House of Lords. Substantial members of the much larger class of landed gentry aspired to a seat in the Commons. These two groups exercised a virtual stranglehold not just on high political office, but also on high military and naval offices. The military and civil powers thus overlapped. Serving officers formed one of the largest professional groups in the eighteenth-century Commons. But land was not the only interest represented in Parliament. Many members of the Lords and the landed gentry also had commercial investments and by 1761 about one in nine MPs was a merchant or a lawyer. This interconnection between landed and mercantile wealth was important because it inclined the governing class to take a broad view of what constituted the national interest.

Each House was responsible for its own affairs but their joint approval was necessary for the passage of legislation. The Revolution Settlement placed no limits on the king's power to dissolve the Commons, but the pressure of business caused by the wars against Louis XIV and the government's need for money ensured that it met annually. Sessions usually began in the autumn at the end of the campaigning season and lasted for between four and five months. In wartime their main business was to vote supplies for the next campaign, a duty which fell upon the Commons for in 1671 and again in 1678 they had resolved that the Lords had no powers to reject or even to amend a money bill. In return for granting supplies, Parliament expected that the executive would keep them informed of their plans. Regular meetings of the two Houses gave MPs and peers the opportunity to press their own, sometimes ill-informed, strategic ideas upon the government.

William inherited a potentially powerful fleet but one which was in some respects badly prepared to fight France. Its main bases, on the Thames and Medway, had been developed in the wars against the Dutch. They were in the wrong place to support a navy which now had to counter the French based at

Brest. The prevailing winds meant that Brest was to windward of the existing English dockyards. Until the English improved their facilities at Portsmouth and developed a new base at Plymouth in the 1690s, the French had the advantage of wind and geography. The Royal Navy was one of England's largest importers of raw materials, employers of labour and biggest shipbuilders. It was controlled by the Board of Admiralty, presided over by the First Lord of the Admiralty. He and his colleagues were responsible for the conduct of naval policy. They were assisted by a number of subordinate boards. The Navy Board, managed by the Controller, was responsible for the general administration of the navy including the making of contracts for stores and the construction of ships and dockyards. Naval finances were the responsibility of the Treasurer of the Navy. In theory he was a member of the Navy Board, but in practice he was independent of it. The Victualling Board ensured, with a growing degree of success, that the fleet was fed, although during the Nine Years' War some commanders were compelled to alter their plans because supplies failed to arrive. In 1689 a temporary Sick and Wounded board was established to tend the navy's casualties.

The system worked if relations between the First Lord of the Admiralty and the heads of the subordinate boards were cordial and if the former had the inclination to master some of the intricate details of the civil administration of the navy. The weakest link in the chain of administration was the way in which ships were armed. The supply of cannon, powder and shot for both the army and the navy lay not with the services themselves, but with a separate organization, the Board of Ordnance. This division of responsibilities was a frequent source of friction. The Ordnance Board enjoyed a reputation for corruption and procrastination which was almost legendary. Some of it was undeserved for there were occasions when other government departments failed to tell the Board what their plans were so that it could place the necessary orders in good time.

Under the later Stuarts approximately a quarter of all government revenue was spent on the navy. The construction and repair of warships and the maintenance of dockyards accounted for about half of all naval spending. The largest dockyards, Chatham, Woolwich, Deptford, Sheerness and Portsmouth, were some of the largest industrial enterprises in the country. Warships were rated according to the number of guns they carried. First (90–100 guns), second (80–90 guns) and third (70–80 guns) were larger than most merchant ships and were usually constructed in one of the royal dockyards. But their building capacity was limited. In 1691 they could build no more than thirteen large vessels simultaneously and in wartime many of their berths were occupied by ships undergoing repairs. The Navy Board turned to private yards to construct the fourth- fifth- and sixth-raters the navy needed to protect commerce. But vessels built in private yards were frequently constructed to the wrong dimensions, were delivered late and were built from inferior materials. The use of the correct materials was crucial if ships were not to be in constant need of repair. Although the navy preferred to use English oak for hulls, most raw materials were imported from New England or, more usually, from the states bordering the Baltic. The fact that such a large proportion of the naval stores the Admiralty needed came from the Baltic gave the English an abiding strategic interest in the region. When the outbreak of the Great Northern War in 1700 threatened to interrupt this trade, the government tried to encourage the trade in naval stores with the North American colonies. But colonial supplies never replaced goods from the Baltic. This was a major strategic weakness. Britain either had to remain on good terms with the Baltic powers or she had to be able to deploy a powerful squadron in the Baltic to overawe them.

A well-constructed ship-of-the-line had a life expectancy of about fourteen years. Ships which had been hastily built with unseasoned timber, as many were in wartime, had a shorter life expectancy. These limits were not set by technological obsolescence. Changes in ship design happened only slowly. It was determined by the fact that wooden ships were liable to two forms of rot, which, if left unchecked could destroy the fleet. Dry rot ate away ships' timbers from the inside just as sea-worms could bore into their timbers from the outside. No satisfactory remedy was ever found to eliminate dry rot. Attacks by sea-worms were particularly prevalent in the warm waters of the Mediterranean and Caribbean. The Royal Navy paid for its interest in those seas with the destruction of whole squadrons of ships until the application of copper sheathing to the hulls of vessels during the American War of Independence helped to reduce the depredations of sea-worms.

In peacetime the navy had little difficulty in attracting able-bodied seamen. In 1688 England's total seafaring population numbered some 50,000 men and the fleet only needed 12,700 men. In peacetime naval pay rates did not lag far behind those in the merchant service. But in every major war until the mid-nineteenth century manning the fleet presented the Admiralty with constant problems. In wartime the wages of merchant seamen and the Admiralty's demand for more hands both rose sharply. By 1695 the fleet needed 48,500 seamen and it could not hope to compete with the merchant service on the open market for labour. The navy could have employed almost every able-bodied merchant seaman in the kingdom. It usually applied the same remedies, offering bounties to attract trained seamen from the merchant marine. But such measures were insufficient and inevitably the navy resorted to the press-gang. Even though the press was only supposed to take up trained seamen it was unpopular. However, as long as the merchant interest in Parliament refused to allow the government to fix a ceiling on the wages they could offer merchant seamen, and as long as the landed gentry continued to abhor anything tending to increase the power of the executive, there was little hope of placing the supply of seamen for the fleet on a more systematic basis by compiling a register of merchant seamen liable to serve in the fleet in wartime. The political nation preferred the press to 'tyranny', especially as the press bore most hard on the inarticulate and powerless. The most telling condemnation of the system was that it failed to fulfil its function of providing enough trained seamen. When many merchant seamen in vital trades had legal protection from impressment and when the Admiralty came up against the fact that the supply of merchant seamen was too small to meet its needs, it had no alternative but to accept landsmen as volunteers. Desertion was an endemic problem. Steps could be taken to discourage it but nothing could ever eradicate it and together with disease and accidents it could decimate a fleet's manpower and limit its operational efficiency.

In April 1689 William III could muster on paper a force of 59,000 subject troops plus a Dutch corps of 15,000 men. It is misleading to talk about the 'English army' during this period. To do so implies a degree of corporate and national identity that the land forces of the Crown did not possess. The basic tactical and administrative units of those forces were the regiment and troop for the cavalry and the battalion and company for the foot. It was to these groups, rather than to the army as a whole, that officers and men owed their primary loyalty. The sons of the landed aristocracy and gentry made up about a quarter of the regimental officer corps but constituted a disproportionately large percentage of the higher ranks of the army. The majority of regimental officers were drawn from the ranks of the lesser gentry, the liberal professions, or trade. They lacked the wealth and powerful patrons (or 'interest') of the first group and were less likely to reach high rank. The remaining officers were either foreign (usually Huguenot) exiles, the sons of army officers, or in some instances were aging subalterns who had enlisted as privates and received commissions when new regiments were raised in wartime.

In peacetime most officers purchased their first commission and, if they had sufficient funds, proceeded to purchase steps up in rank until they became lieutenant-colonels. A soldier as distinguished as the Duke of Marlborough supported purchase because he claimed it minimized parliamentary interference in the running of the army. Purchase meant that the state also escaped having to pay retired officers a pension because they could sell their commissions when they resigned. It also ensured that the army remained politically neutral. Only men who were already members of the political nation could obtain commissions and so the army remained a collection of regiments whose officer corps would not form a corporate body which might set itself in opposition to the civil power. But about one-third of commissions were not purchased. Some officers with powerful patrons received a free commission or a free step up in rank. Officers who lacked wealth and powerful patrons looked forward to vacancies caused by the death of colleagues on active service and toasted the prospect of a bloody war or a sickly season. Free commissions were also granted to officers commissioned to raise new regiments. Promotion above the rank of lieutenant-colonel remained in the hands of the monarch and was determined on the basis of seniority and merit.

At the beginning of this period officership in the army had a venal character. Company and battalion commanders expected to be able to recoup their initial investment not only through their pay but by taking a rake-off from the monies which the government granted them to pay, equip and feed their soldiers. The state was the victim of fraud on a grand scale. Confronted by threats to his throne in Ireland, Scotland and Flanders, William III did not attempt to eradicate these abuses. If the price he had to pay for a loyal officer corps was financial malpractices he was ready to pay it. If abuses such as the sale of commissions to minors, duelling and the taking of leave without permission did not seriously impair the army's efficiency, he turned a blind eye to them. It was only when abuses like the making of false musters (the practice whereby officers inflated the numbers of rank and file serving with their regiments and pocketed the pay of non-existent men) did harm efficiency, that he tried to eradicate them.

The size of the army voted by Parliament increased sharply after 1688. James II had raised a force of about 15,000 men. During the Nine Years' War England became a major military power. Between 1688 and 1697 Parliament voted an average of 76,400 men for the army each year, a figure which rose to an annual average of 92,700 between 1702 and 1713. But these were paper establishments. Recruiting the rank and file was as much a problem for the army as it was for the navy. At the end of each campaigning season battalions abroad sent recruiting parties home to muster more men. Some units even established semi-permanent recruiting depots which operated in England all the year around. Enlistment was for life, although in wartime Parliament sometimes tried to attract more recruits by passing Recruiting Acts allowing men to serve for three years. Men enlisted for a variety of reasons. Some were driven to volunteer by hunger, some were attracted by the offer of a money bounty, others wanted a change from the routine they had known all their lives, or they wanted to get away from a bad marriage. But fewer criminals enlisted than legend might suggest, not least because the army was reluctant to have such unreliable men. But in wartime volunteers were in short supply. To make up their numbers recruiting officers sometimes turned to the press, even though its use by the army was illegal and in the 1690s some regiments also used 'crimps', professional criminals who kidnapped likely recruits and then sold them to the army. In 1702 insolvent debtors were released from prison if they agreed to enlist. When that proved to be insufficient Parliament passed the first of a series of Recruiting Acts in 1704 empowering Justices of the Peace to conscript the unemployed. It remained in force until 1712. Similar legislation was enacted in 1745/6, and 1755/7 and 1778/9.

Despite the best, or worst efforts of crimps and recruiting officers, most units in peacetime and in wartime were usually below their establishment and contained a large proportion of untrained recruits. In peacetime the paper establishments voted by Parliament always comprised a proportion of 'non-effectives', that is fictitious men whose pay was used to generate extra income for their captains and colonels. In wartime battle casualties plus higher rates of sickness and desertion meant that there was an even larger disparity between the paper establishment of units and their real strength. Units abroad could sometimes only be made up to strength by drafting into them trained soldiers taken from units at home, to the great detriment of the latter who were reduced to recruit training depots. Even these desperate measures often failed to meet the deficiencies. The army in Flanders in the Nine Years' War was often 30 per cent below establishment. Shortages of men could have important strategic repercussions. In 1707 the allies lost the decisive battle of Almanzá in Spain because the recruiting system could not supply enough men to maintain the English contingent.

The failure of the army and navy to maintain their establishments was only partly the result of defective recruiting machinery and poor conditions of service. By restricting recruitment to those who could most easily be spared from the workshop and plough, the ruling oligarchy tried to ensure that the direct impact of war on British society was minimized. 'The proper men to recruit and supply your troops', one MP insisted in 1775, 'are the scum and outcast of cities and manufactures: fellows who voluntarily submit to be slaves by an apprenticeship of seven years are the proper persons to be military ones. But to take the honest, sober, industrious fellow from the plough, is doing an essential mischief to the community and laying a double tax.'[2] An effective system of universal conscription would have required a considerable expansion of the machinery of local government, a readiness by Parliament to provide for the families of men who were conscripted and a willingness by the ruling oligarchy to place its own power and privileges at risk. The labouring classes were most reluctant to be the victims of universal training, never mind universal service. Their reluctance to serve in person might have been overcome, but only if the ruling oligarchy had been prepared to preach the kind of secular nationalism which the American colonists adopted after 1775 and which might have made 'the honest, sober, industrious fellow' more willing to enlist. But that would have required that the definition of service in the armed force be changed from being a career to being a civic duty. Such notions were not attractive to the rulers of a hierarchical, deferential and confessional state who wished to restrict the rights of full citizenship to a privileged few and their clients. They preferred instead that the army and navy should face recurrent manpower shortages rather than propagate ideas which might politicize the labouring classes and cause them to question the status quo. The English armed forces existed to maintain aristocratic power, not to undermine it.

This helps to explain why it was a common English practice to hire foreign mercenaries in wartime. They swelled the ranks of the army without denuding the labour market and, a not incidental advantage, they were cheaper than Englishmen. Mercenaries hired from Holland, Prussia, Hanover, Denmark, and a variety of minor German principalities accounted each year for an average of about 30 per cent of the 'English' army between 1691 and 1697 and about 39 per cent each year between 1703 and 1712. They contributed disproportionately to the expeditionary forces England sent to the continent. Between 1691 and 1697 an annual average of about 48 per cent of the army in Flanders consisted of foreign mercenaries, a figure which rose to 59 per cent per annum between 1703 and 1712.

The higher administration of the army was even more divided than that of the navy, for at least the Admiralty exercised some general supervision over the whole system. No comparable body existed to fulfil a similar function for the landforces of the Crown. This mattered little under William, who exercised a close personal superintendence over the army. In theory a number of civil and military officers held overlapping administrative briefs. Under William's successors their actual power depended upon the strength of their personalities, the political support they could muster and whether they enjoyed royal favour. All orders for warlike preparations had to be signed by one of the secretaries of state. Most of the administrative work involving logistical and financial matters concerning the army devolved upon a more junior minister, the Secretary at War. He also had some responsibility for providing medical supplies, uniforms and camp equipment. But he could be eclipsed if the monarch filled the post of captain-general or commander-in-chief. The latter enjoyed great but somewhat ill-defined powers which in the hands of men like Marlborough raised it almost to the status of another Secretaryship of State. The Commander-in-Chief was assisted by an Adjutant-General, responsible for the discipline of the army and by a Board of General Officers, first established in 1705. The Master-General of the Ordnance was responsible for supplying the infantry with weapons and for raising, training, equipping and disciplining the engineers and artillery. The Paymaster General issued money for most of the goods and services the army needed, whilst the Treasury, which exercised its responsibility through the Commissary General, dealt with a wide variety of contingencies which fell to no one else. Rationalization of the supply system was slow. It was not until 1760 that the rising cost of the Combined Army in Germany persuaded the government to give the Treasury a larger role in army supply at the expense of other departments. The result of these numerous and overlapping competencies was that, as one nineteenth-century authority explained, 'an English army ... had no more uniformity of movement, discipline, and appearance ... than one composed of the troops of different sovereign states'.[3]

The practical limitations on the conduct of war meant that as long as the belligerents could maintain a rough numerical equality, the rapid victory of one side or the other was unlikely. The outcome of any battle was uncertain and few generals were anxious to seek quick decisions on the battlefield. The short range of the muskets with which all armies were equipped, and the clouds of choking black smoke they emitted when they were fired, meant that battles were fought at murderously close range. Heavy battle casualties represented a major threat to the hard-to-replace manpower of every army. In 1704 at Blenheim 30,000 of the 108,000 combatants became casualties. Most military writers, and a good many generals, believed that armies should seek to avoid defeat and should try to subsist at the enemy's expense by living off his land whilst manoeuvring to place the enemy's army at a disadvantage. The campaigning season on land and sea was usually confined to the spring and summer. In winter roads were impassable and there was no green fodder to feed horses. Armies could not take to the field until the spring thaw and before the grass had begun to grow. By November they had to return to winter quarters because most roads were impassable and because there was no forage. Troops could rarely march more than 15 kilometres a day because of poor roads and the slow pace at which their artillery and supply wagons moved.

It was no accident that the Low Countries were the site of so many English campaigns after 1688. They were only a short sea voyage from the coast of England. Their harbours were the natural starting point for any enemy attempting to invade England and they were bordered by most of the major continental belligerents. They were flat, fertile and they were crossed by a series of major rivers which ran roughly north-south and formed excellent highways for armies advancing in either direction. It was for that reason that fortresses had been built along the lengths of the rivers Lys, Scheldt, Dender, Senne and Dyle and that the French constructed a series of fortresses from Dunkirk on the Channel coast to Douai to prevent their enemies from invading them by marching down one of the valleys. The French took similar precautions to block the main crossing points along their Rhineland frontier. Consequently

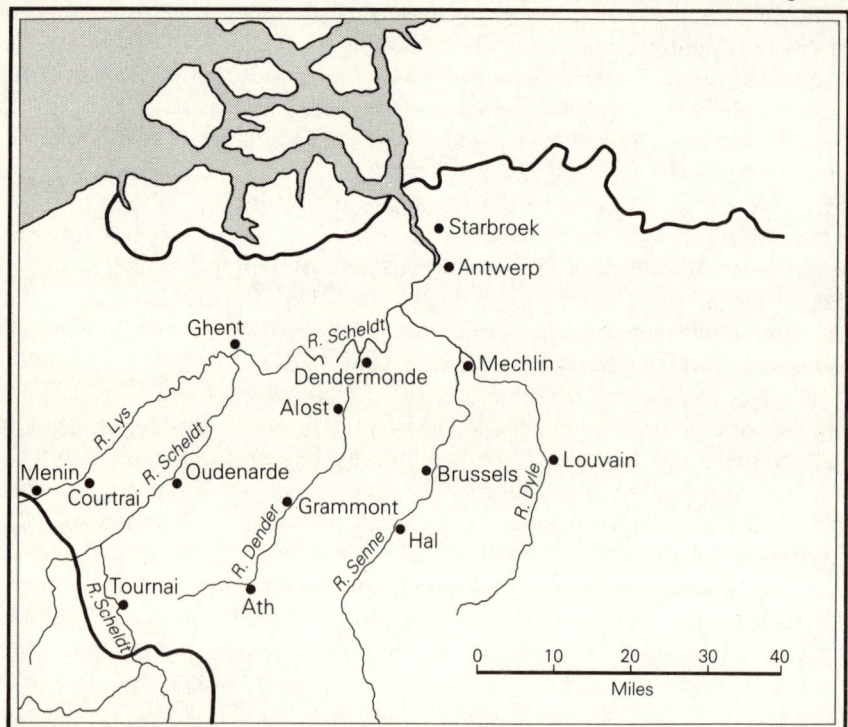

Figure 1 The Low Countries c. 1700

it was impossible for any of France's enemies to gain a quick decision against her. Until the 1790s in every war in the Low Countries the number of sieges far exceeded the number of pitched battles. By 1700 the art of fortification was a long way in advance of the science of gunnery and until the end of the eighteenth century armies were too small to neutralize fortresses by detaching a fraction of their force to mask them so that the rest of the army could by-pass them. Sieges were usually lengthy and costly affairs. The presence of so many fortresses in such a small area meant that it was all but impossible for any general to advance rapidly upon the enemy. After one fortress had been captured another lay just over the horizon blocking the way. Even if by some good fortune a general did succeed in catching his opponent in the open and inflicting a severe defeat upon him, the pursuit of a beaten enemy could itself be an expensive business. Reluctant soldiers were all too apt to take the opportunity offered them to chase the enemy to make good their own escape from the army.

The vagaries of wind, tide and weather and the difficulty of feeding crews and keeping them disease-free, made it difficult for the navy to maintain a continuous close blockade of enemy ports. Fleet actions were usually confined to the summer months because their instability in bad weather made admirals anxious to lay up their larger vessels in harbour between September and April. It was only when the navy began to acquire two-decker 74-gun ships-of-the-line in the 1750s and 1760s that they had vessels able to take on the largest French ships and remain at sea in nearly all weathers. When two fleets joined battle their cannon were inaccurate and lacked the power to penetrate the thick oak planks of enemy vessels at more than 400 yards. Even if ships were holed their crew could often carry out running repairs. Ships' companies might sustain heavy losses but unless their vessel caught fire it was unlikely to sink and in fair weather damaged vessels could often be towed into a port. The unusually heavy losses the French fleet sustained at La Hogue in 1692 were not inflicted by cannon fire but by boarding parties and fireships. The one major tactical advantage that the English did enjoy was that constant practice at sea meant that their training, discipline and gun-drill was superior to that of any other fleet. But between La Hogue in 1692 and the Battle of the Saints in 1782 no British fleet inflicted an overwhelming defeat on its enemies. The tactical initiative of ships' captains was constrained by the Admiralty's *Permanent Fighting Instructions*, issued by Admiral Russell in 1691 and modified by Admiral Rooke in 1703. They remained in force until 1783 and laid down that ships must maintain a rigid line of battle. The inadequacies of the fleet's signalling system, and the fog of gun-smoke created by the fleet's broadsides, meant that enterprising admirals had great difficulty in exploiting any fleeting tactical opportunities because of the difficulty of communicating new orders to their subordinates in the middle of a battle. Admirals were also induced to be cautious by the fact that a crushing victory at sea could alter the balance of advantage between belligerents overnight. Most politicians and admirals, conscious of the time, money and effort needed to create a fleet, preferred to maintain it in being rather than risk it by seeking out and attempting to annihilate their enemy.

Finally, lest some of the preceding comments leave the impression that it was possible for governments to exercise close and continuous control over their armies and navies, it must be emphasized that such was not the case. Strategic communications were slow and uncertain. Before the development of the electric telegraph in the second half of the nineteenth century, orders and information were transmitted by written messages and carried by dispatch riders or packet-boats. In the eighteenth century it could take about two months for orders from London to reach the North American colonies. The sometimes inexplicable hesitations and convolutions of generals and admirals in the pre-telegraph age become explicable when it is realized that the exigencies of war meant that they frequently faced situations in which their instructions were redundant and the government was too distant to provide them with more appropriate orders in good time.

In 1688 William realised that no single state, least of all England, was sufficiently powerful to overcome France. England could match France at sea but the latter's population was approximately twice that of England and her army far outnumbered England's landforces. William could only make good this shortfall by seeking allies and the dominant idea underlying his policy was to create a grand coalition of European states that would be able to field armies in the Low Countries, in Spain, in Germany and in northern Italy. Individually each ally was too weak to defeat France but if they could pose a series of simultaneous threats to her they could, in time, so wear down her power that Louis would be amenable to a settlement which was acceptable to them.

William began creating his coalition in May 1689 when the Austrians and Dutch signed an alliance and pledged themselves to drive France back to the borders she had occupied in 1659. William committed his new kingdom to the alliance in December and in June 1690 Spain, Savoy and Sweden joined them. This marked the beginning of a century of intermittent Franco-British hostility which culminated in 1815 at Waterloo. James had fled to France but in March 1689 lack of men, stores and money meant that the English fleet was too weak to stop him landing in Ireland with money, arms and French troops. Nor could the fleet prevent Louis reinforcing him in 1690. Within a month of his arrival James controlled the whole of Ireland except for Londonderry and Enniskillen. William's eyes were fixed on the war in Flanders and it was not until July 1689 that he sent enough troops to Ireland to lift the siege of Londonderry and so secured a base from which to begin the reconquest. Only in the spring of 1690 did he recognize that his own presence in Ireland was vital if he was rapidly to liquidate the danger from across the Irish sea. In June he crossed over himself, bringing with him considerable reinforcements and routed James's army at the Boyne in July. But Catholic resistance was not ended until the remaining Jacobites in Limerick and Galway were dispersed at the Battle of Aughrim in

July 1691 and the last remaining Jacobite garrison surrendered at Limerick in September. It was only then that William could concentrate his resources on the war in Europe.

While William was winning the war in Ireland, the Anglo-Dutch fleet had lost control of the Channel. In the summer of 1690 the English came nearer to defeat and invasion than at any time before 1940. Shortage of money had delayed the refitting of many vessels and too many of those which were seaworthy had been used to escort William to Ireland or to convoy merchant ships to Gibraltar. Consequently in July 1690 75 French ships-of-the-line encountered only 56 English and Dutch vessels off Beachy Head. The allied commander, the Earl of Torrington, was determined to preserve his fleet in being. He gave the Dutch only half-hearted support when they were engaged and then withdrew to the Downs. Had the French been better supplied they might have made more of their victory by sailing into the Irish Sea and cutting William off from England. Torrington was dismissed but, more usefully, serious steps were also taken to augment the fleet. A major shipbuilding programme was started and new dockyard facilities at Plymouth and Portsmouth were begun or enlarged. By 1695 the base facilities which had served the fleet during the Dutch wars were being extended to form the facilities which were to serve it throughout the French wars of the eighteenth century.

In 1692 Louis prepared to land a Franco-Irish army of 24,000 men in England. He hoped that their landing would be the signal for a rising by the English Jacobites. His hopes were fanciful. The latter lacked competent leaders and an efficient organization. James generated widespread suspicion in England because of his Catholicism, his dependence upon the French and because his public statements wavered between dire threats to punish those who had driven him from his throne and promises to be conciliatory when he returned. The English had seen how easily professional troops had disposed of Monmouth's rebels in 1685 and the vast majority of indigenous Jacobites would not rise without the help of foreign troops. But nothing was more likely to discredit their cause in the eyes of waverers than reliance on Catholic France. In the event their resolution was never put to the test. In May 1692 Torrington's successor, Earl Russell, reaped the early rewards of the new construction programme. When the Anglo-Dutch fleet met the French at Barfleur and La Hogue he used his decisive numerical superiority to board or burn no less than fifteen of the forty-four French ships present for the loss of not a single allied vessel.

The battle marked the end of any immediate hopes of a Franco-Jacobite invasion and also a decisive shift in the balance of naval power. Control of the sea now passed to the allies, or more precisely the English, who had provided two-thirds of the allied fleet. After 1693 the French were so hard-pressed on land that they lacked the funds needed to rebuild their fleet. They avoided set-piece encounters at sea and resorted to attacking English merchant ships with privateers, capturing about 4,000 vessels. This represented the single most damaging campaign against English trade in the sailing era. The Admiralty was subject to vociferous criticism from merchants whose ships were lost. From 1693 to 1694, after a large convoy bound for Smyrna had been intercepted off Lagos, the Admiralty began to develop a more efficient trade protection policy. By 1696 a Council of Trade had been established to advise the Admiralty on how to safeguard trade and the Admiralty itself began to consult with merchants and owners prominent in some trades.

The war had been preceded by a three-cornered trade war between England, France and Holland. Once the war proper began the allies tried to wrest commercial advantage from it, and reduce France's tax revenues, by interrupting her overseas trade. But just because they were at war with France did not mean that their own disputes were forgotten. In 1689 the English induced the Dutch to sign a treaty agreeing to take as prizes all ships of whatever nationality sailing to and from French ports. The English hoped that this would not only hurt the French but would also restrict Dutch trade, to England's own ultimate benefit. But Dutch ships continued to trade with France. Similarly, although they did not like it, the English also had no option but to permit the Danes and Swedes to continue to trade with France. Had they not done so the Danes and Swedes might have withdrawn their mercenary contingents from the allied armies. Whatever commercial advantages the English may have secured at the peace, during the war itself their overseas trade suffered.

Savoy's accession to the Grand Alliance meant that by the summer of 1690 France was virtually surrounded. As long as the alliance remained united the two sides were evenly matched. The inability of armies and navies to achieve rapid victories meant that the war became a conflict of attrition in which the balance of advantage depended upon the length of each belligerent's purse. England's ability to match France rested in large part on the fact that she possessed a more efficient tax-collecting system than did the French. England possessed a representative institution in the form of the House of Commons with undisputed powers to raise taxes. Her economy was more commercialized than that of France and hence it was easier for the English state to tap English wealth. Beginning somewhat falteringly in the Nine Years' War the English government was able to use the security these regular tax revenues gave it to borrow far more extensively and cheaply than their enemies. The government's creditors, unlike their French counterparts, were willing to lend because they knew that they would receive the interest the state owed them on their investments.

William III's effort to bring the full weight of English resources to bear against France precipitated a financial revolution in England. In 1688 he inherited debts of about £2,000,000. Parliament voted £600,000 to defray the cost of the Dutch invasion and another £2,000,000 for the reconquest of Ireland. These sums were of a familiar order of magnitude. But William was soon spending £5,500,000 per year, more than three times what James II had spent. The cost of the Nine Years War, £49,300,000, dwarfed all expectations. The new regime met these bills by expanding its tax base and borrowing money on a hitherto unimagined scale. Between 1690 and 1704 they nearly quadrupled the general level of import duties. These new tariffs were designed to meet the unprecedentedly high cost of the French wars. Protectionism was an accidental by-product of the needs of an Exchequer desperate for cash to fight a war. The English had abandoned tax farming before 1688 and the excise was collected relatively efficiently by a growing band of professional civil servants. In France, where tax farming was still prevalent, a considerable proportion of the revenues which the state might have collected stuck to the fingers of tax-collectors. But despite these relative advantages before 1714 the performance of the customs and excise was erratic and the English government relied upon the land tax which it began to levy at four shillings in the pound in 1692. It remained at that rate until 1697. The land tax was levied on the income from landed property and from certain public offices. Those who paid it resented it and, because they were members of the political nation, they were able to make its collection difficult. In 1693, assuming probably correctly that the only way that they would be able to tax property was with the consent of the propertied classes, Parliament fixed the sum which had to be paid annually by each county and gave the task of assessing what each tax-payer had to contribute to local commissioners. After 1693 no serious attempts were made to revalue property. In every serious international crisis between 1693 and 1765 the tax was levied at four shillings in the pound, a sum which was accepted by government and tax-payer alike as the limit of what was politically tolerable. At that level it produced about £2,000,000 in revenue per annum.

No government could hope to meet the burgeoning cost of war from taxation alone, but the government's ability to tax its citizens also enabled it to borrow from them. During the Nine Years' War William borrowed £16,000,000 to meet the remaining cost of the war. The government expanded its credit operations on a hitherto unheard-of scale. Initially it adopted short-term expedients on the assumption that the war would be over quickly. But by 1693 it was apparent that such an assumption was not tenable and a long-term solution to the problem of borrowing large sums at low interest rates had to be found. William turned to a group of leading financiers for the money he needed. To reassure them that the government would meet its obligations to them, Parliament earmarked specific taxes to pay the interest on the burgeoning national debt and in 1694 they permitted their creditors to establish the Bank of England. The bank lent the government £1,200,000 at 8 per cent interest. The money was forthcoming and thanks to it William was able to win his only major military success on the continent, the capture of the fortress of Namur in 1695. The government also borrowed money from the East India Company in return for confirming its trading privileges.

The national debt rose from £3,100,000 in 1691 to £36,200,000 in 1714. With the benefit of hindsight it might appear that England was able to raise these sums with unparalleled ease. Such a judgement would have surprised ministers caught up in the daily problems of finding the money to pay for their wars. Confronted by service estimates which reached unprecedented levels in wartime, they were nervously aware that they could not gauge just how elastic were England's financial resources. They could never be quite sure that the complaints of the monied interest that the government was asking them to do too much were not the truth, rather than an attempt to blackmail the state into paying them higher rates of interest. The government's credit was not inexhaustible and, especially in wartime, they had to stoop to some dubious practices to extend it. It was not uncommon in the wars against Louis XIV for the pay of soldiers and sailors to be a year in arrears. There were times when ministers could not see where the next penny was coming from and believed that they would have to give up the struggle for want of cash.

In 1691 France had 273,000 men in the field. By 1693 the allies could confront them with 220,000 men, rising to 334,000 by 1695. William's immediate objectives were to keep the allies together and to protect the Spanish Netherlands, for on their security rested the safety of the United Provinces and England. After the Boyne he reinforced the English corps in Flanders until by 1696 over half the allied army in that theatre was in English pay. This campaign marked the first of several occasions when forces paid by England played a major role in an allied military coalition. Louis waged a successful defensive war and the allies lacked the generals and the numerical superiority to overcome him. In 1691 and 1692 superior numbers and better military management allowed the French to steal several marches on their enemies. They got their troops into the field earlier in the campaigning season and were able to take the fortresses of Mons and Namur. But in open battle, at Steenkerk in August 1692 and Landen in July 1693, Louis did not have quite enough men to transform the defeats he inflicted on the allies into decisive victories. William's one indisputable victory in Flanders was the capture of Namur in September 1695. Thereafter shortage of money restricted the operations of both sides.

Steenkerk had important repercussions in England. The Country opposition protested that English lives had been sacrificed by Dutch generals. It became doubly difficult for the government to extract money from the Commons to continue the continental land campaign. Country MPs argued that now England and Ireland were secure, the English should limit their contribution to the alliance to the 10,000 troops and 20 ships they were obliged to supply under the treaty they had signed with the States General in 1678. The rest of their resources should be devoted to a maritime war against France's colonies and seaborne trade. As Admiral Rooke argued, 'blocking up the enemies fleet in their principle port, insulating their coast, burning their towns at the same time, must, in all humble opinion, expose them to the world, make them very uneasy at home, and give a reputation to his Majesty's arms.'[4]

Exactly what that reputation would have been was problematic. The Admiralty realized the vital importance of maintaining a fleet in the approaches to Brest in order to protect England from attack, but the navy was unable to maintain a continuous blockade of the port. Brest faced west and the admirals commanding the blockading squadron lived in perpetual fear of being driven aground by westerly winds blowing off the Atlantic. An amphibious assault in 1694 against the port ended in a fiasco, demonstrating that the exponents of a maritime policy had given no serious consideration to the practical difficulties of landing an army on a defended coast. A similar fate had befallen an expedition in 1693 sent to take the French base on Martinique in the West Indies. There was a pronounced lack of co-operation between the two services and between them and local colonial officials. Soldiers and seamen fell victim to every conceivable tropical disease and the ships operating in the warm Caribbean waters were devoured by sea-worms. This sorry story was to become all too common on other expeditions to the region in the eighteenth century. But the most telling argument against a whole-hearted pursuit of a maritime strategy unencumbered by any significant commitment of troops to the continent was not that it was impractical but that it was politically dangerous. William's objective of driving France back to her frontiers of 1659 could not be achieved unless the Grand Alliance remained united. But England's continental allies could hardly be expected to rejoice if the English devoted most of their men and ships to increasing their commerce whilst they were bled dry waging an expensive and fruitless land war against France.

This is not to argue that the fleet had no role to play in maintaining the cohesion of the alliance. By 1693 William realized that he could not invade France from Flanders and his attention shifted southward. He hoped that not only would a strong allied naval presence in the Mediterranean encourage Spain and Savoy to remain loyal to their allies but that it might even give the Duke of Savoy enough support to enable him to invade southern France. In July 1694 Russell's fleet was dispatched to the Mediterranean where he blockaded the French fleet at Toulon, stopped a French invasion of Catalonia and kept the increasingly hard-pressed Victor Amadeus in the war for another year. Russell overwintered at Cadiz, a major logistical achievement, and returned to the Mediterranean in May 1695. But in October 1695, with his ships badly in need of a major refit and short of sailors, he was compelled to return to England.

By 1693 neither William nor Louis anticipated that their enemy would collapse totally and negotiations for a settlement proceeded as the fighting continued. However, it was not until 1697 that the processes of attrition had sufficiently worn down both sides that they were ready to compromise. Louis wanted peace because France had suffered a catastrophic famine in 1693/4, specie was in short supply, and revenues were falling far short of what the monarchy needed. William too was so short of money that he feared that he might soon have to disband part of his army. But what finally drove him to make peace was the threatened unravelling of the Grand Alliance. In February 1696 French troops embarked at Dunkirk for an invasion which Louis hoped would coincide with William's assassination by Jacobite conspirators. Nothing came of the conspiracy or the invasion but it did persuade William to withdraw twenty battalions from Flanders. In 1694/5 the allies had enjoyed a numerical superiority in Flanders because a large French army was deployed in Piedmont. But the withdrawal of so many English battalions eased the pressure on the French in Flanders and enabled Louis to reinforce his forces facing Savoy. The duke was in a desperate position. The Anglo-Dutch subsidy he was receiving was not sufficient to stave off bankruptcy, his possessions had suffered a series of bad harvests and the allies had just withdrawn their naval support. In June 1696 he made peace. William then tried to maintain pressure on Louis in the south by transferring the subsidy that the duke had received to Austria. But the emperor, without consulting the maritime powers, nullified his intentions by agreeing with the French to neutralize the whole of Italy. By 1697 the French could again concentrate enough troops in the north to outnumber the allies and bring Spain to the point of collapse by breaching her defences in Catalonia.

William thought it prudent to begin serious negotiations before Austria followed Savoy's example and made her own separate peace. He was determined to agree terms with the French and then to impose them on his allies. This was only the first occasion when the English showed themselves indifferent to their allies' interests when it suited them. The Peace of Ryswick was signed in September 1697. The Austrians reluctantly acceded to it in October. France restored some of her more recent gains and Louis recognized William as King of England. But he would go no further. France was not reduced to her frontiers of 1659 and Louis refused to make any stipulations about the legitimacy of William's heirs or to expel James from France.

During the Nine Years' War William had maintained a professional army which was far larger than James II had ever contemplated. William realized that the Peace of Ryswick was little more than an armed truce and he wanted to maintain at least part of that army in peacetime so that he had a cadre which could be expanded when the next round of fighting began. This provoked a bitter pamphlet campaign in 1697/8 in which opponents of a large peacetime standing army like Walter Moyle, Andrew Fletcher and John Trenchard, the author of *An Argument Showing that a Standing Army is Inconsistent with a Free Government and Absolutely Destructive to the Constitution* voiced arguments which were used repeatedly in the eighteenth century. At the heart of the debate were two different conceptions of the ethical basis of the state. Opponents of a standing army feared that it would promote the moral decay of society. A standing army, especially one containing considerable numbers of foreign mercenaries, would encourage corruption and tyranny within the body politic. It would entangle England in expensive continental wars and demand oppressive taxation. It would constitute an enormous engine of patronage and political corruption. Men could be bought with military commissions and lucrative contracts to supply the forces. By these means the Crown might be able to subvert the independence of Parliament. Wars which were ostensibly being fought to defend the liberties of Englishmen against foreign tyrants might instead promote the cause of domestic tyranny. Virtue and patriotism would die if men fought because they were paid to do so and forgot that it was the first duty of all free men to fight in defence of their own liberties. Rather than see their liberties destroyed by a regular army, they insisted that a free people should carry arms in their own defence. The state should be defended by a militia led and manned by men of property and their dependants. These writers might have had little grasp of military realities but their tracts circulated amongst a people who had only to remember the events of James II's reign to understand the potential danger of a standing army.

William's supporters, like Daniel Defoe, rested their case on two premises. They denied that a standing army would be a danger to liberty because it would be under the control of a Parliament who voted funds for its support annually. And they pointed to the imperatives of England's international position and insisted that her liberties could only be defended by a professional standing army. England's new involvement in European affairs and the likelihood that she would soon be involved in another war against France meant that a citizens' militia was not a plausible option. Success in war against the professional army of Louis XIV demanded a degree of training beyond the capacity of a citizens' militia.

Echoes of these arguments were heard throughout the eighteenth century whenever defence policy was debated. In December 1698 the opposition voted to reduce the English army to 10,000 men. When William prevaricated they reduced it to 7,000 men. William had wished to retain a force of 30,000 men but he had to accept these terms. Parliament ensured that William would not be able to maintain even this force without summoning the Commons annually by voting the Crown a civil list of only £700,000 per annum, and they reduced that sum to £600,000 in 1700. William only had himself to blame when he complained that some of his opponents' arguments ignored European realities. His determination to keep the control of foreign and defence policy in his own hands and to keep Parliament in ignorance made it impossible for most members to understand his policy. As he did not even tell his own ministers what he wanted it was not surprising that they were unable to present a coherent argument explaining the king's wishes. As the king refused to educate the public, ignorance and prejudice flourished. It was a lesson which subsequent governments did not always heed. However, after 1699 the forces at the Crown's disposal were augmented by the separate Irish establishment of 12,000 men, paid for by the Irish Exchequer. After every eighteenth-century war the Crown hastened to use the Irish establishment as a convenient place to 'hide' troops from the prying eyes of the English Parliament. The government in London did not regard these forces as constituting a separate Irish army but saw them as part of an imperial reserve which could be sent to England when she was in danger of invasion or to Europe or the colonies if policy so dictated. By the late 1720s the government in London usually met the cost of Irish regiments serving outside Ireland. And furthermore beneath this apparent defeat for the Crown there was a hidden victory. In return for the Crown accepting that Parliament had the right to determine annually the size and cost of the army, Parliament had accepted the principle that England should maintain a peacetime standing army.

Fiscal exhaustion was only one reason why Louis made peace in 1697. He also wanted to disrupt the Grand Alliance because it was apparent that Charles II, the childless King of Spain, would soon die. Charles was the last Spanish Habsburg. He ruled an empire stretching from the Mediterranean to Central and South America and to the Philippines. His death would have repercussions throughout Europe. His closest heirs were Leopold of Austria and the French Dauphin. William was determined that neither France nor Austria should secure the whole of Charles's inheritance intact. If either of them did so they would become an over-mighty power able to dominate the whole of western Europe. Between 1698 and 1702 he tried twice to negotiate a settlement with Louis. The first treaty of partition collapsed when their compromise candidate to the bulk of Charles's inheritance unexpectedly died. But in June 1699 they signed a second treaty. The dauphin was to receive the Spanish Habsburg's lands in Italy and Leopold's younger son, the Archduke Charles, would receive Spain, the Spanish Netherlands and her transoceanic empire. But neither the Spanish court nor Leopold could accept this. Leopold wanted Naples, Sicily and Milan for his heir Joseph and the court wanted an heir who would prevent the partition of the empire. Just before Charles died in November 1700 the court persuaded him to bequeath his whole empire intact to Louis's grandson, Philip of Anjou, on condition that Philip renounced his claim to the French throne. Louis accepted the offer, encouraged by the prospect of a Bourbon on the throne in Madrid and by the Court's threat that if he did not, Charles's empire would go intact to the Austrians.

William's worst fears about French hegemony in Europe seemed about to materialize. But initially many of his English subjects did not share his forebodings. In so far as politicians were concerned with anything other than the quest for power and place, they were concerned with trade, the preservation of social order, diplomacy and war. It is easy to overemphasize the division into Whig and Tory factions which emerged in the Commons in the late seventeenth century and to assume that the groupings constituted something like modern political parties. In fact each faction was composed of two elements. Each contained a group of 'Court' politicians who sought government office and a somewhat larger group of 'Country' members who remained on the backbenches. The 'Country' was distinguished by their steady suspicion of what they believed to be the excessive, growing and corrupting power of the executive, and each party's 'Court' wing could rarely be absolutely sure of their support.

Some of the apparent ideological divisions between these groups was little more than political posturing but by 1699 the Tories had emerged as the more xenophobic and isolationist. They believed that England had fought the Nine Years' War to further Dutch rather than English interests and to line the pockets of William's Whig supporters and Dutch henchmen. Their suspicion of most things foreign expressed itself in the Act of Settlement of 1701, which was to come into effect when the Elector of Hanover succeeded to the throne on Anne's death. It stipulated that the Crown would only be able to make war in defence of Hanover with the express approval of Parliament. They were equally suspicious of the monied interest which the financial revolution had created. By 1709 about 10,000 people had money invested in the machinery of public credit but many Tory squires were groaning under the burden of a land tax set at four shillings in the pound. Jonathan Swift voiced their exasperation in 1711 in *Reflections on the Conduct of the Allies*. 'We have been fighting to raise the wealth and grandeur of a particular family, to enrich usurers and stock-jobbers, and to cultivate the pernicious designs of a faction by destroying the landed interest.'[5]

The Tories were also critical of the subsidies England granted her allies. Whilst the allies were quick to take English money they were slow to do her bidding. They insisted that if England had to go to war she should pursue a maritime strategy, fighting at sea and attacking the enemies' colonies rather than commit an expensive mercenary army to a European land war. Naval campaigns were preferable because they brought tangible gains in the shape of colonies and new opportunities for trade. As one Country Tory explained to the Commons

As we are by nature disjointed from the continent, and surrounded with the sea; it ought always to be a maxim with us, to have as little to do as possible with the disputes among the princes of Europe... soon after the Revolution we... began to interfere in disputes upon the continent, more than we ought to have done; we then began to load our commerce and manufacturers with taxes of various kinds; and we then began to supply the public expense by running in debt yearly; instead of raising the necessary sums within the year... we make ourselves the Don Quixote of Europe... if we leave the continent to take care of itself and confine ourselves to a naval war; we may carry it on with little expense and great success against France and Spain.[6]

By contrast the Court Whigs believed that England's security could not be divorced from the European balance of power. They accepted that to maintain it she would periodically have to dispatch subject troops and subsidies to Europe and act in concert with allies. 'God be thanked', wrote the Whig Thomas Johnson in 1701, 'the Dutch seem resolved to joyne heartily with us against the French.'[7] It was not certain that England's continental allies could withstand the onslaught of their common enemies without direct English military assistance. The conquest of the Netherlands by France or Lombardy by Spain would leave the Bourbons so powerful that they would have little to fear on land. They might be able to exclude English trade from large parts of Europe and eventually they could devote all of their resources to creating a fleet sufficiently powerful to crush the Royal Navy. The Court Whigs were also readier to acknowledge and indeed welcome the monied interest as a necessary ally. They recognized that financial stability and commercial prosperity were essential if England was to become and remain a great power. Money and commerce were important sources of power and no regime could survive for long if it ignored the interests of merchants and financiers. The government's ability to borrow large sums at low rates of interest was vital if it was to wage war in defence of the Revolution Settlement and the Protestant succession. As Charles Davenant had written in his *An Essay upon Ways and Means of Supplying War* in 1695:

> For war is quite changed from what it was in the time of our forefathers; when in a hasty expedition, and a pitched field, the matter was decided by courage; but now the whole art of war is in a manner reduced to money; and now-a-days, that prince, who can best find money to feed, clothe, and pay his army, not he that has the most valiant troops, is surest of success and conquest.[8]

Time and time again in the eighteenth century the same debates reciting the same notions about how Britain could best deploy her resources were repeated.

The Tories launched a furious attack on the secret diplomacy which had produced the partition treaties because they realized that the terms of the second treaty could only have been enforced if England had gone to war. However, Louis's actions soon persuaded many of them that William's forebodings that Louis was a danger to the liberties of Europe, the Protestant succession and English trade, were justified. Louis dispatched French troops to escort Philip to Madrid and to expel the Dutch garrisons from the Spanish Netherlands. He granted concessions to French traders in Spain and secured for them the *Assiento* to transport slaves from Africa to the Americas. He imposed heavy duties on English exports to France and French and Spanish customs duties were aligned in an attempt to exclude Dutch and English traders from their empires. And when James II died in September 1701 he immediately recognized his son as King James III.

The English went to war in May 1702 not to achieve the total overthrow of Bourbon France but to limit Louis's power to his French dominions, to safeguard their own security, to protect and further their own commercial interests and to preserve the Protestant succession. William's chosen tool was to recreate the Grand Alliance. In September 1701 the maritime powers and Austria agreed to fight if necessary to force Louis to accept the partition of the Spanish Empire. They were ready to allow Philip to keep Spain and her transoceanic colonies if he renounced his claim to the French throne. Leopold was to be granted Spain's Italian possessions and the Spanish Netherlands and the Dutch were to receive a strengthened barrier against France in the Low Countries. The maritime powers also claimed the right to seize any Spanish colonies they could capture and secure whatever commercial concessions they could. Although William died shortly before the war began, English strategic policy followed the main lines he had ordained.

Anne did not play such an active political role as William had done and that, combined with the pressure of the wars, tested the higher machinery of government as it had never been tested before. Government business was too complex to be left in the hands of one man or woman for long. The Privy Council was in theory responsible for advising the monarch on all major political decisions. But even before 1688 the full council was too large to dispatch business quickly. Inevitably a group of leading ministers emerged whom the monarch consulted on a more or less regular basis. Under William its membership had fluctuated between nine and fourteen ministers. Under Anne it was supplemented by a still smaller body, the Lords of Committee. Anne did not attend the latter's meetings but she did attend meetings of the larger Cabinet where the final decisions were taken in the light of advice tendered by the Lords of Committee. During Anne's reign the Godolphin and Harley ministries used English ships, soldiers and money to create and hold together an elaborate network of treaties designed to bring the maximum possible number of troops and ships into the war against France. It was only when the burden of the war became too heavy and when their ambitions diverged and the allies showed themselves increasingly reluctant to follow England's lead, that the Harley ministry thought it wise to withdraw from the war. Marlborough had a powerful but not a dominating voice in their counsels, based upon his friendship with the queen and Godolphin and his position as Captain-General and commander of the Anglo-Dutch army. As in the previous war, there was no supra-national allied command and policy had to be settled through a series of war councils, a method bound sometimes to produce serious delays and confusion.

The War of the Spanish Succession, like the Nine Years' War, was also a war of attrition, but this time it lasted long enough to leave France exhausted and allowed England to reap more of the rewards for her efforts. The allies soon secured a measure of superiority at sea. The main French fleet ceased to be an effective offensive instrument after one action off Malaga in 1704. They withdrew to Toulon and never emerged in force again. The Royal Navy dominated the western Mediterranean until the end of the war and England became a major Mediterranean power for the first time. France's naval recovery was hampered because the heavy cost of the land war left Louis with little money to spend on the fleet. But the Royal Navy could not prevent French privateers, assisted by royal vessels, taking more than 3,000 prizes between 1703 and 1708. So heavy were these losses and so vociferous were the merchants who suffered them, that in 1708 Parliament passed a 'Cruisers and Convoys' Act, reserving 43 warships for commerce protection and inaugurating a programme to build more cruisers. The Act served its political purpose in muting merchants' criticisms of the Admiralty, but French privateers shifted their activities to the Mediterranean. However, grievous as the losses of some merchants were, the French *guerre de course* failed to cripple England's overseas trade.

The allied blockade of the enemy's trade was less effective than it had been in the previous war. The Dutch still insisted upon their right to trade with the enemy and when the English tried to blackmail them into compliance with their wishes in 1703, the Dutch outfaced them, insisting that they needed the revenue generated by the trade to pay for the war. And the allies simply did not have enough vessels to blockade the French and Spanish coasts. The navy's record as an offensive weapon was equally mixed. In 1702 an Anglo-Dutch expedition failed to seize Cadiz. Had they done so they would have controlled one end of the rich Indies trade. However, on their homeward voyage they did destroy the Spanish silver fleet in Vigo Bay. In one respect this was a Pyrrhic victory. Most of the precious metal had been landed before the Anglo-Dutch fleet arrived and many of the cargoes they destroyed were owned by English merchants. But the political impact of the battle was considerable. It encouraged both the Duke of Savoy and the King of Portugal to join the allies. The accession of Portugal to the Grand Alliance was significant because it altered its purpose. The Portuguese insisted that the allies must agree to expel the Bourbons from Spain and place the Habsburg candidate, the Archduke Charles, on the Spanish throne. From 1704 substantial allied, and particularly English, forces were committed to the Iberian Peninsula to do this.

In 1702 and 1703 Marlborough drove the French back from their forward positions in Flanders and safeguarded the United Provinces against invasion. But in 1704 the allied position in southern Germany was precarious. Vienna was threatened by the French and their Bavarian allies, who had so intimidated a number of German princes that they refused to join the Grand Alliance. The emperor was short of money and unless the maritime powers gave him direct assistance, he might make peace. Their assistance came when Marlborough marched down the Danube and defeated the Franco-Bavarian army at Blenheim in August 1704. The empire was saved and the Austrians occupied Bavaria until the end of the war. It was the first time a major French army had suffered such a defeat since the 1630s. Henceforth the French were fighting a war to avoid defeat rather than in the expectation of imposing their own terms on the allies. But it was a reflection of the limitations of contemporary military technology and organization, plus France's innate strength, that even though Marlborough had destroyed the French army opposing him, he could not exploit his victory by invading France in 1705.

The Iberian Peninsula seemed to offer greater opportunities than Germany or Flanders. Philip could depend on the support of the Castilian heartland but some of the peripheral provinces welcomed the allies. In 1705 the maritime powers sent a fleet and troops under the Earl of Peterborough to co-operate with the Duke of Savoy in an attack on Toulon. French military pressure on the duke was so great that the operation was abandoned but in October the troops seized the Catalan port of Barcelona. The Catalans declared for Charles and a civil war erupted in Valencia and Aragon. Simultaneously, Philip was menaced from the west by the Portuguese army supported by 5,000 Anglo-Dutch troops under the Earl of Galway. Peterborough persuaded the English government that if he was reinforced he could take Madrid and end the war in a single campaign. They sent the troops and in November 1706 took the momentous step of declaring that Europe would have no peace as long as the French were masters in Madrid. This announcement was made at a moment of euphoria. In May 1706 Marlborough had defeated another French army at Ramillies and conquered most of the Spanish Netherlands and in June Galway had briefly occupied Madrid. The French had withdrawn troops from northern Italy to shore up their northern frontier and left themselves so weak that the Austrians defeated them at Turin in September. The French army retreated across the Alps and Austria was left as the dominant power in Italy.

It seemed as if the programme for which the allies had gone to war in 1702 had been fulfilled. The Dutch occupied their barrier, the English had the security they sought in the Low Countries and the Austrians had most of what they claimed in the southern Netherlands and Italy. But success had so whetted the appetites of the English and Austrians that they wanted more. The 1705 general election in England had strengthened the Whigs and they insisted on 'no peace without Spain'. But events in 1707 demonstrated just how fragile was the Grand Alliance and to what an extent the allied success depended upon their being able to apply continuous pressure on the French along all fronts simultaneously. In March, without consulting the maritime powers, the emperor signed a treaty with France neutralizing the whole of Italy. The strategic repercussions of this agreement were felt in the Netherlands, Spain and southern France. The French were able to reinforce their armies in all three theatres. They could place 100,000 men in the field to ensure that Marlborough could not exploit his victory at Ramillies. In Spain they defeated an under-strength allied army at Almanza in April and ended any real hopes the allies entertained of conquering the country. And they were able to rush just enough troops to Toulon to prevent a combined allied operation from seizing the city.

By 1708 it was apparent that if Spain was to be conquered it could only be done in the Spanish Netherlands. Realizing this, the French tried to weaken the allied army in the Low Countries by mounting a diversion against Scotland. In March they dispatched a small Jacobite expedition which anchored at the mouth of the Firth of Forth. But it did not evoke a rising in Scotland and the Royal Navy arrived before any of the 5,000 French troops on board could land. The ten battalions detached from Marlborough's army to counter it returned to Flanders before the campaigning season began. In July Marlborough defeated a determined French attempt to reconquer the Spanish Netherlands at Oudenarde and exploited his victory by piercing France's frontier fortifications by taking Lille. However, the fortress had served its purpose. It did not fall until December and by then it was too late in the season for Marlborough to exploit his victory.

Marlborough's progress, and the severe winter of 1708/9 which caused widespread destitution in France, encouraged the allies to stand firm on their war aims. When Louis dispatched his foreign minister to the Hague in April 1709, the Dutch demanded terms on behalf of the allies which amounted to a virtual capitulation by France. Savoy and the Dutch claimed enlarged barriers as security against future French aggression and Louis was told to expel James and to recognize the Protestant succession in Britain. He might have been willing to swallow these conditions, but what he would not accept was that Philip had to renounce his claim to the Spanish throne and if he refused Louis was to use French troops to expel him. The talks collapsed. By exposing the allies' unreasonableness they rallied French opinion in defence of their country. Louis was able to raise an army which won a timely defensive victory at Malplaquet in September. The war on France's northern frontier had reached a stalemate.

The French were not the only belligerents who were growing war weary by 1710. The winter of 1708/9 had also brought great hardship to England. Hatred of the recruiting sergeant and the press-gang was growing, merchants were suffering too many losses at sea and the land tax remained obstinately at four shillings in the pound. By 1710 Queen Anne and a large part of the Tory party had come to believe that the Whigs had committed the country to an endless struggle. They blamed the greed of Marlborough, the monied interest, government contractors and allies who were in receipt of English subsidies for the failure to negotiate peace. In August 1710 a political revolution began. The Tory leader Harley constructed an alternative government and in October the Tories won an overwhelming victory in the general election.

But although the new government wanted peace, it knew it would not get satisfactory terms unless it maintained pressure on France. As befitted a Tory administration it devoted more resources than its predecessor had done to securing colonial and commercial gains. But the initiative to do this came as much from the colonists themselves as it did from the government in London. In 1703 the French and their Indian allies had attacked the English colonies of Maine and Massachusetts, but it was not until 1709 that the colonists persuaded the home government to send ships and soldiers to protect them. In 1710 a combined force from the colonies captured Port Royal, the capital of French Nova Scotia. In 1711 the new government tried to drive the French from Canada by attacking Quebec but the expedition was wrecked by bad planning and poor navigation. It ought to have been a timely warning to the exponents of a maritime strategy of the practical problems of fighting a war across an ocean.

In Europe the new government tried to maintain at least a façade of allied unity. It signalled its determination to continue the war by retaining Marlborough in command of the allied army in Flanders for the 1711 campaign. But, despite the fact that the Grand Alliance powers were bound by treaty not to seek a separate peace, Harley and Shrewsbury opened secret negotiations with France in August 1710. Harley realized that the allies could not achieve their aim of 'no peace without Spain'. He was content to revert to the alliance's original aim of partitioning the Spanish Empire. This policy appeared to make even better sense after April 1711 when the Emperor Joseph of Austria died and he was succeeded by the Archduke Charles. The possibility of the same man sitting on the thrones in Madrid and Vienna was no more attractive to the English than that the same man might sit upon the thrones in Paris and Madrid. In October 1711 the French and English signed preliminary terms which gave the English much of what they wanted. Louis recognized the Protestant succession, accepted the separation of the French and Spanish crowns, ceded Newfoundland and Hudson's Bay to England and granted them the *Asiento* and the use of trading stations on the River Plate. The Dutch and Austrians were also granted their barriers.

Britain's allies did not like these terms. But, given the size of England's military, naval and financial contributions to the alliance, they could not force her to renounce them. The final treaty ending the war was signed at Utrecht in April 1713. The Duke of Savoy was given Sicily to counterbalance Habsburg power in Italy and because the English did not want to see the Austrians athwart their Levant trade. The rest of Spain's Italian possessions together with the Southern Netherlands were given to Austria. Philip retained Spain and her transoceanic colonies but renounced his claim to the French throne.

Louis had come to the peace table because his financial resources had been bled dry by a prolonged war of attrition. England's strategic policy between 1688 and 1714 did not conform exactly to either the concept of 'the British way in warfare' or the 'mixed paradigm'. As Table 1.1 illustrates, during the Nine Years' War the government spent only slightly more on sea services than it did on land services and succeeded in striking a rough balance between them. However, during the War of the Spanish Succession spending was more clearly tilted towards the navy. This propensity to spend more on the navy than on the army in wartime remained a feature of British policy until the French Revolution and made Britain almost unique. With the exception of the Dutch during the early eighteenth century, and the French during the American War of Independence, no other state except Britain spent such a high proportion of its defence budget on sea services. In the brief period of peace between 1698 and 1701 the army was reduced to cadre strength and spending on land services as a proportion of total defence spending correspondingly fell. The fall would have been even more pronounced had it not been for the willingness of the Irish Parliament to fund nearly one-fifth of the cost of the Crown's land services. Spending on the navy as a proportion of total defence spending actually rose in peacetime because ships laid up in ordinary and the dockyard support system they needed could not be improvised rapidly on the

Table 1.1 Ratio of Spending on the Land and Sea Services of the Crown, 1688–1712

	Land services : Sea services
1688–97	46 : 54
1698–1701	36 : 64
1702–12	40 : 60

Source: *Parliamentary Papers* 1868–9, xxxv, Public Income and Expenditure.

outbreak of war. Considerable sums of money had to be expended on their maintenance in peacetime throughout the eighteenth century.

The maritime policy advocated by many Tories and Country party MPs made a real but limited contribution to Louis's defeat by eating into French resources. But attacking France's overseas trade would not, by itself, have persuaded Louis to accept the terms he signed in 1713. William and Anne's governments were right to recognize that France's resources were so great that only by creating an anti-French alliance and by forcing the French to dissipate their resources on a number of fronts on land and sea simultaneously, could she be brought to the negotiating table.

English subsidies and her navy did play a role in creating and holding together the alliances but that role was limited and most responsible policy-makers knew it. Too much should not be made of England's propensity to pay others to do her land fighting. The sums allocated to subsidize foreign princes were only a modest proportion of defence spending. England's subsidy policy began in a small way during the Nine Years' War. The published accounts make it difficult to determine how much Parliament voted and how much was actually paid and suggest that about 2 per cent of the money the English spent on the war between 1689 and 1697 was used to purchase foreign military assistance. This is almost certainly a considerable underestimate for it takes no account of the pay due to the foreign troops on the British establishment. Between 1702–12 the sums involved amounted to about 8 per cent of the monies Parliament voted for the upkeep of the armed forces. Subsidies did not buy allied obedience to English wishes. What they did was to facilitate action by allied powers which they believed was in their own interests and which might also be in England's interests. English policy-makers realized these limitations. If they had had greater faith in the efficacy of gold to buy victories, they would have spent more money on their allies. The allied naval victory at Vigo Bay in 1702 did help persuade Portugal and Savoy to join the allies. But in 1704 the navy was of no assistance to the Austrians. Like England's other continental allies, they demanded English troops in the largest possible numbers on the continent. In both wars the English obliged them. Table 1.2 illustrates the average percentage of troops on the English establishment (including mercenaries) deployed in

Table 1.2 Average Annual Troop Dispositions, 1691–7 and 1702–13 by Percentage

	Flanders	England	Colonies and amphibious operations
1691–7	65	32	3
1702–13	58	13	7

Note: Between 1704 and 1712 approximately 25 per cent of troops on the English establishment were in Spain and Portugal.

Flanders, England and overseas each year between 1691 and 1697, and 1702 and 1713. The English committed a major part of their landforces to the continent in both wars, although a disproportionately large share of the troops sent to the continent consisted of foreign mercenaries rather than subject troops. In the brief period of peace between the wars a large part of the political nation showed a marked inclination to withdraw into isolation, a tendency which was only countered by William's stubbornness and the growing obviousness of the threat Louis posed to the liberties of Europe, English trade and, crucially, to the Protestant succession. In both wars the English made their main contribution to the allied military effort in Flanders, although in the second they also made a significant effort in the Iberian Peninsula. The number of troops committed to operations in the colonies or to amphibious operations around the periphery of the enemies' coastline were negligible. These were European wars fought in Europe for European objectives.

It is tempting to condemn the Earl of Oxford (the title Harley assumed in May 1711) for cynically abandoning England's allies in 1713. In fact he should be given credit for recognizing the limitations which technology, politics and finance placed on warfare as an instrument of policy in the early eighteenth century. His major achievement was to reduce England's war aims to within practical limits. Utrecht secured most of the major objectives for which England had gone to war in 1702. French power was checked and a balance of power was established in western Europe. The French wars of 1689–1713 marked the emergence of England as a great European power, a fact underlined by the way in which the Treaty of Utrecht was largely dictated by England and France. In the next half century England also began to emerge as a major imperial power.

2 War for Empire, 1714–63

Between 1714 and 1763 Britain emerged as Europe's leading imperial power. She did not do so by disengaging from the European alliance system so as to be free to devote resources to expanding her interests outside Europe. On the contrary, membership of a series of European alliances was fundamental to her ability to expand her extra-European interests. Without European allies she would have been compelled to devote too many resources to defending her interests in Europe to have been able to look further afield.

Under the early Hanoverians the ultimate direction of defence policy was the responsibility of the king, the First Lord of the Treasury, and the secretaries of state. The Secretary for the Northern Department was usually responsible for relations with Russia, the Baltic, Holland and Germany. His colleague, the Secretary for the Southern Department, was answerable for relations with Spain, France, Italy and the Ottoman Empire. This division of responsibilities sometimes made the pursuit of a coherent policy difficult until one secretary achieved a dominant position. In the later 1740s and early 1750s the Duke of Newcastle engineered the dismissal of no less than three of his colleagues before he secured a compliant partner in the shape of the Earl of Holderness. Major overseas expeditions involving both services were usually the responsibility of one of the secretaries of state, who signed orders directing the naval and military commanders. A secretary of state's powers were never unfettered, as Pitt the Elder discovered. At least during the later stages of the Seven Years' War, when Pitt was always careful to keep the service ministers informed of Cabinet decisions, the system worked with reasonable efficiency.

Ministerial deliberations were constrained by what was acceptable to Parliament and the wider political nation. After 1714 the Tory party lost its Court wing and became an opposition Country party. The ministers of the first two Georges were almost entirely Court Whigs. Suspicion of foreigners and of any attempt by the administration to augment the army or to send subject troops or subsidy forces to the continent became part of the stock-in-trade of 'patriot' politicians who opposed the government. They were only reflecting the prejudices of a political nation which extended far beyond the walls of Whitehall and Westminster and which no administration could ignore. In 1714 approximately one in five adult males could vote and the electorate numbered about a quarter of a million. There were some questions upon which they could and did express strong prejudices. The widespread fear of a large standing army remained. Anti-popery coupled with a wider xenophobia also ran deep and produced passions which could be exploited by the government to generate a powerful ground swell of anti-Bourbon sentiment. But the opposition could also exploit them to encourage suspicion that the first two Georges wanted to place Hanover's interests before those of Britain.

After 1714 the idea that Britain's security was bound up with the preservation of a balance of power was widely, but not universally, accepted. In 1734 Newcastle wrote that 'we are and must be ... concerned for the Balance of power, on which our own peace and security entirely depend.'[1] But some 'patriot' politicians professed to believe that Britain need not actually act to keep the balance. Britain was not the only state which might be threatened by an over-mighty France. She could leave it to France's continental neighbours to coalesce against her if she threatened their liberties. Those who did believe that Britain had to exert herself to maintain the balance were divided over how she should do so. The success of the Grand Alliance in containing Louis XIV tempted statesmen like Newcastle to try to repeat the same policy in the 1740s and 1750s. He met with little success. A more practical option after 1714, because it took account of the fact that not every other power agreed with Britain that France was the most pressing and constant threat to their security, was to give support to the most powerful state that could be found ready to resist France. In the 1730s and 1740s that meant Austria.

The navy emerged from the wars against Louis XIV with its prestige enhanced. Before 1688 the social gap between gentlemen and 'tarpaulins' – experienced seamen commissioned from the lower deck or from the merchant marine – was wide. But by 1714 the tarpaulins aspired to gentlemanly manners and officers of gentle birth had acquired professional competence. The navy now offered a vocation acceptable both to the sons of the aristocracy and gentry and a career for talented men of quite humble birth for, unlike the army, commissions could not be purchased; they had to be earned. In 1667 Samuel Pepys, the Secretary of the Admiralty, introduced an examination in seamanship for all aspiring lieutenants. No candidate was permitted to present himself for examination until he had served a minimum period at sea. The system imposed a minimum standard of professional competence throughout the officer corps. Few men were attracted to a career on the quarter-deck by the pay. Until 1694 it had compared badly with that offered in the merchant service. Because fleets were expensive to maintain, at the end of each war the government laid up most of its warships and paid off their officers and crews. However, in 1694 the pay of commissioned officers was almost doubled and the half-pay system, which hitherto had applied to only a fraction of the officer corps, was eventually extended to apply to all captains and many lieutenants and masters. They now received a retainer even when they were not employed in peacetime. This ensured that the navy could become a lifetime's profession. Once they had received their commissions officers were encouraged to devote themselves to their professions by the prospect of the far higher rates of pay and allowances they might receive if they attained the rank of post-captain. Promotion to that rank depended upon a mixture of competence, luck and patronage. Promotion to flag rank depended on seniority. The result was that the naval officer corps was divided into a myriad of shifting and amorphous cliques which reflected and paralleled the political structure of the nation at large. But that did not mean that the rich and well-connected were promoted whether or not they had any professional skills. No patron readily sought the promotion of an officer who was incompetent lest his protégé's failure should redound to his own discredit. The advantage of such a system was that talented officers like Rodney, who became a rear-admiral at the age of 40, could reach flag rank when they were still in their prime.

For the lucky few a naval career could bring them a fortune from prize-money. It was granted to the officers and crew of any ship, together with their squadron or fleet commander, when they captured an enemy vessel. It was intended to promote zeal in the face of the enemy. The extent to which it helped to promote Britain's broader strategic interests was sometimes questionable. At times it may have discouraged captains from slugging it out with heavily armed enemy warships for fear that even if they were victorious their own vessels would be too badly damaged to pursue the rich prizes the enemy might be convoying. Parliament recognized that this was a problem and in 1740 it granted £5 'head money' for every man on board an enemy warship which was taken, sunk or burnt. Some officers ignored orders because of the chance to take a rich prize. The eighteenth-century Admiralty had few coercive powers over its officers and, given the fact that sailing ships were subject constantly to the vagaries of wind and weather, commanders on distant stations had ample latitude to interpret their orders as they saw fit. The Admiralty had to persuade them to obey orders by handing out the carrots of promotion, honours and potentially lucrative postings. The obverse of this was the propensity of officers to argue with the Admiralty about postings they did not want. Service in the Mediterranean was much sought after because of the rich pickings it offered. Service in the West Indies was shunned because, despite the chance of taking a rich prize, disease was all too likely to kill an officer before he could spend his windfall.

The navy continued to experience considerable difficulty in manning its vessels with experienced seamen in wartime. The problem was not insoluble. Bounties and the press could find sufficient men. Between 1738 and 1747 the number of seamen on the fleet's books rose from 16,800 to 48,200. But eighteenth-century administrations worked slowly and meant that men could not be found quickly. When seamen were found desertion remained endemic and scurvy, dysentery, fever and typhus continued to kill them in large numbers. The problem of disease was most acute when the fleet was being mobilized on the outbreak of war. Large numbers of recruits, often dressed in filthy clothes, came on board ship for the first time and brought with them innumerable diseases. Some attempts were made to safeguard seamen's health by improving their diet. In 1759 Admiral Hawke largely succeeded in eliminating scurvy as an operational problem during the second half of the Seven Years' War by insisting that the crews of his vessels blockading Brest should be served with fresh vegetables four times each week. But the permissive spirit which permeated so much eighteenth-century administration meant that this was usually done on the initiative of individual officers rather than throughout the fleet by order of the Admiralty.

Part of the navy's successes after 1714 was due to the fact that its support structure was now more developed. By the 1740s Portsmouth, Plymouth and Sheerness cleaned, refitted and repaired the home fleet, whilst Deptford, Woolwich and Chatham built ships-of-the-line, conducted major repairs and prepared stores for dispatch to other yards and to squadrons operating overseas. Harwich on the East Anglian coast and Kinsale on the Irish coast were used as bases for cleaning cruisers. In general they performed their tasks efficiently. If there were some complaints about excessive costs, it was conceded that their workmanship was superior to that offered by private yards. Sea officers believed that dockyard overhauls took too long, but some of these delays were the fault of captains who were too slow to prepare their own vessels for docking. After 1714, as the navy assumed an increasing role outside home waters, it also established bases overseas. Cruisers stationed in the North American colonies used the facilities offered by New York, Boston, Philadelphia, Charleston and, after 1749, Halifax in Nova Scotia. The East Indies squadron used Trincomalee in Ceylon and vessels in the West Indies used Port Royal, Jamaica and English Harbour, Antigua, where facilities were expanded after 1725 because trouble with Spain seemed to be a continual threat. Vessels in the Mediterranean used Gibraltar or, for preference, the superb natural harbour at Port Mahon on Minorca. At most of these bases ships' bottoms could be cleaned and repairs performed, stores were replenished and sick and wounded seamen placed in hospital. No other navy could match these overseas base facilities and although none of them could perform a major dry-dock overhaul, they did obviate the need to send vessels home for minor repairs and so they enabled the Royal Navy to keep its vessels on distant station for longer than its opponents.

The fact that Britain usually won most of her major naval engagements in this period was due neither to the superior training of her officer corps nor the superior design of her ships. Most British first- and second-raters were so badly designed that they could not open their lower gunports in anything but calm weather and were so difficult to man that they rarely left port. The three-decker third-raters carried too many guns and were unstable gun platforms because they heeled over excessively even in moderate winds and sea conditions. British naval officers did not receive a better formal training than their French or Spanish counterparts. The British officer corps was more socially cohesive in 1740 than it had been in 1670 but it was also riven by professional and political rivalries. But thanks to the high esteem in which the navy was held it did attract young men of talent. It is not difficult to see that the administrative structure supporting the fleet was illogical and in some respects even ramshackle. However, it served it well and by the middle of the eighteenth century the British were able to keep at sea the largest fleet in the world. The crucial advantage the navy enjoyed compared to its enemies was that its officers and seamen had greater sea-going experience. Year in and year out Britain kept more ships at sea than either France or Spain. There was no substitute for daily sail and gunnery drill at sea if captains wanted an efficient ship's company. Only an admiral who had supreme confidence in the seamanship of his subordinates would have done what Admiral Hawke did at Quiberon Bay in 1759 when he committed his fleet to a stern chase to leeward in a gale. The efficiency of the fleet in both peace and war was a reflection of the fact that the political nation was willing to spend comparatively lavishly on it. Without sufficient funds the fleet could not have been kept at sea for the lengthy periods which it was. It was above all lack of money which robbed French and Spanish fleets of much of their efficacy.

The social composition of the officer corps of the early Hanoverian army was little changed from what it had been before 1714. After 1714 the stimulus which war gave to efficiency was removed and many of the abuses which had existed before 1714 might have flourished still more widely. That they did not was largely the work of the first two Georges and the Duke of Cumberland. But they had an uphill struggle for the army was well represented in Parliament where army officers formed the largest single professional group in the Commons. The Crown tried to reduce the perquisites which company and troop commanders had been able to garner. Although the colonels escaped almost unscathed, this campaign to lessen corruption laid the groundwork for the House of Commons' more radical intervention into the regimental economy during and after the American War of Independence. George I detested the purchase system but the adamantine way in which eighteenth-century Englishmen clung to their property meant that he could not abolish it. The most he and his successor could do was to regulate it and prevent private individuals conducting business behind the Crown's back. In 1720 and 1722 Royal Warrants were published listing the rates at which commissions could be purchased. Prices varied depending upon the social standing of particular regiments. To prevent rich but inexperienced officers jumping up the promotion ladder the warrants stipulated that an officer could only sell his commission to another officer holding the rank immediately below him – i.e. a major could only sell his commission to a captain and not to a lieutenant – and they gave the Crown the right to select and approve the vendor's successor. But within twenty years the cash sums they stipulated were being exceeded so at the end of the Seven Years' War the Secretary at War, Lord Barrington, issued a revised list of prices. It, too, was soon being ignored.

The Hanoverians recognized that purchase was inimical to the morale and efficiency of their officer corps because many officers were too poor to purchase promotions. They had some success in ensuring that deserving officers of limited means and influence got at least some advancement and that young officers with deep purses but little experience did not monopolize the higher ranks of the army. Of the 290 men appointed to colonelcies between 1714 1763, 240 had served for at least fifteen years. But it was true that the rich and well-connected formed a 'fast stream' within the officer corps and left behind a much larger group of poorer but experienced officers in the lower ranks. However, in wartime the expansion of the army hastened the rate of promotion even for officers without wealth or influence. The result was that the early Hanoverian army was led by officers of considerable experience and no little merit. The system was not perfect and sometimes deserving officers who lacked means or influence were unfairly treated. But as in the navy, an officer with energy and talent who attracted influential patrons could rise to the top quickly. James Wolfe was a lieutenant at 15 and a major general at 32. The disadvantages of the purchase system must also be measured against the alternative. Purchase did not apply in the artillery or the engineers and it was no accident that both corps contained too many officers who were too old for duty in the field.

The establishment of the British army was reduced in 1714 to 22,000 men. It rose during the Jacobite emergency of 1715 but between 1722 and 1739 it remained fixed at 18,000 men, although it was augmented by the 12,000 men of the Irish establishment. By European standards the army of the first two Georges hardly made Britain a formidable military power. The king of Sardinia maintained a similar number of troops. But the Hanoverian monarchs did make a serious effort to maintain its readiness for war. Between 1716 and 1720 George I began to employ general officers to conduct an annual inspection of all regiments on the home establishment to determine whether they were fit for service. In 1728, at George II's instigation, the Board of General Officers issued the first new drill instructions since 1690. The Duke of Cumberland issued a second set in 1748. However, it was one thing to promote reforms on paper but it was quite another to see that they were put into practice, especially when the peacetime routines and duties of the army stood in the way of regular training. The greatest obstacle to making preparations for war in peacetime was Parliament's insistence that the army be reduced to cadre strength after each war. The army was never capable of delivering a considerable, never mind a knockout blow, against any opponent at the start of a war because regiments were too busy absorbing and training large numbers of raw recruits. Serious preparations for war were also hampered by peacetime patterns of duty. About a quarter of all infantry regiments served abroad garrisoning the empire, a quarter were in Britain and the remainder were in Ireland. Training facilities on overseas stations like Gibraltar were at best cramped and often non-existent. It was not until 1749 that Cumberland began a limited system of rotating units between home and overseas stations. Hitherto it had not been unusual for units in colonial garrisons to be abroad for over a decade without relief. Units at home which might have enjoyed more opportunity to train often found themselves doing the work of policemen because until the middle of the nineteenth century Britain lacked an effective civilian police-force. Lack of time, inadequate training facilities in colonial garrisons and the need to absorb large numbers of untrained men at the outbreak of each war, were the real reasons why the peacetime training of most regiments was insufficient and that of the remainder barely adequate. What is surprising is not that the army sometimes performed poorly on the battlefield but that it often performed as well as it did.

At the outbreak of each major war the government augmented the strength of its landforces in three ways. It brought existing units up to strength, it raised new units and it hired foreign mercenaries. Table 2.1 shows the mean number of men voted by Parliament during each of the major wars in which the British were engaged between 1714 and 1763. The government continued to restrict recruiting to the economically marginal. In 1756 the Duke of Newcastle deprecated forming even a part-time militia because 'It would breed up our people to a love of arms, & military government; & divert them from their true business, husbandry, manufacture, &.'[2] Recruiting foreign mercenaries therefore remained an attractive option, as Table 2.2 indicates.

The British could not disengage from Europe after 1714. The new dynasty gave the British a new interest in Europe, the defence of King George's German possessions, the Electorate of Hanover. It was not universally welcomed. The Act of Settlement in 1701 had stipulated that the new monarch must not wage war for anything other than British interests without the express sanction of Parliament. Under the first two Georges opposition politicians accused the king's British ministers of subordinating Britain's interests to those of Hanover.

Table 2.1 The Mean Number of Men Voted Annually by Parliament for Selected Wars, 1714–63

Date	Men
1718–20	26,403
1726–9	35,354
1739–48	79,563
1755–63	129,034

Table 2.2 The Mean Percentage of Foreign Troops on the British Establishment Voted Annually by Parliament for Selected Wars

1718–20	24
1726–9	18
1741–8	23
1756–63	30

But any British minister who wished to retain his post had to take account of his royal master's fondness for the Electorate. Almost as soon as George I ascended the throne his conduct illustrated just how the concerns of the Electorate and Britain might diverge. George wished to deprive Sweden of the small German territories of Bremen and Verden. But Britain's dependence on Baltic naval stores and cereals, not to mention the ministry's wish to discourage the Swedes from involving themselves in Jacobite intrigues, demanded peace in the Baltic and a rapid end to the Great Northern War. The need to seek support in the Baltic and the need to underwrite the Utrecht settlement in the south encouraged Viscount Stanhope, the Secretary of State for the Northern Department, to rebuild the alliance system that the Tories had dismantled. In 1716 he signed the Treaty of Westminster with Austria. In return for Austrian support in the Baltic, the British agreed to support Austrian ambitions in the Mediterranean. Stanhope then negotiated a new barrier treaty with the Dutch, but his major policy departure was to sign a treaty with France. The two powers were drawn together by a common desire to contain the revisionist ambitions of Spain. In November 1716 the old enemies became allies and, when they were joined by the Dutch in January 1717, a new triple alliance had been created.

The Anglo-French alliance was significant for the British because it protected Hanover, it meant that the Jacobites would not receive French support and it secured Britain's naval predominance. During the War of the Spanish Succession she had dominated the seas not because her fleet had overcome the enemy in battle but because of the diplomatic constellation in Europe. She was allied to two of the continent's major naval powers, Portugal and the United Provinces. The Spanish were engaged in a civil war and the French made their major effort on land. After 1714 the treaty enabled the British to dispatch their fleet overseas without worrying that they might be invaded from across the Channel. But the apparent ease with which the Royal Navy overshadowed other navies bred exaggerated expectations that Britain could solve her foreign policy difficulties through the use of her fleet. In practice the fleet alone was rarely effective. After 1714 the British only achieved their objectives when they could employ a judicious mixture of naval power, diplomacy and usually someone else's army.

The limitations of British naval power were illustrated in the aftermath of the Treaty of Utrecht. Between 1715 and 1717 powerful squadrons of the Royal Navy operated in the Baltic to check the Swedes. In 1716 Parliament voted a quarter of a million pounds 'to concert such measures with foreign powers as may prevent the design of Sweden for the future'[3] and by 1717 George had achieved his war aims. When Charles XII died in December 1718 Sweden's growing exhaustion and the navy's ability to prevent the Russians from crushing the Swedes produced a series of peace treaties in 1719 and 1720 which ended Sweden's hostilities with all her enemies. But what the fleet could not do without the support of a powerful army was to roll back Russian expansion. Events in the Mediterranean pointed to a similar lesson. Spain still coveted Sicily. The powers tried to deter her by signing a new Quadruple Alliance in August 1718. But the treaty, and the threat of British naval intervention were insufficient and the Spanish seized Sardinia and Sicily from the Duke of Savoy. The British reply was belated because they did not have a naval base in the Mediterranean where they could permanently station a powerful squadron. Although they had acquired Gibraltar and Minorca at Utrecht, neither was entirely suitable because both depended on imported grain from North Africa and were open to enemy attack. When they did muster a squadron the British were able to destroy the Spanish fleet off Cape Passaro in August 1718. But they then had to endure a lengthy conflict whilst an Austrian army actually reconquered Sicily. Nor did the fleet make Britain secure against invasion. A Spanish attempt to land a force of Jacobites in England was upset by adverse weather but they did land a small force in Scotland. The invaders were only finally crushed when troops overcame them at Glenshiel in June 1719. Spain did not finally capitulate until she was confronted by a French invasion across the Pyrenees in 1720.

The Spanish did not remain content for long. In 1725 they negotiated treaties of peace, trade and alliance with the Austrians. In 1726 the Russians and a number of smaller German princes joined them. The British viewed this with alarm. The new arrangement shattered the Quadruple Alliance, endangered the balance of power and threatened them with intensified Flemish commercial activity in the Spanish Empire. In September 1725 the British responded by forming the Alliance of Hanover with France and Prussia. The Dutch joined them in 1726 and the support of Sweden, Denmark, Hesse and Brunswick was purchased by subsidies. Between 1726 and 1729 a state of undeclared war existed. The fleet mounted a series of naval demonstrations off the coast of Spain and in the West Indies. Although the latter operation, involving the blockade of Porto Bello on the Isthmus of Panama, cost the lives of large numbers of the seamen involved, it did play an important role in preventing the crisis from escalating still further. Spain and Austria lacked the money they needed to mount an aggressive war effort and looked to the Indies to make good this deficiency. By paralysing the flow of specie to Spain, the navy crippled their efforts and the Spanish could only retaliate by besieging Gibraltar. Because the Spanish could not lend them the money they needed, by the spring of 1727 the Austrians were losing their taste for their new allies and agreed to open negotiations. Spain had little choice but to follow their example and in March 1728 they agreed to cease hostilities.

The entire episode seemed to vindicate the faith of many Englishmen in the efficacy of naval power. However, as peace negotiations became protracted, the British government faced increasing criticism at home because of the continuing heavy cost of the war. The land tax had been raised to four shillings in the pound to raise the money to subsidize the allies, hire Hessian mercenaries, augment the army and fit-out the fleet. In 1729/30 a growing domestic crisis reached a head. Sir Robert Walpole was able to oust his rival Viscount Townshend and effect a reconciliation with Spain. Walpole's overriding passion was peace. If he secured it the land tax could be reduced, trade would prosper and the Hanoverian dynasty could be made more secure. He achieved his aims. The Treaty of Seville signed in November 1729 meant that the French and British had detached Spain from Austria. In return they allowed Spanish troops to occupy the Duchies of Parma and Piacenza. This was unacceptable to the Austrians and raised the spectre of war in central Europe to solve the Italian problem. Walpole deftly avoided it by negotiating a *rapprochement* with the Austrians behind the back of France. By the Treaty of Vienna of 1731 the Austrians agreed to stop all talk of a marriage alliance between Austria and any other great power, to allow the Spanish into the duchies and not to permit the Flemings to compete in the Spanish Empire.

Walpole had succeeded in resolving the major problem which had beset central and southern Europe since 1725. With the danger of war averted he could demobilize the army and navy and reduce the land tax to one shilling in the pound. But the British paid a high price for this settlement. Peace with Spain did nothing to defuse the growing antagonism between the two powers over Britain's illegal trade with Spain's American colonies. As part of their agreement with Austria, the British had to make a serious commitment to central Europe by guaranteeing the Pragmatic Sanction, recognizing the indivisibility of the Austrian Empire and the rights of the emperor's daughter, Maria Theresa, to succeed to the Austrian dominions. But most important of all, Walpole's efforts left the Anglo-French alliance in tatters and the era of Anglo-French co-operation was ended. Within two years the two Bourbon courts had signed a family compact and begun to increase their naval armaments. The strategic consequences of this shift in diplomatic alignments were immense. With the Bourbon powers potentially hostile, and with the United Provinces much weaker than they had been during the wars against Louis XIV, Hanover was vulnerable and Britain had lost the naval predominance she had enjoyed since the Battle of Malaga. It was therefore not surprising that Walpole did all he could to keep Britain free of continental conflicts. Until 1739 he succeeded. Hoping that the Habsburgs and Bourbons would exhaust themselves, to Britain's ultimate benefit, Walpole stayed neutral during the War of the Polish Succession which broke out in 1733. Walpole's boast to the Queen in 1734 that 'Madam, there are fifty thousand men slain this year in Europe, and not one Englishman' appealed to a British public afraid that British interests might be subordinated to those of Hanover. But his calculations were wrong. The Austrians were defeated, France secured the Duchy of Lorraine and emerged as the effective arbiter of Europe.

Mercantile complaints that the Whig government was placing the continental interests of the Hanoverian dynasty before those of British merchants became part of the 'patriot' critique of Whig rule under Walpole and were exploited by the parliamentary opposition. After the peace of Utrecht the trade of the French colonial empire in the West Indies expanded rapidly and British merchants were concerned about growing competition with the French in the 1720s and 1730s. The French had the advantage that their colonies were more populous, fertile and possessed more cultivable land than did those of their British competitors. Throughout Europe the British faced increasing French competition in re-exported colonial goods. And in the North Atlantic the French were expanding the foundations of their naval power as growing numbers of Breton fishermen, using the fortress of Louisburg on Cape Breton as their base, began to exploit the fisheries of the Grand Banks off Newfoundland. But it was in the Spanish Empire that commercial rivalry first spilled over into open war. The interests of Britain and Spain conflicted at several points. The Spanish continued to resent the British occupation of Gibraltar. There were constant disagreements over the frontier of British Georgia and Spanish Florida and, most important of all, the Spanish resented the way in which British traders from Barbados, Jamaica and New England tried to increase their illegal trade with Spanish America. The episode during which Captain Jenkins's ear was allegedly sliced off was only one of a series of clashes which took place between British interlopers and the Spanish *garde costa* in the Caribbean. By 1738 Anglo-Spanish relations had reached a crisis. The economic importance of the illegal trade was not so great as to justify war. The damage a war would do to Britain's legitimate trade with the Hispanic world would certainly outweigh any direct economic gains Britain might make. But the interloping merchants were able to exploit the political climate of the late 1730s to secure support. Mercantile lobbies all over the country, fearful that they were about to be squeezed out of the colonial trade by the French and Spanish, pressed for war. The press portrayed the conflict as a struggle between slavery and liberty in which Britain's national honour was at stake. The parliamentary opposition, led by politicians as skilful as the Elder Pitt and Carteret, exploited these sentiments to embarrass the government. Walpole tried to stop the agitation by dispatching a squadron under Admiral Haddock to threaten the Spanish coast. But he remained anxious to avoid war and he almost succeeded. He negotiated a convention with Spain by which they were to have paid compensation to the British and in return the British South Sea Company would have paid its debts to the Spanish government. But the South Sea company, supported by a bellicose public, refused to honour their obligations and when the Spanish in turn refused to ratify the treaty, the public outcry in Britain forced the government to declare war.

Unlike many Englishmen, Walpole had a shrewd appreciation of the limitations of British naval power. But the apparent ease with which the fleet had achieved Britain's political objectives since 1714 and popular stories and ballads of the successes of Elizabethan buccaneers, blinded most of the public to the problems of mounting combined operations in the tropics four thousand miles from Britain. The War of Jenkins's Ear which began in 1739 was the first war the British had fought primarily to acquire a West Indian empire. Its supporters looked upon the Spanish Empire as a fruit ripe to be plucked. The opposition believed that key points like Havana, San Domingo and Cartagena could be annexed with little difficulty and would produce great profits. But not only did they underestimate Spain's strength in the Caribbean, they also failed to appreciate the logistical and medical problems which any large expedition operating in the region would face.

The Walpole ministry was not incompetent nor did it lack strategic direction. But in 1739, as it tried to wage war on the other side of the Atlantic, it had to move rapidly from a peacetime to a wartime footing. This was a task no previous British government had attempted. On paper the Royal Navy possessed a comfortable margin of superiority over the Spanish. But the government could not deploy all their forces against Spain for fear that Britain herself would be left vulnerable to a French invasion. Even so the British began the war with a striking success. Intent on crippling Spain's ability to make war, they tried to throttle her trade with the Indies. In November 1739 Admiral Vernon captured Porto Bello before Spanish reinforcements could arrive. Commodore Anson, who had been sent to take Panama, failed to do so but after rounding Cape Horn he did succeed in disrupting Spanish trade in the Pacific and eventually circumnavigated the globe. But thereafter the British war effort in the West Indies was a dismal failure. Both the army and navy were short of men and time was needed to augment them. By contemporary standards the administration of the army and navy was not defective but the system could not respond quickly to the unprecedented demands placed upon it to support a huge expedition in the Caribbean. It took nearly a year to organize the dispatch of 11,000 troops to support Vernon. When they arrived all chance of achieving surprise had passed and they were devastated by yellow fever. In March 1741 an attack on Cartagena was an expensive failure. Subsequent efforts to capture Cuba and Panama also failed. By the end of 1742 the British ceased offensive operations in the Caribbean and Spain continued to receive the treasure which she needed to fight the war. In Britain the public's facile belief in the efficacy of British naval supremacy received a rude shock. Walpole had only agreed to the Caribbean venture because public expectations meant that if he did not 'his opposers would take the Advantage of troubling him'.[4] But as the king's first minister it was he who had to take the blame for policies which he had opposed in the privacy of the cabinet. In February 1742 he resigned.

But by then the war with Spain had merged into a larger European contest. Charles VI's death in October 1740 and the accession of Maria Theresa to the Habsburg's throne encouraged Spain, France, Bavaria and Prussia to try to divide her inheritance between them. In December 1740 Frederick II of Prussia began the war when he invaded Silesia, Austria's richest province. Faced with a war in the Caribbean which was already stretching Britain's resources, Walpole temporized, hoping that moral pressure might induce Frederick to withdraw. It did not and by May 1741, after the defeat of Austria at the Battle of Mollowitz and with the possibility of a Franco-Prussian alliance drawing closer, Walpole could wait no longer. If a balance of power was to be maintained, and

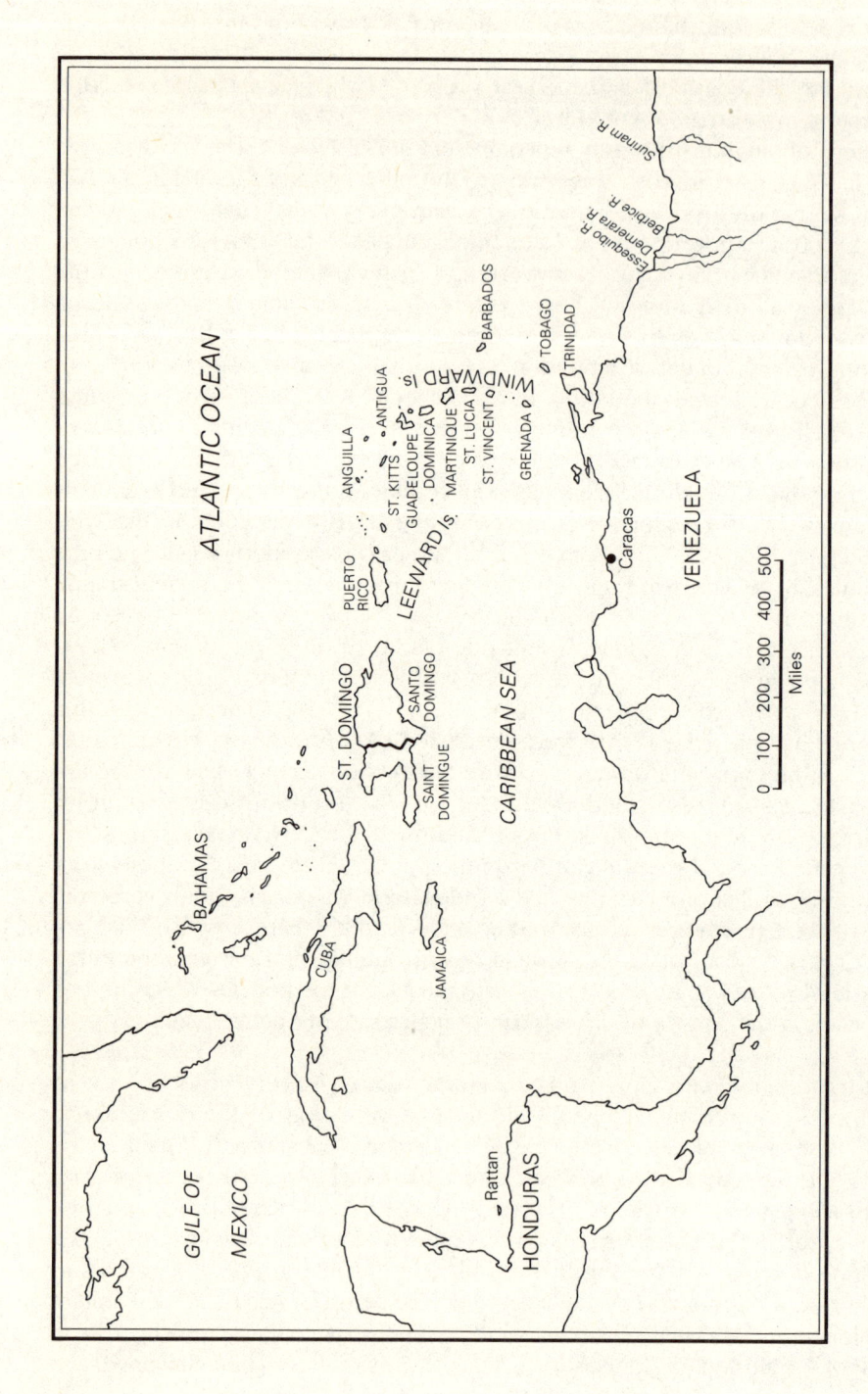

Figure 2 The Caribbean

if the French were to be kept out of northern Italy and the Austrian Netherlands, the Britain would have to give Austria direct military support. 'America', as the Lord Chancellor, Lord Hardwicke, remarked, 'must be fought for in Europe'.[5] But the British could not act effectively upon the continent without allies and as one minister had written in October 1740, 'if the Powers now concern'd will not enter into any measures for the preservation of the Balance of Europe, which is now in imminent Danger, His Majesty must be obliged to confine his case to the security of his own subjects, without interesting, or concerning himself, about the fate of Europe in General'.[6] The government began to assemble an expeditionary force of 12,000 men. Although large by British standards, it was small by continental ones and with Austria apparently on the point of defeat, there was little hope that any other European powers would throw in their lot with them. George II, in his role as Elector of Hanover, refused to employ his 25,000 Hanoverian troops to assist the Austrians and declared his Electorate neutral. In doing so he crippled the British government's efforts to create an anti-French coalition. The army stayed at home.

The situation began to improve early in 1742. This was not due to Walpole's resignation and the fact that control of war policy passed into the hands of Lord Carteret, George II's favourite. It happened because Maria Theresa temporarily neutralized Prussia by negotiating a convention with her in October 1741. This freed the Austrian army to operate against the French and by the middle of 1742 they had driven the French backwards and occupied Bavaria. In September 1742, sweetened by the offer of further British subsidies, Austria went further and made peace with Prussia. It was these more propitious circumstances which made it possible in 1742 for the British to send to Flanders 16,000 British troops, supported by Danish and Hanoverian mercenaries, to form the Pragmatic Army. In 1743, under the command of George II, they advanced into Germany and in June defeated the French at Dettingen. George might have pursued the French into their own country but did not do so because Britain was not yet at war with France. She was acting as an Austrian auxiliary and no British policy-maker wished to provoke a French declaration of war. But although the victory did not give the British any significant military advantage, it did strengthen Carteret's hand when he negotiated the Treaty of Worms with the Sardinians and Austrians in September 1743 to provide for the defence of northern Italy against the combined Bourbon forces.

But Carteret's triumph was brief because Prussia's neutrality was brief. In 1744, fearful of the growth of Austrian power in Germany, Frederick II organized the League of Frankfurt to resist it and in August he invaded Bohemia. Carteret's hope that Austria would invade France from the east was still-born. The Bourbons reacted to the setbacks of 1743 by signing a new family compact designed to enable them to prosecute the war against Britain more vigorously and launched new offensives in the Low Countries and Italy. After the failure of their operations in the West Indies the Royal Navy spent most of 1742–4 convoying merchant ships, trying to intercept Spanish treasure fleets, supporting the Austrian army in northern Italy and observing the enemy fleets in Brest, Toulon and Ferrol. In February 1744 Admiral Mathews failed to prevent the escape of the Franco-Spanish fleet from Toulon and the French were able to assemble an invasion flotilla at Dunkirk. In March they finally declared war on Britain and Hanover. It was difficult for the government to sustain popular support for an expensive policy of military intervention on the continent which seemed incapable of delivering any tangible victories and appeared to leave Britain open to invasion. Many Englishmen suspected that British troops and gold were being sent to the continent to protect Hanover and by December Henry Pelham and the Duke of Newcastle had created a new 'broad bottom' administration without Carteret.

The new ministry was divided over the proper course to follow. Pelham had never liked the continental war but his brother Newcastle was committed to it. The French followed their declaration of war by invading the Netherlands and promised to prolong the fighting just when the British were beginning to contemplate peace. Marshal Saxe owed his victory at Fontenoy in May 1745 not only to the tactical ineptitude of the allied commander, the Duke of Cumberland, but more significantly to the fact that the French outnumbered their enemies. In August 1744 the Austrians had recalled their troops from France's frontiers to meet the renewed threat from Prussia. In the wars against Louis XIV the British had spent a larger proportion of their resources on sea services than on the army. Between 1739 and 1748 those priorities were maintained. Britain's commitments in the West Indies meant that between 1742 and 1748 she committed about one soldier in three to Flanders compared to about two in three in Marlborough's wars. The result, given also the growing financial weakness of the Dutch, was that by 1745 the allies could not match the French army in Flanders. By 1746 Saxe could deploy about 120,000 men there compared to the allied force of 80,000 men.

But the most pressing threat to Britain came in July 1745 when Charles Edward, the Young Pretender, landed in Scotland. This was the most serious invasion the Jacobites ever mounted. The Hanoverians overcame it because for most Englishmen and Scotsmen the prospect of a Catholic prince on the throne was no more acceptable in 1745 than it had been in 1688. After the Jacobites took Edinburgh and marched as far south as Derby, scarcely 150 miles from London, the English rallied to the Hanoverian dynasty. Demonstrations of loyalty were not just confined to the ruling oligarchy. Even in Scotland support for a Jacobite restoration turned out to be negligible. Not one of Scotland's great magnates supported the Pretender. It was the lack of popular support in England that more than anything else persuaded the Jacobites to turn back to Scotland when they had reached Derby. News that they had done so persuaded the commander of the French invasion force destined to land on the south coast of England to abandon an attempt at a Channel crossing even though the winds were in his favour and had blown Admiral Vernon's blockading squadron off station. Newcastle tipped the military balance in favour of the Hanoverians by recalling the army from Flanders and summoning 6,000 Dutch troops. The navy played a limited but significant role in defeating the rebellion. After Charles Edward retreated into Scotland it could not totally block his communications with France. But it did reduce the supplies of gold and food he received and command of the coastal waters around Scotland ensured that the Hanoverian forces under Cumberland were properly supplied. It was the lack of cash to pay his troops which persuaded Charles Edward to gamble on defeating Cumberland's forces at Culloden in April 1746 and gave Cumberland the opportunity to defeat him. The episode was not without some strategic significance for the detachment of the British contingent meant that the Pragmatic Army was further weakened. Frederick II had inflicted sufficient defeats on the Austrians to persuade them to make peace in December 1745 and after Fontenoy Saxe was able to take control of the whole of Belgium. In February 1746 he occupied Brussels and the Bourbons defeated the Sardinians at the Battle of Bassignano in northern Italy.

One of the few bright spots for the British was the capture of Louisburg in June 1745. Louisburg was the only French naval base on the North American coast and it guarded the gateway to French North America. It was taken by 4,000 New England militiamen protected by a small squadron dispatched from the West Indies. Its fall ended hopes of an early peace. It encouraged Englishmen to look towards North America, rather than the West Indies, as somewhere to satiate their imperial ambitions. And it encouraged Tory spokesmen like Pitt the Elder to insist that Britain should withdraw from the fruitless land war in Europe and open a new front against the enemy in North America. The British were not able to do this because mounting large-scale colonial expeditions took time and patience, commodities which were in short supply by 1746. They also required the practical elimination of the French and Spanish navies. But the British did not achieve naval superiority quickly or easily. During the early years of the war enemy squadrons seemed to come and go at will. In 1741 the Spanish were able to transport 12,000 troops from Barcelona to Genoa by sea because the British squadron attempting to blockade Cadiz and Cartagena was too weak to intercept the combined Franco-Spanish squadron convoying them. After 1742 the Admiralty took care to reduce their commitments in the West Indies and deployed more vessels in the western Mediterranean. As in previous conflicts the French resorted to a *guerre de course* against British merchant ships and for some time British losses mounted. It was not until 1745 that the Admiralty began effectively to blockade the main French fleet. Frigates were stationed to maintain a close watch on Rochefort and Brest while a powerful squadron of ships-of-the-line was deployed off the south-west coast of England to intercept the French fleet if it left harbour. The policy was successful but it was only in 1747 that Anson and Hawke finally succeeded in cutting French communications with North America and the West Indies.

A successful colonial war also required that Britain's allies must be able to hold the ring against France in Europe. They could not do so. In 1746/7

Newcastle's strategy rested on two pillars. He wanted to keep Britain's allies united and he wanted to delay any serious peace negotiations until the allies had won some significant victories in Europe to improve their bargaining position. He could do neither. Liège fell to Saxe in October 1746 and by July 1747 he was on the point of taking the fortress of Maestricht, the key to the Dutch Republic. The Austrian contingent with the Pragmatic Army was below its establishment. The Dutch had practically no army ready and told the British that without a large loan they would have to seek terms from the French. Parliament was not prepared to find the money. France wanted peace because she was suffering a serious fiscal crisis and a famine and hoped that by offering her enemies moderate terms she would be able to shatter the anti-Bourbon coalition. Peace negotiations had begun between Britain and France in 1746. They had stalled because Newcastle insisted on retaining Cape Breton but the news from Holland made him realize that it was time to make concessions. The British negotiators could not disrupt the Bourbon family compact, they recognized that their Dutch allies were a broken reed and that the Austrians were dissatisfied with the way London had compelled them to cede Silesia to Prussia. Britain agreed to surrender Louisburg in return for France evacuating Flanders and Madras in India. Prussia was the only state to gain much from the war. The Treaty of Aix-la-Chapelle ending the war was signed in October 1748, product of a stalemate. It marked an uneasy truce in Anglo-French relations and their antagonism, both in Europe and in the colonies, remained unresolved.

After 1748 the British sought to avoid another war with France by demonstrating that they would not permit the French to bully them. In Europe they attempted to deter the French by reinvigorating the Grand Alliance with Holland and Austria. Outside Europe they defended what they thought were their colonial rights. Britain now possessed an extensive empire in the Caribbean and on the mainland of North America. From Georgia to New York British settlers had begun to reach the eastern boundaries of the Appalachian Mountains. They were in contact with the Indian peoples of the interior, exchanging furs for guns, cloth, hardware and rum. They were meeting increasing competition from the French who had extensive settlements in Canada and wished to connect these settlements with their southern settlements in Louisiana by establishing a line of forts down the Ohio valley. Both nations believed that trade enhanced their power and in the early 1750s commercial rivalry spilled over into violence in the disputed regions of the Ohio valley, the Great Lakes and Nova Scotia. Newcastle, who became the king's first minister in March 1754, had been convinced since 1749 that the French would resume the war with Britain just as soon as they had manoeuvred themselves into a stronger position than they had enjoyed in 1748. The intelligence which colonial governors sent to London seemed to prove France's aggressive intentions. Newcastle wanted to avoid a general war. But he believed that unless French attempts to encircle the British colonies were defeated, when the war he feared did begin, the colonies would fall. Their loss would be a major blow to British power because he was convinced that in the last war it had only been Britain's maritime strength and her victories in America which had enabled her to check France.

In August 1753 the government ordered all colonial governors to use force to repel French encroachments into territory the British regarded as their own. In May 1754 troops commanded by George Washington were sent from Virginia where they clashed with the French at Fort Duquesne in the Ohio valley. This local conflict escalated into a world war. In September Newcastle's government decided to send Major-General Braddock with two regiments to the Ohio valley as a signal to the French that Britain would maintain what she believed to be her rights. But far from being deterred by this show of force, the French responded by assembling a fleet at Brest and Rochefort. They hoped that a show of naval force would intimidate the British into seeking a negotiated settlement. Newcastle feared that if the French continued their naval preparations and the negotiations failed, the French would be able to reinforce their forces in Canada unhindered and the balance of power in North America would have tilted in their favour. Braddock's troops sailed in January and in March they were followed by a fleet under Admiral Boscawen with orders to stop the French reinforcing their garrisons. But most of the French fleet evaded Boscawen and the French reinforced their colonies. The British abandoned hope of negotiations and in July 1755 the Cabinet ordered the fleet to attack the French in European waters.

The British hoped to fight a colonial and maritime war but the French would not let them for they retaliated by threatening Hanover. Traditionally the British had defended the Electorate by treaties with the Dutch and the Austrians. But in 1755 the Dutch wanted no more part in European wars and the Austrians were more concerned with expelling Frederick the Great from Silesia than fighting in defence of Hanover. The British therefore tried to protect the Electorate by signing subsidy treaties with the Hessians and Russians. The latter agreement caused Frederick the Great to fear that he might soon be confronted by a combined Anglo-Russian-Austrian force. In January 1756 he therefore seized a British offer that the two countries should agree to maintain the peace in Germany by promising not to attack each other's territories and to resist the passage of foreign troops through Germany by force.

The Convention of Westminster ignited a diplomatic revolution in which Newcastle succeeded in destroying the system of alliances which he had regarded as vital to Britain's security. It convinced the Austrians that Britain would not help them to reconquer Silesia. In May 1756 they signed the first Treaty of Versailles with France, agreeing not to menace each other's territory and to send troops or subsidies if either signatory was attacked by a third party. Fearful that the French would now try to invade Britain, Newcastle asked the Dutch to provide the 6,000 troops they were bound to supply to her under their treaty of 1678. They refused and broke the link between the maritime powers which had been forged in 1688. A fortnight later Britain declared war on France. Newcastle hoped to wage it by creating another grand alliance. But his ambition only demonstrated his insular egotism. Not every power shared his view that the containment of France should be their first and overriding priority. In Russian eyes Britain was now useless as an ally against Prussia and Russia reconciled herself to France by signing the Treaty of Versailles in December 1756.

Newcastle next briefly considered abandoning the continent to France and waging a purely maritime war. But Britain did not have enough ships or soldiers to do so. Braddock's forces had been routed on the Monongahela in July 1755. At sea the French could concentrate their resources against Britain and the British had to retain their fleet and army at home to counter the threatened invasion. Consequently in the Mediterranean Admiral Byng could not be reinforced in time and when the French landed on Minorca he failed to drive their ships away and the British garrison surrendered in May 1756. Britain was only saved from isolation by the recklessness of Frederick the Great who thought he was about to become the victim of a combined attack by Austria, Russia and France. In August 1756 he struck out against Austria by invading Saxony and threatening Bohemia in the hope that if he acted quickly he could defeat one of his enemies before the others were ready to help them. But although he occupied Saxony his attack only served to call into being against him the hostile combination he had most feared.

Braddock's defeat and the loss of Minorca led to the collapse of the Newcastle ministry. After a brief interim administration led by the Duke of Devonshire, Newcastle returned to the Treasury and one of his foremost critics, William Pitt, became Secretary of State for the Southern Department. Pitt did not enjoy full and unfettered control of foreign and defence policy. Government business was too large and complex to be guided by one man and strong-minded colleagues like Lord Anson, the First Lord of the Admiralty, could not be bullied by anyone. The ministry agreed that trade was the ultimate source of British power. As the Earl of Holderness, the Secretary of State for the Northern Department, wrote to the British ambassador in Berlin in July 1757, 'We must be merchants while we are soldiers... our Trade depends upon a proper exertion of our Maritime strength.'[7] To protect Britain's trade and to contain the French fleet, Anson reverted to the policy which had succeeded during the final stages of the previous war and established a strong squadron in the Western Approaches. In North America the government wished to recover their rights as defined by the Treaty of Utrecht and to establish a frontier contiguous with the St Lawrence and the Great Lakes. The main area of disagreement concerned Britain's policy towards the continent. George II wanted ministers who would do all they could to safeguard Hanover. Some ministers at least initially believed that Britain could best do this by confining herself to assisting her continental ally with subsidies. But others believed that she must dispatch troops as well as money. Britain could not detach herself entirely from the continent and fight exclusively at sea and in the colonies because so much of Britain's trade was with her European neighbours. By the time Britain had destroyed France's overseas trade and occupied her colonies France might have become master of the continent. If that happened Britain might, as in 1748, again be forced to surrender her colonial spoils in return for France giving up her gains in Europe. Pitt, whilst never embracing the king's views about Hanover, gradually moved towards the second school of thought.

But of even more fundamental importance in determining the course of strategic policy at the start of the war was the habitual weakness of the British army. As usual it took time to recruit enough men to complete cadre regiments and to raise new units. The government's first task was to safeguard the home islands and so free troops and ships for service overseas. The Jacobite invasion of 1745 had underlined Britain's vulnerability and, confronted by another threatened invasion in 1757, Parliament passed a Militia Act to raise 37,000 militiamen. The Act did not mark a significant departure from the principle that war must impinge as little as possible on the civilian population, or at least on the productive sections of it. The Militia was not a system of universal conscription for home defence. It was a tax, levied in men or, increasingly, money, on particular localities. Each county was given a fixed number of men it had to levy. Although recruits were chosen by lot, only the poor, and therefore presumably the least economically productive, had to serve. Their better-off neighbours could pay a fine or buy a substitute to serve in their place. The militia served several purposes. It freed regulars for service abroad and it prevented public panics about an invasion which might otherwise have hamstrung the war effort by destroying public credit. As Holderness wrote in October 1755, 'Public credit is our very being, and there is no answering for the effects which a panick [sic] taken here might have upon those objects which are the basis of our strength and grandeur.'[8] Its supporters also claimed that it would obviate any further increases in the size of the regular army, increases which would place still more politically corrupting patronage in the hands of the executive. And it meant that the German mercenaries who had been summoned to Britain in 1756 could be sent back to Germany where they countered the French threat to Hanover, and protected Frederick's flank, by forming an Army of Observation under the Duke of Cumberland.

In 1757 such hopes as the government had for some rapid successes crumbled. In June the Austrians expelled Frederick from Bohemia and occupied Berlin. The British could afford him little help. Cumberland's force was much too small to check the French. In July he was defeated at Hastenbeck and could only save the electoral army by signing the Convention of Klosterseven. In September the French occupied Hanover and the Army of Observation was disbanded. Frederick looked in vain for effective military assistance from the British. In September they mounted the first of several amphibious raids against the French coast, designed partly to cause a 'diversion of the forces of the enemy' from Germany and partly because Pitt needed to reassure the public that he was committed to a 'patriotic' maritime strategy.[9] The first target was the naval base of Rochefort. The operation ended in fiasco. When the expedition arrived its commanders believed the French defences were much stronger than in fact they were and that the water was too shallow to allow their ships to move inshore and protect the landings with their gunfire. After deliberating for five days they tamely returned home. In 1758 similar raids were mounted against St Malo, where a considerable number of privateers were burnt, and Cherbourg, whose fortifications were razed. In strategic terms the raids were a failure. The French knew that the outcome of the European war would be decided in Germany, not on the Atlantic coast, and hardly a soldier was withdrawn across the Rhine to counter them. Anson refused Frederick's request for a British squadron to protect his Baltic coast because he had too few ships to protect Britain. The squadron he had deployed to blockade Brest was too weak to contain the French fleet and between December 1756 and May 1757 a considerable number of vessels escaped to North America. The British sent an expedition to Louisburg but when they arrived their commanders were not prepared to risk landing for fear that the French fleet might cut their communications with Britain. It was the French who took the offensive in America, seizing Fort William Henry near the headwaters of the Hudson River and threatening to march south to New York and cut the British colonies in two. With the British unable to intervene on the continent or even to cause the French serious problems in North America, Frederick had to save himself, something he did by defeating the French at Rossbach in November and the Austrians at Leuthen in December.

Frederick's victory enabled the British to begin to rebuild their position on the continent. At the insistence of his British ministers, George II repudiated the Convention of Klosterseven and British subsidies, granted, according to Pitt, 'upon the grounds of fatal necessity' enabled the Army of Observation to be reconstituted under Ferdinand of Brunswick.[10] It operated to protect Hanover and Frederick's western flank from the French. Whilst Ferdinand contained a growing number of French troops, Frederick continued to resist the Russians and Austrians. In April 1758 Britain and Prussia cemented their better relations by signing a subsidy treaty. Both parties agreed not to conclude a separate peace, the British granted Frederick an annual subsidy of £670,000 and dispatched a small force of British troops to Emden.

The British were simultaneously planning an ambitious three-pronged offensive in North America. Reinforcements of regulars and enough specie to induce the colonies to raise about 20,000 troops from their own resources were sent from Britain. This marked an important development because the government's readiness to pour money and men into the colonies reversed the assumption that they should not drain but must contribute to the military strength of the empire. The repercussions of this decision were to have momentous consequences after 1763. Plans were prepared for 25,000 regulars and provincials under Lord Abercromby to advance via Lake George, Fort Ticonderoga and Crown Point to Montreal and Quebec. Jeffrey Amherst, supported by a fleet under Admiral

Boscawen was to take Louisburg and a smaller force was ordered to take Fort Duquesne. More realistic planning and more adequate forces than in 1757 meant that this time the British achieved at least a measure of success. The navy ensured that the attack on Louisburg would not be thwarted like the last for fear of the untimely arrival of the French fleet. In April Admiral Hawke scattered a convoy meant to reinforce French forces in Canada and in the Mediterranean Admiral Osborne blockaded part of the French Mediterranean fleet in Cartagena and then repulsed a force sent to relieve them. Louisburg fell to Amherst in July. The British now controlled the gateway to the St Lawrence and in November Forbes captured Fort Duquesne. But by then the main British overland thrust had already failed for in July the French repulsed Abercromby when he tried to storm Fort Ticonderoga.

These successes whetted the government's appetite. In December Pitt issued orders to his commanders in North America which were similar to those they had already received. Amherst, who replaced the disgraced Abercromby, was to march overland to Montreal. A smaller overland expedition was to take Niagara, a post which controlled the Great Lakes and was a vital link in French communications with the Ohio. But the bulk of the regular army in North America was given to James Wolfe, who was ordered to take Quebec by an amphibious assault down the St Lawrence. Pitt also mounted two new overseas expeditions against the French colonies of Gorée on the West African coast and Martinique in the Caribbean. He hoped that their fall would cripple the French slave trade and ruin the economy of the French sugar islands. That in turn would reduce France's trade, would further curtail her ability to pay for her war effort and they might become bargaining counters which could be exchanged for Minorca. The decision to mount these expeditions marked a significant change in British policy. Hitherto they had been fighting a defensive war in Europe and America. Henceforth their aims were increasingly offensive as they sought to add territory which would show a profit to the British Empire.

In 1759 the French were convinced that the war in Germany was only being maintained by British gold and so they decided to strike at the heart of her credit. They reduced their commitments in Germany and prepared to mount a cross-Channel invasion. By February 1759 rumours that the French intended to unite their Mediterranean and Atlantic fleets had reached London. The government's credit did indeed fall but they staved off disaster. The militia was called out to restore public confidence and the navy wrecked the French plans. Anson reinforced Boscawen in the Mediterranean and this enabled him to defeat the French Mediterranean fleet off Lagos in August. Anson also dispatched a powerful squadron under Hawke to blockade Brest. In September a gale blew Hawke off station and permitted the French West Indian squadron to enter the port. The combined fleet then left port and rendezvoused with transports carrying troops which were to land in Scotland. But in November Hawke caught the convoy in Quiberon Bay. Six of the eighteen French ships-of-the-line were captured, sunk or foundered. The battle not only ended any possibility of a

French invasion but it also ensured that they would not be able to reinforce their colonies. That was fortuitous because in September Wolfe had captured Quebec and although the expedition sent to Martinique had found the island too heavily defended, it had taken Guadeloupe instead. By the end of 1762 the British had added Belle Isle, Grenada, St Lucia and Martinique to their conquests.

Meanwhile in India a separate war was being conducted which illustrated the danger of assuming that before the coming of the electric telegraph in the mid-nineteenth century the government in London could exercise close control over colonists and commanders abroad. The East India Company had established trading stations in India in the seventeenth century. The death of the Muslim Emperor Aurangzebe in 1707 marked the beginning of the disintegration of the Muslim empire into a number of warring and semi-independent 'country powers' and in the eighteenth century the company was able to expand its influence in the face of an indigenous population which was divided against itself. The British originally came to India to trade, not to seek dominion. They concentrated their trade in parts of India, such as the Carnatic and Bengal, where the native regimes were small, weak and compliant. But the French also took advantage of these same conditions to establish their own trading posts at Pondicherry and Chandernagore, near the British posts at Madras and Calcutta. The company's board of directors in London, anxious to avoid the great expense of providing adequate fortifications for their trading posts, was slow to perceive what was glaringly apparent to its governors on the spot. The French presence in India represented a real threat to the company's trade. When the War of the Austrian Succession spilled over to India, the East India Company was ill-prepared to meet the French threat. In 1746 Madras fell to the French with hardly a shot being fired and later in the same year a handful of French soldiers and French-trained Indian troops defeated a much larger army of Britain's Indian allies. The French did not win because they possessed superior weapons but because they had instilled European-style training and discipline into their indigenous troops. Endless drill meant that their army was mobile, disciplined and able to act in concert under fire. By contrast the Mogul forces were an ill-disciplined feudal levy. They were unpractised in battle-drill and found it difficult to move with swiftness or precision across a battlefield. They were all too apt to melt away in confusion when confronted by a setback or the desertion of some of their senior leaders.

Although Madras was returned to the company in 1748 the company's representatives in India took the lesson of its loss to heart. An unofficial war continued between the French and British in India throughout the early 1750s. The company began to use its superior financial resources to raise its own European-trained regiments of sepoys. By 1759 they had five sepoy regiments and were in a position to challenge not only the French but also some of the smaller Indian states. In 1756 the Nawab of Bengal, assisted by French military advisers, seized Calcutta. The company dispatched a force of 2,000 sepoys and 900 Europeans to retake it. At the Battle of Plassey in 1757 Clive defeated the Nawab's army which outnumbered his own by ten to one. The company was now the *de facto* ruler of Bengal, one of the richest provinces in India. It used its new tax revenues to augment its own army so that by 1765 it had ten regiments of sepoys. After Quiberon Bay the Royal Navy prevented the French from reinforcing their forces in India and the government dispatched a single battalion of the king's troops to reinforce the company's army. The fall of Pondicherry in January 1761 marked the destruction of French power in India. The British had become masters of a considerable part of northern India.

By the end of 1759 Britain had achieved her original war aims. The problem now facing the ministry was how to sustain their efforts for long enough to achieve a satisfactory peace settlement which would permit them to retain most of their gains. This was difficult as the immediate impact of their victories was to widen the scope of the war. In 1759 Charles III became King of Spain. He was alarmed at the extent of Britain's colonial conquests, resentful of her continued occupation of Gibraltar and fearful that her growing power would threaten his own empire. In August 1761 he signed a family compact with Louis XV and agreed to make war on Britain by May 1762. Pitt wanted to cripple Spain's war-making ability by launching a pre-emptive strike against her South American treasure fleet but neither his colleagues nor the new king, George III, would agree and in October 1761 he resigned. Confronted with growing difficulties in financing the war against France, the last thing that Newcastle wanted to do was to add to Britain's enemies. But in the face of Spain's warlike preparations he could not remain idle. In January Britain declared war on Spain, 6,000 British troops were sent to protect Lisbon from the Spanish and by October the British had added Havana and Manila to their colonial conquests.

In Germany the war had reached a stalemate. The Anglo-Prussian alliance had always been unstable. The two partners had different strategic priorities: Britain's main concerns were colonial and maritime and her main enemy was France; Prussia was fighting a land war against Austria and Russia. Quiberon Bay enabled the British to reinforce Ferdinand with British troops who had been kept at home to meet a French invasion. By 1760 he had a force of some 22,000 British and 58,000 German troops. In 1760 and 1761 Frederick and Ferdinand were able, with increasing difficulty, to resist their assailants. But in January 1762 the Tsaritsa Elizabeth, who had been the driving force of the anti-Prussian coalition since 1759, died. By May 1762 her successor had signed a peace treaty with Prussia. Victory in America made the costly and apparently indecisive war in Germany unpopular in Britain, especially with George III and his favourite, Lord Bute. The growing cost of the war convinced Newcastle that it would be wise for Britain to cease her efforts in America and concentrate instead on the war in Germany. That was anathema to Bute and the king. Newcastle resigned when his colleagues refused to renew the Prussian subsidy treaty. Bute was then able to negotiate peace preliminaries with France which formed the basis of the Peace of Paris signed in February 1763. Pitt, now in opposition, was critical of the treaty on the grounds that it restored too much to France. But when he had begun secret negotiations with the French himself in 1761 he also had realized that Britain could not have peace unless she returned at least some of her conquests. Pitt's argument that restoring Martinique, St Lucia and Gorée to France and granting her fishermen access to the Newfoundland fisheries, meant that Bute had returned to France the foundations of her maritime and imperial greatness, was grossly exaggerated. This was a small price to pay for retaining St Vincent, Grenada, Dominica and Tobago, and for achieving military security for the North American colonies by retaining Canada and the American hinterland up to the Mississippi. Britain also returned Belle Isle to France in exchange for Minorca and Havana to Spain in exchange for Florida. In India the French retained their existing trading posts but on condition that they did not fortify them. They thus became British hostages. Britain's acquisitions in Canada and India were significant because they marked the beginning of the end of Britain's purely salt-water empire. Henceforth she had to defend a territorial as well as a seaborne empire. Nor did Britain cynically abandon her faithful Prussian ally. France agreed to evacuate all her forces from Germany and when Prussia made peace with Austria she lost nothing because the Anglo-Prussian treaty had ended.

Pitt's advice amounted to a call for an indefinite prolongation of the war in the hope of utterly destroying French maritime and commercial power. That was not a practical aim. Even if she had been shorn of all her overseas possessions, metropolitan France would have remained a formidable power. Britain's loss of her American colonies in 1783 did not reduce her to the status of a second-rate power and there is no evidence to suggest that the loss of Martinique or Gorée would have crippled France either.

Pitt said that America was won in Germany. That was trite but true. Britain did owe her successes in part to the presence of European allies able to absorb some of her enemies' forces. But she also owed much to her ability to mobilize her own wealth, her navy and army and the resources of her colonies. The navy's record was one of growing success. After Quiberon Bay the French naval threat was almost eliminated. The French did mount another *guerre de course* against British trade but the British blockade and the care with which the Admiralty co-operated with the mercantile community to organize convoys, meant that losses were kept within acceptable limits. Consequently Britain's overseas trade continued and her credit and expanding tax revenues enabled the government, albeit with growing difficulties, to raise the taxes and loans they required to continue fighting and to subsidize their allies until France was prepared to negotiate acceptable terms of peace.

The navy also helped cripple France's ability to pay for her war effort. During the War of the Austrian Succession it had failed to intercept the

Spanish treasure fleet and it was not until the establishment of a strong western squadron that French trade with the West Indies was disrupted. But during the Seven Years' war the navy enabled the British to mount a successful attack on France's colonial empire. It had a considerable impact on France's ability to make war. In the 1740s and 1750s the French Crown relied increasingly on loans raised from amongst the rich merchants who traded with Canada, the West Indies and India. By disrupting this trade, the British were able to curtail France's ability to finance her war efforts. The Seven Years' War cost the French government about twice what the War of the Austrian Succession had cost them. But in the 1740s they had reached the politically practical limits of taxation. Heavier taxes would undermine the privileges which sustained the wealthiest and most powerful groups of *ancien régime* France. The French tax system was riddled with exemptions and anomalies and the government could only borrow large sums at ruinously high rates of interest and by the end of the decade they were virtually bankrupt. The British never had to follow the example the French set in 1759 when they had to pass a law protecting the government from prosecution for debt by its own creditors.

The British government's ability to tax and borrow on a lavish scale was crucial in enabling them to outlast their enemies. After 1714 the significance of the land tax diminished. The steady imposition of new imposts meant that the excise became the single most important source of revenue until Pitt the Younger introduced an income tax in 1799. The level of per capita taxation in eighteenth-century Britain was about twice what it was in France. The British government's success in taxing its citizens also enabled it to borrow from them. About three-quarters of the additional revenues needed to finance the War of Jenkins's Ear, the War of the Austrian Succession and the Seven Years' War was raised by borrowing. No government was able to raise loans so cheaply or lavishly as was the British. Despite the multiplying national debt, interest rates on government loans fell and the government's credit remained good enough for them to attract considerable sums of Dutch as well as British money. But Britain's financial resources were not inexhaustible, or at least governments did not think they were. In 1748 Lord Chesterfield wrote that 'if there is not a certainty of peace in three or four months...an entire stagnation of all credit, if not bankruptcy, is universally expected.'[11] Even so Britain never faced the stark choice which confronted France of starving one service so they could continue to pay for the other. The French dilemma was made doubly difficult because during the Seven Years' War they were compelled to dissipate their resources by fighting on two fronts, at sea and in their colonies against the British, and in Germany against Frederick the Great and Ferdinand. They chose to devote the bulk of their resources to the army and to starve their navy. By 1760 the French could only spend 9 million livres (half a million pounds) on their fleet, compared to the £3.64 millions voted by Parliament for the Royal Navy.

Between 1714 and 1763 Britain came as close as she ever did to pursuing consistently over time 'the British way in warfare', but even in this period there were anomalies in her behaviour. As befitted a power seeking to expand its overseas interests but unable to do so by disengaging from the European alliance system, Britain made no major continental commitment in two of the four wars in this period (the War of the Quadruple Alliance and the Anglo-Spanish War of 1726/9). But she did commit a considerable body of troops to the continent in both the War of the Austrian Succession and the Seven Years' War. Table 2.3 illustrates the average percentage of troops on the British establishment (including mercenaries) deployed each year in Flanders, Britain and overseas in the wars in question.

The high proportion of troops retained at home between 1718 and 1720 and 1726 and 1729 reflected the government's unwillingness to become engaged in extensive land operations. The troops kept at home during the War of Jenkins's Ear, the War of the Austrian Succession and the Seven Years' War reveal their doubts about the ability of the navy to safeguard Britain against invasion. These calculations take account of the militia in the Seven Years' War when it was embodied, but they do not take account of the regiments on the Irish establishment except when they were transferred to the British establishment for use in Britain or abroad. Nor do they take account of the colonial levies raised in America, or the sepoy regiments raised by the East India Company. Until Pitt came to power British landforces in North America typically consisted of a number of royal regiments supported by a larger force of provincials. In 1711 of the 12,000 troops dispatched to Quebec under Walker 7,000 were provincials. In 1745 Louisburg was taken by a force of about 4,000 New England volunteers. No royal troops were used during the operation. It was only under Pitt that the king's army began to play a predominant role and even in 1758/9 strong provincial support was still necessary. Wolfe's army which took Quebec in 1759 consisted almost entirely of the king's regiments but Amherst's army consisted of 6,000 regulars and 5,000 provincials and the force with which General Forbes had taken Fort Duquesne in 1758 consisted of 1,600 regulars and 5,400 provincials. Similarly at Plassey 2,000 of the 2,900 troops

Table 2.3 Annual Average Percentage of Troops Deployed between Particular Theatres in Selected Wars, 1718–63

	Europe	Britain	Colonies and amphibious operations
1718–20	0	74	26
1726–9	0	83	17
1739–48	36*	39	32
1756–63	21**	33	26

* 1742–8 only.
** 1758–63 only.

under Clive's command were sepoys. Without the supplies and manpower the colonies provided it is doubtful if the British could have waged a successful war effort so far from their home base. Critics of Britain's apparent propensity to send troops to the colonies rather than commit them to the continent sometimes overlooked the fact that a large proportion of the troops who fought in North America, and the overwhelming majority of those who fought in India, were recruited on the spot. These forces were not automatically interchangeable. No one ever seriously entertained the notion of sending colonial levies raised in North America to Europe. The British government was in no sense exercising a strategic 'option' when it chose to raise men in Massachusetts. If they did not serve in North America or the Caribbean, they would not serve anywhere.

The British spent little on their allies during the War of the Quadruple Alliance but between 1727 and 1729 Parliament voted £650,924 to hire German mercenaries, a sum equal to slightly less than 4 per cent of total government spending on land and sea services. Britain's propensity to rely on foreign mercenaries when they sent forces to the continent reached its peak in the middle of the eighteenth century. Between 1742 and 1747 about 52 per cent of the British forces in Flanders were foreign mercenaries. That figure compared to about 74 per cent of the British forces in Germany between 1758 and 1763. The proportion of the defence budget used to pay others to fight on Britain's behalf also reached a peak between 1739 and 1748 when subsidies and the cost of hiring mercenaries accounted for 12 per cent of the defence budget. However, during the Seven Years' War the proportion of defence spending devoted to this purpose fell to approximately 7 per cent.

The pattern of spending on land and sea services was reasonably consistent with the notion that the British pursued the 'British way in warfare' in this period. Table 2.4 shows that in both peace and war policy-makers consistently preferred to spend money on the navy rather than on the army. Throughout this period the navy regularly absorbed about three-fifths of total defence spending

Table 2.4 Ratio of Spending on the Land and Sea Services of the Crown, 1713–63

	Land services : Sea services
1713–17	47 : 53
1718–20	35 : 65
1721–5	41 : 59
1726–9	40 : 60
1730–8	41 : 59
1739–48	38 : 62
1749–55	36 : 64
1756–63	43 : 57

Source: *Parliamentary Papers* 1868–9, xxxv, Public Income and Expenditure.

compared to the two-fifths which was spent on land services. The army's share of defence spending would have been even smaller had it not been for the fact that in peacetime the Crown was able to shift a large part of the burden of supporting its landforces on to the Irish Exchequer. In peacetime the Irish tax-payer met on average nearly 22 per cent of the cost of the landforces of the Crown. But in wartime, when regiments on the Irish establishment were transferred to the British establishment and sent abroad, the Irish paid on average for only 14 per cent of the cost of the army.

At the end of each war the British were careful to husband their resources by reducing spending on their armed forces and the army always bore the brunt of these reductions. The British could afford to reduce defence spending in peacetime without excessive risk because, until the mid-nineteenth century, Britain was protected by her island geography from the constant fear of the sudden descent of a hostile invader. Until the invention of the steamship and the railway it was impossible for any power to threaten the home islands without first making lengthy preparations which were hard to conceal and which would give the British time to prepare their defences. Until then the British did not have to spend lavishly on their defences in peacetime for fear that they might be the victims of a sudden attack which would cripple them before they were ready to fight. The political nation found large loans and heavy taxes acceptable in wartime because, with varying degrees of enthusiasm, most of them accepted that they had to borrow and tax on such a scale or face defeat. But heavy taxes were never popular and the fear that Britain might one day sink beneath a mountain of debt was often repeated. When peace came Parliament was always anxious to reduce borrowing and to cut taxes. As long as a portion of the fleet and a cadre of trained troops were standing by, Britain could not be defeated quickly. That did not mean that the armed forces were ever cheap in peacetime. Even in the peaceful 1730s they still accounted for about half of the government's spending. The price of husbanding resources in peacetime was that there was inevitably a time-lag between a declaration of war and the moment at which the army and navy were ready for offensive operations.

The British were never able to disengage from Europe so as to be free to devote themselves to imperial expansion. They could not ensure their own security in a European war or divert a large proportion of their armed forces to operations outside Europe unless they had continental allies. Without the Grand Alliances of the Nine Years' War and the War of the Spanish Succession, without the Anglo-Austrian alliance during the War of the Austrian Succession and without the Anglo-Prussian Alliance during the Seven Years' War, the British would never have been able to wear down France's ability and will to continue fighting. Without European allies able to tie down the French army in Europe, the Commons would not have voted to send an average of one British soldier in three to the colonies during the War of Jenkins's Ear and the War of the Austrian Succession and one in four during the Seven Years' War. The reason why Britain had to maintain this continuous involvement was simple, for as

Newcastle told Charles Fox in 1756 'We are not singly a match for France'.[12] Just how precarious Britain's position could be when she lacked European allies became apparent during the American War of Independence.

3 The American War of Independence, 1763–83

Clausewitz believed that before 1793 war had been an affair for governments alone but that during the French Revolution 'Suddenly war again became the business of the people' who threw the full weight of their nation's might into their struggles.[1] In fact the break between the limited wars of the eighteenth century and an era of unlimited war beginning in 1793 (and temporarily ending in 1815) was less sharp than he suggested. Its beginnings can be discerned during the Seven Years' War. The means which the combatants adopted may have been limited but for at least one belligerent, Prussia, the ends were not. The anti-Prussian alliance tried to deprive her of more than just a province; they wished to reduce her to the ranks of a second-rate power. And had he looked across the Atlantic, Clausewitz might have noticed that in the 1770s and 1780s the Americans had already shown how the full weight of the people might be thrown into a national war effort. The American War of Independence was unlike the wars which had been fought in Europe for dynastic aims earlier in the eighteenth century. It was not so much a struggle for territory as a contest for the political allegiance of the American people. The Americans proclaimed that they were fighting to liberate themselves from the despotism of British rule. The great cause for which they believed they were fighting filled enough Americans with sufficient patriotic zeal to enable the Congress to mobilize the colonies' resources in a way which had not been seen in Europe since the Thirty Years' War.

Between the end of the Seven Years' War and the beginning of the War of Independence Britain endured the longest period of diplomatic isolation in peacetime that she experienced in the eighteenth century. The Seven Years' War left a legacy of irreconcilable Bourbon animus at a time when no European power had a compelling interest in allying with Britain. France and Spain embarked on an ambitious naval rebuilding programme so that one day they might have their revenge. Prussia had been offended by the way in which Britain had broken with her in 1762. The Dutch remained unwilling to expose themselves to French hostility by siding with Britain. The Austrians saw an alliance with France, rather than with Britain, as the best safeguard for their interests in northern Italy and the Low Countries and the British were no more willing to underwrite Russian ambitions at Turkey's expense than the Russians were to underwrite Britain's security by acting as a counterbalance to the Bourbons in western Europe. The decade before the outbreak of the American war was almost the only period in the eighteenth century when the British tried to maintain their security without the assistance of allies and by relying solely on their own forces. After 1763 the British government recognized that their security depended upon the maintenance of a navy capable of defeating the Bourbon fleets and upon convincing the French and Spanish that they would use naval force if necessary to uphold their rights. But they were almost equally anxious to persuade them that Britain's maritime pre-eminence did not pose such a serious threat to their interests that they must go to war to reduce it. It was a policy which demanded careful statesmanship and a willingness to spend lavishly on the fleet. A series of naval mobilizations in 1764/5 and in 1770 over disputes concerning the Honduras, Turks Island, the Gambia and the Falkland Islands, appeared to demonstrate its success. In reality they only showed that the Bourbons were not willing to push matters to extremes over issues of secondary importance until their naval rearmament was complete.

In such a hostile world no British government could afford to neglect the colonies. The expensive and victorious war which they had just concluded in North America and the Caribbean convinced them that their international status depended upon the security of their colonies. Nothing else could explain Britain's rise 'from the third or fourth Place in the Scale of *European* Powers' to 'a Level with the most Mighty in Europe'.[2] Their problem after 1763 was, in the words of Lord Bute, to meet the twin challenges of 'security and economy'.[3] Between 1739 and 1763 the North American colonies had been the site of almost constant military activity. Problems associated with imperial defence superseded purely economic matters in the minds of policy-makers in London when they looked at the British settlements. Relations between Britain and her colonies had begun to deteriorate during the mid-century wars. The cost of defending the colonies rose from £148,000 per annum during the War of the Austrian Succession to £998,000 per annum during the Seven Years' War. It was hardly surprising that the British were apt to complain that the colonies were not playing their full part in paying for the burden of imperial defence. The Peace of Paris brought some relief but it was unlikely that the burden of colonial defence would drop to its prewar level. During the war the British had signed treaties with a number of Indian tribes in the trans-Appalachian region assuring them that the British would leave them in the possession of their lands if they deserted the French. In 1763 the imperial government tried to make good their promise by fixing the watershed of the Appalachians as the western limit of British expansion. To ensure that the colonists kept to the terms of the treaty, and to subjugate the disaffected inhabitants of Britain's new possessions in Canada and Florida, General Amherst estimated that the British would have to maintain 10,000 troops in North America. The revolution was in part the product of a crisis brought about by the problem of how to meet the extra cost of imperial defence after 1763.

Between 1763 and 1765 George Grenville's government inaugurated a series of measures designed to bring greater unity to the empire and to reduce the cost of empire to the British tax-payers. The peacetime establishment of the army reflected a new design for imperial defence. After 1763 the army was reduced but more of the newly raised corps survived than at the end of past wars. Between 1763 and the resumption of fighting in North America in 1775 the army was composed of twenty-seven regiments of cavalry and seventy-seven infantry battalions, and averaged about 45,000 men. More than a third of the foot served abroad. In 1769 the Irish establishment was raised to 15,000 men to provide a hiding-place for part of this larger force and after 1765 another fifteen battalions were stationed in the North American colonies. The latter represented a large increase in the size of the American garrison.

The post-war officer corps was also larger, numbering some 2,800. This was not simply a reflection of the larger establishment. Although the manpower of most units was reduced to cadre strength, they maintained a higher proportion of officers on the active list than hitherto so that they could be expanded at the start of the next war. Other aspects of the army did not change. The purchase system remained as prominent as it had been before 1755 but despite the expansion of the peacetime army, it continued to be led in the most part by competent career officers who still required long service before they reached field rank. Units remained short of men, even after their establishments had been reduced, and too many men in the ranks were recruits. Peacetime training continued to be interrupted by operations in support of the civil power. Field days were infrequent and large formations were rarely brought together for training. Regiments which served overseas in peacetime were in an even worse position than those at home as regards men and training facilities but some attempts were made to overcome these problems by extending the system of imperial rotation to include Ireland, the Caribbean and North America.

Amherst had estimated that the postwar garrison of North America would cost £300–400,000 per annum. In fact the average annual cost of the army in North America between 1763 and 1764, and 1774 and 1775 was nearly £390,000, or about 4 per cent of the national budget. Parliament's powers over the colonies were ill-defined. Although there was some opposition to taxing the colonies, most members of the political nation in Britain were convinced that Parliament had the authority to do so. In the 1760s the British government not only attempted to tighten controls on American trade, it also twice tried to make the colonies contribute to their own defence by imposing new taxes on them. But each of the thirteen mainland colonies had developed its own representative assembly and the colonists were convinced that their assemblies were true parliaments where they could exercise their rights as Englishmen to assent to taxes or not as they chose. The removal of the French and Spanish threats to their security left them free to concentrate their attention on the British. The Stamp Act of 1765 and the Townshend duties of 1768 were both rendered nugatory by colonial resistance. The royal officials who attempted to gather the monies due to the Crown were intimidated by violence. Parliament's attempts to impose new taxes on the colonies only succeeded in uniting them in a way in which military threats from the French and from the American Indians had never done. These crises might not have led to an open breach between Britain and the colonies but for the fact that beneath the ostensible issues both sides believed that principles which were vital to their security and liberty were at stake. The colonists saw in Townshend's attempt to make royal officials independent of the colonial legislatures a potentially fatal threat to colonial self-government and the political liberties which they had won from the Stuarts. By 1772 the government in London believed that if they granted the colonists' demands it would presage the break-up of the imperial commercial system and Britain would lose the economic wherewithal she needed to remain a great power.

The centre of colonial opposition to British initiatives was Boston. In 1773 a group of Bostonians made clear their displeasure with Parliament's attempt to give the East India Company a monopoly on the sale of tea in America by tipping one of the company's cargoes into Boston harbour. Lord North's Cabinet had little time for conciliation. Between 1766 and 1776 successive British governments believed that they were confronting a problem of how to enforce law and order in the colonies. They were convinced that once the colonists' legitimate grievances had been met only a few recalcitrants would continue to resist their lawful governors. But the destruction of the tea in Boston Harbour showed that the recalcitrants were more numerous and commanded more sympathy than the government had supposed. Encouraged by misleading reports from colonial governors and officers who had served in America in the last war that the propertied classes in the colonies were on the side of the imperial government, and believing that the colonies were so divided amongst themselves that they could never unite against the British, the Cabinet decided to take a firm line. They assumed that the unrest was centred on Boston and that the other colonies were alarmed by the latest violence in the city. If Boston could be isolated and punished the remaining colonies would be intimidated into submission. In 1774 Parliament voted to close the port until its inhabitants had recompensed the East India Company for the tea they had destroyed, to remove the customs house and the seat of government from Boston to Salem, and to replace the colony's elected council with one nominated by the Crown. The success of this policy rested on the ability of the British to deploy overwhelming force to suppress the insurgents in and around Boston. But General Gage, who was sent to the city with a commission as governor, believed that only four regiments would suffice to restore order.

This combination of determination backed by inadequate force was counter-productive. The imperial government's attempt to coerce Boston and to rewrite the Massachusetts charter convinced many colonists that the British were intent on threatening the liberty of every colony. Local popular assemblies were summoned in each colony to elect members to attend a congress to give shape to their resistance. The first Continental Congress met in Philadelphia in September 1774. It promulgated a Declaration of Rights insisting that as the colonies were not represented in Parliament only their own assemblies had the right to tax them and it encouraged colonial legislatures to resist the royal government. By the end of 1774 revolutionary committees were active in almost every colony organizing troops and military stores.

In February 1775 Parliament declared that the New England colonies were in rebellion. But they failed to realize just how widespread was the resistance to British rule. North believed that the rebellion was centred on Massachusetts and that it could be overcome with a judicious mixture of firmness and what he took to be conciliation. Most British policy-makers believed that the great mass of the American people were loyal to the Crown. This erroneous assumption survived throughout the war and underlay almost every major decision they took. They also believed that the colonial militia could not resist British regulars. North did not believe that he had to send a major expedition to America or to engage in a regular war on the other side of the Atlantic. He was convinced that the troops the British already had in New England could crush the rebellion by mounting what was no more than a large-scale police action. In January 1775 he ordered Gage to stop the colonists forming armed bands, to seize their magazines and to arrest the rebel leaders in Massachusetts. He then expected the rebellion to collapse. If the colonists acknowledged Parliament's supreme authority and made permanent provisions for the support of their civil government, their judiciary and the cost of defence, the imperial government would try not to raise taxes in the colonies by Act of Parliament. His concessions were too little and too late for they met none of the colonists' grievances.

In April 1775 Gage tried to seize the rebels' main supply dump in Massachusetts at Concord. On 19 April British regulars met colonial militia and exchanged the first shots of the war at Lexington. The outcome of the skirmish was indecisive. But it could be interpreted as a victory for the rebels in that the British had failed to achieve their purpose and it did immense harm to the British cause. Within weeks of Lexington rebel committees drove royal officials from most of the colonies. Unlike most popular revolutionary movements the Americans began the war in control of a large military machine in the form of the colonial militia. It had many inadequacies when confronted by regular troops; but it proved a more than adequate bulwark against American loyalists and British attempts to engineer a counter-revolution. The Americans had secured their *de facto* independence more than a year before they published the Declaration of Independence. The task now facing the British was to discover a way of depriving them of it.

The second Continental Congress met in May 1775, transformed itself into a revolutionary government, and began to raise the Continental Army. The rebellion in America was unprecedented because a conflict between an ideologically motivated insurgent population and a metropolitan state 3,000 miles away had never before been seen in the *ancien régime*. But for a long time the British acted as if they were embarking upon the kind of limited war they had fought so successfully since 1689. Many of the strategic lessons of past wars did not apply or should not have been applied. But past precedents were the only guide the British had and it was upon them that they based much of their strategy.

The rebels launched an abortive invasion of Canada and besieged Gage in Boston. Gage was unwilling to attack the colonists whilst there was the slightest chance of finding a peaceful political solution. It was only the outbreak of actual fighting in July 1775 that made the Cabinet realize that they were engaged in something more than a large-scale police action. The king was determined to bring his rebellious subjects to heel but he never aspired to control the strategic direction of the war. North was diffident of his own abilities as a war leader and largely confined himself to managing Parliament. The conduct of British strategy thus fell to several hardline ministers, the two secretaries of state, Viscount Weymouth and the Earl of Suffolk, the Earl of Sandwich, the First Lord of the Admiralty and Lord George Germain who became the Secretary of State for America in November 1775. Although their mutual relations were often marred by friction, in 1775 they were agreed that they were faced by a conventional war which could be fought and won upon conventional lines. They remained convinced that the centre of the rebellion lay in New England and agreed that their proper course was first to quarantine the New England states from the remaining colonies. Gage recommended that the rebels could be brought to surrender if the British shifted their base from Boston, where the population was hostile and the terrain made an advance into the interior impossible, to New York. The rebels' resources could be depleted by occupying Rhode Island and by blockading the New England coast. Troops from New York were to advance up the Hudson valley to isolate New England from the middle colonies whilst troops coming south from Canada were to attack the frontiers of Massachusetts and Connecticut.

Initially the government had been confident that the troops would play a secondary role in returning the colonies to British rule. Many Englishmen shared Amherst's view that the Americans made poor soldiers, for 'if left to themselves [they] would eat fryed Pork and lay in their tents all day long'.[4] The crisis had been provoked by the government's determination to retrench its military spending. North, anxious to win support in a House of Commons where the government's majority was by no means always secure, did not want to provoke opposition by a hasty and expensive mobilization of the armed forces. It was an indication of the extent to which the British government underestimated the military problem confronting them in the colonies that they believed they could suppress the rebellion with only a partial mobilization of their military and naval resources. Existing regiments were brought up to strength but before 1778 only one new regiment was raised. Recruits were found by the customary methods of offering bounties for volunteers. Rather than dig deeper into Britain's own human and financial resources, the ministry preferred the cheaper course of looking abroad. In 1776 agreements were signed with Hesse-Cassel, Hesse-Hanau, Waldeck and Brunswick for 18,000 German mercenaries. By the end of the war over 29,000 German soldiers had served in North America. They constituted an average of 15 per cent of the troops in British pay during each year of the war but nearly 45 per cent of the forces they sent to North America. In 1775/6 there was a gradual increase in the proportion of the British army serving in North America (including Canada) from about 1:4 to about 1:3. The campaign of 1777/8 marked the high point of Britain's military commitment to the reconquest of the thirteen colonies. On the eve of France's entry into the war Parliament had voted to send nearly 42 per cent of the army to North America, but thereafter the proportion dropped sharply. France's entry into the war caused a dissipation of Britain's military resources and meant that her best chance to reconquer the colonies had gone. But remembering the very significant role provincial corps had played in conquering the North American empire before 1763, perhaps the government's greatest error was their failure to produce a coherent plan to organize loyalist sympathizers in the colonies. The few loyalist provincial corps which were assembled in 1775/6 were formed on the initiative of the loyalists themselves.

The navy also suffered from a slow start. In the decade of peace after 1763 the naval budget dropped from £5,900,000 in 1762 to only £1,500,000 in 1768. The ratio of spending on land and sea services between 1764 and 1774 was 39:61 in favour of the navy. That ratio became even more favourable to the navy during the war, shifting to 33:67 between 1775 and 1783. But even before France declared war her latent hostility hampered the navy's freedom of action against the colonists. In 1775 the Admiralty was content to dispatch cruisers to North America but it retained most of its ships-of-the-line at home. The Americans had no navy but they had a large seafaring population and a long tradition of smuggling and privateering. During the war they put all three to good use. In 1775 the Royal Navy could barely protect ships entering Boston Harbour. Although the navy attacked some American coastal towns, the British squadron in North American waters was too small, too undermanned and too poorly supplied either to mount a successful blockade of the American coast or to stop munitions reaching the rebels from abroad. The British could have done more but in 1775/6 North, concerned that the high cost of sending an army to the colonies would make the war unpopular at home, chose to mobilize only a fraction of the fleet. It was not until the end of October 1776 that intelligence reports that the French were augmenting their own fleet finally enabled Sandwich to persuade his colleagues to put the fleet at home on a war footing. It was not until 1778 that the British began to lay down a significant number of new ships-of-the-line.

In October 1775 Gage was superseded by Sir William Howe. Between 1775 and his recall in the spring of 1778 Howe had a better chance than any British general of crushing the rebellion. His recall in 1778 coincided with France's entry into the war. Had he destroyed Washington's field army before Saratoga, rebel morale might have collapsed. Guerrilla warfare might have continued but Germain believed that once the Continental Army and the Congress had been dispersed, policing could be done by loyalist militia supported by a stiffening of regulars. The Crown might have regained the colonies. Howe realized the extent of the support that the rebellion had achieved but his understanding of the political and military problems facing the government prevented him from seizing the initiative and crushing the Continental Army. He was a conventional European strategist. He believed that his proper function was not to seek out and destroy Washington's army unless he could do so at minimal risk to his own forces. In March 1776 Germain informed him that there was no possibility that the government would be able to recruit all the troops Parliament had voted and Howe felt he dare not risk the disintegration of his own army so far from home. Unlike the rebels he was not prepared to mount offensive operations in the winter, preferring instead to maintain his army in winter quarters until the spring came. Throughout the winter of 1775/6 his army remained idle in Boston. He was hamstrung by shortages of supplies and by the slow arrival of the reinforcements he requested because the Navy Board and the Treasury had great difficulty in assembling the necessary tonnage to carry them. His failure to attack the rebels besieging Boston enabled Washington to prepare his troops and to gather together the largest army the Americans put into the field throughout the entire war.

Howe abandoned Boston in March 1776, taking his men to Halifax in Nova Scotia for reorganization. He did not land at New York until July. In the meantime in June a small expedition attacked Charleston in South Carolina in the hope of establishing a rallying-point for southern loyalists. The attack was repulsed but this failure did not destroy British faith in the strength of southern loyalism. They were encouraged by the fact that some loyalist bands did indeed attack the rebels in the colonies. They blamed the loyalists' defeat on the fact that British regulars arrived too late to assist them. Farther north, Howe seemed to have more success. In August, barely a month after the Congress had issued its Declaration of Independence, he defeated the Continental Army at the Battle of Long Island. Had he exploited his victory he might have destroyed Washington's army. But he did not. The commander of the Royal Navy in North American waters was Howe's brother, Lord Richard Howe. The brothers believed that the war must end in a political settlement that would reconcile the colonists to British rule. Admiral Howe had been sent to America to negotiate peace by first accepting the colonists' surrender. The campaign which the brothers waged in 1776 was designed to promote reconciliation between the warring parties and a restoration of British authority. Although they knew that some use of force would be necessary to induce the colonists to accept British authority, they also knew that each battle would be another obstacle on the way to reconciliation. The general therefore tried to use his troops to demonstrate the majesty of British power over the widest possible swathe of American territory so as to encourage the loyalist population and to prove to the rebels that their cause was hopeless. He wanted to wear out the rebels rather than engage them in a major battle, to exhaust their resources and, when the time seemed ripe, to make peace overtures to them. He achieved only limited success. He occupied New York and Long Island, drove the rebels back into Pennsylvania and established a line of posts across New Jersey to provide security for loyalists and British foraging parties. The rebel militia which had controlled the state disintegrated. It was replaced by a loyalist militia and the government granted pardons to all civilians who took an oath of allegiance. By October 1776 the Howe brothers had 32,000 men at New York supported by seventy-three warships (about 45 per cent of the Royal Navy's total fleet). This represented Britain's biggest military effort since the Seven Years' War. But the fleet was still far too small to blockade the American coast and support the army, and the military setbacks Howe's troops had inflicted upon the rebels did not make them amenable to compromise. In September 1776 Admiral Howe approached the Congress with peace proposals. They were rejected. The Congress had decided that any terms which did not acknowledge American independence were unacceptable.

By failing to destroy the Continental Army in the summer of 1776 the Howes lost the best chance the British ever had to defeat the revolution. Congress rejected their terms because the brothers had failed to strangle the colonies' economies or to destroy the Continental Army. In trying to wear down the enemy's resources the British had pursued the same strategy which had brought them so much success in their earlier wars. It had worked against European enemiees because the latter had solidly structured fiscal systems and the fighting took place in clearly defined and quite small cockpits. But the American colonies were not small and their fiscal, and indeed governmental systems were anything butt solidly structured.

Throughout the war Washington tried to make the Continental Army resemble a conventional European army. But he was sufficiently flexible not to be wedded to European military practices. He campaigned in winter and he used the militia as irregulars to attack isolated parties of British troops and to terrorize loyalists into quiescence. Above all, he did not attempt to confine the American war effort to the men of his own class and the dregs of colonial society. He tried to mobilize men of all social classes by appealing to political principles supposedly held in common by all Americans. He was not entirely successful, and despite much rhetoric about the civic duty of all men to fight for their country, the Continental Army came to contain a disproportionately large number of the poor and propertyless. But, compared to the British army, the rebel forces also contained a disproportionately large leavening of solid citizens. The willingness of the Congress to draw upon men of all social classes enabled the Americans to mobilize a much higher proportion of their human resources than their opponents. Between 1:2 to 1:2.5 white American males of military age served at one time or another in either the Continental Army or the militia. By comparison only about 1:9 British males of military age served in the regular army, the militia or the navy.

But even though Washington disposed of a higher proportion of American resources, the population of the colonies was so much smaller than that of Britain that he could never hope to overwhelm the British by weight of numbers. Nor, he realized after the fall of New York, would the Continental Army be able to match British regulars in the discipline they needed to defeat them in a conventional battle. His main concern was to maintain the Continental Army in being for fear that if the British smashed it, American morale would collapse and the revolution would expire. After New York he waged 'a war of posts', attacking isolated British detachments in an effort to sustain American morale and to hasten the day when British patience was exhausted and they abandoned the reconquest of the colonies. The geography of the colonies meant that he could trade space for safety in a way which few generals in western Europe could do. The Low Countries measured about 200 miles by 200 miles whereas the colonies measured about 1,000 miles from north to south and, at their widest point, about 300 miles from east to west.

The Americans had a second advantage which most European states did not enjoy. Their war efforts were constrained by the state's ability to raise taxes and to borrow the money it needed to maintain its armed forces. Within broad limits all European governments wished to minimize the impact of war on their own societies and recognized the overriding need to maintain a stable currency. When their tax revenues ran out and they had reached the limits of what they could borrow, they made peace rather than resort to the wholesale debasement of their currencies. The British fought Louis XIV and Louis XV to a standstill because they had pursued strategies which left their enemies bankrupt and unable to buy the goods they needed to maintain their armed forces. They tried to do the same when they fought the Americans. The latter had few industries capable of manufacturing the kinds of hardware their troops needed. At the end of 1780 Washington had to disband part of his army for lack of clothing. He never managed to maintain more than 19,000 regulars in the field, supported by a varying number of militia. However this time the British strategy failed. The Royal Navy's blockade was so porous that the colonists had little difficulty in sustaining themselves on arms smuggled from Holland and France. Between 1775 and 1778 the Royal Navy dared not intercept significant numbers of neutral ships carrying munitions to the colonies for fear that they would provoke the French to declare war. Their forbearance did not prevent the French from providing the colonies with generous credits totalling $8.16 million from 1776 to 1782.

But that was only a small fraction of the money Congress spent on the war. The colonies had always been short of specie and even before the revolution they had depended to a much greater extent than any European power on paper money. As the Congress did not have the power to raise taxes, it had no option other than to continue this practice after 1775. It soon discovered that the printing-press was a potent weapon. Although the continental bills began to depreciate at the end of 1777, they enabled the fledgling rebels to mobilize their resources to resist the British with a rapidity that more traditional means would never have permitted. By 1780 80 per cent of the funds Congress had raised to fight the war took the form of continental bills. When they had depreciated almost to nothing by 1780, Congress resorted to price-fixing, forced collections and requisitioning to secure supplies for the army. At first impressment of goods fell upon loyalists but soon it extended to patriots. Unlike the Bourbons or the British the Americans were not fighting to defend an existing polity. They were fighting to create a new one and they were not prepared to allow inflation or bankruptcy to stop them.

As the British could not starve or bankrupt the colonies into submission their only remaining option was to try to regain their loyalty. In 1776 General Clinton wrote of the need 'to gain the hearts & subdue the minds of America'.[5] Senior officers like Clinton believed that could most easily be done by treating the majority of presumably loyal Americans leniently and by curbing the propensity of their troops to plunder. But many of their subordinates advocated a much harsher policy in the expectation of cowing the civilian population into submission. Leniency towards former rebels also offended loyalists and loyalist militia went out of their way to mete out retribution. Consequently the conflict was not only a war for American independence from Britain, it was also a civil war between Americans. Former rebels and neutrals often found that submission to the British brought them few advantages and they faced the hard choice between fleeing from their homes into rebel-controlled territory or resistance to the British.

During the Seven Years' War the army had purchased the supplies they wanted from a friendly local population in the colonies. But in 1775 the local population was anything but friendly and rebel committees soon stopped local supplies reaching Gage's troops. The British had to try to supply themselves from Britain. The first attempt to do so, a convoy which sailed from Britain in the autumn, illustrated the practical problems they encountered. The convoy was scattered by a gale and a number of vessels which did reach American waters were taken by American privateers. One reason the British decided to shift their base from Boston to New York in 1776 was because they believed that the army would have a better chance of supplying itself from local resources in New Jersey and Rhode Island. The British did try to live off the land, but that meant they had to disperse their army. That gave the rebels the opportunity to inflict an infinite number of casualties on small parties of soldiers and occasionally to defeat larger bodies of troops by massing a superior force against them. Two of the earliest of these encounters took place in December 1776 and January 1777 when Washington won two minor but politically and psychologically important victories over British detachments at Trenton and Princeton. The

British evacuated most of New Jersey, leaving the loyalists with the choice of retiring with them to New York or remaining and facing rebel retribution. Like the evacuation of Boston, the retirement from New Jersey appeared to demonstrate that the British were incapable of protecting their friends and so made it more difficult to organize the loyalists into a meaningful political movement as a counterweight to the rebels.

The withdrawal to New York also made it harder for British foraging parties to find supplies. Even so British soldiers probably went hungry less often than their enemies. For all its shortcomings the British logistical apparatus performed wonders in supplying what was by contemporary standards a huge expeditionary force 3,000 miles from home. But even that was not enough. The British problem was not how to secure their daily supplies, but how to create a sufficiently large reserve to enable them to mount sustained mobile operations to trap an enemy like Washington who was determined not to give battle if he could avoid it. Before France entered the war both Howe and Clinton insisted that they must have a reserve of six months' supplies. The Americans did their best to make this build-up impossible by dispatching privateers to European waters. After France entered the war and her fleet too threatened their transatlantic supply lines, the British commanders in America wanted to double their stocks. Before 1775 the Treasury had been responsible for the administration of contracts to supply the army but during the war it was also saddled with the responsibility of finding new sources of supply and arranging their storage and transportation. It was ill-prepared to meet this challenge and slow to adapt to new problems. Inadequate accounting procedures, poor quality control of the provisions, shipping shortages, badly organized and inadequately protected convoys, the propensity of naval captains to impress the crews of victualling ships and the fact that the department itself never seriously tried to create a stockpile of supplies in America, meant that the army rarely had the supplies its generals demanded. The army in America only had sufficient stockpiles of supplies to wage a mobile war against the Continental Army for twenty-three of the seventy-nine months the war lasted. When supplies were adequate, in 1776 and 1777, the army moved. But from 1778 to the middle of 1781 they only reached the required level on three occasions. It might be suggested that the army's demands were excessive and that Washington was prepared to operate on a much more hand-to-mouth system. But such criticisms fail to take account of an important psychological difference between the two sides. The Americans were operating at home. The British were fighting in hostile territory 3,000 miles from home and with the Atlantic Ocean at their backs. Their generals demanded large stockpiles of supplies as much because they afforded them badly needed psychological reassurance as because they gave them the means to mount offensive operations.

In 1777 Germain, prompted by one of Howe's subordinates who had returned from America, Sir John Burgoyne, decided to make a determined effort to destroy the Continental Army. British forces were to continue to harass the coasts of New England but the main British effort was to be a two-pronged offensive against the rebels. One army under Burgoyne was to march south from Canada whilst Howe's troops were to march north up the Hudson valley. Germain assumed that the threat that the two might meet near Albany would force the Continental Army to give battle to prevent the British from isolating New England. The plan miscarried because Germain failed to ensure that Howe would co-operate with Burgoyne. Howe knew that he could expect few reinforcements from Britain in 1777 and he believed that his troops were too few to defeat the Continental Army. He wanted to leave a small force at New York and to move most of his troops by sea to Philadelphia. From there he hoped to be able to augment his forces by recruiting from amongst the supposedly loyalist population of the Delaware valley. The loyalists would free British regulars from garrison duties and by the end of the year he hoped to be able to occupy most of Pennsylvania, New Jersey and New York. Germain's mistake, which Burgoyne shared, was to believe that Howe could complete his southern campaign and then return north in time to meet Burgoyne. Neither man insisted that Howe had to return from Philadelphia in time to assist Burgoyne. The basic cause of the failure of the 1778 campaign was that Burgoyne and Germain both underestimated the Americans' strength and believed that the British could accomplish not one but two campaigns against two separate objectives.

Howe embarked his army for Philadelphia in July 1777. He went via the Chesapeake in the hope of cutting Washington off from his main magazines in Pennsylvania. This threat did force Washington to stand and fight but although the British won the Battle of Brandywine in September 1777, Howe again failed to turn Washington's defeat into a rout. Furthermore, the navy had so few ships in American waters that they had to lift their blockade so they could escort the army from New York to the Chesapeake. Burgoyne had begun his invasion in June with 7,000 troops. He was not perturbed at the likelihood of receiving little assistance from Howe for he expected that the population of northern New York would show themselves to be loyalist. They did not. Rebel militia attacked his flanks and menaced his lines of communication with Canada. Personal honour, professional ambition and the mistaken belief that British regulars could defeat the rebels in open battle drove him on towards Albany. He marched as far as Saratoga where an American army under General Gates forced his surrender in October 1777.

France had been granting covert assistance to the colonies since 1776. The French naval rearmament programme was due to be completed in time for the 1778 campaigning season. News of Saratoga arrived at an opportune moment. It enabled the bellicose French foreign minister, Vergennes, to begin to overcome the hesitations of both Louis XVI and eventually of the Spanish government about committing their countries to the conflict. Vergennes tried to frighten them into believing that if they did not ally with the Americans, Saratoga might induce Britain and the rebels to reach a compromise peace and then together attack the Bourbons' Caribbean colonies. For the time being the Spanish refused to be persuaded but Louis XVI was won over. In February 1778 France and the rebel colonies signed a treaty of amity and commerce and agreed not to make a separate peace with Britain. Without the money, troops and naval support which France gave the colonies it is unlikely that they would have gained their independence. France entered the war with limited aims and means. She wanted revenge for 1763 by depriving the British of their monopoly of American trade. But she did not seek to crush the British, believing that at some point in the future she might require their assistance to curb Russia's growing ambitions in eastern Europe. For the time being peace on the continent was vital for France because her finances had not recovered from the Seven Years' War and she could not afford to maintain a large army and a powerful fleet on a war footing simultaneously.

Saratoga did not persuade the British to abandon the war for America but it did force them to reappraise their strategy. The likelihood of France's entry into the war persuaded North that the time had come for Britain to negotiate with the colonies, for the cost of fighting an expanded conflict would far outweigh any possible benefits. 'Great Britain will suffer more in the war than her enemies... not... by defeats, but by an enormous expense which will ruin her, and will not in any degree be repaid by the most brilliant victories.'[6] The king dismissed such sentiments as worthy only of a shopkeeper but none the less in 1778 Parliament repealed the 1774 Coercive Acts, offered the colonies freedom from parliamentary taxation and sent a peace commission to America under the Earl of Carlisle to discuss terms with the colonists. Their proposals, which reached Congress simultaneously with the Franco-American treaty, were soon rejected.

France's entry into the war marked the bankruptcy of the policy the British had pursued since 1763 of relying on a naval deterrent without continental allies to contain the Bourbons. It also transformed what had been a colonial war in North America into a global war fought around the coasts of Europe, in the Caribbean and in India. During the Seven Years' War the British had waged such a war successfully but then they had a continental ally in the shape of Prussia who tied down and exhausted a considerable part of their enemies' resources. That had permitted them to concentrate a large proportion of their own resources in what was for them the main theatre of operations, North America. But during the War of Independence the British had no allies and their difficulties were made worse in April 1779 when Spain joined the allies. In 1780 the British added to their own problems by declaring war on Holland in the hope of ending Dutch economic assistance to the rebels. In the same year most of the other major European maritime powers united against British pretensions to interrupt their trade to form the Armed Neutrality. Table 3.1 indicates how the naval balance of power began to shift against Britain when the Spanish became allied to France.

Table 3.1 Shifts in the Naval Balance of Power 1778–82 measured in Ships-of-the-Line

Year	France	Spain	Holland	Total Allied	British
1778	52	n.a.	n.a.	52	66
1779	63	53	n.a.	121	90
1780	69	48	n.a.	117	95
1781	70	54	13	137	94
1782	73	54	19	146	94

Spain's contribution to the allied effort should not be discounted. Her operations against Gibraltar and Minorca contained a considerable number of British troops and ships in European waters. The Spanish governor of Louisiana proved to be one of the war's most successful generals, waging a campaign in the lower Mississippi valley which tied down a considerable number of British troops and which culminated in the expulsion of the British from the Gulf coast. Spanish ships constituted part of the fleet which blockaded the British at Yorktown in 1781 and formed part of a Franco-Spanish fleet which menaced the English coast. The Dutch also added to Britain's problems. The British were able to capture the Dutch colonies of St Eustatius in the Caribbean and the port of Trincomalee in Ceylon. But the forces diverted to do so, just as the ships which the Royal Navy had to retain in the North Sea and Channel to counter the enemy fleets which threatened Britain herself, might have sufficed to tip the naval balance of power in North American waters and to have saved the British army at Yorktown.

In 1778 the Admiralty had to try to make up for the tardy mobilization of 1775–7 and the fleet had to operate in three more theatres where British interests were menaced by the French and Spanish: the Channel, Gibraltar and the West Indies. The navy might have been able to make a better showing against the Bourbon fleet had its dockyard support been more efficient. The weakest point in the British shipbuilding industry was not the construction of new vessels but the repair and refitting of existing ones. Once the American war started the royal dockyards devoted most of their capacity to repairing and refitting ships. The Navy Board turned to merchant yards for most of the new small vessels and many of the new ships-of-the-line it required. Between 1775 and 1783 the royal and private yards outbuilt the French and Spanish yards, producing 181 vessels, including 36 new ships-of-the-line. Between 1778–1782 they also succeeded in fixing copper sheathings to 82 ships-of-the-line and 231 smaller vessels. This was the most important technological innovation which ships experienced in the eighteenth century. It kept vessels relatively free of weeds, it improved their sailing qualities and it protected their timbers from being eaten by sea-worms.

Although the reliance on private yards for much of this construction took some of the pressure off the royal yards, each ship-of-the-line still spent on average one year and eighty-five days during the war in harbour being repaired or refitted. These delays were not caused by shortages of raw materials. The war with the colonies did not cripple the fleet by depriving it of masts and spars from New England. The navy continued to get what it wanted from the Baltic. The delays were partly caused by the dockyard authorities' reluctance to take on more labour because they knew that it would be difficult to reduce their establishment after the war. The introduction of piece-work in the yards might have increased labour productivity but failed to do so because the Navy Board simultaneously placed an upper limit on what each shipwright could earn. But short-sighted management was not the only reason why so many ships were laid up for so long. Sea officers were often reluctant to join their ships when they were being made ready for sea. When they were present they sometimes delayed work by insisting on time-consuming modifications to their ships. The Admiralty wasted some of the yards' capacity by permitting private owners to have their merchant ships refitted in them. Even if the Navy Board had been able to turn ships around more quickly, or build even more vessels, finding sufficient seamen, keeping them healthy and preventing them from deserting, would have placed a ceiling on the size of the fleet.

The French had spent lavishly on rebuilding their fleet after 1763 and could put about 70 ships-of-the-line to sea in 1779. The Spanish contributed another 50. And unlike during the Seven Years' War, they could sustain this effort for some time, although by no means indefinitely, because they did not have to divide their resources between the land and the sea. But in the long term the British enjoyed certain advantages which allowed them to defeat this challenge. They had a larger pool of trained seamen than their enemies, better access to Baltic naval stores and a much larger dockyard system. Bourbon resources were not automatically interchangeable between the army and the navy. No amount of Bourbon gold could suddenly transform soldiers into trained seamen. The result was that by 1782 the Royal Navy was a match for the allied fleet. But by then in the colonies it was too late. Yorktown had fallen. In the crucial period between 1779 and 1782, the North administration's decision to undertake only a partial mobilization of the fleet meant that the Royal Navy was outnumbered by between 20 to 50 ships-of-the-line. Even superior training and discipline could not make good such a deficiency.

The army was also only fully mobilized after the Bourbons began to enter the war. Between 1778 and 1781 no fewer than 31 foot and 4 new cavalry regiments were raised. The voluntary recruiting system could not sustain such a force unaided and Press Acts were enforced in 1778/9. The Acts did not impose a universal obligation to serve, applying only to 'all able bodied loose idle and disorderly persons, [and] vagrants'.[7] Their operation was restricted to the economically marginal region of Scotland and to London, which had a large vagrant population whose absorption into the army would have minimal impact on the economy. They were also suspended during the summer so as to minimize any impact recruiting might have on the harvest. The main result of this legislation was to increase voluntary recruiting from amongst the urban poor who, fearing that they might be taken as conscripts, preferred to volunteer and receive a bounty. The government remained insistent that the war should disrupt civil society as little as possible. Recruiting remained confined to those men whose absence from the plough or the workshop would matter the least.

During the war the establishment rose to 30 cavalry regiments and 118 infantry battalions. Between 1775 and 1782 the augmenting of the regular army, the hiring of mercenaries and the calling out of the militia meant that numbers of troops voted by Parliament for the British establishment rose from about 45,000 to over 180,000 men. In theory that should have been an ample force to crush the rebels, but it was not. The decision to carry out a more complete mobilization was only taken in 1778. But the entry of France and Spain into the war forced the British to disperse their military effort in the same way that it compelled them to dissipate their naval effort. Only about one in three soldiers on the British establishment served in the North American colonies (including Canada) between 1779 and 1781. About a quarter of the entire British army consisted of militiamen who did not serve outside Britain. Even those units which were sent to the colonies were short of men. Units about to be sent abroad often had to be made up with drafts from other units, a process which had a deleterious impact on morale. Eventually 11 battalions in the colonies had to be broken up and their men used to fill gaps in the remainder. Only limited relief was provided by the loyalists who served in the provincial corps which the British raised in the colonies for their numbers fell far short of what the British had anticipated. In the summer of 1777 only 3,000 provincials were under arms. By 1780 the figure had risen to 10,000 but it went no higher.

With a population of nearly 11 million the British should in theory have experienced little difficulty in recruiting sufficient men to keep their units up to strength. That they were not able to do so was only partially due to defects in their recruiting machinery. More fundamentally it was due to the unwillingness of the ruling oligarchy to propagandize the kind of secular nationalism which their American enemies were so ready to disseminate. They did not do so because such notions were not attractive to the rulers of a confessional Protestant state and because such ideas might have politicized the labouring poor and caused them to question the status quo. They paid for their determination to maintain the status quo at home with the loss of the colonies. Shortage of manpower did limit British freedom of action in America. Throughout the war British commanders were inhibited from acting boldly because the British army was so small that it could not afford even a victory if it was bought at the cost of too many casualties.

After Saratoga the centre of British policy shifted to the Caribbean and the southern colonies. The sugar islands were important to Britain because, as George III remarked, 'If we lose our Sugar Islands it will be impossible to raise money to continue the war'.[8] Conversely if France lost her Caribbean colonies she would lose the revenues she needed to maintain her fleet. The British might even be able to compensate themselves for any losses they sustained in North America by completing Pitt's work and expelling the French from the Caribbean. Clinton was told to send 3,000 troops to protect Florida and 5,000 troops to mount a pre-emptive strike against the French island of St Lucia. Sandwich explained the significance of these orders in a dispatch to Howe: 'The object of the war being now changed, and the contest in America being a secondary consideration, our principal object must be distressing France and defending... His Majesty's possessions.'[9]

The British did not abandon the war in America. The government knew that they could not raise enough troops from their own resources to defend the United Kingdom and their colonies and bases in Canada, India, the Mediterranean and the Caribbean, and defeat the rebel colonies so they turned to the loyalists of the southern colonies to help them. The king and Germain had always seen the southern colonies as the rebels' weakest point. They hoped that they might be able to exploit fears of a slave rebellion and the Indian tribes menacing the colonies to the west to bring them to heel one by one. In March 1778 the ministry told Clinton that henceforth he would have to rely much more on the navy and local American resources to crush the rebellion. Clinton was ordered to withdraw from Philadelphia and concentrate his forces at New York and Rhode Island. He was told to increase economic pressure on the rebels by raiding and blockading their ports from New York northwards and to encourage his Indian allies to attack the colonies' western frontiers. Considerable British forces had to be left in New York to contain the Continental Army, which was itself reinforced by 5,500 French regulars in August 1780. In the autumn he was to embark 7,000 regular troops and send them to the southern colonies to operate in conjunction with local loyalists to liberate Georgia and South Carolina. Their policy was to drive the rebel main force from one colony at a time, establish loyalist militia units to secure the king's peace, restore civil government and then to expand British control outward behind a screen of British regulars. If this policy succeeded it would also have the incidental but important result of strengthening support for the government's policy in Parliament by making clear to the ministry's critics that the war had to be continued for the sake of the majority of loyal colonists who had been tyrannized by a handful of ruthless rebels. The political survival of the ministry and victory in America therefore depended upon Clinton successfully mobilizing the loyalists.

The success of this strategy depended on the Royal Navy's ability to secure naval superiority in the western Atlantic. In 1778 the French hoped to win the war in a single campaign. But in July the Brest and Channel fleets fought an indecisive action off Ushant. The French also dispatched a fleet across the Atlantic under Admiral d'Estaing with orders to scatter Howe's squadron and blockade the British army in New York until it surrendered. But he failed and in November he sailed for the Caribbean where he arrived too late to prevent the British from taking St Lucia. This proved to be a mixed blessing.

The presence of d'Estaing's fleet meant that the British no longer enjoyed naval superiority in the Caribbean and in June and July 1779 the French occupied Grenada and St Vincent. The troops sent to St Lucia had to remain as a garrison and were lost to Clinton. But the French navy's failure to defeat the Royal Navy in either the Caribbean or the Channel made it imperative for the French to secure the support of Spain, for without Spanish ships the French would be outnumbered. The Spanish had no interest in American independence. They did, however, want to regain Gibraltar and Minorca from the British and to make their American empire secure by regaining Florida. Britain refused to buy Spain's neutrality by returning Gibraltar and Minorca and so she accepted French entreaties for an alliance. Her price was high. Not only did she want help in obtaining her objectives, but she also insisted that the French should co-operate in invading Britain. The Spanish remembered the depredations the British had wrought throughout their empire in 1762 and were anxious to bring the war to a rapid conclusion to prevent the same from happening again. The Franco-Spanish alliance was signed in April 1779. In August their combined fleet of 66 ships-of-the-line appeared off the Devon coast. The 39 ships of the Channel fleet were far to the west and did not know of the enemy's presence. Only the lack of provisions, the spread of disease throughout the Bourbon ships and bad weather prevented a successful invasion.

After 1779 the allies made no more attempts to invade. The mere threat that they might try again was enough to force the British to retain a large part of their fleet at home. It might have been possible for the Admiralty to reduce this new challenge by concentrating their vessels in home waters and maintaining a close blockade of the French Atlantic ports. But Anson had only been able to do this in the Seven Years' War because Admiral Hawke had enjoyed a sufficient margin of superiority over the French to enable him continuously to return storm-damaged ships to port for repair. In 1779 Sandwich knew that the British did not enjoy a similar superiority. He was determined to preserve the fleet intact and fear of the wear and tear that a close blockade would impose on ships persuaded him not to attempt it. Instead he concentrated the Channel fleet in Torbay where it was safe from storm damage and deployed other squadrons in the West Indies and North America and periodically dispatched a squadron to relieve Gibraltar. The result was that the Channel fleet was so far distant from the enemy's ports that it could not prevent the escape of French squadrons and the overseas squadrons were too weak to be certain of defeating the enemy if they met them.

On the American mainland the strategy of pacification began successfully. In December 1778 Savannah fell to the British, rebel resistance began to collapse in parts of Georgia and the British began to organize loyalist militia. However, the reappearance of a more numerous rebel militia encouraged the loyalists to desert and by the end of 1779 the British controlled little territory outside Savannah. In February 1780 Clinton himself came south with large reinforcements and in May he captured Charleston together with the main rebel army in the southern colonies. It was the most serious defeat the rebels suffered throughout the war. In June Clinton returned to New York, leaving Lord Cornwallis in command in the south with orders to extend his conquests to the north whilst retaining the gains he had already made and in particular securing his base at Charleston. By midsummer the whole of South Carolina appeared to have been pacified but the military situation in the middle colonies seemed at a stalemate. The British were extending their military control northwards from South Carolina and the Continental Congress appeared to be losing control of the country's resources thanks to the apparent mismanagement of its financial policies.

But pacification failed. By refusing to give battle Washington kept the Continental Army intact and compelled Clinton to retain a large part of his force in the middle colonies. Clinton could not attack and scatter the Continental Army because the reinforcements he needed to do so were committed to the war in the Caribbean and the defence of Gibraltar and Minorca. In 1780 Cornwallis had only 28 per cent of the British regulars in North America. That was not enough, especially as active loyalists proved to be much less numerous than the British had hoped. Only about one in five white Americans belonged to loyalist families and in no colony did loyalists outnumber their rebel neighbours. The loyalists were weak because before 1778 the British had exaggerated their numbers, taken them for granted and done little to encourage them to organize themselves. By 1779 it was perhaps too late to expect very much from them, not least because the rebels' confidence had received such a boost by their victory at Saratoga and the French alliance. When Cornwallis did make a serious effort to organize the loyalists in South Carolina, his attempt was hampered by a lack of trained officers, muskets and horses.

The British and their loyalist auxiliaries were too few to extinguish the last remnants of rebel resistance in the south in 1780/1. The longer the war lasted the more frustrated the British became and the more inclined increasing numbers of British officers were to mete out harsh treatment to the civilian population in the hope of cowing them into submission. Clinton tried to curb the excesses of the loyalist militia and the regulars but too few subordinate officers shared his views. Many Americans who might have remained neutral were driven into the arms of the rebels in self-protection. Small bands of rebel partisans remained in hiding and when they emerged and coalesced they were able to overwhelm isolated loyalist forces. In 1780/1 a ferocious guerrilla war spread throughout the Carolinas and Georgia as loyalists and rebels fought each other. Behind a screen of militia and guerrillas the rebels were able to place another regular army in the field in central North Carolina led by Nathanael Greene. In 1781 Cornwallis, a headstrong man with scant sympathy for the patient policy Clinton had ordered him to pursue, recalled his mobile columns and tried to destroy Greene's army. He failed twice, at Cowpens and Guilford Court House. He merely increased his own casualty list and moved through North Carolina so rapidly that he could make no real attempt to organize loyalist forces in the region. Clinton insisted that he should not advance into Virginia until he had pacified the Carolinas because to march into Virginia without doing so would mean that he would lose all contact with his base at Charleston. But personal relations between the two men had broken down. Cornwallis ignored Clinton's strictures and, on his own initiative, shifted the focus of the war to the Chesapeake.

By the summer of 1781 Cornwallis's army had shrunk to less than 2,000 men but when it joined with British forces in Virginia and was reinforced it rose to 8,400 men. Cornwallis needed a new base on the coast and the fleet needed a good harbour. After the British evacuated Rhode Island in 1779 the nearest safe anchorage was in Halifax, Nova Scotia. New York was never satisfactory because the harbour had a dangerous bar. Cornwallis and Clinton thought that Yorktown would suit the needs of both services. In fact it proved to be a trap. Admiral Rodney, the commander of the British West Indian squadron, knew that his French counterpart, de Grasse, intended to sail north but assumed that he would do so with only part of his fleet and that he would send the rest to France for refitting. He therefore detached five of his own ships-of-the-line and, before poor health forced him to sail to Britain, sent his second in command, Sir Samuel Hood, north with 14 ships-of-the-line. But de Grasse had taken his whole fleet of 28 ships-of-the-line to the Chesapeake. When Washington heard of the imminent arrival of the French fleet in American waters, he marched his army around New York into Virginia to besiege Cornwallis in Yorktown. Clinton did nothing to stop him, assuming wrongly that Cornwallis would be quite safe because the Royal Navy could prevent the French from cutting his seaborne communications. But the navy had been forced to divert so many ships to relieve Gibraltar, protect Minorca (which was lost to the Spanish in 1782), and safeguard home waters that the French fleet in American waters now outnumbered them. In a tactically indecisive battle at the mouth of the Chesapeake in September the French drove off the British fleet and gained temporary control of the bay. In October 1781 Cornwallis surrendered.

The Americans and their French allies had not destroyed the British army in America. Cornwallis's force accounted for only about a fifth of all British troops in the colonies and the British still had about 28,500 troops in garrisons in Canada, New York, South Carolina, Georgia and East Florida. Yorktown was a decisive defeat because it undermined Britain's will to reconquer the colonies. The victory came at a very opportune time for the allies. The Americans were nearing the end of their resources. France's finances were in imminent danger of collapse. A major British victory, or even a continuation of the stalemate, might have persuaded the French and the Americans to accept British peace terms.

The outbreak of the war in 1775 and the Declaration of Independence in 1776 weakened the position of America's friends in Britain. The treaties of 1776 to hire German mercenaries passed easily through both the Commons and Lords.

It was not until Saratoga and France's entry into the conflict that the war in the colonies began to be seriously unpopular. The king's friends remained opposed to granting the colonies their independence. The opposition was divided. The Chathamites were ready to go no further than renouncing Parliament's right to tax the colonies and to revoke the measures which had ignited the rebellion. The Rockinghamites were, reluctantly, now ready to grant the colonies their independence. But the most serious threat, not just to the North administration but to the whole basis of aristocratic government, came from outside Parliament. In the 1740s the growth of the popular press and the spread of coffee-houses and clubs in London and major provincial cities had laid the foundations for the growth of a new popular political consciousness which was increasingly critical of Whig men, measures and taxes. The growth of this new radicalism was hastened, especially in London, by the trade depression which followed the end of the Seven Years' War. The period from 1765 to 1774 saw an important development in the ideology of radicalism. Before the 1760s such demands as there were for parliamentary reform had revolved around the ideas of the Country party's programme to purify the Commons by the removal of placemen and the calling of more frequent general elections. But by the late 1760s the expulsion of John Wilkes from the Commons, contrary to the repeated wishes of the Middlesex electorate, had raised the question of whether Parliament represented the interests of the people or those of a narrow oligarchy. The American colonists' critique of virtual representation and their insistence that there should be no taxation without representation struck a receptive chord amongst unenfranchised tax-payers in Britain.

By the late 1760s parliamentary politicians were increasingly alarmed. Their critics were not plebeian. Typically they were newspaper owners, urban merchants, brewers, innkeepers who could no longer tolerate patrician leadership. The American war gave their ideas added appeal. Between 1775 and 1782 central government spending nearly tripled, rising from £10,400,000 to £29,300,000. They financed it by their now traditional methods of raising taxes to the extent that the country gentlemen in Parliament would allow and meeting the rest of the cost of the war by borrowing. The national debt rose from £127,000,000 in 1775 to £232,000,000 in 1783 and by 1779 the government's credit was becoming strained. The price of 3 per cent stock fell from 86 in 1776 to 54 in 1782. North raised the land tax to four shillings in the pound and imposed new indirect taxes to meet increasing interest payments. But, anxious to minimize the impact of the war upon civil society, until 1780 he tried not to tax articles of common consumption and as he remained committed to a stable currency the government did not attempt to relieve the burden of the war which fell on the tax-payers by printing paper money.

Heavier taxes were one reason for tax-payers' complaints but equally important was the fact that their money seemed to buy no results. In 1779 North's disastrous handling of the war provoked a group of Yorkshire freeholders led by the Reverend Christopher Wyvill to organize a nation-wide movement to challenge the domination of politics by the aristocracy. It was the very respectability of the Yorkshire Association and its sister movements which made it such a powerful challenge to aristocratic government. Their demands combined the Country programme for economical reform with radical demands for a reform of the system of representation in order to reduce the patronage and corruption available to the government and to increase the influence of the electorate over the executive.

The only way in which the North administration could have diminished the appeal of their critics was by winning the war in America. The victories in the southern colonies in 1780 went some way towards re-establishing its prestige in the Commons and the country. In September the government held a general election in the hope of capitalizing on this trend but they were disappointed. Those constituencies where the electorate were able to express their own preferences gave their verdict against the government. The country gentlemen were growing weary of the war. But even so, the new Commons supported its continuation until Yorktown. But then it was apparent that after seven years of war and the loss of two armies, all the British had to show for their efforts were the footholds they retained around Charleston, New York and East Florida. After 1778 the government had justified continuing the war by claiming that they were morally obliged to protect American loyalists. Yorktown exploded the myth of the all-pervasiveness of American loyalism. Most members of the political nation now wanted to end the war in America to enable Britain to concentrate her resources against France and Spain. In February 1782 those independent MPs usually favourably disposed to the king's ministers withdrew their support and the Commons passed a resolution condemning an attempt to continue to prosecute the war in America. In March, after the news was received that Spain had taken Minorca, the North ministry resigned.

It was replaced by a new administration under Lord Rockingham which confronted two choices. Either the government secured peace in America and salvaged what it could in the war against the Bourbons or it would face a powerful threat to oligarchical rule at home. It chose peace with America coupled with a brief and successful effort to protect the remainder of the empire. Less than a month before it took power, the offices of secretary of state had been reformed. Henceforth the Home Secretary was responsible for domestic and colonial matters whilst a single Foreign Secretary guided foreign policy. The latter post was held by Charles James Fox and the former by the Earl of Shelburne. The policies of the two men were in sharp contrast. Fox wanted to recognize American independence at once, hoping that the Americans would abandon the war and Britain could concentrate her efforts against the Bourbons. Shelburne preferred a more cautious policy, granting recognition of American independence only as part of a comprehensive peace settlement with the colonies which would ensure cordial postwar relations between Britain and the new nation.

In the middle of this dispute, and when the British had begun tentative negotiations with the allies, news arrived in Europe from the West Indies which strengthened the hands of the British negotiators. Early in 1782 the British had suffered a series of defeats in the Caribbean. But in April 1782 Admirals Hood and Rodney regained most of what the British had lost by defeating a French fleet in the Battle of the Saints, south of Guadeloupe. In July Rockingham died and was replaced by Shelburne, who now controlled Britain's peace policy. At the end of July he accepted the necessity of recognizing American independence. He accepted the colonists' claim to all territory up to the Mississippi and the Great Lakes and admitted them to the Newfoundland fisheries. Shelburne hoped that these concessions would pave the way for close postwar economic ties between the two nations and would persuade America's European allies to accept a quick peace for fear that if they did not the Americans would abandon them and enable the British to switch more of their efforts to the West Indies.

The French also wanted peace. There was a growing crisis in eastern Europe which seemed to presage a growth of Russian power. The restoration of British naval power at the Battle of the Saints threatened their Caribbean possessions. The morale of their fleet was collapsing and there was an increasing probability that French and Spanish finances would be exhausted before Britain's. When the French began to negotiate they dragged the Spanish in their wake. France had to be content with the return of St Lucia and the retention of Tobago, an enclave around Pondicherry in India and fishing rights off the Newfoundland coast. The Spanish were unable to recapture Gibraltar, which was finally relieved in October 1782 but they were placated when Britain allowed them to retain Minorca and Florida. The British would not return Gibraltar and they regained the islands they had lost in the Bahamas. The final peace treaties with the United States, France and Spain were signed in September 1783. Peace with Holland had to wait until May 1784.

The War of Independence was only superficially a war fought for the possession of territory. At a more profound level it was an ideological struggle between monarchism and republicanism. The Americans' triumph was not inevitable. Independence movements do not invariably succeed. They can be quashed on the battlefield, as the experience of the Confederacy in 1865 and the Boers in 1902 demonstrated. The proper object of the British army in America should have been the undermining of the rebels' morale by the destruction of the Continental Army. The colonists themselves were able to mobilize support for their cause through their militia. Had Washington's field army been destroyed, the British might then have been able to do the same for their cause using the loyalist militia. The British might have succeeded in destroying the Continental Army, at the Battle of Long Island, for example, in 1776, but only if they had been prepared to take bold offensive action and perhaps to risk the destruction of their own army. But Gage, Howe and Clinton had learnt their strategy in the limited wars of the mid-eighteenth century. They were only too well aware of just how difficult it was for the home government to recruit the troops they needed. They preferred caution to boldness. They have sometimes been castigated for being excessively timid and for failing to move quickly to exploit favourable circumstances. Such charges fail to take account of the practical and psychological problems they faced. The army in America was plagued by the same problem of desertion which it had suffered from in earlier wars. Its officers were still reluctant to unleash their troops in pursuit of a defeated enemy lest their own men deserted in droves. They were operating in hostile country, with the Atlantic Ocean at their backs and at the tip of a 3,000-mile-long supply line. Despite undoubted inefficiencies the British logistical system performed wonders in supplying an army so far from its base. Nothing like it was seen again until the major Allied amphibious operations of the Second World War. But their success was only qualified. All too frequently they lacked the stockpiles of supplies without which they could not move rapidly in any direction. In the colonies the British army's reliance on foraging produced hostility from many of those who had their goods and foodstuffs seized and drove even those who wanted to remain neutral into the hands of the rebels for protection. And, by forcing the British so often to disperse their troops into small parties, it gave the rebels the opportunity to wage 'a war of posts', a strategy which was well suited to their lack of formal military training. The British committed two errors in their dealings with the loyalists: they turned to them for assistance too late, in 1778, when they should have done so in 1775; and then they relied on them too heavily.

In the decade before the outbreak of the War of Independence the British attempted to maintain their own security without the assistance of continental allies for almost the only period in the eighteenth century. The Bourbons' entry into the war in 1778 and 1779 demonstrated the bankruptcy of that policy. Naval power alone was not sufficient to deter great power rivals bent on revenge for the Treaty of Paris and convinced that Britain's predicament in North America and their own naval rearmament gave them a reasonable chance of securing it. It forced the British to alter their war aims. After 1778 America became a secondary theatre of operations as resources were shifted to the Caribbean, the western Mediterranean and home waters. Britain was incomparably richer and more populous than the thirteen colonies. By all the canons of eighteenth-century warfare they should have experienced little difficulty in bringing the rebels to heel before 1778. But the Americans were not bound by the nostrums of an ideology which dictated that the social and economic impact of war on civil society must be minimized. From the beginning of the war they were willing to mobilize a much higher proportion of their human and economic resources than were the British. With a population of nearly 11 million the British should in theory have experienced little difficulty in recruiting sufficient men to crush the rebels. That they were not able to do so was only partially due to defects in their recruiting machinery. It was due to a failure of perception and a failure of political will. Before 1778 they underestimated the magnitude of the task confronting them and only partially mobilized their resources. And even after 1778 self-imposed limitations restricted what they could do. But to have done more would have required them to propagandize the kind of secular nationalism which their American enemies were so ready to disseminate. The British already had a stable polity and notions of liberty and equality were not attractive to its rulers. Their fears that widening military obligations might have dangerously democratic implications were justified. In 1780 the radical Westminster Committee, linking a demand for manhood suffrage with the fact that almost every adult male was now liable for militia service, demanded rhetorically 'Shall a man therefore be thought unworthy of a suffrage in the election of his representative, and at the same time shall his fellow citizens entrust to his fidelity and courage whatever they hold dear?'[10]

American economic mobilization was not restricted by traditional British restraints. The Americans resorted to paper money at the beginning of the war whilst throughout the conflict the British mobilized their resources through loans and taxes. The result was that although in theory the British could dispose of far more men and supplies than the rebels, shortage of specie and ultimately the unwillingness of lenders to lend more to the state except at ruinously high interest rates, hamstrung the British. The Americans had discovered that the printing-press was a potent weapon. Unlike the British they were not prepared to allow their war effort to be limited and circumscribed by the fear that paper money might produce inflation and social disruption. Although their human and industrial resources were much less than those of Britain, they could at least partially redress the balance by mobilizing a much larger proportion of what they had.

The British war effort accorded in several respects with the notion of the 'British way in warfare'. Bereft of continental allies, they committed no troops to the continent. Defence spending favoured sea services at the expense of land services by a ratio of 67:33. By 1777/8 the Commons had voted to concentrate nearly 42 per cent of their troops in North America. But thereafter the proportion fell to about 1 in 3 as France's entry into the war caused a dissipation of Britain's military resources. Fear of invasion was one reason why after 1778 nearly half of the men under arms remained in Britain. But against these important manifestations of a 'British way in warfare' it is worth noting that the British relied on foreign assistance far less in this war than they had done in any war since 1688. Mercenaries constituted an average of 15 per cent of the troops in British pay during each year of the war and whilst they averaged about 45 per cent of the troops in North America, that too was a smaller figure than for any expeditionary force Britain had sent abroad since 1688. The British spent only £5,400,000 in paying others to fight for them, a sum equal to slightly less than 3 per cent of total defence spending during the war. Britain's war effort was more 'British' in this war than in any war since 1688.

4 The French Revolutionary and Napoleonic Wars

Pitt the Younger did not rush headlong into a war against revolutionary France. The political nation had not lost its dislike of continental entanglements. In 1789 the French Revolution did not threaten Britain's European interests. Many Englishmen believed that the French were doing what the British had done during the Glorious Revolution and welcomed the consequent upheavals in France, believing that they would weaken their rival. Even when the French National Assembly declared war on Austria and Prussia in April 1792, abolished the monarchy and established a republic, Pitt did nothing. He would not go to war to save the French monarchy. The government was only prepared to act if Britain's own security was threatened by French expansion beyond her frontiers. In the summer of 1792 Prussian and Austrian troops invaded France. In September their armies were stopped by the French at Valmy. As winter approached, and as disorders in Paris mounted, the allies decided that it would be wisest to allow the revolution to do their work for them by making France still more vulnerable. In the meantime they turned their attention to Poland which had first been partitioned in 1772. In 1792, much to the alarm of Prussia and Austria, the Russians invaded the truncated Polish state. The Second Partition of Poland came at a fortuitous time for the revolutionaries. Following the allied withdrawal after Valmy, the French invaded the Rhineland, annexed Nice and Savoy and occupied the Austrian Netherlands and the port of Antwerp. They then threatened to pursue the retreating Austrians into Holland and they opened the Scheldt to trade.

The revolution now began to pose a direct threat to British security, her commercial interests and the legitimacy of the Hanoverian regime. On 19 November the French National Convention issued decrees offering fraternity and assistance to all the peoples of Europe who wished to rid themselves of their tyrannical monarchies. The opening of the Scheldt was done in violation of the Peace of Westphalia and threatened to re-establish Antwerp as a commercial rival to Amsterdam and London. Holland was of vital concern to Britain. Her harbours would make an excellent starting point for an invasion of the British Isles. In 1787 France and Britain had signed a convention and France renounced any intention of interfering in Holland's internal affairs. A year later Britain had ended her post-War of Independence isolation by signing a Triple Alliance with the Dutch and Prussians obliging them to defend the republic against French attacks. By November 1792 ministers were concluding that disaffection at home might have to be dealt with in the context of war abroad. From 1790 to 1792 radical reform societies, inspired by the publication of Tom Paine's *The Rights of Man* and the success of French armies, had begun to enlist support from amongst the tradesmen and shopkeepers of some British towns. The Convention's decrees of 19 November offering their support to just such anti-aristocratic movements came at a time when the government was receiving reports of crop failures, strained commercial credit and food riots and when rumours were circulating that the radicals were stockpiling weapons. Pitt informed the French that, if they withdrew their troops from the territory they had occupied and renounced the decrees, Britain would recognize the republic. The French refused. On 1 February 1793 they declared war on Holland and Britain and called upon their peoples to topple their governments.

The French republic threatened not only Britain's security interests in western Europe but also the stability of the Hanoverian regime. The Jacobites had only sought to replace one royal dynasty by another. The French republic wanted to abolish monarchy, aristocracy and the Anglican Church. But even though Britain was now involved in an ideological conflict in defence of the foundations of the British state, that did not mean that the government mobilized all possible resources in its own defence. With only the precedents of the eighteenth century to guide him, Pitt began the war convinced that France would not be able to sustain her war effort for long. Judged by the standards of the *ancien régime*, France's finances were in chaos and her army was disintegrating. But in August 1793 the French began to demolish the fiscal and human barriers which had inhibited the states of *ancien régime* Europe when they mobilized for war. By decreeing that 'all Frenchmen are permanently requisitioned for service into the armies'[1] they declared that everyone, no matter how rich or poor, owed military service to the state. In time the rich found ways to avoid serving in person, but even so after 1793 the French army was able to call upon a far larger manpower pool than ever before. In 1694 Louis XIV had raised about 300,000 troops. In the eighteenth century France's population increased by about 30 per cent. But by the spring of 1794 she had 750,000 men under arms. Conscription was placed on a more systematic footing in 1799 and Napoleon extended it to many of the countries he annexed or occupied. Between 1800 and 1812 he enlisted 1,300,000 men in his army. More than half of the 614,000 soldiers of the Grande Armée which invaded Russia in 1812 were drawn from France's allies and satellites. The revolution fed these huge forces by a combination of paper money, requisitioning inside France and by levying contributions and plunder from the countries it conquered. This was made easier by the growing agricultural surplus which western Europe was producing in the second half of the century. Campaigns were made to pay for themselves and show a profit.

Napoleon's victory over Prussia in 1806 yielded a net profit of fr. 359,000,000, the equivalent of about half the total income of the French state in 1807.

The revolution gave the French armies an enormously increased resource base upon which they could draw. Their mobility was rarely blocked by fortresses because they had sufficient men to detach part of their force to mask them. French armies could seek out and destroy their enemies in battle for they knew that their losses could easily be made good. In the Napoleonic era armies were on average three times as large as they had been in the eighteenth century and they fought pitched battles six times more frequently. It was not until the French army became bogged down in the Iberian Peninsula after 1808 and the Grande Armée was destroyed in Russia in 1812, that the human and economic resources of France and her satellites began to be exhausted. The French made war an affair of the whole nation and drastically altered its objectives. Instead of using the limited resources of the *ancien régime* to achieve limited objectives, the French republic and its imperial successor sought to destroy their enemies' means and will to resist. But their ability to wage war on a such a vast and intensive scale ultimately proved counter-productive. It encouraged them to lose sight of the fact that the purpose of war was not military victory, but the security offered them by a more stable peace. The French sought to impose one-sided settlements on the states they vanquished. That only encouraged the defeated to repudiate the agreements France had forced upon them at the first opportunity and so ensured that Europe was racked by a generation of war.

In 1793 British strategic policy was made by three men, Pitt, the Foreign Secretary Lord Grenville and Henry Dundas, who was the Home Secretary until the summer of 1794 and President of the Board of Control of India from June 1793. In July 1794 the Portland Whigs joined the government and the Duke of Portland replaced Dundas as Home Secretary. In order to retain Dundas at the centre of the conduct of the war, Pitt created the new office of Secretary of State for War and the Colonies for him. This Cabinet endured with some changes for the next six years. The smallness of this inner group of ministers might have promoted rapid and decisive decision-making but for the personalities and ideas of the men involved. Pitt was a brilliant finance minister but he knew himself to be no war leader. By the late 1790s Dundas and Grenville differed about the objects for which Britain should be fighting. Dundas believed that the policies which had been so successful in Britain's wars against the Bourbons would also work against the revolution. Britain could achieve an advantageous settlement if she expelled France from the Austrian Netherlands and if she dispatched expeditions to the East and West Indies to disrupt French trade and increase 'our own National Wealth and Security'.[2] But Grenville came to recognize that the new regime in Paris was different from its royal predecessors. Hemming France in behind strategic frontiers and weakening her trade would not eliminate the challenge posed by the republic. A secure peace could only be achieved if the regime in Paris were toppled and replaced by a government prepared to abide by the terms of the treaties it signed. The entry of the Whigs made little difference to the conduct of the war except that as Secretary at War William Windham was a powerful voice in favour of assisting counter-revolutionaries in both France and French-occupied Europe.

The pattern of defence spending between 1784 and 1792 reverted to the eighteenth century peacetime norm. The ratio between land services and sea services was 32:68 in favour of the navy. After 1783 the army was reduced to 81 infantry battalions and 30 cavalry regiments and returned to its peacetime duties. Between a half and a third of all infantry battalions served abroad. The American war had so drained the army of trained manpower that until the end of the 1780s most battalions were below establishment and contained a high proportion of raw recruits. Problems caused by the shortage of manpower were compounded by the fact that uniformity of drill broke down during the American war. In 1778 the concentration of a considerable number of troops in southern England ready to meet a French invasion gave the War Office the chance to introduce new drill regulations. But because such a large part of the army served abroad during the American war, and because rotation between home and overseas stations was slow after 1783, some battalions never became familiar with the new regulations. The uniformity of drill which the War Office had worked so hard to achieve since the 1720s collapsed in the 1780s and the ability of units to operate in harmony was undermined. No serious effort was made to overcome this problem between 1783 and 1792 because the army was without a professional soldier as commander-in-chief. New regulations were not issued until 1792, too late to be disseminated throughout the army before the start of the next war. The weaknesses and omissions of years could not be made good overnight, a fact made all too apparent by the poor showing of the army sent to Flanders under the Duke of York in 1793.

The navy had fared better than the army in the decade after 1783, perhaps because of the close interest Pitt took in the fleet. Starting in 1785 the civil affairs of the navy were the subject of a series of searching parliamentary inquiries established to reduce waste and extravagance in public expenditure. Pitt sympathized with these objectives. Throughout his peacetime premiership he was anxious to bring prosperity to the nation and to reduce public spending. But he was determined that spending must not be cut at the expense of the navy's efficiency. Between 1784 and 1788 he raised its peacetime establishment from 15,000 to 20,000 men and 34 new ships-of-the-line were built between 1783 and 1790. That fact, together with two war scares with Spain and Russia in the preceding three years, meant that in 1793 the navy was better prepared for war than at the beginning of any previous war in the eighteenth century. It had 93 ships-of-the-line supported by a substantial stock of stores and equipment and the extensive dockyard network which had been created in the eighteenth century. A ship-of-the-line required repairs and refitting on average every two-and-a-half years in wartime. It was a measure of the dockyards' efficiency that despite the enormous wear and tear the fleet suffered, between 1794 and 1801 they were able to keep on average 75 per cent of the navy's ships-of-the-line and 83 per cent of its frigates in commission each year. But that did not mean that the navy was without its problems. The peacetime building programme had given priority to ships-of-the-line rather than to cruisers and throughout the wars officers echoed Admiral Collingwood's complaint in 1809 that 'My distress for frigates and small vessels is extreme'.[3]

From 1793 to 1795 the services relied upon their traditional methods of raising men. The Admiralty offered bounties to volunteers and Parliament relaxed the Navigation Laws, permitting ship-owners to man their ships with crews three quarters of whom were foreigners so as to facilitate the enlistment of trained British merchant seamen in the fleet. But the fleet's manpower needs rose from 45,000 in 1793 to 100,000 in 1795 and far exceeded the numbers of volunteers available. Resort had to be made to the press. In one respect the manning problem became easier than in earlier wars. After 1799 the Admiralty issued oranges and lemons on a regular basis. That step, together with a variety of *ad hoc* measures taken by a few more enlightened sea officers, went some way towards reducing the number of men lost to sickness. Without these advances in naval medicine and hygiene it is doubtful whether the fleet could have maintained the continuous blockade of the French coast that it mounted for much of the war.

The augmentation of the army also began along traditional lines. In 1793 the government hired over 28,000 German mercenaries. Grenville defended doing so on traditional grounds that highlighted the government's belief that it was engaging in another in a series of limited wars. He claimed that employing mercenaries meant that the British would not be compelled to enlist 'our own youth from the plough, & the loom, and thereby not merely put a stop to our domestic industry, but also drain the island of its population, and diminish our natural strength'.[4] But some enlistment of subject troops was inevitable. When the post of commander-in-chief had fallen vacant in 1783 the control of army patronage fell into the hands of the Secretary at War, Sir George Yonge. He used it ruthlessly for political ends. When he began to raise more troops in 1793 he did so by raising new regiments rather than augmenting existing ones. Commissions created by augmenting existing regiments could not be sold. They were granted free to the next senior officers in the regiment or to deserving officers from outside it. But commissions in new units could be sold and it was the cheapest way of raising troops. It enabled the War Office to amass a fund from which it could pay bounties to encourage men to enlist in the ranks. But many of the new regiments were little more than hollow shells lacking sufficient rank and file and led by inexperienced officers. By 1795 the work of regimental recruiting parties seeking volunteers, assisted sometimes by crimps who kidnapped recruits and sold them to the army, had swollen the ranks of the regular army from about 45,000 to 125,000 men. But even so between 1795 and 1797 the regular army was still 50,000 men below strength.

Britain's early failures sprang from three facts. Ministers lacked an adequate knowledge of the mechanics of war and their ignorance made them ready to embark on operations which were impractical. The prevalent belief in a short and limited war did nothing to encourage Pitt to overcome his natural hesitancy and impose a clear list of strategic priorities on his colleagues. The result was that the government dispersed Britain's limited means among too many objectives. But, most important of all, ministers underestimated the magnitude of the task confronting them. Between 1793 and 1795 they believed that the revolution had weakened rather than strengthened France's ability to make war. They were slow to realize that the revolution had liberated forces in France which made her far less vulnerable to strategies designed to bring her to the conference table by exhausting her fiscal resources. Pitt boasted that he could predict to the day when France's finances would collapse and she would have to make peace. His friend William Wilberforce had a shrewder appreciation of the dynamics at work in France: 'But who was Attila's Chancellor of the Exchequer?' he once asked.[5]

In February 1793 Dundas told the Commons that the government's objective was 'to bring down every power on earth to assist them'.[6] Between March and August they signed bilateral conventions with Russia, Prussia and Austria, agreeing to act in concert and not to make a separate peace until France had surrendered her conquests. The one feature of Britain's traditional practice which was missing were subsidies to the great powers. Pitt expected a short war and saw no need to spend the nation's capital lavishly. The conventions provided a framework for co-operation but they did not explain how the allies were to act in concert. This encouraged the British to dissipate their limited resources between four theatres. They knew that the Austrians would gladly exchange the burden of defending the remote Austrian Netherlands for Bavaria. In order to dissuade Vienna from disengaging from the region, Grenville promised that British troops would be employed to enlarge the Austrian Netherlands at France's expense and the king's son, the Duke of York, was sent with a small army to the Low Countries to co-operate with the Prussians and Austrians in attacking France's northern frontier.

In the south agreements Britain signed with Spain, Portugal, Sardinia and the Kingdom of Naples had direct operational implications. The agreements with the Iberian powers helped to establish a cordon to prevent the French Mediterranean fleet breaking out into the Atlantic. The British promised the Sardinians they would send a fleet to the Mediterranean to help them to recover Nice and Savoy. In August Anglo-Spanish forces attacked Toulon as part of what the British hoped would be a concerted allied offensive in southern France. In December troops intended for the Duke of York were dispatched to assist French rebels fighting republican forces in the Vendee. In November 1793, in the expectation that the French colonial empire would fall like so many ripe apples into their lap, Sir Charles Grey was sent to the Caribbean with 6,000 men to occupy the major French Caribbean islands. The British did not expect to win the war by fighting in the Caribbean. But they did hope to improve their own security by depriving France of this nursery for her seamen and to win the peace by augmenting their own trade.

The prospect of a rapid French collapse in 1793/4 proved to be illusory. The Terror gripped France as the revolutionaries expunged domestic opposition and mobilized their resources for the war. In December 1793 the allies evacuated Toulon because the Austrians, Sardinians and Neapolitans failed to send the necessary troops to help their allies to hold it. The troops the British sent to Cherbourg to assist the rebels arrived only after the latter had been crushed. The government could not find the reinforcements York needed to assist the Austrians in breaching France's frontier and the Anglo-Austrian force was checked by the French in May 1794. That setback might not have been decisive but for the fact that a few weeks earlier Polish insurgents had taken control of Warsaw. Henceforth the minds of the Austrians, Prussians and Russians turned away from the French frontier and focused on Poland. By October the French had occupied Brussels and Antwerp, invaded Holland, driven the British and Dutch back across the River Waal and the Austrians back across the Rhine. The Prussians did nothing, ostensibly because of the late arrival of a promised British subsidy. By April 1794 Grey had taken some of the smaller French Caribbean islands and the capital of Sainte Domingue, the richest of the French colonies. But Pitt's satisfaction was short-lived. Success in the Caribbean depended upon the navy's ability to prevent the French sending assistance. The Admiralty, anxious to spare their ships the full rigours of a close blockade, only mounted a distant blockade of Brest. Lord Howe's Channel fleet anchored in Torbay whilst frigates watched Brest. The policy was a qualified success. When a French squadron escaped from Brest to escort a homeward-bound grain convoy, Howe intercepted it and on 1 June 1794, in the first fleet action of the war, captured or destroyed seven French ships. However, he could not prevent a French squadron from escaping to the Caribbean and retaking Guadeloupe. At the beginning of 1795 British forces in the Caribbean facing this counter-attack were being decimated by disease and had to contend with a series of slave revolts which threatened their hold on their own West Indian possessions.

In 1795, when it was apparent that the French would not collapse before the first allied assault, the First Coalition began to crumble. Pitt failed to stop the rot by offering Prussia a subsidy to continue fighting. In January 1795 Russia, Austria and Prussia began the Third Partition of Poland. The Prussians, anxious to consolidate their new gains, were the first partner to defect from the coalition, making peace in April 1795. The collapse of the alliance between 1795 and 1797 marked a new stage in the development of Britain's war effort. It meant that the war would not be over quickly and that Britain would have to mobilize her resources more fully if she were to survive. Fortunately for the army Yonge left office in July 1794 and in February 1795 the Duke of York became commander-in-chief. He held the post until 1809 and did more than any man to improve the efficiency of the army. He ensured that children and incompetents holding commissions were kept away from the troops, and he tried to produce efficient units from the mass of weak battalions Yonge had created. By 1795 the country had been drained of volunteers. The government, which was increasingly short of money, could not pay sufficiently large bounties to attract enough recruits. They tried to overcome this problem in two ways. In 1795 York carried out the largest draft of the century, breaking up a quarter of all the foot regiments and dispersing their men amongst the rest of the army to bring the remaining battalions up to strength. Pitt resorted to a limited form of conscription for the fleet and for home defence. He introduced two Quota Acts permitting the government through the magistracy to raise landsmen for the fleet. As in the case of the militia, men were permitted to pay a substitute if they could afford to do so. In 1797 he augmented the home defence army on the cheap by raising 60,000 supplementary militiamen who were given a brief period of training before being released from the service. By February 1799 the militia had trebled in size since the start of the war.

The most remarkable feature of the British response was that the regime was able to do this without resorting to methods which would have undermined the political structures they were seeking to defend. French notions of liberty, equality and fraternity had only a limited appeal in Britain. Even before war broke out the ruling oligarchy began to close ranks in the face of a common danger. When the Whig MP Edmund Burke published his *Reflections on the Revolution in France* in November 1790 it was not taken seriously by many of his party colleagues. Charles James Fox claimed that the doctrine of the rights of man propagated by the French was the basis of the British constitution. But with the outbreak of war Fox found himself in a minority. The government used the law to repress radical clubs and built barracks to stop soldiers being infected by radical notions. But they did not appeal directly to the great mass of middle-class opinion nor did they attempt to spread nationalistic propaganda amongst the labouring classes. The same fears which had held them back during the War of Independence persisted. Their determination to restrict active citizenship to the landed elite and their clients made it impossible for them to issue a blanket appeal to all classes to serve the state. The only outlet for popular nationalism which wartime governments felt safe in sponsoring was the cult of monarchy. In 1795, when the Commons were discussing paying the Prince of Wales' debts, Pitt insisted that national security necessitated that the state had to maintain the monarchy in splendour as a counterblast to radical republicanism.

The government could afford this somewhat lackadaisical attitude because the war tapped the strains of popular Francophobia which had been present in Britain throughout the eighteenth century. In November 1792 anti-reform opinion outside Parliament began to mobilize itself in the form of loyalist associations. Led by local elites and with their members drawn from amongst the middle classes, they demonstrated that most men of property were united behind the government and placed the radicals' boast that they spoke for all men of intelligence in its proper perspective. By 1794, with the exception of a handful of Foxites, most members of the political nation saw the French, rather than an over-mighty British monarchy, as the greatest threat to their liberties. Conservative writers like Burke contrasted French poverty and anarchy with Britain's prosperity and liberty and produced a convincing and sophisticated response to French propaganda and British radicalism. The Anglican Church sustained pro-war sentiments, celebrating days of national thanksgiving during which Anglican ministers dwelt upon French wickedness and portrayed Britain as an instrument of divine retribution.

The government's role was to create a framework within which society's traditional rulers, the landed aristocracy, country gentlemen, Anglican parsons and municipal corporations, could organize to suppress dissidents and rally opinion behind the status quo. In 1794 Pitt introduced legislation to encourage local elites to raise volunteer corps. They were part of an attempt to create a national conservative coalition. In the event of a French invasion they were to become the executive arm of committees of loyalists charged with repressing sedition and ensuring that British Jacobins did not disrupt the army's communications. The government took care to ensure that the 100,000 men who served in volunteer units between 1793 and 1801 included a high proportion of men of property who would be willing to perform these policing functions. Their bright uniforms were mute but vivid testimony to the strength of the status quo. But by affording the *nouveaux riches* of Georgian England an opportunity to give practical expression to their patriotism, and thus on one level to claim parity with the landed classes, they represented a small break with the principle that service in the armed forces was a career rather than a civic duty.

The forced evacuation of York's army from the continent in February 1795 presented the British with strategic and logistical problems which they could not overcome until 1808. The British army would always be too small by itself to defeat the forces which France could muster. After 1795 the first priority of successive governments was to form a coalition with at least two of the three eastern powers so that their armies could contain a large part of the French army. When such a coalition existed they were willing to dispatch part of their own army to the continent to support their allies. When the coalitions collapsed, as they did in 1795, 1800 and 1806 the British army was withdrawn before the French could overwhelm it. Without allies, the British had no option other than to wage a maritime war. They augmented their own defences and reduced the possibility that France might invade Britain by mounting operations to weaken the enemy's own fleet and those of her allies. They secured overseas bases to deny them to the French and they attacked enemy colonies to protect Britain's own colonies and to increase their own ability to finance their war effort by opening new markets for British trade.

This strategy emerged between 1795 and 1798. In May 1795 the Dutch changed sides, giving the French control of the Dutch fleet and the British promptly launched a pre-emptive strike against the Dutch colonial empire.

An expedition from Britain occupied the Cape of Good Hope to safeguard the route to India and forces of the East India Company captured the Dutch bases at Trincomalee in Ceylon and Malacca on the southern end of the Malay peninsula. Britain's position in the Caribbean was already under threat when Spain added to her difficulties by leaving the coalition in July 1795 and ceding San Domingo to France. In August 1796 she allied herself with France and in October declared war on Britain. Pitt dispatched 31,000 men under Sir Ralph Abercromby to the West Indies with orders to put down the slave revolts in Britain's own islands, prevent the French occupying San Domingo and to take the Dutch colonies of Surinam and Demerara. Between April and June 1796 Abercromby occupied Demerara, St Lucia, Grenada and St Vincent but Guadeloupe and San Domingo remained in French hands. The West Indian campaign augmented British trade and increased her ability to finance a long war. But between 1793 and 1801 it cost the lives of 87,000 to 97,000 soldiers and sailors. Fear of service in the Caribbean was one reason why the regular army experienced such difficulty in recruiting sufficient men in the 1790s. The campaign diverted a considerable part of the British army away from Europe and it provided French propagandists with an easy target. In 1800 the British ambassador in Vienna reported that 'We are represented as making war, and inciting all other nations to join us, merely for its profits'.[7] But even if the tens of thousands of men involved had been sent to Europe, they would have been too few to have made a significant difference to the outcome of the continental land war where the decisive factor was that the French army was numbered in hundreds of thousands.

Throughout 1795 the Austrian and Russian armies had remained practically motionless as their governments haggled over the exact terms of the partition of Poland. In 1796, before they could take the initiative, General Bonaparte swept through northern Italy, forcing Sardinia to make peace, obliging the pope to yield territory to France and compelling the Austrians to accept a truce in April 1797. The British could do nothing directly to help the Austrians beyond offering them a loan which fell far short of the sum they had demanded. By signing the Peace of Campo Formio in October 1797 Austria gained Venice, Dalmatia and Istria and the French promised that they would use their best efforts to allow her to acquire part of Bavaria and Salzburg. In return Austria abandoned her Belgian provinces and recognized the two puppet states the French had created in northern Italy, the Cisalpine republic, which dominated the Po valley and the Ligurian republic (Genoa).

The British government was more concerned with threats nearer home. Lack of military success abroad, the danger of invasion, domestic unrest, mutiny in the navy and growing financial problems all combined to persuade the government to seek peace in 1796/7. In 1794 they had already banned the United Irishmen, a group of Irishmen who wished to end British rule in Ireland. Its leaders went underground and began to establish arms caches and to form military cadres in preparation for a revolution. Some of them were ready to accept French help to establish an independent Irish republic. The governments in London and Dublin knew of their machinations. The Directory believed that Ireland was the weakest link in Britain's defences and ordered the Brest fleet to convoy 20,000 troops to Ireland. In December 1796 the French succeeded in evading the Channel fleet's distant blockade and only bad weather prevented them from landing in Bantry Bay. In Britain the mid-1790s were marked by a series of poor harvests and rising food prices which provoked sporadic unrest and riots. In October 1795 the king was surrounded by a mob chanting 'No Pitt, no War, Bread, Bread, Peace, Peace'.[8] The government suspended habeas corpus and introduced Bills strengthening the law of treason and banning seditious meetings. But the most serious threat to national security occurred in April and June 1797 when the fleet at Spithead and the Nore mutinied. The men complained about poor food and clothing, lack of leave, harsh discipline and low pay. Ministers had to hasten supplementary estimates through Parliament to meet the men's demands for increased pay. As a precaution they also raised soldiers' pay.

Finally by early 1797 the government's credit appeared to be exhausted. When Pitt came to power he was anxious to reduce the burden of the national debt and in 1786 he established a sinking fund to liquidate it. In 1793 he planned to pay for the war by raising loans coupled with a moderate increase in taxes to fund the added interest payments. He raised £74,400,000 in loans between 1793 and 1796. The land tax already stood at four shillings in the pound so to find the money he needed to support the funding system he continued his pre-war policy of spreading the load of taxes on as many luxury items as possible. But just what burden property could bear before it crumbled was unclear. In 1776 Adam Smith argued in his *An Inquiry into the Nature and Causes of the Wealth of Nations* that wars were economically wasteful because they diverted capital from productive enterprises and multiplied the numbers of unproductive labourers. Some political economists believed that Britain could not fight a long war and that the economy would be crushed under the growing burden of the public debt. At the beginning of 1796 the Bank of England was so concerned at the ratio of its liabilities to its assets that it tried to ration the amount of short-term credit it offered the government. This only gave further encouragement to merchants and manufacturers who demanded an end to the war. In February 1797 commercial confidence had sunk so low that when a small body of French troops landed on the Welsh coast there was a run on gold which so depleted the bank's gold reserves that the government had to suspend cash payments and issue bank notes in small denominations. The result further fuelled inflation and by 1811 the paper pound had depreciated by about 20 per cent. But by expanding credit without the constraint imposed by the obligation to make payments in gold, it helped the country pay for the most expensive war it had ever fought. Inadvertently, Pitt had stumbled on one of the secrets of a successful wartime fiscal policy.

But that was not yet apparent. In 1796 and 1797, fearing that Britain would be unable to continue the war alone, Pitt made two attempts to negotiate peace terms. The government was ready to leave France master of western Europe by accepting French control of the Low Countries, but they sought to balance those losses by retaining Trinidad, Ceylon, the Cape of Good Hope and one of the French islands they had taken in the Caribbean. However, the *coup d'état* of Fructidor in September 1797 brought to power a group of politicians supported by Bonaparte who wanted not only the domination of western Europe but also the destruction of the British Empire. The British negotiators were recalled and when Pitt met Parliament in November 1797 he could convincingly blame the French for the collapse of the talks.

In February 1797 Sir John Jervis had defeated the Spanish fleet off Cape St Vincent and thwarted a second French attempt to invade Ireland. The battle marked the start of a new era in British naval operations. It was distinguished by a greater willingness to assume risks and a greater ability to seize fleeting opportunities to impose a crushing tactical defeat on the enemy. At the 'Glorious First of June' Howe had beaten a French fleet of equal size but had allowed the grain convoy they were escorting to escape. At Cape St Vincent Jervis engaged a Spanish fleet of 28 vessels with only 15 British ships-of-the-line. St Vincent, the title Jervis took when he was ennobled, and his protégé Nelson, brought to naval warfare the same determination to annihilate the enemy that the French had brought to land warfare. St Vincent had relied upon the fact that the amendment of the old fighting instructions, the adoption of new signal books and the superior seamanship of his fleet, would together enable him to outmanoeuvre the enemy. His confidence was justified. Nelson was able to break the Spanish line and the British vessels engaged the enemy at close range. In October 1797 Admiral Duncan added to Britain's maritime security by defeating the Dutch fleet at Camperdown. For the moment the government's fears of an overwhelmingly powerful naval concentration had passed. That, plus the fillip the two victories gave to national morale, meant that for the time being demands for an early peace subsided.

In 1797/8 the British mobilized men and money so they could fight alone. In December 1796 Pitt had raised a 'loyalty loan' of £18,000,000 in less than a day, which seemed to indicate that there was still considerable support for the war. But the government spent over £57,000,000 in 1797. Borrowing on this scale drove interest rates up to ruinously high levels. To save the government's cheap credit he had to borrow less and tax more. Pitt's new proposals showed that the government now accepted that they were engaged in a struggle for national survival. In 1798 the assessed taxes were trebled, the land tax, which hitherto had been voted annually, was made permanent, and in December Pitt introduced a new tax on incomes above £60 per annum. Although the income tax was not an immediate success, by 1800 the whole package had achieved Pitt's aim. Without these new taxes the British would have been unable to sustain their own efforts or to subsidize their allies on the lavish scale they adopted after 1810.

The collapse of the First Coalition and the abortive peace negotiations of 1796/7 left Grenville more than ever convinced that peace with the Directory would never be more than an armed truce and that only the toppling of the existing regime and the restoration of the Bourbons would produce a lasting peace. He believed that the First Coalition had crumbled because the allies had lacked an agreed political aim and a common strategy. He attempted to avoid the same mistakes by creating a four-power concert which would impose a territorial settlement on France and then establish a collective security system to forestall future French aggression. He faced some formidable obstacles, not the least of which was that although the powers were suspicious of France, they remained almost equally suspicious of each other. Until the end of his life Pitt was determined to expel the French from the Low Countries and a consistent theme in his diplomacy was his desire to create a northern alliance with Prussia and Russia. Between 1795 and 1805 he sent no less than five missions to Berlin armed with promises of subsidies and territory if the Prussians would co-operate. But although the Prussians wanted to expel France from the Low Countries they remained neutral for fear that war would endanger their recent gains in Poland. The British had to fall back on Austria but Anglo-Austrian relations were bedevilled by the Austrians' refusal to meet their financial obligations under a loan convention of 1795. The Russians would not act except in concert with the Austrians and by the summer of 1798 Grenville had made little progress in breaking this impasse.

The French broke it for him. In May 1798 they abandoned their plans to invade Britain and turned east. Bonaparte left Toulon with 35,000 men to occupy Egypt. Simultaneously French agents from Mauritius threatened Britain's position in India by starting negotiations with Tipu Sultan of Mysore. Dundas persuaded the Admiralty to send Nelson to the Mediterranean to stop Bonaparte. But Nelson arrived too late and, after occupying Malta, Bonaparte landed at Alexandria in July 1798. Campo Formio had given France control of the major routes through northern Italy to the rest of the Peninsula. In 1798 they occupied Rome, Switzerland, Tuscany and Naples and the Ionian Islands and it appeared that they were determined to dominate the Levant. This alarmed Tsar Paul I who had succeeded his mother Catherine in 1796. On 1 August 1798 Nelson destroyed Bonaparte's fleet at Aboukir Bay, stranding him in Egypt and giving Britain command of the Mediterranean. Between December 1798 and January 1799 Nelson's victory enabled Grenville to sign treaties with Russia, Turkey and the Kingdom of the Two Sicilies. Pitt hoped the allies would agree to reduce France to her pre-revolutionary frontiers and block her expansion by creating powerful barrier states along her borders. The Dutch republic could be strengthened by union with Belgium. Piedmont should be liberated and strengthened by union with Savoy. Austria could be granted territory northern Italy as compensation for her losses in Belgium. Prussia might induced to join the coalition by compensation in Germany. But the Prussians remained so suspicious of Austria that they could not be bought and Austria remained isolated until February 1799 when French troops crossed the Rhine and compelled her to declare war. But even then her objectives differed from Britain's. The latter wanted to overthrow the regime in Paris. All the Austrians sought was to push the French back across the Rhine, preserve their army intact and defend their hereditary territories.

In the summer of 1799 Austro-Russian forces drove the French back across the Rhine and inflicted heavy defeats on them in northern Italy and Switzerland. Grenville hoped that the Swiss campaign would be the prelude to an allied invasion of France. He thought that the Directory was at the end of its resources and that a counter-revolution was fermenting inside France. Grenville had hoped that the Prussians would liberate Holland. When they refused he decided that it would have to be done by an Anglo-Russian expedition. But the regular army was hardly in a fit state to embark upon a major continental campaign. Although about 150,000 men had enlisted in the regular army between 1793 and 1798, desertions and losses sustained in the West Indies meant that at one moment in 1798 there were only 8,500 regular infantry in Britain. To make good this shortfall the government embodied the Supplementary Militia. They hoped that once militiamen had been removed from their civilian surroundings and had a taste of army life, they would be ready to enlist in the regulars. In June 1799 they therefore reduced the militia to 66,000 men and allowed militiamen to join the regular army. For the first, but not the last time, the militia became a recruiting depot for the regulars and enabled the government to cobble together an expedition of 30,000 men for Holland. In return for a subsidy of £44,000 per month, the Russians supplied another 11,000 men.

The Second Coalition collapsed for many of the same reasons which had destroyed its predecessor. The Austrians, determined to maintain their army intact, did not follow up the allied victories in Switzerland and northern Italy with enough vigour to stop a French recovery. In August 1799 French troops regained control of the major Alpine passes and in September they defeated a Russian army at Zurich before a second Russian force could arrive from northern Italy to help them. The Anglo-Russian expedition to Holland sailed in mid-August. It reawoke Austrian interests in the Austrian Netherlands and they began to shift a large part of their army from Switzerland to the lower Rhine. That hamstrung Austro-Russian co-operation and ended any possibility that the allies could invade France through the Jura in 1800.

The Anglo-Russian expedition illustrated the immense practical problems of waging amphibious warfare along the European coast. The hardest task the planners faced was to find sufficient shipping. Each infantryman required a modest one-and-a-quarter tons of shipping but as a single cavalry regiment needed 20,000 tons, the British contingent was accompanied by only one squadron of cavalry and depended upon local Dutch resources for its transport. The Transport Board could not find sufficient shipping to enable the force to be carried in a single lift and the troops had to be shuttled across the North Sea. British amphibious operations had succeeded in the past when they had been

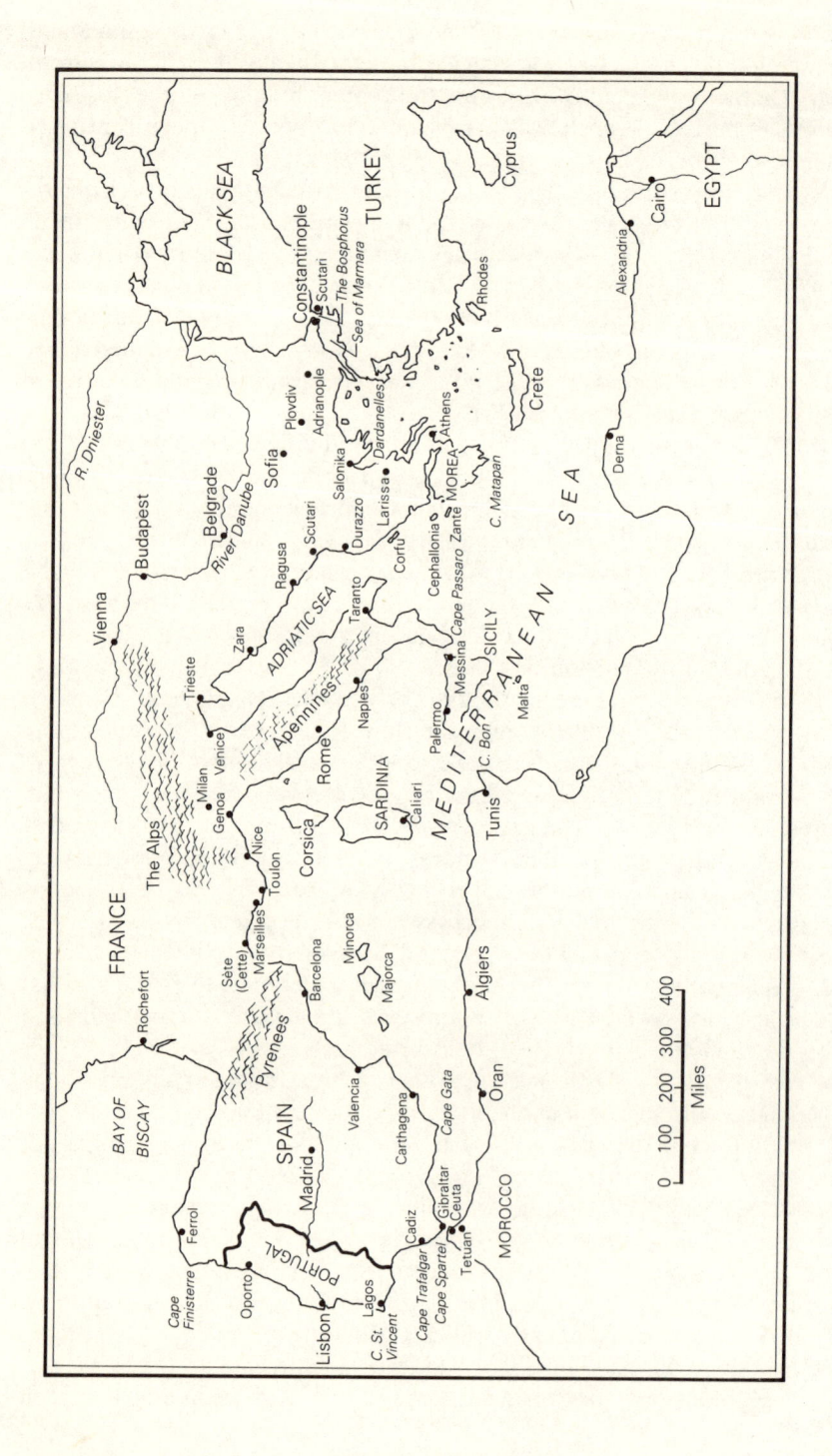

Figure 3 The Mediterranean

directed against targets where the navy could deprive the enemy of supplies and reinforcements. The only way those circumstances could be replicated on the European mainland was if France's lines of communication were attacked by the indigenous population. It was imperative that any landing take place in the midst of a friendly population. But the House of Orange was far from being popular with all Dutchmen, there was no rising to help the allies, and the French were able to summon sufficient reinforcements to hold Amsterdam. The expedition was evacuated in November and the whole episode ended with the Russians and British blaming each other for their failure.

The government was now more than ever divided about its objectives. Grenville saw the war as an ideological struggle which could only be ended satisfactorily by the overthrow of the regime in Paris. Dundas continued to believe that Britain was engaged in a limited conflict for power and wealth which could be ended by a compromise peace. This division bedevilled British policy until the Peace of Amiens. In November 1799 Bonaparte, who had escaped from Egypt, made himself First Consul and offered to negotiate peace. The military situation still seemed propitious and Pitt refused. Grenville and Windham rushed military supplies to rebels in western France. They also wished to bribe Austria to co-operate by offering them Piedmont and the Netherlands and to negotiate a subsidy treaty to create a polyglot army of Russians, Bavarians, Swiss and French émigrés to reconquer Switzerland and invade France. But the tsar had lost patience with his allies and withdrew from the coalition. Russia's defection left Austria dependent upon British support. In June 1800 the Austrians obtained an additional subsidy of £2,000,000 on condition that Austria did not make a separate peace before February 1801. But the same week this agreement was signed Bonaparte destroyed Austria's military power in northern Italy at Marengo. After one more French victory at Hohenlinden in December 1800, the Austrians were ready to accept Bonaparte's terms. The Peace of Luneville, signed in February 1801, reaffirmed France's ascendancy over the Italian peninsula and enabled Bonaparte to begin to redraw the map of Germany.

The British could do little to prevent the collapse of the Second Coalition. Dundas feared that France might soon be able to challenge Britain's maritime power by concentrating her own resources on rebuilding the French navy and exploiting the maritime resources of her conquests. He advocated attacking enemy squadrons in harbour and mounting offensives in the colonies to extend Britain's own commerce and expand her ability to fight alone. In January 1801 Russia, Prussia, Sweden and Denmark, who between them could, in theory, maintain a fleet of a hundred ships-of-the-line, formed a League of Armed Neutrality in protest at the way in which Britain exercised her belligerent rights at sea. By insisting that neutral vessels should be permitted to carry enemy property to enemy ports and that naval stores did not constitute contraband, the league threatened the basis of British naval power. They retaliated by sending a fleet to Copenhagen which forced the Danes to capitulate. That, together with the death of Tsar Paul and his replacement by Tsar Alexander, wrecked the league.

In the meantime the British were busy extending their dominions in India under the guise of defending it from the French. The Battle of the Nile had not diminished Dundas's fears for India. After the passage of the 1784 India Act India was subject to dual government. In theory the governor-general in Calcutta was responsible to the Board of Control in London. In practice the latter could only exercise a remote supervisory role over him. That was significant because the two parties could not agree on what was the most pressing danger to British rule in India or on how to meet it. The government in London thought it was self-evident that the East India Company's trading enterprises required peace if they were to prosper and therefore deprecated a forward policy which might involve the company in expensive wars inside India, especially as they thought that the external danger from France was the most serious threat to India. When Bonaparte landed in Egypt Dundas had believed that he intended to march overland to Sind. In fact Bonaparte intended – as the East India Company predicted – to take the sea route from Suez and land on the west coast of India where he might receive support from the Maratha Confederation or Tipu Sultan. A squadron of British ships operating in support of the Turks had blocked Bonaparte's passage north through Syria at Acre and in 1801 15,000 British troops had landed at Alexandria and forced the surrender of the remnants of the French army.

In the meantime Portugal, Gibraltar and the Cape had all been stripped of troops to reinforce India. The men on the spot in India welcomed the reinforcements but they had different priorities. From 1765 until the final establishment of British paramountcy in 1818 with the crushing of the Maratha Confederation, successive governors-general were far more concerned at internal rather than external threats to British rule. In 1798 Lord Mornington (soon to be created the Marquis of Wellesley), who was governor-general from 1798 to 1805, thought it was self-evident that the company's commerce would not be secure if rival powers in the subcontinent threatened it. That does not mean that he and his successors discounted the French threat. Most governors-general did not believe in the possibility of a direct French invasion of India, but they did fear that the spread of French influence amongst the states of the subcontinent would inspire them to attack the British. Wellesley did not believe that threats to British rule could be countered by remaining on the defensive as London enjoined and wanted to defend the company's territories as far from Calcutta as possible. But it was only by stressing the reality of a French threat that he and his successors could persuade the government in London to sanction the expense involved in pursuing a forward policy in the subcontinent.

Wellesley began gathering princely allies by signing subsidiary treaties, granting Indian princes security against all comers by stationing a detachment of the company's troops on their territory. In return each prince agreed to supply them either in cash or by alienating part of his territory to the British. Every treaty gave the company more revenue to expand its army. He then proceeded to use these troops and the recently arrived British reinforcements to crush Britain's most dangerous internal enemies. He formed an alliance with the Nizam of Hyderabad, defeated Tipu Sultan in 1799 and annexed the Carnatic in 1801. The resources of southern India could now be used to safeguard Britain's position in central and northern India. In 1801 fears of an invasion by Zaman Shah of Afghanistan encouraged the company to establish a *de facto* protectorate over Oudh in northern India. Wellesley then turned his attention to the Maratha Confederation in central India. They were a dangerous threat because their armies were organized and disciplined by European or Eurasian officers on European lines and it was not until 1818 that one of Wellesley's successors, Lord Hastings, subdued them. Their defeat meant that all India up to the Sutlej river was under the company's direct or indirect control and that the British were the paramount power in the subcontinent. It also meant that the nature of the problem of the defence of British India as it had existed since 1765 had changed. After 1818 the British in India no longer feared a threat from any of the Indian states unless there was a possibility that the latter could combine with a hostile power outside India or unless such a threat coincided with a mutiny in the company's army.

By the spring of 1801 the war had reached a temporary stalemate. Britain and her empire were secure from French invasion but France dominated western Europe. Bonaparte wanted to consolidate his rule and Pitt's government had resigned less than a week before the Treaty of Luneville was signed because George III refused to accept Catholic emancipation. Pitt's administration was replaced by a government under Lord Addington which signed a truce in October 1801 and a peace treaty at Amiens in March 1802. The British agreed to return all the colonies they had seized except Trinidad and Ceylon and promised to withdraw from Malta within three months. The French promised to evacuate Egypt (where in fact their army had already been defeated), the Papal States and Naples. The French were left in possession of the Low Countries, they had expanded to their natural frontiers along the Rhine and controlled the Swiss passes and most of northern Italy. Pitt's government had gone to war to safeguard British security. The Peace of Amiens represented a measure of their failure to do so. To Grenville, Windham and Dundas it was a bitter blow, leaving the British Empire open to French attack and giving Britain little or no compensation in the colonies for the trade and security she had lost in Europe.

Bonaparte soon made it apparent that peace with Britain would bring an acceleration, not a cessation, of French expansion. In 1801 Spain and Portugal had ceded Louisiana and Portuguese Guiana to France. France had already obtained Haiti from Spain and she now regained Tobago from the British. To underline his determination to create a Caribbean empire, in November 1801 Bonaparte dispatched an expedition to suppress a Negro insurrection on Haiti. He also sent ships and troops to reoccupy French posts in India and tried to increase French trade and political influence with the Ottoman Empire. British manufacturers were incensed when they discovered that high tariffs excluded their manufactured goods not just from France but also from Spain, Holland and Italy. By the end of 1802 not only had France occupied Piedmont, Parma and Switzerland, she also refused to withdraw French troops from Holland.

The Addington government never regarded the Peace of Amiens as anything more than a truce and in May 1803 they had become so exasperated by the way in which Bonaparte was flouting the spirit of the treaty that they declared war. The one positive gain the British had made was that Napoleon's obvious arrogance in attempting to exclude British trade and influence from Europe united public opinion in Britain against him. Men who had opposed the Revolutionary Wars supported the war against Napoleon. The new war acquired some of the overtones of a crusade fought to resist French despotism which threatened the liberties not just of Britain but of the whole of Europe. After 1815 Napoleon admitted that his aim had been 'to reestablish the kingdom of Poland as a barrier against the Muscovite barbarians, divide Austria, establish client states in Italy, declare Hungary independent, break up Prussia, form independent republics in England and Ireland, control Egypt, drive the Turks out of Europe, and liberate the Balkan nations'.[9] In response to this patriotic sentiments ran through all levels of British society. Anti-war opinions did not disappear after 1803 but, except in times of extreme economic hardship, their expression was more muted than it had been. As a letter-writer to *The Times* explained in 1812, 'We are engaged in a war – a war of no common description – a war of system against system in which no choice is left us but victory or extirpation'.[10]

Unlike Pitt and his colleagues in 1793, in 1803 Addington assumed that the war would be prolonged. He mobilized the armed forces to secure Britain against invasion, blockaded the French fleet in port, swept her commerce from the seas, reoccupied the colonies which Britain had surrendered at Amiens and looked for continental allies. He was bolstered in this by the fact that there was now a growing body of evidence about the remarkable rate of economic growth which Britain had attained during the early stages of the Industrial Revolution. This enabled Addison and his successors to overcome the fears which had been expressed in the late 1790s that a prolonged war would bankrupt Britain. The 1801 census provided the first reasonably accurate assessment of the size of the population. The Inspector-General of Imports and Exports collected figures demonstrating the growth in British overseas trade and in 1799 the Dean of Bristol published calculations indicating that Pitt had underestimated the national income by nearly one-third. Addington had repealed Pitt's income tax in 1802 but he reintroduced it in a new and more successful form in 1803 and laid the foundations for the achievements of British war finances over the next twelve years. Between 1799 and 1808 the government's income doubled. Without this increasing revenue the government would never have been able to borrow as heavily at it did to maintain a fleet of nearly 100 ships-of-the-line, an army (including militia) numbering on paper over 350,000 men in 1814 and to subsidize her allies to the tune of about £35,000,000 between 1810 and 1815.

After the Treaty of Amiens the militia was stood down and the regular army reduced. But the latter's peacetime establishment of 132,000 men, nearly three times what it had been in 1793, was evidence of Addington's suspicion that the peace would not last. About 50,000 regulars had been retained abroad and enough men were in the West Indies to enable the British to take St Lucia, Tobago and Demerara on the outbreak of war. Faced with the prospect of having to fight the French without continental allies, the government's first concern was to augment the army and auxiliary forces to resist an invasion. They enacted legislation which represented the closest approach to military conscription that any British government was to adopt until January 1916. In July 1803 a Levée en Masse Act was passed requiring lords lieutenant to prepare lists of all males in their counties between the ages of 17 and 55. These men were placed in one of four categories depending upon their age, marital circumstances and the number of their children. But it was unnecessary to summon conscripts for between May and December 1803 some 380,000 men joined volunteer corps. Between 1803 and 1805 Britain came the closest she ever came before 1916 to being a nation in arms. But the landed oligarchy did not like the democratic implications of what they had done. The volunteers afforded the *nouveaux riches* an opportunity to give practical expression to their patriotism and to claim parity with the landed classes. In 1804 one MP described them as 'Armed Parliaments'.[11] It was no accident that as soon as the immediate danger of invasion had passed in 1806, the government began to disband them.

Addington also strengthened the regular army. Realizing that militia colonels hated their battalions being milked for recruits for the regulars he raised a new force, the 'Army of Reserve'. Like the militia men were conscripted into it by ballot but could purchase a substitute. They could not be forced to serve outside the United Kingdom but could volunteer to do so. In time the regulars secured 19,500 recruits from this force. When York received these men he did not form them into new regiments but used them to form second battalions for existing regiments. In a foretaste of the post-1871 Cardwell system, these units sometimes became depot battalions for their sister battalions. It took some time before these new levies were efficient but by October 1805 the government was sufficiently confident of them to plan to denude the country of regular troops by dispatching 60,000 troops to the north German coast.

When he formed his government Addington, anxious to add some prestige to what was otherwise a lacklustre Cabinet, had made St Vincent First Lord of the Admiralty. In 1802 St Vincent demobilized the fleet and then embarked on an ill-advised attempt to reform the dockyards. As a consequence, when war broke out in May 1803 the yards lacked many of the skilled shipwrights and the seasoned timber they needed to keep the fleet in good repair. It was no accident that Pitt was able to bring down the Addington government in May 1804 by attacking the way in which it had permitted the fleet to deteriorate.

Pitt replaced St Vincent with Lord Melville (the title Dundas had assumed in 1802). Henceforth the yards were only slightly less successful than they had been during the Revolutionary War in keeping the fleet seaworthy. Between 1804 and 1814 they managed to keep each year an average of 69 per cent of the navy's ships-of-the-line and 79 per cent of its frigates in commission.

Pitt's return to power coincided with Bonaparte's coronation as emperor. For a year Britain had fought alone as Napoleon prepared an invasion army at Boulogne. Britain was rescued from her isolation by French activities in the Morea and on Corfu and quarrels with Russia over the status of the Ionian Islands which persuaded Tsar Alexander that French ambitions in the Levant threatened Russian interests. In the autumn of 1804 he signed a secret alliance with Austria to protect Naples from French attack and suggested to Pitt that they should form an alliance which might be the basis for the re-establishment of the European balance of power. Pitt's reply, embodied in a state-paper of January 1805, reflected many commonplace British assumptions about European international relations. The aim of the alliance ought to be to contain, not to destroy French power and France should be restrained by the creation of a series of barrier states around her frontier. The tsar did not take kindly to his proposal as it entailed the aggrandizement of both Prussia and Austria. Only Napoleon's rapacity in annexing Genoa broke the log-jam and persuaded Austria and Russia to ally with Britain. That the three powers were allies should not obscure the fact that each still had different objectives. The Russians hoped to reunite Poland under their protection and to acquire Constantinople, the Austrians wanted to regain their former ascendancy in Germany and Italy and the British wanted to defeat Napoleon and reduce France to her former frontiers.

By July 1805 Napoleon had enough landing-craft assembled at Boulogne to carry 150,000 troops across the Channel. But he dared not put to sea until he had gained at least temporary control of the Channel. Britain's first line of defence were her squadrons blockading Brest and Toulon and, after Spain's declaration of war against Britain in December 1804, Cadiz and Ferrol. But the government knew that the navy alone could not prevent an invasion. In 1803/4 the Ordnance Board began to erect a series of Martello towers along the coast of Sussex and Kent and later along the coast of East Anglia. These small forts were completed too late to play any part in persuading Napoleon to abandon his invasion attempt in the autumn of 1805. But after the Treaty of Tilsit in July 1807 they did give the British a new strategic flexibility. By making it too dangerous for Napoleon to attempt an invasion across any beach which the Boulogne flotilla could reach, they freed a considerable portion of the regular army for overseas service. In 1805 Napoleon hoped to secure a brief period of command of the Channel by combining his scattered squadrons and overwhelming the Channel fleet. He ordered the Brest squadron to break out, raise the blockade of Ferrol and then sail with the Spanish to the West Indies. Simultaneously the Toulon squadron was to evade Nelson's blockade, rendezvous with the Cadiz fleet and also sail to the West Indies. Napoleon assumed that the combined fleet would compel the

British to weaken their Channel fleet by sending part of it in pursuit. He hoped that before pursuer and pursued could meet, the combined fleet would have returned to the Channel to cover the passage of the French army to England.

The Brest squadron failed to break out but the Toulon squadron did so, combined with the Spanish from Cadiz and then sailed to Martinique. But the British refused to be decoyed. Rather than weaken the Channel fleet, the new first lord, Lord Barham, strengthened it. Nelson followed the French Admiral Villeneuve to the West Indies. As soon as Villeneuve learnt of his arrival he set course for Ferrol. But Nelson arrived in European waters before the combined fleet and by mid-August Napoleon's grand design to lure the Channel fleet away from its station had failed. Britain's defences were concentrated in the vital approaches to the Channel and the immediate danger of invasion had passed two months before Trafalgar. At the end of August, with Austria threatening Napoleon abandoned the invasion. The Grande Armée broke camp and began to march towards the Danube and he ordered the combined fleet to convoy troops to Naples. That gave Nelson his opportunity to annihilate the combined fleet at Trafalgar in October 1805.

The strategic results of Trafalgar should not be exaggerated. The immediate danger of invasion had passed before the battle and it did not extinguish French naval power. Until the Spanish national rising in 1808 the Mediterranean fleet had to blockade the remnants of the combined fleet in Cadiz. After the Treaty of Tilsit Napoleon could draw upon the shipbuilding resources of most of Europe to prepare another invasion armada. The battle also had little impact on the continental land war. It did not persuade the Prussians to join the coalition and it did not prevent Napoleon forcing the surrender of an Austrian army at Ulm and defeating a combined Austro-Russian army at Austerlitz in December 1805. The war demonstrated the limitations of British amphibious warfare. The British army was too small to operate on the continent without allies. Pitt intended to dispatch 60,000 men to the north German coast but the government recalled them in February 1806 for fear that the French would now be able to crush them. A smaller force of Russian and British troops landed at Naples in November 1805 but the tsar quickly agreed to an armistice and the Russians retired to Corfu. The British were left to garrison Sicily which henceforth became the pivot of their strategy in the Mediterranean, a granary for the British naval base on Malta and a barrier against French advances towards the Levant and India.

The Austrians accepted the humiliating terms of the Peace of Pressburg and Pitt died in January 1806. But Austerlitz did not mark the collapse of the Third Coalition. Grenville succeeded Pitt as Prime Minister and became the leader of the 'Ministry of All the Talents'. Until his death in September 1806 the Foreign Secretary Charles James Fox pursued a policy of limited war combined with attempts to negotiate a peace. But he was determined to do both in combination with Russia and the peace negotiations failed in the summer of 1806 precisely because Napoleon tried to separate the allies. In December 1805 Napoleon had granted Hanover to Prussia as the price of her neutrality while he dealt with

Austria and Russia. In the course of the abortive talks with Britain he offered to restore the Electorate to George III, an offer which incensed the Prussians. In September 1806, without waiting for Russian troops they sent an ultimatum to Napoleon. He retaliated with appalling rapidity, crushing the Prussian army at Jena in October and extinguishing Prussian resistance by occupying Berlin at the end of the month. The Russians were now menaced not only in Poland but also on their southern frontier. After Austerlitz the Turks, anxious to escape from Russian tutelage and fearful that Napoleon might otherwise attack their Balkan possessions, closed the Dardanelles to Russian ships. The last thing the British wanted was a Russo-Turkish war which would divert Russian troops from Poland, alienate Austria and possibly cause the collapse of the Ottoman Empire. In February 1807 a British squadron appeared off Constantinople in an attempt to force the Porte to climb down. But news of Jena encouraged the Turks to resist and the Russo-Turkish war became a reality.

Russia was now bearing practically the whole burden of the land war alone. French troops crossed the Vistula and engaged the Russians at the indecisive Battle of Eylau in February 1807. The British afforded their ally little help. In January 1807 Fox's successor, Viscount Howick, shunned Russian requests for financial assistance. The running-down of the volunteers meant that few troops could be spared to go abroad. Those that could be mustered were not sent to the coast of France, as the Russians asked, but were dispatched to seize Buenos Aires and Alexandria. Both operations ended in ignominious withdrawal. The tsar regarded them as proof that the British were more concerned with enriching themselves overseas than in defeating Napoleon. In July 1807, after the Battle of Friedland, he made peace at Tilsit.

Napoleon saw the peace as a way of waging war against Britain. In November 1806 he had promulgated the Berlin Decrees, closing the ports of Europe to British trade. He hoped to force Britain to submit by strangling her trade. Alexander promised that if Britain refused his mediation he would declare war on her. Sweden, Denmark and Portugal were also to be compelled to follow suit. The collapse of the Russian alliance meant that Britain once again had a maritime war thrust upon her. The Continental System threatened to starve and bankrupt Britain into submission. Tilsit meant that Napoleon could use the fleets and shipbuilding resources of the whole of Europe to outbuild the Royal Navy. In 1807 Napoleon had 37 ships-of-the-line. By 1813 he had over 80 with another 35 under construction. The Royal Navy's margin of superiority was less than decisive. It reached the limit of its expansion in 1808 when it had 113 ships-of-the-line. The British might have been able to build more ships, but they could not man them. The possibility that Britain might be overwhelmed at sea existed as long as the war lasted.

The British could not afford to ignore these threats to their maritime and economic security. Grenville, and his successor after March 1807, the Duke of Portland, retaliated against the Berlin Decrees with their own Orders-in-Council in 1807. They prohibited all trade, whether carried by neutrals or belligerents, between enemy ports and declared that neutral ships could only trade with France if they first called at a British port. They overcame the worst effects of the Continental System by smuggling and by opening new markets. Portland's Foreign Secretary, George Canning, mounted pre-emptive strikes against neutral fleets which Napoleon might have used against Britain. The Danes refused to surrender their ships to Britain so the British attacked them at Copenhagen in August 1807. In November 1808 Alexander fulfilled his promise to Napoleon by declaring war on Britain, but the Russian fleet was too small by itself to shut the Baltic and in the spring and summer of every year until 1812 a powerful British squadron convoyed large fleets of merchant ships into the Baltic. Napoleon met a similar setback in Portugal because the Portuguese government refused to break with Britain. French troops invaded the country but the Royal Navy reached Lisbon first. In November 1807 they offered the Portuguese king the choice of sailing with his fleet to Brazil or of seeing his capital bombarded. The king chose Brazil, Napoleon lost the use of 8 Portuguese and 7 Russian ships-of-the-line anchored in the Tagus and the British gained access to Brazilian markets.

The campaign in the Iberian Peninsula which the British waged in conjunction with the Portuguese and Spanish between 1808 and 1814 was the brainchild of Portland's Secretary of State for War, Lord Castlereagh. In May 1808 Napoleon forced Carlos IV of Spain and his son to abdicate and proclaimed his own brother Joseph king of Spain. The Spanish resented this foreign intrusion into their affairs and resisted the French troops sent to place Joseph on his throne. The Peninsula represented the kind of theatre of war which the British had been seeking since 1795. In Portugal they could establish a secure bridgehead and in the Portuguese army they found troops who could take the place of the mercenaries they had hired regularly since 1689. The Peninsula was surrounded by sea on three sides and so it afforded the British one of the best opportunities they ever had to exploit their sea-power. The navy convoyed merchant ships carrying food to feed the allied armies and prevented the French from moving men and supplies around the coast. The war was especially debilitating for the French because, although their men were masters at living off the land, most of Spain was too poor to support an army of any size. The Spanish national rising ensured that the small Anglo-Portuguese army could not easily be overwhelmed by a larger French army. Spanish guerrillas and regulars forced the French to disperse much of their army to defend their vulnerable lines of communication. In 1810 the French had 350,000 men in Spain but Marshal Massena could concentrate only 90,000 of them to invade Portugal. The rest had to be employed on counter-insurgent duties. The Iberian Peninsula enabled the British to do something they had not been able to do since the start of the war, to maintain a lodgement on the continent without an alliance with the eastern powers.

Even so the initial British foray into the Peninsula almost ended in disaster. In July 1808 Sir Arthur Wellesley (who was created the Duke of Wellington in

1814), was sent to Lisbon with 17,500 men to assist the Portuguese and Spanish to regain their independence. When a further 10,000 men arrived command devolved upon Sir Hugh Dalrymple. Shortly before Dalrymple assumed command, Wellesley defeated the French at Vimiero. Dalrymple became a plausible scapegoat for the way in which many of the fruits of that battle were thrown away under the terms of the Convention of Cintra. In fact Wellesley bore a much greater share of the responsibility for the convention than either he or the government, of which he had been a member, were prepared to admit. In the meantime the Spanish had forced the French to retire beyond the River Ebro and in October the British sent Sir John Moore to the Peninsula with orders to co-operate with the Spanish in expelling the French. Moore's brief foray into Spain ended in January 1809 when a reinforced French army forced him to evacuate his troops from Corunna.

This first Iberian campaign served one purpose. In 1808 Canning had granted the Spanish money and weapons because he hoped that by keeping resistance to Napoleon alive in one part of Europe it might persuade other powers to oppose him. In April 1809 Napoleon's commitment to Spain did encourage the Austrians to try to wipe out the humiliations of Pressburg by allying with Britain and invading Bavaria. But the actual help the British gave them was minimal. In December 1808 they had asked for a subsidy of £7,500,000, far beyond anything the British could supply. When it was not forthcoming they asked the British to launch a diversionary attack on the north German coast. The Cabinet preferred to mount diversions in the Low Countries and in the Peninsula. In July 1809 40,000 troops were sent to seize Antwerp in the largest amphibious raid the British mounted before the Second World War. But it sailed too late to help Austria. Napoleon defeated them at Wagram on 5 July. The British troops got no further than the island of Walcheren where 'Walcheren fever', a mixture of dysentery and malaria, killed 4,000 and left another 11,000 sick.

The Walcheren expedition deprived the army in the Peninsula of a considerable body of trained troops and was of no appreciable assistance to Austria. In April 1809 the Portland government sent Wellesley back to Lisbon with orders to defend Portugal but not to venture into Spain without express orders. The government, which was already weakened by the Walcheren expedition and a duel between Castlereagh and Canning, could not survive Portland's fatal illness and collapsed in September 1809. For a month Britain was without a government until Spencer Perceval formed one. Castlereagh was replaced at the War Office by Lord Liverpool, who was a steadfast supporter of the Peninsula campaign both now and when he succeeded Perceval after the latter was assassinated in 1812.

The campaign needed supporters in high places after 1809 for it did not bring rapid results. In the summer of 1809 Wellesley expelled the French from Portugal but he was too weak to advance to Madrid. By the end of 1809 the French had besieged the Spanish junta in Cadiz where it remained, supplied by the Royal Navy, until the French abandoned the siege in August

1812. In 1809/10 Wellesley began to mobilize Portugal's resources to resist the anticipated French invasion. Sir William Beresford used British cash to raise 50,000 Portuguese troops and in 1810 Wellesley created the lines of Torres Vedras, a fortified barrier stretching from the River Tagus to the sea, to protect Lisbon. In September he repulsed a French army at Busaco and then retreated behind his fortifications, stripping the country in front of them bare of food and transport. He encouraged the Portuguese people and militia 'to do the enemy all the mischief in their power ... not by assembling in large bodies, but by impeding his communications, by firing upon him from the mountains and strong passes with which the whole country abounds, and by annoying his foraging and other parties that he may send out'.[12] Wellesley's own supplies were secured by the Royal Navy and he waited in safety behind the lines until March 1811 when the starving French retreated to the Spanish frontier. He followed them in an attempt to occupy the border fortresses of Badajoz, Almeida and Ciudad Rodrigo. Once he had done so he would be able to advance into Spain. Almeida fell in May 1811 but the others remained in French hands until the spring of 1812. When Badajoz did fall, Castlereagh, who had rejoined the government when Liverpool became Prime Minister, persuaded his colleagues to increase the Spanish subsidy and provide equipment for 100,000 troops so that Wellesley could augment his Anglo-Portuguese army with Spanish regulars. But the proximity of decisive success was deceptive. Although Wellesley defeated the French at Salamanca in July 1812 and occupied Madrid, the French were still able to regroup their scattered armies and again drove him back to the Portuguese frontier.

By the end of 1812 the Peninsular campaign had liberated Portugal and Spain south of the Tagus, denied Napoleon the use of 24 Spanish and 5 French ships-of-the-line in Cadiz harbour and compelled him to commit a large part of his army to a pitiless war of attrition waged by Wellesley's field army and Spanish guerrillas. Its international political repercussions were even more significant. Hitherto French propagandists had been able to portray Britain as 'perfidious Albion' – ever ready to use her own troops to take rich enemy colonies but never willing to commit them to the Continent to confront the might of France. Between 1793 and 1808 there was some justification for these charges. Throughout the entire war about 30 per cent of the army remained in Britain and in the 1790s about a third of the army served in colonial theatres. From 1793 and 1794 slightly less than a third of the army was committed to Flanders, but thereafter and with the exception of the brief foray into Holland in 1799, British troops in any numbers were absent from the continent until 1808. However, between 1808 and 1814 about one-fifth of the British establishment was committed to the Peninsula. By 1812 Wellesley had kept his army in the field against Napoleon for three years, longer than any of France's other enemies. Together with his Spanish and Portuguese allies they inflicted 164,000 casualties on the French. It was enough to begin to give the lie to the jibe that the British would fight to the last allied soldier.

And the British did this despite the fact that the Peninsular War was inordinately expensive and they were called upon to pay for it when their own economy was experiencing dramatic fluctuations. In 1807/8 the economy was depressed and petitions and mass meetings were organized in northern manufacturing towns expressing dismay at the length and cost of the war and at corruption in high places. The economy improved in 1809/10 when the USA lifted a trade embargo it had imposed to protest against the way in which the belligerents interfered with their trade and the Peninsular campaign opened South American markets to British exports. But in 1810 Napoleon tightened his control over northern Germany and the Netherlands, the British harvest was poor and the USA reimposed their non-intercourse legislation in protest at Britain's refusal to abandon the Orders-in-Council. British exports fell and by 1811 she faced a serious trade depression and high unemployment. Specie was so short between 1806 and 1812 that the British had to ration the financial assistance they gave their allies and by 1812 the pay of the army in the Peninsula was four months in arrears. Groups of merchants and manufacturers blamed their difficulties on the orders in council and insisted that they be abolished. The labouring classes reacted with a combination of petitions and food riots and in the textile districts Luddites attacked factory machinery. In June 1812 the government had to deploy 12,000 troops in the disaffected areas and revoked the Orders-in-Council.

The revocation of the Orders-in-Council coincided with a breakdown in Franco-Russian relations. Although Alexander excluded British shipping from Russian ports, British cargoes still entered Russia in neutral ships and in June 1812 Napoleon invaded Russia with 614,000 troops to plug this hole in the Continental System. A month later Russia made peace with Britain. This *rapprochement* occurred at an opportune moment. The revocation of the orders came three weeks too late to prevent President Madison from declaring war on Britain in retaliation against the way in which she interfered with American trade and impressed American sailors. The British had not sought this war, their army in the Peninsula was dependent upon grain imported from New England, and they had neither the ships nor the troops to wage more than a limited campaign in North America. The British knew that the New Englanders deplored the war and so they tried to employ just enough force to persuade the American people to induce their government to make a quick peace. The commander of the North American squadron was ordered to blockade the North American coast, to permit licensed trade between New England, Spain and Portugal and to negotiate an end to the conflict.

However, the Americans were not willing to submit to British terms. In 1812 the British repulsed three American invasions of Canada but at sea they did not have things all their own way. The American fleet was smaller than the Royal Navy's North American squadron, but it contained the world's fastest and most heavily armed frigates. In 1812 and 1813 they exerted an influence on the war out of all proportion to their numbers, making it impossible for the British to establish an effective blockade for fear that if they dispersed their ships along the coast they would be overwhelmed piecemeal. The naval balance of power in North American waters only began to tilt in Britain's favour in the spring of 1813. Napoleon's invasion of Russia led to the dispatch of 15 Russian ships-of-the-line to co-operate with the British in the North Sea. Early in 1813 that enabled the Admiralty to send sufficient reinforcements to the east coast of America to neutralize the American frigates and blockade the Delaware and Chesapeake. Troops from the West Indian garrisons and, after Napoleon's surrender in 1814, from Wellington's army, conducted a series of amphibious raids along the coast intended to divert American forces from Canada and to bring the war home to the civilian population in the hope that their war-weariness would persuade their government to make peace. In 1814 the British extended the blockade to the whole American coast and the raiding policy was intensified, culminating in an attack on Washington in August 1814. However, a subsequent raid on Baltimore failed, as did an offensive against New Orleans and another on Lake Champlain. The British had paralysed American overseas trade and accelerated the collapse of her finances but they could not exploit their advantage. The Americans controlled the Great Lakes and an invasion overland from Canada was impossible. The war had more in common with the limited conflicts of the eighteenth century than with the period of total war which began in 1793. Both sides recognized that the conflict had reached a stalemate and they made peace in December 1814.

By the end of 1812 Napoleon's retreat from Russia had degenerated into a rout as the Grande Armée disintegrated. But there was no guarantee that the tsar would do more than expel the French from Russian soil and then guard his own frontier so in 1813 Castlereagh expended British subsidies and supplies on a lavish scale to ensure that the war on the eastern front continued. In February 1813, when the Prussians changed sides and allied themselves with Russia, Castlereagh quickly sent them 100,000 muskets. In March he promised the Swedes £1,000,000 by October if they put 30,000 men in the field to assist Russia. But negotiations with the Russians and Prussians were prolonged because the British were short of the specie needed to pay the huge subsidies they demanded. In the summer of 1813 the Russians and Prussians were defeated by Napoleon at Lutzen and Bautzen and without consulting the British envoy who was in Germany they signed an armistice with the French to last for six weeks. The Austrians were still neutral and a negotiated peace between Napoleon and the two eastern powers appeared to be a distinct possibility.

But in June the situation was transformed by Wellington's victory at Vittoria which finally destroyed Napoleon's power in the Peninsula. The authority which Vittoria gave British diplomacy, plus Napoleon's stubborn refusal to agree to any settlement acceptable to the three eastern powers, broke the diplomatic stalemate. Castlereagh concluded the Reichenbach treaty with Prussia and Russia.

In return for credits totalling £5,000,000 they promised to maintain 100,000 and 200,000 troops respectively in the field and not to make a separate peace. In August Austria joined the Fourth Coalition, promising to place 150,000 men in the field in return for a British subsidy of £1,000,000. In October the allies destroyed Napoleon's power in Germany at Leipzig and by November he was in retreat across the Rhine and Wellington had invaded southern France.

However by December each ally was increasingly concentrating on their own national objectives, offering Napoleon the opportunity of destroying the Coalition piecemeal if he was ready to satisfy some of them. To prevent that the Cabinet sent Castlereagh to Germany with orders to distribute up to £5,000,000 in subsidies to keep the allies united. The result was the Treaty of Chaumont signed in March 1814. In return for British cash each ally agreed to maintain an army of 150,000 men in the field, to remain at war until Napoleon surrendered and to maintain their alliance for twenty years after the conclusion of the peace. A few weeks after the treaty was signed Napoleon had surrendered and was on his way into exile. When he returned from Elba in March 1815 the four powers reactivated the treaty. Since there were only 47,000 British and Hanoverian troops in Flanders, the British tried to make good the shortfall by hiring German mercenaries. The allies' strategy called for the establishment of an unbroken line of troops along the French frontier. When Napoleon invaded Belgium in June Wellington and Blücher's Prussians were already in position. On 18 June a polyglot army of British, Dutch, German and Belgian troops under Wellington, assisted by Blücher's Prussians, finally defeated Napoleon at Waterloo.

France had threatened Britain's physical and economic security on several occasions in the century before 1793. But the revolutionary and Napoleonic regimes represented threats of an altogether different order. Not only did they menace Britain's physical security and her right to trade with whomever she pleased, but they propagated political doctrines which promised to tear apart the social and political fabric of British society. They posed the most formidable threat the British state had faced since the Spanish Armada. It was this realization which called forth an unprecedented mobilization of British resources. By 1809 Britain had 817,000 men under arms – 300,000 regular troops and embodied militia, 130,000 seamen and marines, 198,000 local militia and 189,000 volunteers. About one in six adult males of military age was in uniform. The most remarkable feature of this response was that the Hanoverian regime mounted it without resorting to methods which undermined the basis of the social and political system they were defending. The extension of military service was not accompanied by an extension of political rights. Service in the navy, the regular army and the militia remained a career rather than a civic duty. Only the volunteers breached this principle and it was a measure of the seriousness of the peril they faced that the landed oligarchy was ready to accept the arming of the people on such an extensive scale. 'I am well aware', Dundas wrote, 'of the danger of entrusting arms to the whole population without distinction; but serious as is the danger, it is nothing to the risk we should run if, when invaded by the enemy, we were unprepared with any adequate means of defence'.[13]

But despite their willingness to undertake such an extensive mobilization, the British were never under any illusion that they could defeat France alone. British strategic policy exhibited several of the features of the 'mixed' paradigm during these wars. Between 1793 and 1802 spending on land and sea services almost exactly balanced in the ratio 51:49 in favour of land services. But between 1803 and 1815 the ratio was 57:43 in favour of land services. After 1793 the British government's first priority was to form a coalition with at least two of the three eastern powers so that their armies could maintain an eastern front and contain the largest possible portion of the French army. When they succeeded in doing so they dispatched part of their own army to the continent. In 1793/4 the Commons voted that about 30 per cent of the troops on the British establishment should serve in Flanders. (That compared to the annual average of about 13 per cent they voted for the West Indies between 1794 and 1798.) But the majority of the troops of York's army (58 per cent) were German mercenaries. When the Coalitions collapsed the British army was evacuated before the French could destroy it. The maritime war which the British conducted when they lacked continental allies was pursued from necessity, not choice. Without continental allies they had to strengthen their own defences and reduce the possibility of a French invasion by attacking enemy squadrons, by removing neutral and allied ships from French control, by securing bases overseas which the British themselves needed to exercise their sea-power and by mounting offensives against enemy colonies to extend their commerce. Sea-power alone was not the decisive weapon which brought about Napoleon's downfall. As often as not a British victory at sea was followed by an equally crushing French victory on land. Britain's colonial conquests in the West Indies, the 'Glorious First of June', Cape St Vincent and Camperdown did not prevent the collapse of the First Coalition. The Battles of the Nile and Trafalgar did not save the Second and Third Coalitions.

The role of British sea-power until 1808 was primarily defensive. It shielded Britain from the worst consequences of the defeat of her continental allies. But the fleet alone could not safeguard Britain from invasion, as the French expedition to Bantry Bay in 1796 had shown. It was for that reason that between 1793 and 1808 the British kept at least 1 in 3 of their troops at home. The military value of some of the militia and volunteers has often been questioned. But they served one vital function. Together with the regulars they ensured that if the French did mount a serious invasion they would have to come in such large numbers that they would need to assemble so many transports and so many warships to escort them, that their chances of evading the Royal Navy would be minimal.

After 1808 both the fleet and the regular army could play a more offensive role. The Iberian Peninsula was exactly the kind of theatre of operations which the British had sougght since 1795. In Portugal they established a secure bridgehead and in the Portuguese army they found troops who could take the place of the Germann mercenaries they had hired in the eighteenth century. The Peninsula gave the British one of the best opportunities they ever had to exploit their sea-power. The navy prevented the French from moving men and supplies arround the coast and compelled them to use roads which were subject to frequent attacks from Spanish guerrillas. The guerrillas made possible Wellington's survival by supplying him with much valuable intelligence and preventing the French from concentrating their superior numbers and crushing his field army. Between 1808 and 1814 the Commons voted annually to deploy about one fifth of the troops on the British establishment in the Peninsula. Excluding the Portuguese troops who were under Wellington's command but not part of the British establishment, only 10 per cent of this force consisted of foreigners, making Wellington's field army one of the most 'British' expeditionary forces the British had ever committed to the continent. Between 1808 and 1812, for the first time since the start of the war, the British could maintain a lodgement on the continent without an alliance with the eastern powers.

Between 1793 and 1815 the British spent nearly £65,800,000 on subsidies. High as that sum was it represented only about 8 per cent of the £830,000,000 they spent on the war. Expenditure on this scale was made possible by four things: an economy which, despite the strains placed upon it by the Continental System, was growing by leaps and bounds during the initial stages of the Industrial Revolution; a tax system of unparalleled efficiency which enabled the government to raise a much higher proportion of its income from revenue in this war than in any previous conflict; the suspension of cash payments in 1797 which fostered economic development at home and enabled the government to export specie abroad to subsidize the allies; and after 1802 the growing confidence, buttressed by the calculations of political economists, that Britain had the economic capacity to carry such a burden. But gold alone would not have created and held together the final coalition. Wellington's army, which cost the Treasury twice what it spent on subsidies after 1808, and his Peninsular victories, gave Castlereagh's diplomacy an authority which no previous British diplomat had enjoyed.

5 The Era of the 'Pax Britannica', c. 1815–80

The development of British defence policy between 1815 and 1880 continued to be determined by domestic political circumstances and the security needs of Britain and her empire. The French wars were the most expensive Britain had ever fought. Between 1793 and 1815 the national debt had almost quadrupled. By 1816 the cost of servicing it threatened to swallow up the whole of the state's ordinary revenues. Pressure to reduce public spending, of which defence spending was the largest component, came from plebeian radicals, political economists and country gentlemen who disliked paying high taxes. Such pressure was even harder to resist after 1832 when the Great Reform Act nearly doubled the size of the electorate.

In 1789 Jeremy Bentham, author of *Plan for a Universal and Perpetual Peace*, argued that universal peace would come when all powers abandoned their colonies and alliances, reduced the size of their armed forces and adopted free trade. In the 1790s Tom Paine taught plebeian radicals that mankind would live in harmony were it not for the vested interest which princes, diplomats and soldiers had in promoting wars to enrich themselves. In the early nineteenth century Adam Smith's ideas gained wide currency amongst political economists. James Mill and David Ricardo insisted that war was the single greatest obstacle to the growth of prosperity for it diverted resources from more profitable investments. One consequence of this was that in 1814, against the wishes of the Liverpool government, the Commons voted to abolish the income tax. But it would be a mistake to assume that postwar governments disarmed or that they did so because they were carried away by the twin tides of political economy and radical agitation. After 1815 defence spending did fall from its inflated wartime levels but it had done so in every period of peace following a major war in the eighteenth century. When a Select Committee on finance argued in 1818 that the government should remember

> that not ships and stores, and military arrangements, are alone necessary for the safety and glory of the country in the event of war; but that finances recruited during peace, and wealth and industry generally diffused through the nation by all

practical savings of expense and consequent diminution of burdens, are at least of equal importance, while they mainly contribute towards the happiness of all classes of society at the present time

it was only restating a consensus about Britain's peacetime defence policy which had been arrived at a century earlier.[1]

The burden of defence was both heavier and lighter than it had been in the past. In the fifty years after 1815 the real economic cost of defence was probably less than it had been during those periods when Britain was at peace in the eighteenth century. From 1815 to 1865, thanks to the burgeoning wealth generated by the Industrial Revolution, defence absorbed only about 2–3 per cent of Britain's gross national product, compared to approximately 4.5 per cent in 1790. However, contemporaries were apt to ignore such niceties. Tax-payers only knew that the financial cost of defence had multiplied. In the peacetime years 1784–92 defence spending averaged about £7,200,000 per annum. Between 1816 and 1824 annual defence spending measured in real terms was over 220 per cent higher. Governments after 1815 were not able to spend as much on defence as they wished. But, as George I might have told them, that was not a new phenomenon. However, the way in which the defence estimates were spent after 1815 was significantly different. Throughout the eighteenth century when Britain had not been at war against a great power, Parliament had habitually voted more money for sea services than for land services. That pattern was reversed between 1816 and 1895. If spending during the Crimean War is excluded, the ratio of spending on land and sea services was 58:42.

The era of the 'Pax Britannica' was not peaceful. Between 1815 and 1880 the British fought thirteen major wars. They are listed in Table 5.1. The table includes only those wars in which British forces suffered at least 1,000 fatalities in battle or in which at least one other great power was involved. Between 1837 and 1880 Britain also fought nearly 150 smaller campaigns in which her casualties fell below that figure. The suggestion that Britain was at peace after

Table 5.1 British Wars, 1815–80

1817–18	Second Maratha War
1824–6	Second Burmese War
1838–42	First Afghan War
1840–1	Egyptian War in alliance with Russia and Austria against Mehemet Ali
1839–42	First Opium War against China
1845–6	First Sikh War
1848–9	Second Sikh War
1854–6	Crimean War in alliance with France against Russia
1857–9	Indian Mutiny
1856–60	Third Opium War in alliance with France (1859–60) against China
1879	Zulu War
1879–81	Second Afghan War
1880–1	First Anglo-Boer War

1815 betrays a Eurocentric view of British history. What distinguished this era in British defence policy from the century before 1815 was that, with the exception of the Crimean War, all of Britain's opponents were non-European powers.

In 1815 Britain did not enter into a new era in which her ruling class forsook what one historian has called the 'strategic view' of foreign policy which had dominated their actions in the eighteenth century. Nor did they undergo a spiritual revolution which encouraged them to disarm and abandon the pursuit of national interests in favour of a quest for higher moral goals.[2] To accept this view of British policy and to see 1815 as marking a major watershed in the way in which the British employed their armed forces, is to mistake the rhetoric of a handful of politicians like Richard Cobden and the Manchester School for the reality of government policy and to overlook the strong elements of continuity between the eighteenth and nineteenth centuries. No British government after 1815 based its policies on the principle of complete non-intervention advocated by the Manchester School. British statesmen were quite capable of pursuing simultaneously both what they conceived to be Britain's national interests and high moral principles. Commerce, Christianity and civilization were synonymous to the Victorians. If missionaries brought Christianity to non-Christians they believed they would not only show them the path to eternal life but also the way to unlimited social and economic progress. Commerce was the best means to open non-Christian communities to the gospel. The fact that societies like China were opened to western commerce and missionary activities by war embarrassed some Victorians, but it did little to diminish their enthusiasm for the outcome.

This chapter will explain why the British could devote a great part of their armed forces to campaigns far from Europe. It will show the way in which domestic political circumstances and the needs of the empire combined to determine the evolution of the armed forces between 1815 and 1880. And it will analyse the role played by the armed forces in the expansion and consolidation of the British Empire.

Britain was able to gear much of her defence policy to goals outside Europe because the Vienna settlement of 1815 did more than put an end to a generation of European warfare. It ushered in an era when Europe was noticeably more peaceful for longer than at any time in the eighteenth century. Between 1715 and 1792 the European states suffered about 1,900,000 battlefield deaths. In the century after 1814 that figure dropped to 635,000, despite the fact that the population of Europe probably doubled over the same period. The Vienna settlement created a balance of power in Europe which endured, with some modifications, until the late 1860s. It guaranteed the security of all of the great powers and the establishment of the Concert of Europe introduced a dynamic element into the international system which, despite the wars of the mid-nineteenth century, generally enabled its members to settle their differences without recourse to war. The settlement created or guaranteed the existence of a number of medium-sized states like the Kingdom of the United Netherlands, Switzerland and the German Confederation, which acted as intermediaries between the major powers. They were sufficiently strong to resist French or Russian expansion but not so strong as to be a threat to their neighbours. The eighteenth century had been marred by a series of wars in the Americas, the Caribbean and India between European states. These conflicts were not replicated in the nineteenth century. The Napoleonic Wars marked the end of the Anglo-French struggle which had begun in 1689 for colonial and maritime dominance. By 1815 Britain had won, a fact underlined by the territorial spoils she garnered at the peace – West Indian islands, Cape Colony, Heligoland, Malta, Ceylon and Mauritius. By 1815 Britain had a base in every ocean of the world except the Pacific and her domination of the world's oceans meant that Europe was effectively cut off from the extra-European sources of conflict which had afflicted her in the eighteenth century. Britain made her naval and commercial dominance acceptable to the other powers in a way in which it had not been in the eighteenth century by gradually adopting free trade. The Royal Navy, which had been much criticized by continental nations in the eighteenth century for the high-handed way in which it enforced Britain's belligerent rights, won acceptance after 1815 by its role in policing the sea-lanes of the world.

British policies in Europe did differ from those of the three conservative great powers, Prussia, Russia and Austria. Between 1820 and 1822 the British withdrew from the congress system when the eastern powers tried to use it as a vehicle to repress liberal and nationalist movements on the continent. Foreign Secretaries like Canning and Palmerston insisted that 'changes which foreign Nations may chuse [sic] to make in their internal Constitution and form of Government, are to be looked upon as matters with which England has no business to interfere by force of arms'.[3] But withdrawal from the congress system was not synonymous with withdrawal from the European state system. Britain had no aggressive ambitions in Europe after 1815, but she did retain substantial interests on the continent and she did not retreat into isolation. Europe remained her richest market and the only region from which the security of the home islands could be threatened. Until the aftermath of the Crimean War the British acted vigorously if they believed another state might be about to upset the balance of power. If treaties signed in wartime or in direct anticipation of war are excluded, between 1815 and 1880 the European great powers signed six defensive alliances, one neutrality pact and five ententes which involved at least two of their number. Britain was a member of three of the alliances and three of the ententes. She was not especially less prone to become involved in the European state system than the continental great powers. Austria joined four alliances, two ententes and one neutrality pact. Prussia joined four alliances and two ententes. Russia joined three alliances, one neutrality pact and four ententes and France joined two alliances and two ententes. But between 1859 and 1870 the Vienna settlement was revised wholesale and Britain was unable to prevent it. Her inability to act was not so much the product of a deliberate decision by her policy-makers to disengage from Europe as a reflection of a structural change in the European state system. After the Crimean War Russia ceased to be the gendarme of Europe and joined France as a revisionist power. The collapse of the Anglo-French alliance meant that the British lacked what they had always required to make their intervention effective, the troops of a continental ally.

Possession of an extensive empire did not allow the British to retreat into imperial isolation. On the contrary it compelled them to continue to be involved in European power politics. The British perceived France and Russia as their most powerful rivals. The French threat was probably exaggerated but old habits of enmity died hard. If French ambitions in Egypt and Syria, dating from Napoleon's invasion of Egypt in 1798, were ever fulfilled, France could represent a real threat to British India. But in the late 1820s the French bogey began to be replaced by the Russian bogey. The government in London feared an external threat and suffered nightmares that if Turkey collapsed under tsarist pressure or if Persia fell under her domination, Russian troops might march down the Euphrates, establish a naval base at the head of the Persian Gulf and cut Britain's communications with India. The Turkish Empire in Asia was the first line of defence of British India and the need to sustain it was the underlying reason why Britain engaged in the Crimean War, the only great-power war she fought in this period. More normally, however, the British defended India by either courting one rival at the expense of the other or by attempting to work with both. Thus in July 1827 the British signed a treaty with Russia and France to bring about a settlement of the war between the Greeks and Turks. In 1840 Palmerston concluded an agreement with Prussia, Russia, Austria and the Ottoman Empire which led to the British deploying warships in the eastern Mediterranean against France's client, the ruler of Egypt, Mehemet Ali. And in 1878 Disraeli pledged Britain to the defence of Turkey-in-Asia if she were attacked by Russia.

The continuity between pre-1793 and post-1815 defence policy was best captured by the Secretary at War, Sidney Herbert. In 1854 he explained that the reason why Britain was only prepared to fight a small war at the start of each large war was that 'through every Government and every Parliament we have always had the same stereotyped system of economy in military affairs'.[4] After 1815 policy-makers had to try to fulfil two different commitments. They could not for long forget that the European states retained a latent capability to menace Britain's own security. This became especially pressing from the mid-1840s when the French began to build steam warships which might make possible a sudden invasion, a 'bolt from the blue'. That was one reason, although not the only one, why Britain could never be entirely denuded of regular troops. The second was that dependence upon the army to maintain public order was not immediately removed by the passage of the Metropolitan Police Act in 1829 or the Municipal Corporation Act in 1835.

Policy-makers had to balance those demands against the equally pressing demands for the services of the army and navy outside Europe to police and expand the empire. In 1793 Britain possessed twenty-six colonies. By 1815 she had forty-three and in the next fifty years the empire expanded by an average of 100,000 square miles each year. Britain's eighteenth century salt-water empire had been transformed. She was now also a great land power and each new acquisition needed a garrison. In 1792 the regular army had numbered about 45,000 men. When the army of occupation was withdrawn from France in 1818 the regular army was reduced but it still numbered about 100,000 men. Growing imperial commitments combined with the need for more troops to counter domestic unrest in Britain, led to a gradual increase in its strength so that on the eve of the Crimean War the army's establishment was nearly 153,000. In addition, on the eve of the Indian Mutiny in 1857 the East India Company maintained about 300,000 sepoys and 15,000 European troops. Far from being a military pygmy Britain most nearly approached matching the landforces of the other European great powers between 1815 and 1854. If the total manpower of the Crown's and company's forces are combined the landforces of the British Empire were larger than those of Prussia (200,000) or Austria (350,000), although they remained smaller than those of France (570,000).

Beyond Europe the army and navy were employed to further Britain's economic interests by policing her existing empire and expanding her spheres of informal control. The spread of free trade was not synonymous with the spread of peace, a fact that was grasped by the free-traders themselves. As Richard Cobden said in 1857, 'The manufacturers of Yorkshire and Lancashire look upon India and China as a field of enterprise which can only be kept open by force.'[5] The Guards and most cavalry regiments were retained at home but three-quarters of all infantry regiments were deployed abroad as imperial garrisons. Between 1818 and 1837 units abroad could expect to spend nearly thirteen years in exile before they were rotated home. Communications difficulties made it imperative that troops be scattered around the frontiers of the empire rather than be concentrated at home ready to be sent to any trouble spot. Before the extension of the electric telegraph to India, Australasia and the Far East in the 1870s it might take as long as eight months for a communication to reach New Zealand and for a reply to be received in London. In the empire the army garrisoned naval bases, protected settlers and quelled native unrest. By 1853 about 23,000 troops were stationed across the world, from Nova Scotia to Hong Kong, fulfilling these functions. A further 27,000 troops of the Crown's army were in India and until the 1860s about 50,000 troops were in the settlement colonies in Australasia, South Africa and Canada. Despite the extent of these commitments, the British did not develop a coherent philosophy of imperial defence, although in the late 1840s the Secretary of State for War and the Colonies, Lord Grey, tried to formulate one. He insisted that the dominant force of British sea-power justified the withdrawal of some, although not all, troops from the white colonies to create a large disposable force in Britain. The troops withdrawn could be replaced by locally raised militia and fortifications. Some progress was made in this direction but not as much as Grey had hoped. Wellington reminded the government of the role played by the colonial militia during the American War of Independence and the Horse Guards deprecated too much reliance on local forces because they were sedentary units which could not be moved across the globe as strategy dictated. It was not until the 1860s that overwhelming financial stringency finally dictated the removal of the regulars from the self-governing colonies which then became responsible for their own internal defence.

Troops and ships were also employed to expand the limits of British influence. The Foreign Office believed that it had performed its proper task when it had secured equality of opportunity for all traders and stayed aloof from promoting individual commercial enterprises. However, legislation freeing British overseas trade from restrictions was not always enough by itself to enable British goods to penetrate foreign markets. Between 1816 and 1842 British exports to Europe and North America rose comparatively slowly. The protectionist policies adopted by many European states after 1815 was a powerful incentive for the British to extend their trade into underdeveloped countries outside Europe. Underlying this policy was the fear, particularly strong in the 1830s and 1840s at the height of the chartist agitation, that unless government could ensure a plentiful supply of jobs and of cheap food, domestic social order would collapse. It was not coincidental that Palmerston's interventionist policies, signalled by the Anglo-Turkish Commercial Convention of 1838 and the first Opium War, were at their most intense between 1838 and 1841 when Britain was disturbed by the first wave of chartism. His objective was to create a group of economic satellites managed by British clients and able to provide the markets and cheap raw materials and food-stuffs which Britain's growing population demanded. In the case of Turkey the British also hoped that by opening the country to Western commerce they would promote political stability and maintain the Ottoman Empire as a barrier against Russia. Although the Manchester School clouded the adoption of free trade with much rhetoric suggesting that it would lead to a millennium of world peace, the underlying reason why politicians as hard-headed as Liverpool and Palmerston promoted it had much to do with a shrewd appreciation of how Britain's economic security could best be assured. Outside India and her formal settlement colonies in Canada, Australasia and South Africa, Britain sought to expand her informal empire by acquiring small entrepots from where she could command the world's maritime trade routes. These did not require large and costly garrisons (although they did require some garrisons) and they promised rich rewards by enabling British merchants to monopolize trade in the surrounding region. Sir Stamford Raffles, who negotiated the acquisition of Singapore for the East India Company in 1819, explained that the company's purpose 'is not territory, but trade; a great commercial emporium, and a *fulcrum* whence we may extend our influence politically as circumstances may hereafter require'.[6] Thanks to their new acquisitions the British were able rapidly to expand their trade with Siam and the Philippines. But in general they were reluctant, for financial as much as for moral reasons, to use force to impose free trade on other governments. However, not all indigenous regimes were willing to accept the supposed benefits of British trade and they sometimes resisted British economic penetration to the point where the British had to use force to open their markets and to keep them open. Thus the East India Company exported opium to China, despite the repeated edicts of the Chinese government banning the trade. The ending of the company's trading monopoly in 1833 opened the China trade to all comers and enormously increased the quantities of opium which were smuggled into China. Relations between the two countries became so bad that in 1839 Palmerston resorted to force, blockading the Chinese coast and ordering the navy to seize Hong Kong as a base for operations. The first Opium War brought considerable benefits to British trade. Hong Kong became a free port and under the Treaty of Nanking signed in 1842, the Chinese were compelled to open a number of their ports to British trade.

It would be wrong to suggest that every episode which led to the expansion of the British empire was directly related to the home government's desire to give greater scope for British trade. The looseness of London's control over its officials on the periphery of the empire makes it a mistake to assume that the initiative in making policy always lay wwith the government in London. In the age before the telegraph the difficulty of communicating with colonial governors gave officials on the frontiers of thhe empire wide scope for pursuing their subimperialist policies. In New Zealand in the early 1860s the gggovernor-general, Sir George Grey, used his monopoly of communications with London to disseminate entirely erroneous allegations of hostile Maori intentions so that London would send him the troops he craved to invade Maori territory.

Indian officials enjoyed a similar latitude. The expansion of British-controlled territory towards the north-west frontier owed little to commercial considerations. The priorities of the British rulers in India had differed from those of the government in London before 1815 and they remained different after 1815. For Calcutta the most pressing threat to British rule came from inside the subcontinent. The final destruction of the Maratha confederation in 1818 meant that the British rulers of India no longer feared the separate Indian states, but they were worried about Muslim conspirators, popular disturbances, or, most dangerous of all, a mutiny within the Indian regiments of the company's army. The government in India did not discount the Russian threat but, as had been the case with the French menace before 1815, they defined it in a different way. The British in India were well aware of how few they were and of the sometimes fragile basis of their power. They did not believe that there was a pressing risk of an actual Russian invasion. The real danger was that the spread of Russian influence into Persia or Afghanistan would cause unrest inside India which would necessitate higher military expenditure and ultimately make India unprofitable. They were therefore determined to maintain British prestige. It was vital that British rule should not be successfully defied by any indigenous power, for if it was the Indians might lose their belief in Britain's invincibility and the main prop which buttressed British rule could crumble. They wanted friendly regimes in Persia and Afghanistan able to block the advance of any hostile powers and were determined, if their power were challenged, to retaliate quickly. Shortly after Lord Auckland arrived in India as viceroy in 1836 it was apparent that Persia, with Russian encouragement, wanted to annex the Afghan province of Herat to compensate for territory she had recently lost to Russia. Auckland was alarmed because he was simultaneously receiving reports of disaffection in several Indian states and feared that if Afghanistan lost Herat the resulting disturbances would spill over into India. He decided that preventive action was necessary and in 1838 he tried to depose the Amir of Afghanistan and to establish a pro-British puppet regime at Kabul. The result was a military disaster culminating in the destruction of a whole British army when it retreated from Kabul in 1842. However, this setback did have one positive result. Until the late 1870s the British in India and London realized that the logistical difficulties which faced any army operating in Afghanistan meant that India could not be successfully invaded across her north-west frontier.

But the Afghan War did not mean that they ignored the frontier or that the government in India adopted a policy of masterly inactivity. Denied a buffer in Afghanistan and fearful that the dent in British prestige might encourage Muslims beyond the Indus and their co-religionists in India to mount a holy war against British rule, Auckland's successors were determined to secure control of the approaches to the north-west frontier and to refurbish their tarnished prestige. As Auckland's immediate successor Lord Ellenborough wrote, 'our supremacy rests upon the opinion hitherto entertained of our invincibility'.[7] In 1843, in search of an easy triumph, and without consulting the government in London, Ellenborough annexed Sind. From 1845 to 1846 and from 1848 to 1849 Ellenborough's successors, Lords Hardinge and Dalhousie, waged wars against the Sikhs, whose army was in a state of unrest. There had been a series of mutinies in the company's Bengal army and both men feared that if they did not act, the bad example set by the Sikh army might encourage worse insubordination amongst the company's troops. Furthermore, British control of the Punjab would establish a barrier between the Muslims of Afghanistan and those of India.

In Southern Africa land hunger rather than a strategic threat was the main motor driving British imperialism and calling for the employment of troops. In 1836–7, 1845, 1846–7 and 1850–3 British troops in South Africa repeatedly attempted to find and maintain a strategic frontier which would separate Boer settlers in search of land moving north from Bantu settlers also in search of land moving south. Land hunger could also cloak other, more complex motives for territorial expansion. Between 1843 and 1848, 1860 and 1861, and 1863 and 1866 British troops fought a series of campaigns with the Maoris of New Zealand. The settlers' desire for land was matched by their determination to impose British law, administration and 'civilization' on the Maoris. Finally the armed forces engaged in a form of gunboat diplomacy to mount punitive expeditions against indigenous rulers who had wronged British citizens or who had refused to accept British trade.

Between 1815 and 1854 the armed forces had two missions, home defence coupled with the maintenance of public order, and policing the empire. The possibility that the British might have to dispatch an army to Europe gradually faded from sight. The higher administration of Britain's landforces did not become noticeably more rational in the early nineteenth century. The army continued to be administered by different departments each acting more or less independently of the other. The Secretary of State for War and the Colonies retained responsibility for its overall size, the Secretary at War was responsible for finance and the passage of the annual Mutiny Act and the Treasury was responsible for the Commissariat. The Home Secretary controlled the use of troops inside Britain and the Commander-in-Chief at the Horse Guards oversaw the discipline and efficiency of the infantry and cavalry but had no authority over troops in the colonies or over any expeditionary forces. During the Crimean War, the Commander-in-Chief relied upon the press for his information about events before Sebastopol. Responsibility for the arms and equipment of the whole army, together with the discipline and efficiency of the artillery and engineers, rested with the Master-General of the Ordnance. The work of individual departments, especially those concerned with transport, medicine and supply, was impeded by overlapping spheres of competence. The continued tension between the professional and civil administrators of the army made it impossible to formulate coherent strategic policies. In 1837 a Royal Commission recommended that the Secretary at War should become a Cabinet minister responsible to Parliament for all matters concerning the army and that he should be the channel through which the Cabinet could pass its orders to the Commander-in-Chief. Such an organization would have enabled the government to determine the exact cost of the army and to present a single army estimate to Parliament annually. Its recommendations were rejected, largely because the Duke of Wellington threw his prestige behind the argument that the Secretary at War would become too powerful, the Commander-in-Chief would be powerless and a deliberative chamber like the Commons was not a suitable body to exercise executive control over the army. Underlying his objections was the fear that if the reforms succeeded the army would be entirely subordinated to a government dangerously bent on economy. Nothing was done until the Crimean War demonstrated that although this structure was just capable of sustaining an army devoted to police functions at home and in the colonies, it could not support an army fighting a major European power.

There were few significant changes in the social composition of the army's officer corps or its rank and file after 1815. The great majority of officers continued to be drawn from the ranks of 'gentlemen'. The purchase system remained in operation until 1871, although after 1842 cadets from the Royal

Military Academy, Sandhurst, could obtain a free commission. During the Crimean War, as in previous wars when the army had been rapidly expanded, there was a considerable increase in the number of free commissions granted. Even the abolition of purchase did not bring about a noticeable change in the social make-up of the officer corps. Before and after 1871 subalterns required a private income to make good the inadequacies of their pay. Those who discovered that their incomes were insufficient to permit them to live like gentlemen in Britain opted to serve in India where the cost of living was lower. The social composition of the officer corps, its domination by 'gentlemen' and the existence of the purchase system until 1871 did not preclude the development of professional skills amongst officers any more than it had done in the eighteenth century. Long tours of duty in remote colonies encouraged officers to turn in upon their regiments. But it was a parochial professionalism centred on the regiment and the demands of imperial campaigning. Because these operations rarely involved large numbers of troops, colonial fighting provided little incentive for the army to develop the kind of general staff which might be needed to command a large army intended to meet a European enemy.

Throughout the century the army faced the problem of trying to meet too many commitments with too few troops. By the 1840s it needed between 11,000 and 12,000 recruits annually to make good its wastage. Improving employment prospects in Britain combined with emigration from Ireland and Scotland, meant that in peacetime the number of recruits usually fell about 2 per cent short of the army's needs. In 1847, in an attempt to attract a better class of recruits by making enlistment seem less like a life sentence, recruits were given the option of enlisting for ten years in the infantry or twelve in the other arms of service. Viscount Howick, the Secretary at War who sponsored the Bill, also hoped that it would create a reserve of time-expired men who could be recalled to the colours when needed. But few men took advantage of the new terms, a better class of recruit was not attracted and the reserve created amounted to a paltry 3,000 men. Higher rates of pay which would have allowed the army to compete with civilian employers might have helped, but the governing classes were unwilling to pay the market rate for military labour. Colonial operations and garrison duties represented a heavy drain on the army's manpower, not because large numbers of men were killed by shot and shell but because they were the victims of disease. Canada, Malta, or Gibraltar were comparatively healthy overseas stations but West Africa or Jamaica could decimate whole battalions in a year. In the 1840s the War Office at last awoke to this problem and in the Western hemisphere introduced a formal system of rotating battalions through a ten-year cycle between healthy and unhealthy stations. The result was a drop in the mortality rate which represented the saving of a whole battalion each year.

Nor did Howick's innovation do much to enable the recruiting system to augment the army's numbers rapidly in an emergency. In March 1855 it needed

90,000 more men but the ordinary recruiting machinery could only secure 4,500. The Crimean War was the first major European war which the British army fought without resorting to some form of compulsion to fill its ranks. It did utilize foreign manpower to make good these deficiencies and looked to German mercenaries for the same reasons its forefathers had done so in the eighteenth century. Enlisting foreigners was preferable to using compulsion to enlist British artisans because it minimized the deleterious impact of the war on the British economy. But the German states refused to permit the British to recruit in their territories. The small foreign corps raised did not number more than 10,000 men and did not serve in the Crimea. The Crimea thus became the first European war which the British fought with an army which was almost entirely British.

The early Victorian navy was not a huge and impressive force dedicated to fleet manoeuvres. It was a small force of mostly small ships. In 1815 the Admiralty recommended that the peacetime fleet should be reduced to 102 ships-of-the-line and 110 frigates and asked for an ambitious building programme to replace older vessels. Shortage of money meant that this programme was never completed and between 1830 and 1834 the Whig first lord, Sir James Graham, reduced the fleet to 58 ships-of-the-line and 59 frigates. The navy estimates reached their lowest point of the century, £4,500,000, in 1835. These reductions did not mean that Britain unilaterally disarmed herself at sea nor that after 1815 successive governments had so reduced the size of the fleet that Britain's security was at risk. The French, Russians and Americans retained powerful fleets. In 1833 the French had 34 ships-of-the-line and 37 frigates; the Russians had 36 ships-of-the-line and 23 frigates and the Americans had 8 ships-of-the-line and 10 frigates. The demand for 'cheap government' was never permitted to go so far that the navy would have been unable to counter these potential enemies even though the margin left for contingencies beyond these threats was sometimes small.

Graham was also responsible for a major reform of the central administration of the navy. Hitherto the navy had been controlled by a two-tier administration. The Board of Admiralty, composed mostly of naval officers and presided over by a politician, the first lord, had been responsible for overall policy, including warship design and strategy. Its decisions were executed by a number of subordinate boards, the most important of which were the Navy and Victualling Boards. In 1832 Graham abolished the subordinate boards. Five members of the new Admiralty Board became responsible for the duties which hitherto had been performed by the old boards. Graham hoped that this centralization would accelerate naval administration and produce greater economy by preventing conflicts of authority. The system worked well enough in peacetime but faltered under the pressure of business created by the Crimean War. The sea lords were overwhelmed by administration and were too busy to advise the first lord about strategy. Graham had unwittingly abolished the Admiralty's only mechanism for considering general policy and he did so just when the application of industrial technology to naval warfare was making such deliberations all the more necessary. There was no naval staff to advise the first lord and during the Crimean War Graham opposed even the idea that one of the professional members of the board should join with a group of senior army officers to concert their plans.

The worst defects of these arrangements did not become apparent until 1854 because between 1815 and 1853 the major tasks of the Royal Navy were to act in support of British diplomacy and to suppress piracy and the African slave trade, not to engage a first-class European power. Between 1815 and 1853 the navy dominated the waters around Europe and enabled British diplomats to interfere, with varying degrees of success, in the internal affairs of Holland, Belgium, Spain, Portugal, Greece and the Ottoman Empire. It also assisted the spread of British trade in South America, around the coast of Africa, in the Indian Ocean, in the East Indies, and around China, Australasia and the Pacific. But the navy by itself was not omnipotent and some states were less susceptible to naval coercion than others. During the Syrian crisis of 1839–40 the navy forced Mehemet Ali to conform to the wishes of the concert powers by bombarding the coastal fortress of St Jean d'Arce. But the strategic situation in that conflict was peculiarly suitable to the exercise of naval power. The Egyptian army's communications ran along the coast where they could be bombarded from the sea and the navy had the assistance of Turkish troops to occupy the fortress after they had bombarded it. When the navy was not able to summon the assistance of friendly troops it was less successful. In 1823 the Austrians were able to ignore British protests and crush a revolution in Piedmont. In 1825 the French defied British wishes and sent an army across the Pyrenees into Spain and in 1830 the Royal Navy could do nothing when a Russian army crushed Polish rebels. These failures underlined the lessons of Britain's eighteenth-century European wars. If the British lacked troops of their own, or allies who possessed an army, their ability to intervene in continental affairs was limited. It was a lesson which was reinforced during the Schleswig-Holstein crisis of 1864. Palmerston threatened the Prussians with naval intervention if they occupied the duchies but Bismarck called his bluff, a fact the Prime Minister ruefully admitted in August 1864 when he told an audience that 'Ships sailing on the sea cannot stop armies on land'.[8]

The Crimean War highlighted the problems facing the fleet on mobilization against a European power. Since 1815 so many ships had been scattered in small squadrons across the globe that there had been few opportunities for practising fleet manoeuvres. Station keeping was made more difficult because some ships were steam-driven and others relied upon wind power. Manning and officering the fleet was also a problem. After 1815 the eighteenth-century practice of hiring seamen when a ship was commissioned and discharging them at the end of each commission had continued. In 1853 boys of 16 or 17 were given the opportunity of enlisting for two years' training and then for ten years' continuous service. However, this innovation came too late to solve the manning problem on the outbreak of war. To man the expanded fleet in 1854 seamen had to be recruited on an *ad hoc* basis. Merchant seamen were reluctant to enlist because the Admiralty was tardy in offering them the traditional bounty. It was politically impossible to impose the press so recourse was had to enlisting over-age coastguards. The navy-list was top heavy with elderly officers who had served in the Napoleonic War and had remained on half-pay, waiting in vain for promotion. Promotion from captain to flag rank continued to depend upon seniority and the flag-list was packed with aged officers. When the Admiralty tried to find a vice-admiral to command the Baltic fleet it had no option other than to employ the 68-year-old Sir Charles Napier because he was the only vice-admiral under 70 who was not already employed.

The Aberdeen government went to war against Russia in March 1854 because the Russians had occupied the Danubian principalities of Moldavia and Walachia and because their attack on the Turkish fleet at Sinope in November 1853 had demonstrated that Russia was now a major naval power that threatened British naval supremacy in the eastern Mediterranean. The government sought to destroy Russian naval power in the Black Sea and to prevent the Russians advancing farther in the Balkans. To do so they tried to create a great coalition and to persuade Sweden, Austria and Prussia to open a northern and central front against the Russians so as to draw their forces away from Turkey. To encourage the neutrals the British sent a fleet to the Baltic where it blockaded the Russian fleet, disrupted Russian trade, captured the fortress of Bomarsund on the Aland Islands in August 1854 and tied down powerful Russian forces in Finland and around the Baltic coast. But the defences of the main Russian naval bases in the Baltic were too formidable to enable them to repeat their success at Bomarsund. Naval power did not induce the Swedes, Prussians, or Austrians to become active belligerents, although Austrian pressure did persuade the Russians to evacuate the principalities in August 1854.

The French and British concentrated their main forces in the Black Sea. In London, Graham, rather than the Duke of Newcastle, the Secretary of State for War, formulated British strategy. Graham wanted to destroy the Russian naval fortress of Sebastopol because it would wreck Russian naval power in the Black Sea and eastern Mediterranean, it would reduce her ability to interfere in Turkish affairs and it would ensure that the Danube remained open to shipping. Even before the Russians evacuated the principalities, the government had decided to follow Graham's advice. In September 1854 the British and French landed an expeditionary force in the Crimea. The British contingent numbered 27,000 men. The consequence of the army's concentration on imperial operations since 1815 was that it was ill-equipped to fight a European power. Only two of the five generals who commanded the infantry divisions had ever before led anything larger than a battalion. The allies overcame three Russian attempts to drive them out of the Crimea, at the Alma in September, at Balaclava in October and at Inkerman in November 1854. They might have been able to storm Sebastopol after the Battle of the Alma but they advanced too slowly and gave the Russians time to prepare their defences. The allied expedition faced the perennial problem of amphibious expeditions in the age of sail: they had been unable to bring sufficient horses and land transport with them to enable them to advance swiftly. They had to rely on what they could acquire in the Crimea and that was a serious handicap because local resources were scarce. The allied army had to settle down to a lengthy siege, an operation made even longer by the fact that they also had too few troops to invest it completely. Sebastopol did not fall until September 1855. But, paradoxically, the allies' inability either to storm or effectively to invest the city proved to be the key to their success. In the winter of 1854/5 the Russians were able to reinforce and resupply the fortress but at a terrible cost. The hardships of the journey south decimated the Russian army even before it reached the port. The allied army, supplied from the sea with increasing efficiency after the winter of 1854/5, lost about 60,000 men. The Russians lost nearly half a million men. Even so the fall of the fortress did not immediately induce them to sue for peace. What finally persuaded them to negotiate was a combination of the news that Palmerston, who had become Prime Minister on the fall of the Aberdeen government, had renewed his search for allies, that he wanted to attack St Petersburg and the knowledge that Russia's supplies of war materials and money were nearly exhausted. The Treaty of Paris ending hostilities was signed in March 1856.

The Crimea had highlighted the shortcomings of a colonial army sent to fight a European war. The reports of *The Times*' correspondent with the army, W. H. Russell, showed that the commissariat, transport and medical services were inadequate to sustain the troops. Radicals blamed the purchase system and demanded its abolition, believing that it advanced the wealthy at the expense of the meritorious. In January 1855 the Aberdeen government had been brought down by a vote in the House of Commons in favour of establishing a Select Committee to inquire into the state of the army before Sebastopol. Aberdeen was succeeded by Palmerston who was pledged to reform the army's administration. The process had in fact begun in 1854. Three months after the start of the war the Secretary of State for War and the Colonies had been deprived of his duties in respect of the army and a new Secretary of State for War was created. His office was soon amalgamated with that of the Secretary at War and by 1858 he discharged all the civil functions of the army. Its military functions remained the responsibility of the Commander-in-Chief but for the first time they now included responsibility for the engineers and artillery. The failure of the staff in the Crimea led to the establishment of a Staff College at Camberley in 1858, although attendance at the college was not made a prerequisite of staff appointments and nearly fifty years were to elapse before the army acquired a fully functioning general staff. These reforms, coupled with the end of the war in March 1856, the army's success in crushing the Indian Mutiny, and victories in China in 1860, on the north-west Frontier in 1863, and in New Zealand from

1860 to 1864 caused the army reform movement to disintegrate in a cloud of public complacency.

The millennium envisaged by the radicals never arrived. Defence spending fell to £12,000,000 in 1836, the lowest level it reached throughout the nineteenth century. But it began to rise even before the Crimean War. In the late 1830s and 1840s increasing numbers of troops were needed to quell chartist demonstrations. Just as they were subdued, events in France in the late 1840s and 1850s persuaded the government to vote a further increase in the size of the army to deter a possible French invasion. This trend was accelerated by the Crimean War, the Indian Mutiny and the fears aroused by the foreign and naval policies of Napoleon III in the late 1850s and early 1860s. The growing bill was paid for in part by the income tax which the Conservative Prime Minister Sir Robert Peel reintroduced in 1842. Peel intended the tax to be a temporary expedient to sustain the government's revenues until his other fiscal innovations had made good the receipts lost by the abolition of most tariffs. His political heir, William Gladstone, who was Chancellor of the Exchequer between 1852 and 1853 and again from 1859 to 1865, tried and failed to fulfil his mentor's wishes. Defence costs absorbed a third of the budget in the 1850s and 1860s and explained the great importance financial reformers placed on cutting the defence estimates. More than half the cost of the Crimean War was met from current revenue. Britain found herself able to win it without incurring a crippling increase in the national debt and, what was equally significant, the public paid up with hardly a murmur. The rhetoric of 'cheap government' did not disappear overnight in the 1850s but one of the legacies of the war was to increase, within limits, the public's tolerance of higher spending. Thanks to the economic boom which Britain had experienced since 1849, the government could afford guns *and* butter. In March 1857 Palmerston's government was defeated in the Commons on a resolution moved by Cobden condemning its policy of bombarding Canton. But in the resulting general election Palmerston won a resounding victory and Cobden lost his seat. Even Gladstone recognized that the policies of the Manchester School did not find favour with the electorate but he never understood this new mood. When he returned to the Treasury his subsequent budgets were formulated according to principles he explained to an audience of businessmen in 1859. They were determined 'by the sentiments of the people'. If they wanted thrift he would oblige. But if they did not 'it is vain to look to the Chancellor of the Exchequer to stem such a tide of feeling'.[9]

The application of industrial technology to maritime warfare also had repercussions for the estimates. In the mid-1840s technological developments began to revolutionize naval warfare. The French started to build steam-powered warships and the security which the navy's sail-powered fleet had afforded Britain since 1815 was called into question. The Royal Navy quickly adopted the same technologies, and in some cases actually introduced new technologies before the French. But steam-powered vessels were more expensive than vessels which relied on sails, a fact which helped to double the naval estimates between 1840 and 1860. Nor did the higher estimates buy much psychological reassurance. In 1846 an engineer and Peninsular veteran, Sir John Burgoyne, wrote to Wellington complaining about the lack of fixed defences along the south coast. The duke concurred with Burgoyne's criticisms and insisted that Britain's defences were too weak to resist a French invasion. His reply was leaked to *The Times* and started the first invasion panic of Victorian Britain. The Chancellor of the Exchequer, Lord John Russell, proposed the unpopular expedient of raising the income tax to pay for a reorganized militia and increased navy estimates. The fall of Louis Philippe in 1848 dampened fears for the time being but the panic was typical of those which followed. It was begun with a pronouncement by a major public figure. It was underpinned by a new technological development but rested on little real consideration of its implications, nor was any attempt made to view the situation from the perspective of the putative enemy and to consider if he could, or even wished, to invade. Louis Napoleon's seizure of power in 1851 produced a second scare and caused a public debate which suggested that although the navy remained Britain's first line of defence, by itself it might not suffice and that the regular army at home was too weak to be of much assistance. The government opted to build fortifications to multiply the effectiveness of the troops they had and raised large numbers of part-time, and cheap, militiamen. In 1851 although there were 13,600 yeomanry available the militia barely existed even on paper, for in 1829 the Wellington government had suspended the militia ballot. It remained moribund until the passage of an Act in 1852 to raise 80,000 men, by the ballot if necessary but preferably by enlisting volunteers. So pronounced was the fear of invasion and so strong were the patriotic sentiments of the nation during the Crimean War that the ballot never had to be used. During the war the militia not only freed regulars for service abroad, it also provided 33,000 recruits for the regular army.

The militia was largely rural-based and its officer corps was socially exclusive. It gave little scope for the urban middle and working classes to demonstrate their patriotism or respectability. In the mid- and late 1850s such people began to pepper the Horse Guards with requests that they should be permitted to form volunteer corps just as their ancestors had done during the Napoleonic War. The commander-in-chief, the Duke of Cambridge, deplored the suggestion on the grounds that they would constitute 'an armed and a very dangerous rabble'.[10] But in the late 1850s and early 1860s the speed of technological change quickened. Napoleon III's foreign policy seemed to be dangerously expansionist. The development in France of a railway and telegraph system and construction work at the port of Cherbourg seemed to make it possible for the French to mass a large army on the Channel coast for an invasion of Britain with hardly any warning. In 1859 Britain and France each possessed thirty steam-powered wooden battleships. The French then launched the world's first steam-powered iron-clad, *La Gloire*, proof against shot from any existing gun and able to cross the Channel in defiance of the wind. The First Lord of the Admiralty started another invasion panic by conceding that the navy could not defend Britain's coasts. Palmerston established a Royal Commission on the defence of the United Kingdom. Basing their report on the assumption that the fleet might have been defeated, decoyed away, or crippled by a storm, the commissioners reported that the navy alone could not secure the defence of the country and recommended that the major ports should be fortified. The Admiralty rejected this 'brick and mortar' policy and responded by increasing their building programme and launching HMS *Warrior*, a vessel superior to *La Gloire*. But Palmerston agreed with the Royal Commission and inaugurated an expensive programme of fortifications.

The Royal Commission's conclusions dominated British strategic thought for the next thirty years. The navy, which had traditionally been Britain's first line of defence against invasion, was no longer thought to be adequate. Britain had to be transformed into a fortress bristling with guns. Troops were necessary to man these defences and they could only be had at reasonable cost by raising volunteers. In May 1859 Tennyson published his poem 'Form, Riflemen, Form' in *The Times* and the War Office bowed to public pressure and ordered lords lieutenant to form volunteer corps. Volunteers were exempt from the militia ballot but were liable to be called out in an emergency. Except when they were embodied they could resign if they gave two weeks' notice. To ensure that arms did not fall into the hands of the labouring poor the government insisted that volunteers would be required to purchase their uniforms themselves. The panic faded in the mid-1860s. By 1864, although Britain had fewer iron-clads than the French, their fighting power was superior. The volunteers were initially popular and by 1868 nearly 199,000 men had enlisted. But by then the corps had undergone an important change. Volunteering carried little social status for the upper middle classes and by the mid-1860s their interest in it had diminished. Increasingly the rank and file were drawn from amongst the ranks of urban artisans, attracted to the movement partly by the opportunity it gave them to demonstrate their patriotism and respectability but also by the social facilities volunteering offered them. But their military role was unclear. They had originally been established as a home defence force but after Prussia's victories over Austria and France in the 1860s their skills as marksmen seemed less than sufficient to fulfil that task. The question of who precisely was responsible for the defence of the home islands against a full-scale invasion was not settled until the 1890s.

Palmerston's fortifications cost £11,000,000 and the defence estimates rose from £20,700,000 in 1859 to £25,900,000 in 1865. The pressure this placed on the budget was one reason for the reforms which began to overtake the armed services in the 1860s and 1870s. The army in India was paid for by the Indian tax-payer but the cost of the forces stationed in other parts of the empire was paid for by the British Treasury and absorbed about one-third of the military budget in the 1850s. At a time when the white settlement colonies were claiming a larger measure of self-government it was probably inevitable that their garrisons would be the first target for British politicians in search of economies. This process had been started by Lord Grey, the Secretary of State for War and the Colonies between 1846 and 1852. The Australian colonies, which were not menaced by any external power or by powerful indigenous tribes, were the first to be deprived of their regular garrisons. The settlement of boundary disputes with the USA in 1842 and 1846 facilitated a reduction of the Canadian garrison. The Crimean War accelerated the withdrawal and also encouraged the Canadians and Australians to form their own militia for local defence. However, the establishment of a Colonial Office separate from the War Office in 1854 made the problem of determining the size of colonial garrisons more complex. The difficulty that the War Office experienced in persuading some colonial governors, notably Sir George Grey at the Cape, to release troops to go to India to suppress the mutiny, encouraged the Secretary of State for War, General Peel, to insist that an interdepartmental committee be established in 1859 to investigate the responsibility of the War Office and the colonies regarding military expenditure. It discovered that despite efforts to reduce colonial garrisons outside India, they were still absorbing 50,000 regulars at an annual cost to the British tax-payer of about £4,000,000 and that annually the colonies only contributed £380,000 to their own defence. This persuaded the Commons to establish its own Select Committee on Colonial Military Expenditure in 1859 under the chairmanship of Arthur Mills MP. In 1862 the Mills Committee recommended a continuation of Grey's policy on the grounds that, although the British had a duty to protect those colonies which were threatened by external aggression, the presence of a garrison of British regulars in the self-governing colonies merely served to dissuade them from helping themselves.

The navy had not figured in the deliberations of the Mills Committee but it did not escape from the forces tending to reduce British expenditure on the defence of the self-governing colonies. Between 1835 and 1860 the number of warships stationed outside European waters roughly doubled. The navy's vessels were scattered in small squadrons across the globe. Ships-of-the-line were maintained in home waters in case of a recurrence of a major naval building programme by Britain's European neighbours, but for policing the empire what was required were small vessels, which could operate in shallow coastal waters. During the Crimean War British yards launched 156 small but powerful shallow-draught warships, each mounting one or two heavy guns. These gunboats and gun vessels were ideally suited to enable the navy to perform its role as the policeman of the world's coasts. By the 1860s and 1870s these vessels and their direct descendants formed the bulk of the fleet.

They were the answer to an economist's prayer, for they were cheap to build and easy to man. The 1860s and 1870s were not a period of stagnation for the navy. A Royal Commission on manning reported in 1859 and between 1860 and 1866 a series of Naval Discipline Acts were passed to attract volunteers to the navy by humanizing discipline and improving living conditions on the lower deck. The problem of how on mobilization to increase rapidly the seamen on the fleet's book also began to be surmounted in 1859 by the formation of the Royal Naval Reserve. Volunteers from amongst experienced merchant seamen were granted a retainer in peacetime and obliged to perform one month's drill each year aboard a warship. By 1878 the RNR could provide the fleet with about 18,000 seamen. The manning problem was also eased by the fact that Gladstone and Disraeli reduced the establishment of the navy from 75,000 to 60,000 men.

From the mid-1860s Gladstone and Disraeli also competed with each other to reduce the navy estimates. They were assisted by a favourable international situation. France's defeat in 1870–1 left her with little energy to spare on her fleet and the Russians and Americans both seemed content to neglect theirs. But it was Hugh Childers, the First Lord in Gladstone's first administration, who had the greatest impact for good or ill on the navy. Not only did he close Deptford and Woolwich dockyards, he also tackled the task of redistributing the fleet with more vigour than any of his predecessors. Childers and his successors succeeded in reducing the size of the permanent squadrons stationed abroad, arguing that British prestige could be equally well maintained at less cost by smaller permanent squadrons supported by visits from a flying squadron. The number of vessels on foreign stations fell by nearly 40 per cent in the decade after 1865. Equally significant was the way in which Childers restructured the Board of Admiralty. Anxious to place Admiralty administration on what he believed were more business-like lines, he merely ensured that the board as a collective body practically ceased to exist. Under his regime individual members of the board met the First Lord separately. No mechanism for collective deliberations existed and even less attention could be paid to matters of general policy than under the system established by Graham in 1832. Still without a naval staff, the board became even less capable of taking a comprehensive view of rapid changes in the naval situation.

Although the Commons had adopted the resolutions of the Mills Committee in May 1862, it was to be some time before they were put into practice. A reduced garrison was retained in Canada in the early 1860s for fear that she might become involved in the American Civil War and then it was reinforced in the mid-1860s to counter the threat of Fenian raids. In New Zealand the Maori Wars tied down 10,000 troops in the mid-1860s. It was not until the formation of the first Gladstone administration in 1868 that the government acted decisively to end the garrisoning of regular troops in the self-governing colonies. They did so as part of a much larger package of army reforms which was devised by Gladstone's Secretary of State for War, Edward Cardwell. Cardwell was responsible for four major reforms: the introduction of short service enlistment to enable the formation of a new army reserve; the localization of the home army so that each regiment was accorded a specific territory from which to draw its recruits and was affiliated to local auxiliary forces; the abolition of purchase; and the centralization of army business under the secretary of state.

Army reform had hardly figured in the Liberal party's election propaganda and Cardwell did not enter the War Office with preconceived ideas beyond a desire to cut the estimates. He therefore accelerated the withdrawal of garrisons from the self-governing colonies and by 1870 he had reduced the forces committed to colonial garrisons (excluding India) to 25,700 men and cut the estimates by £2,200,000. But the recall of these garrisons did not mean that the army no longer had to provide men to garrison the rest of the empire. Finding recruits was a constant problem. Long-service recruiting had failed to meet the army's manpower needs in the 1860s. Conscription on the Prussian model was impractical. Two or three years' service with the colours would be too brief to permit troops to be trained and then shipped out to the colonies. But the introduction of short service might encourage more men to enlist, would facilitate the formation of a larger reserve of ex-regulars and would further reduce the estimates by cutting the cost of pensions. The Army Enlistment Act of 1870 did not establish a standard period of six years' service with the colours followed by a similar period in the reserve. The terms were flexible and could be varied according to the army's needs and long-service enlistments for twelve years were still permitted. Cardwell hoped to create a reserve of 60,000 men which would not only permit him to reduce the cadre of home-based units but would also enable him to bring them up to strength quickly in an emergency. By 1895 the first-class army reserve contained almost 83,000 men. However, it had been created at the expense of the line army. Cardwell had estimated that 32,000 recruits would be needed annually to create the reserve and supply the drafts for units overseas. The army rarely met that quota. After 1870 men who might have stayed with the colours for twenty-one years now passed into the reserve after only a decade.

The recruitment and retention of the other ranks was made easier by the increasing paternalism, often the product of evangelicalism, of many officers. Generals like Wolseley, Roberts and Buller insisted that the army would never be able to attract sufficient recruits unless pay and conditions of service were improved. Some enlightened officers tried to wean their men away from more dissipated pastimes by establishing regimental libraries and sponsoring organized sports. Slowly their reforms helped to make army life slightly more attractive for the rank and file. Net pay was increased gradually in the second half of the century and improvements were slowly made in the heating, lighting, ventilation and size of barrack accommodation. Flogging was restricted and finally abolished in 1881. The mortality rate of the army at home improved considerably after the Crimean War. The army's success in suppressing the Indian Mutiny and in policing and extending the frontiers of the empire in the second half of the century were vividly reported in the press and did much to make it an increasingly popular national institution. But what such reports did not do, even when coupled with these reforms, wass to transform the army into an attractive career for all but a tiny proportion of the 'respectable' poor.

The reforms of the central administration of the army during and after the Crimean War had left the relationship between the commander-in-chief at the Horse Guards and the secretary of state at the War Office ill-defined. The War Office Act of 1870 finally subordinated the commander-in-chief to the secretary of state. But Cardwell had to buy off Cambridge's opposition in such a way as to leave him still in a strong position. Cambridge refused to become merely the secretary's military chief of staff and Cardwell had to grant him an unlimited tenure of office with wide powers over discipline, appointments and promotions. Cardwell had no doctrinaire objections to the purchase system. In 1870 he tried to persuade Parliament to abolish the rank of ensign so that he could reduce the number of subalterns as part of his larger plan to cut the cadre establishment of batttalions. His proposal failed because he was only willing to compensate officers who lost their commiissioons at the regulation price and many of them had paid more than that. In 1871 he therefore chose to abolish the whole purchase system because the prevalence of over-regulation prices was blocking his wider reform plans. He never shared the radicals' hope that the abolition of purchase would transform the social composition of the officer corps and it did not. He had hoped that it would begin a new era of professionalism because promotion by merit would demand that officers pay greater attention to their professional duties. He was disappointed. Cambridge deplored selection as the basis for promotion, believing that it smacked too much of favouritism and political jobbery. He relied upon seniority and so mediocre officers could still be found in command of battalions and promotion probably became slower. It would have been even slower had it not been for the introduction of regulations in 1877 imposing compulsory pensionable retirement on captains and majors after set periods of service.

Cardwell's final reform was the fusion of regular, auxiliary and reserve forces by the localization of the army. The Localization Act of 1872 established sixty-six territorial districts. Each district formed the base for two line battalions, two militia battalions and a number of volunteer units. It delimited a recruiting area for every unit and formed a permanent depot and training centre for recruits. Cardwell hoped that linking line and auxilliary units might improve the efficiency of the latter and that the battalion at home would supply drafts for its sister battalion abroad. His first wish probably was fulfilled but his second was not. Localization as a way of supplying adequate drafts for units overseas would only have worked had there been a numerical balance between the line units in Britain and overseas. But a series of small colonial wars in the 1870s meant that by the end of the decade there were 59 battalions at home and 82 overseas. Home battalions were often reduced to skeletons in an effort to keep their sister units supplied with drafts.

With the exception of the abolition of purchase, the Cardwell reforms were generally, although not universally, well received by the press and Parliament. Until the end of the century Cardwell's supporters claimed that he had preserved the voluntary system, enabled Britain generally to win a series of colonial wars and to meet the security needs of the empire and kept the estimates within reasonable limits. In fact localization, in many ways the key to maintaining an efficient army at home and abroad, had begun to fail within five years of Cardwell's leaving office. Nor, thanks to the continued tenure of Cambridge at the Horse Guards until 1894, did the reforms infuse the officer corps with a new spirit of professionalism. The old professionalism which had existed even under the purchase system remained but the promotion of meritorious officers may in some instances have actually been held back after 1871 because of the duke's reliance upon the principle of seniority.

It has sometimes been too readily assumed that rich and powerful European nations were inevitably victorious when they confronted poor and weak Indian principalities or African tribes. But the Italians' experience in Ethiopia in 1896 should warn against such facile generalizations. There were a number of reasons why the British won most of their nineteenth-century colonial wars, not all of which were directly connected to the professional prowess of their armed forces. Domestic opposition to colonial wars was rarely prolonged or successful. Although some radical politicians in the first half of the nineteenth century regularly called for a reduction in the army estimates, Britain's colonial wars met with little opposition at home. They were cheap in terms of British lives and they cost the British tax-payer remarkably little. This was partly a reflection of the fact that the number of troops involved was usually quite small. The largest expeditionary force sent from Britain to conduct a colonial campaign between 1815 and 1899 was the army dispatched to Egypt in 1882 which numbered only 35,000 men. Wherever possible the army continued its eighteenth-century policy of employing indigenous or colonial forces in preference to British soldiers. At the beginning of the two Sikh Wars Sir Hugh Gough, the British commander, mustered 4 British and 13 sepoy Indian battalions in 1845 and 5 British and 16 sepoy battalions in 1848. Although the size of the Indian army was limited after the mutiny, it was still sufficiently large to enable Indian units to take part in at least ten expeditions outside India between 1859 and 1899. Ten of the 14 infantry battalions the British employed in Abyssinia in 1867–8 were Indian units.

The cost of colonial wars to the British tax-payer was less than it might have been because part of the burden was borne by the Indian tax-payer. The East India Company's army was financed by the Indian tax-payer who also paid the cost of the Crown's forces in India. By 1841 the East India Company was spending annually about £9,000,000 on its army. After the amalgamation of the company's and the Crown's army following the mutiny, the government of India continued to meet the cost of its indigenous regiments and granted the British

Treasury an annual capitation fee of £10. for every British soldier stationed in India. However, the British tax-payer did have to meet most of the cost of the Crown's forces at the Cape and in Australia, New Zealand and Canada. The wars themselves were cheap compared to Britain's eighteenth century wars, although that did not stop the Treasury from trying, often unsuccessfully, to recoup some of the costs from colonial governments. The first Afghan War cost about £8,000,000, the campaigns fought along the frontiers of Natal and Cape Colony from 1835 to 1851 cost about £2,000,000. The Abyssinian expedition of 1867–8 cost about £8,600,000, but the cost of the Indian troops employed was met by the Indian government. Wolseley's campaign against the Ashanti in 1873–4 was a bargain, costing only £900,000. Sums of this magnitude might cause tax-payers and chancellors to grumble but they would certainly never bring Britain to the verge of bankruptcy.

Generalizations about the actual conduct of the colonial campaigns which the British fought are made difficult by the enormous variety of opponents they faced and the terrain over which they fought. Some, like the army of Arabi Pasha who resisted the invasion of Egypt in 1882, possessed the weapons and training of a European army. The Afghans had the arms but not the organization of European forces. The Zulus' discipline approximated to that of a European army but they had few European weapons. The Maoris resisted the British by building earth and timber fortifications which were proof against British artillery, the Pathans fought in the hills of the North-West Frontier and the Ashanti fought in the forests of West Africa. But several elements were common to many of these campaigns. Geography and climate were often as formidable an adversary as the enemy and could impose their own constraints on the conduct of operations. The British usually assumed the strategic offensive at the earliest possible stage of each campaign for fear that if they tarried too long their seeming hesitation would encourage more malcontents to join the opposition. Battle in the open was the best way in which the British could make their generally superior discipline tell by imposing the largest possible casualty list on the enemy, so preventing a recurrence of trouble. It was for that reason that astute enemies like the Maoris avoided such encounters. But against an enemy like the Maoris the British had another advantage. Maori society produced little in the way of the kind of economic surplus needed to maintain a professional army in the field indefinitely. Warriors could not afford to leave their fields untended for too long. The British, by contrast, could maintain troops in the field indefinitely and apply continuous pressure on their enemies until the process of attrition had worn them down.

Until the 1830s the British had owed their military successes against African and Asiatic powers not to superior numbers or technology but to their superior organization, discipline and tactics. But in the second quarter of the nineteenth century European technology also began to work in their favour. In the era of sailing ships, the navy's power had not extended far beyond the coastline for sail-powered warships were difficult to manoeuvre up the winding rivers which led to the interior of continents. But steam-power opened up the rivers of the world. In 1824 the East India Company mounted the first modern river war when they used three small wooden-hulled steamers to sail 500 miles up the Irrawaddy in the course of the first Anglo-Burmese War.

The Victorian army was not a technological anachronism. Continuous colonial warfare ensured that the British remained at least on a par with their continental neighbours and meant that they were sometimes ahead of them in the adoption of new weapons. Before the middle of the nineteenth century British troops did not enjoy a significant technological superiority over non-Europeans. Smooth-bore muskets had an effective range of about 100 yards and could be fired only two or three times a minute. Muzzle-loading rifles, which were employed by some British units during the Napoleonic Wars, had a longer range but a slower rate of fire. Two inventions transformed the military potential of the infantryman in the mid-nineteenth century, the copper percussion-cap and the cylindro-conoidal bullet. The first invention greatly reduced the rate of misfires and the second gave the infantry a weapon with an effective range of about 500 yards. However, rifles were still slow to reload but the problem was overcome in the 1860s when the Royal Laboratory at Woolwich developed the Snider-Enfield rifle, a breech-loader firing a brass cartridge with an effective range of 1,000 yards. It represented a quantum leap in weapons technology. It only required the invention of smokeless powder in 1885, the addition of magazines to transform single-shot rifles into repeaters and the development of machine-guns for the gun revolution to be complete. The ease with which small British forces defeated much larger enemy armies in the Ashanti War of 1873–4 and the Zulu War of 1879 demonstrated the extent of the technological superiority they now enjoyed. It reached its apogee at Omdurman in 1898. Kitchener's army, equipped with breech-loading repeating rifles, 20 machine-guns and rifled artillery, killed 11,000 of the 40,000-strong Dervish army for the loss of only 48 British soldiers.

The logistical obstacles the army frequently faced were overcome with a mixture of science and improvisation. Until the 1850s the most effective defence West Africa enjoyed against British penetration was malaria. But by the 1870s Europeans venturing into the region began to use quinine successfully as a prophylactic and the death-rate from fever dropped. The Victorian army habitually campaigned in regions of the world which, by European standards, lacked any communications infrastructure. It had to organize the means of its own mobility before it could begin to campaign and its needs were often enormous. Napier's 13,000 combat troops in Abyssinia were supplied by over 36,000 animals and 49,000 supply personnel. The army's transport system was often improvised on the spot because no uniform arrangements would have sufficed to meet the different demands of the theatres in which it operated. The apparent ease with which the British often won their battles was in some respects deceptive. It was only made possible in the first place because the army overcame the diverse logistical difficulties which confronted it.

The mid-Victorian army and navy were effective and economical instruments of British imperialism. However, by the late 1860s some perceptive observers who examined the wars of German unification, were beginning to recognize that armed forces designed for these missions might not suffice in the future. These wars were won by large conscript armies and the spread of such organizations to the other European powers was bound to diminish the military potential of Britain's smaller professional army. The British might have been able to make good some of the deficiencies of the Cardwell system, and particularly the army's inability to expand its numbers beyond a certain level, if they had been able to mobilize more imperial, and particularly Indian, resources. British politicians were apt to see the Indian army as an almost inexhaustible imperial reserve, largely because its numbers were not voted upon by Parliament, because its cost, and the cost of the British troops stationed in India, were met by Indian tax-payers and because Indian troops were used outside India on several occasions after 1857. In reality, after the mutiny and until the First World War forced their hand, the Victorians and Edwardians were careful to restrict the number of troops they raised in India and the uses to which they put them. In the early nineteenth century an Indian soldier was thought to cost only half as much as a British private and the East India Company's army made Britain a major military power east of Suez. But in November 1858, after the mutiny, the company's army was disbanded. All but 5,000 of the company's Europeans took their discharge and the remainder became part of the Crown's army. As a precaution the number of sepoys was also sharply reduced in order that the ratio of Indian to European forces could be fixed at about 2:1. In 1869 there were 64,800 European and 120,000 Indian troops in India. To preserve internal order, and if necessary overawe the Indian part of the army, all artillery, arsenals and fortresses were concentrated in European hands. Indian battalions were usually brigaded with European battalions so that no important station would be without reliable European troops. In 1867 a Commons Select Committee tried to determine if it might be possible to use Indian troops on general service outside India and to garrison certain colonies. But after hearing the evidence of the viceroy, Sir John Lawrence, who deprecated using Indian troops to garrison European colonies 'on the ground that the impression upon the native mind, derived from a closer view of European institutions, would be the reverse of favourable', the committee recommended that they should only be used in non-European colonies and in small numbers.[11] The need to maintain domestic tranquillity inside India took precedence over the wholesale exploitation of India's military potential. Between 1815 and 1880 that hardly mattered. The defence of the empire had been a manageable task because it had rarely been menaced by another great power. How it would continue to be defended in an era when changes which were inimical to British interests were occurring in the international environment remained to be seen.

Britain did not pursue a policy of diplomatic isolation after 1815. She was hardly less ready than the other great European powers to involve herself in the ententes and alliances of the European state system. Her security continued to rest upon the preservation of the balance of power in Europe and she safeguarded that balance by judicious interventions in the diplomatic system rather than by remaining aloof from it. The Crimean War represented Britain's one major military foray to the continent. Her conduct exhibited some, but not all of the features of 'the British way in warfare'. Her original expeditionary force of about 27,000 men represented only about 16 per cent of the regular army on the British establishment. The bulk of the army remained in the colonies or at home. Had it not been for the presence of a larger French force, Sebastopol would probably have remained in Russian hands. But the army in the Crimea was a British force, unsupported by foreign mercenaries. The era considered in this chapter represented the period of Britain's undisputed naval supremacy. It was therefore ironic that it was distinguished by the fact that the eighteenth-century peacetime norm, when spending on sea services regularly exceeded spending on land services, was reversed. After 1815 Britain was a great land power and her empire needed garrisons.

The paradigms outlined in the introduction to this book were hypotheses designed to analyse the way in which Britain conducted her great-power wars. But with the exception of the Crimean War Britain did not engage in any great-power wars during this period. The poor showing of the army during the war was not simply the result of a penny-pinching Treasury. The Crimean War was an aberrant experience for the Victorian armed forces. They were not designed to fight a first-class European power on the continent. Notions of a 'British way in warfare' drawn from Britain's experiences of fighting European powers, are not an appropriate tool to analyse her experiences in the colonies. British forces were intended to police the empire and to meet what was in reality the remote contingency of an attack on the home islands, functions they fulfilled with considerable success between 1815 and 1880.

6 The Rise and Fall of the 'Blue Water' Policy

Between 1815 and 1880 Britain was basking in a benign international and economic environment. She was growing richer thanks to the Industrial Revolution, she could fund her services and her security was only intermittently threatened by another great power. However, starting in the 1860s with the unification of Italy and Germany, this congenial world order began to crumble. By the 1880s imperial rivalries, the establishment of conflicting alliance blocs in Europe and an arms race induced by new technologies and the growing belief, prompted by the spread of social Darwinist ideas about the inevitability of war, were combining to render her defence policies obsolete. This happened just when her growing dependence on imported foods and raw materials was adding to her vulnerability. Policy-makers had to search for a new strategic synthesis to safeguard Britain and her empire.

Since the report of the Royal Commission on the Defence of the United Kingdom of 1859, thinking about defence policy had revolved around the notion that Britain was a fortress to be defended by the army and the volunteers. The navy only had itself to blame for the way in which it had been relegated. Naval officers were too absorbed in understanding new technologies to spend much time considering how they ought to be applied to the defence of Britain and her empire. A 'bricks and mortar' policy was appropriate when foreign powers posed only an intermittent threat to the home islands and hardly any threat at all to Britain's imperial possessions. But in the late 1870s that was no longer the case. Egypt was an important British interest, even before the opening of the Suez Canal in 1869, because it represented the shortest route to India. Since 1838 Britain had based her Mediterranean strategy upon her predominant naval power, the maintenance of Turkish power as a check on Russian expansion and on tacit acceptance that she would share paramountcy with France at Cairo and Constantinople. At the Congress of Berlin in 1878 Disraeli tried to prop up the Turkish Empire as a barrier to Russian expansion. He guaranteed Asiatic Turkey against the Russians and occupied Cyprus as a base from which to launch a riposte if the Russians continued their advance towards the Straits.

Gladstone fought the 1880 election on a platform condemning Disraeli's apparent willingness to threaten war in disregard of the rights of other nations, but his own government was dragged into one costly foreign entanglement after another. Egypt was legally part of the Turkish Empire and in the 1860s and 1870s the British and French had worked together to transform the Egyptian regime into a liberal and, after its bankruptcy in 1875, solvent state. What they succeeded in doing was laying the foundations for a nationalist backlash against Western control which culminated in a revolt by the Egyptian army in 1881. Gladstone was reluctant to intervene directly in Egyptian domestic politics but his Whig colleagues insisted that Britain could not afford to stand on the side-lines for fear that if they did nothing, the French might act unilaterally and gain control of the Canal. After trying and failing to secure French co-operation and waiting in vain for the Turks to put down the revolt, the Cabinet reluctantly agreed to invade Egypt to crush the nationalists and install a more pliant regime in Cairo. The invasion culminated in Wolseley's defeat of the nationalist army at Tel-el-Kebir in September 1882. But the political and diplomatic cost of the operation was high. The British looked in vain for a pro-British ruler who could govern the country without their assistance and so began an occupation of Egypt which lasted for nearly seventy years.

Hardly had the British established a new regime in Cairo than their empire was menaced in Asia. Since the end of the first Afghan War the British had accepted that geography made a direct Russian threat to the north-west frontier of India unlikely. In 1863 the Russian frontier was 500 miles from the Oxus. But twenty years later when the Russians annexed Bukhara, the Afghan and Russian frontiers were coterminous and the government of India was once again fearful of Russian influence in Afghanistan. Disraeli's administration failed to persuade the Amir of Afghanistan to accept the guidance of a British agent to keep watch on Russian intrigues and in 1878 the viceroy failed to force an adviser on him at the point of a bayonet. British prestige had been dented and had to be restored. In November 1878 the British declared war on Afghanistan and in 1879 placed a new amir on the throne who would accept British control over his foreign policy.

But in 1884 the Russians annexed Merv, began to march towards Herat and in March 1885 clashed with Afghan troops at Penjdeh on the Afghan border. After occupying Egypt the British could not now expect the sultan to act as the first line of defence of the British Empire. The fact that the Turks were improving the fortifications of the Dardanelles whilst ignoring those along the Bosphorus threw doubt upon the practicality of countering the Russian advance by threatening her Black Sea coast. Sir Frederick Roberts, the commander-in-chief in India in 1885, believed that India had to be defended as far forward as possible, for even a minor British military setback along the Indian frontier might encourage disaffection in India and a second mutiny. Until 1885 Gladstone and some of his ministers had been sceptical of arguments in favour of defending India in Afghanistan. But the Penjdeh incident removed this issue from party politics.

Both Gladstone, and Salisbury when he succeeded him in June 1885, agreed that Herat had to be defended. This crisis was settled by negotiation. But for the next twenty years British defence planners were left with the seemingly insoluble problem. How could the British, who possessed a large navy but only a small army, defend a lengthy land frontier in Asia against a power with a much larger army which was consolidating its advances by laying railways and making itself increasingly invulnerable to amphibious attack?

The potential dangers of this new international environment were brought home to politicians and the public in the early 1880s. Seen against the background of the Anglo-French estrangement, the possibility that a Channel tunnel might be constructed ignited another invasion scare in 1882. In September 1884 W. T. Stead, editor of the *Pall Mall Gazette*, alerted his readers to the fact that for several years the French had been engaged in a major shipbuilding programme and had almost as many capital ships as the British. Faced with the possibility that they might have to engage in war with two European great powers simultaneously, the Gladstone government added £5,500,000 to the navy estimates spread over the next five years. That satisfied the public's agitation, but there was no guarantee that another panic might not erupt in the future. The re-emergence of a major threat to British security from two continental powers left the British with four possible options. They could resolve their difficulties with their rivals by negotiation. They could seek allies with whom to share their defence burdens. They could counter their rivals by spending more on defence. Or they could reshape their defence policy so that the army and navy were better prepared to overcome the problems now confronting them.

In the 1880s and 1890s the British enjoyed only mixed success when they attempted to resolve their difficulties with their rivals by negotiation. Since 1879, when Germany had allied herself with Austria-Hungary, the great powers of continental Europe had begun to be divided into two alliance systems. The Russians joined the two autocratic powers in 1881 to form the League of the Three Emperors and in 1882 Germany, Austria and Italy formed the Triple Alliance. The League of the Three Emperors crumbled in the early 1890s and this enabled France to break out of her isolation by forming an entente with Russia in 1891, a military convention in 1892 and in 1894 the two powers formed the Dual Alliance. Two power blocs, the Dual Alliance and the Triple Alliance, now confronted each other.

Britain remained formally aloof from both blocs. Her occupation of Egypt made a *rapprochement* with France difficult and the diplomatic costs of the Anglo-French estrangement were high, for Bismarck exploited it to extract colonial concessions from the British in Africa and the Pacific. But the men who dominated British politics in the closing decades of the century had reached maturity before 1850. They formed their vision of Britain's place in the world before the structural changes which transformed the European state system in the 1860s and 1870s had occurred. Gladstone continued to place his faith in the Concert of Europe even after it was past its zenith. Salisbury based his foreign policy on a more pragmatic *realpolitik*. Neither man was an isolationist who believed that Britain could safely ignore what happened on the continent. But neither thought that the new diplomatic constellations which were emerging in Europe in the 1880s required Britain to become tied to one or other of the alliance blocs. Salisbury believed that working arrangements, like the Mediterranean agreements of 1887 with Austria-Hungary and Italy, were acceptable, but binding alliances involving a definite military commitment to a continental power were not necessary. In Asia he tried to exclude Russian influence from India's neighbours and in Africa he ensured that Britain controlled those regions essential to her imperial communications. In South Africa he clung tenaciously to the Cape. In North Africa he maintained British control over the Canal and by 1898 the British had advanced deep into the interior of Africa and conquered the entire Nile valley for fear that if they did not control the head-waters of the Nile, some other power would do so and undermine their control of Egypt by depriving her of water.

Diplomacy did not offer an easy solution to the problems of British defence policy. Nor could the British spend their way out of trouble. The economic predominance the Industrial Revolution had conferred upon Britain began to slip in the 1860s as industrialization gathered pace in Europe and the United States. Whereas in 1870 Britain accounted for 32 per cent of the world's manufacturing capacity and 25 per cent of world trade, by 1913 the comparable figures had fallen to 15 per cent and 14 per cent. But Britain's relative decline as a world economic power was accompanied by a rise in her net national income (measured at 1900 prices) from £622,000,000 in 1865 to £1,750,000,000 in 1900. In theory a great deal more wealth was available to spend on defence. In practice the sums governments were prepared to devote to defence were restricted by prevailing economic ideas. By the late 1880s the growth of public spending, which was caused not only by growing defence budgets but also by the determination of politicians to placate the new electorate created by the 1867 and 1884 Reform Acts by some measures of social reform, was causing politicians and Treasury officials increasing concern. In the 1850s the central government's budget had averaged £59,600,000 per annum. By 1887 the budget had reached £87,000,000. Both Liberal and Conservative politicians feared that Britain might be reaching the limit of her financial resources and that further increases in public spending could only be met by new methods of public finance which would sap the nation's wealth-creating capacity.

Liberal fiscal orthodoxy, accepted by both major political parties, dictated that the state should limit its interference in the economy. Minimal government spending was desirable because it would leave money to fructify in the pockets of the people. Budgets ought to be balanced, peacetime spending should be met from tax revenues and long-term borrowing should be avoided in peacetime so as to preserve the government's credit for wartime expenditure which might be too large to be met from taxation. Indirect taxes on articles of consumption should be kept as low as possible, not only for social reasons but also because it was necessary to avoid the temptation of imposing them as a form of tariff. Direct taxes on incomes should also be kept low so that they could form a financial reserve which the government could draw upon in wartime to cover the interest payments on any wartime loans. Although government revenues rose in the early 1890s, by 1895 Treasury officials were afraid that in the near future they would not increase sufficiently rapidly to meet growing spending. The range of options open to the government was narrow. An increase in the income tax would annoy wealthy voters and eat into the state's wartime fiscal reserves. Increasing existing indirect taxes might cause consumption, and therefore revenue, to drop. New indirect taxes might appear to be a step towards protection; and any increase in indirect taxation was bound to encounter political opposition from the consumer. Suspension of the Sinking Fund would reduce the government's ability to borrow in an emergency.

The government could neither negotiate nor spend its way out of difficulty. Defence planners therefore had to reshape defence policy so that both services were better prepared to overcome the problems created by this new international environment. Some publicists had already begun to develop the concept that imperial defence should be based on coherent planning and preparations involving the adoption of consistent plans by the army and navy. In 1867, when a Royal Marine captain, John Colomb, published a short book entitled *The Protection of Our Commerce and Distribution of Our Naval Forces Considered*, the navy found a voice to challenge the prevailing army-centred view of defence policy. Colomb argued that Britain owed her position as a world power to the fact that she was a worldwide trading empire. Her security depended upon safeguarding the home islands, her imperial possessions and the maritime communications which linked them. A policy which concentrated overmuch on the defence of the home islands was inadequate because it would jeopardize Britain's overseas interests. Colomb insisted that it was necessary to consider the empire as a single unit. As a maritime empire, Britain had to give precedence to her navy. An invasion of the British Isles would succeed only if an enemy first wrested control of the seas from the navy. The navy had to be concentrated around the English Channel, both to protect Britain from invasion and to safeguard shipping as it approached that most important bottle-neck. But trade in distant waters also required protection and that could best be effected by stationing warships in secure bases overseas. That insight was not new. The navy had needed such overseas bases in the eighteenth century. What was new was Colomb's insistence that the introduction of steam-powered vessels, which could only carry a limited supply of coal, made the possession and security of such bases doubly important. Colomb was not an anti-army advocate. He recognized that soldiers were needed to garrison overseas bases and to prevent enemy raids on Britain, a function most 'blue water' theorists thought could be fulfilled if enough troops were retained at home to deal with an enemy force of 10,000 troops. And they were needed to wage small colonial wars and to mount amphibious operations against the enemy's shore in conjunction with the fleet. After 1872 he also began to argue that as the empire represented a single commercial unit, it was only proper that the colonies should contribute in proportion to their means to the cost of imperial defence.

Colomb had hoped that his theory, by defining the roles of the army and navy, would produce harmony between the two services. It did the opposite. His argument that Britain was a great maritime empire ignored the fact that she was also a great continental land power in India. His attempt to dismiss the problem of Indian defence in a phrase, 'India must stand alone' was not a recipe for a coherent policy.[1] In this and subsequent works Colomb and other thinkers like his brother Admiral P. H. Colomb and Mahan, whose books were enthusiastically received in Britain in the 1890s, developed ideas about imperial defence which formed the basis of what was called the 'Blue Water' School. The war scare with Russia of 1878-9 led to the establishment of a Royal Commission on the Defence of British Possessions and Commerce Abroad presided over by Lord Carnarvon which endorsed Colomb's ideas and they were popularized by pressure groups like the Navy League, founded in 1895 and the Imperial Federation League and the Imperial Federation (Defence) Committee. They warned that without careful preparations Britain and her empire might find themselves defenceless in the face of the kind of lightning attack that had caused the defeat of Prussia's enemies between 1864 and 1871.

In the 1880s such preparations were hampered by the almost complete absence of inter-service co-operation and the lack of trained staff officers at the War Office and Admiralty. The course at the army's Staff College became much more practical and produced a steady, albeit small, flow of able officers. But students were given little encouragement to study larger questions of imperial defence and their usefulness to the army remained limited. The War Office and Admiralty established their own intelligence departments, the former in 1873 and the latter in 1887. Both produced valuable intelligence reports, but neither service possessed a planning staff to use them or a department charged with policy-making, operational planning and inter-service liaison. In 1885 a Colonial Defence Committee was established but its task was not to offer strategic advice to the Cabinet but merely to gather and circulate the work of government departments on particular aspects of colonial defence.

Few soldiers looked kindly upon a theory of imperial defence which relegated the army to second place. The quarrel between the 'Bricks and Mortar' and 'Blue Water' Schools came to a head between 1886 and 1889. It was settled in favour of the latter. In 1886 the Director of Military Intelligence told a Commons Select Committee that he might have only one week's warning of an invasion and that three corps of regulars and three corps of volunteers would be required to protect London. The debate became a public issue in 1888. The 1888 fleet manoeuvres seemed to show that, at a time when the French and Russians were increasing their naval strength, the Royal Navy was too weak to blockade even a single enemy in port and continue to perform its other wartime functions. Both the Commander-in-Chief, the Duke of Cambridge and Wolseley, now the Adjutant-General, highlighted the danger of invasion and condemned ministers for trying to win political popularity by cutting the service estimates. In December 1888 Edward Stanhope, the Secretary of State for War, provided the army with a statement of its purposes which gave a high priority to home defence, placing it after the need to give aid to the civil power and to garrison the empire, but before the likelihood that it might have to furnish an expeditionary force to be sent to the continent. This order of priorities endured until 1906. The Admiralty replied that a successful French invasion presupposed the destruction of the entire Royal Navy, something they refused to contemplate.

The Salisbury administration came down on the side of the 'blue water' theorists. In March 1889 it opted for a 'blue water' strategy, marked by the introduction of a Naval Defence Act costing £21,500,000 to be spread over five years. It also insisted that Britain had to maintain a fleet of battleships which was the equal of the world's next two largest fleets. As a consolation prize the army received a mere £600,000. The decision to maintain the navy on a two-power standard was consonant with the dominant image of naval warfare, popularized by Mahan, that command of the seas would result from a series of decisive battles fought between fleets of capital ships. In the 1890s the standard was accepted by both political parties as a symbol of British maritime superiority and as the ultimate guarantee of the security of the empire. It was originally invoked against France and Italy, the second and third naval powers. But in 1893 Italy's place was usurped by Russia and the Russians established a squadron at Toulon to co-operate with the French Mediterranean fleet. Gladstone was content to ignore this threat but when the majority of his Cabinet insisted that the navy had to be augmented he resigned. The First Lord, Lord Spencer, promptly laid down seven new battleships and a number of smaller vessels.

Salisbury's second initiative had been to establish a Royal Commission under the Marquis of Hartington to investigate the army and navy and their relationship with the Treasury. The commission issued two reports, in 1889 and 1890. It discovered that the formulation of a coherent imperial defence policy was hamstrung by the jealousies of the defence departments. They were determined to safeguard their own particular responsibilities and there was no consultation between them. Nor was any person or committee charged with preparing imperial defence plans. To perform that function the commission recommended that a defence committee of ministers and service personnel should be established with powers to examine the service estimates before they were submitted to the Cabinet, to advise the Cabinet on defence matters and to devise a plan for imperial defence. The post of Commander-in-Chief ought to be abolished and his roles parcelled out amongst the members of a new War Office council. Finally, the commission suggested that a general staff ought to be established to study the empire's military needs, to advise the secretary of state and liaise with the Admiralty.

The commission's main report could have represented a major advance towards establishing a more rational machinery for defence planning. But its recommendations were emasculated by two dissenting reports. Lord Randolph Churchill recommended that the separate service ministries should be united into a single Ministry of Defence presided over by a minister who was both an MP and a senior service officer, whilst Sir Henry Campbell-Bannerman, a former Liberal Secretary of State for War, deprecated the establishment of a general staff because he feared that it would take control of military policy out of the hands of civilian politicians. Campbell-Bannerman's suspicions were symptomatic of a problem which was to bedevil the development of defence policy until after 1918. Before the mid-nineteenth century Britain's civil and military elites overlapped. Between 1734 and 1832 one MP in six had held a commission in the army. The commanders of many of the expeditions which Britain had sent to the continent were men like William III, Marlborough and Wellington. They were both politicians and soldiers and personified the overlap of the two elites. Bitter and prolonged struggles between the military and the civil power had been rare. However, in the second half of the nineteenth century the expansion of the electorate, the declining economic and political power of the landed gentry and the increasing prevalence of middle-class 'professional' politicians like Campbell-Bannerman meant that the two elites became divorced and communications between them were marred by mutual suspicions. The eventual solution which brought the two elites into more amicable communication again was the development of bureaucratic committee structures through which the military and their political masters could attempt to resolve their disagreements. But until these structures began to function with some degree of efficiency in the 1920s and 1930s, the two elites were frequently at loggerheads. It was no accident that this period was marred by incidents like the Curragh 'mutiny' of 1914 and the bitter intrigues of Haig, Robertson and Lloyd George between 1916 and 1918.

However, neither Churchill nor Campbell-Bannerman was responsible for scotching the Hartington Commission's main recommendations. That distinction fell to the queen and the Duke of Cambridge, who claimed that the monarch's constitutional position would be undermined if the office of commander-in-chief were abolished. To their voices were added those of Roberts and Wolseley, both of whom wanted to succeed Cambridge. Salisbury compromised. He established a War Office Council, but retained the commander-in-chief as its first military member and did not set up a general staff. In 1891 a Joint Naval and Military Committee was formed but it confined itself to technical matters concerning the defence of ports and coaling stations. In 1895 Salisbury's nephew A. J. Balfour, who had a passionate interest in defence questions, persuaded the Prime Minister to establish a permanent Defence Committee of the Cabinet. But the fact that it was presided over by the Duke of Devonshire, and not by the Prime Minister, was an indication of Salisbury's lack of enthusiasm for such bureaucratic initiatives and the committee was relegated to settling inter-departmental disputes rather than trying to concert imperial defence policy.

More might have been achieved towards creating a more rational approach to defence planning if the fiscal pressures of the early 1890s had been maintained. But they were not. The defence estimates rose in the late nineteenth century from £25,200,000 in 1880 to £40,200,000 in 1898. But the share of public spending which defence absorbed rose less steeply and a 'blue water' policy seemed to have reduced the threat of bankruptcy produced by spiralling estimates. Although there were some criticisms of the shortcomings of the Cardwell system, judged by results it appeared to work. The army was generally victorious in the series of colonial campaigns it fought in Africa and Asia between 1882 and 1899. The two-power standard seemed to have given the navy an adequate margin of superiority over its rivals.

The appearance of success was deceptive. An immediate fiscal crisis was only postponed by a fortuitous growth in prosperity and revenues between 1896 and 1899. Increasing estimates did not mean that the British were purchasing a greater measure of security. The application of industrial technology to weapons systems meant that individual units faced more rapid technological obsolescence as rival powers introduced warships or rifles which could sail faster or shoot farther. Nothing added so much to the growing feeling of insecurity as the fear that unless the British purchased the latest technology their empire might be ruined. But each new generation of weapons was more expensive than the system it replaced. The *Warrior* launched in 1860 cost six times as much as a late-eighteenth-century wooden ship-of-the-line. By 1888 the newest generation of capital ship cost twice as much again. Too much concentration on the need to match the French and Russian fleets hid the fact that Britain's global naval predominance had slipped. In 1883 she had possessed 38 capital ships compared to the 40 maintained by the combined fleets of France, Russia, USA, Japan, Germany and Italy. By 1897 the latter nations combined possessed 96 capital ships compared to Britain's 62. On land Britain's adherence to voluntary recruiting at a time when her European neighbours had adopted conscription meant that a wide gap had opened between British military manpower and that of her potential European enemies. By 1897, when the British army, including the first-class army reserve and the Indian troops of the Indian army numbered about 420,000 men, Russia possessed a war establishment (that is, standing forces plus mobilizable reserves) of about 4,000,000 men, France of 3,500,000 men, Germany of 3,400,000 men and Austria of 2,600,000. men. If the British ever engaged in a prolonged continental land war in Europe or Asia against one or more of these powers, they would either have to raise a conscript army or enlist the support of an ally who had one.

It took the imperial crisis of 1899–1902 to demonstrate that a 'blue water' policy could not defend Britain and her empire. The manpower demands of the Boer War exceeded anything the War Office had contemplated. By 1900 Britain was bereft of an efficient home defence force. The army began the war without a strategic appreciation or a plan of campaign and its operations were hampered at every turn by inadequate numbers of trained staff officers. After the three defeats which the army suffered in the 'Black Week' of December 1899 there was a storm of criticism in the press and Parliament. The government promptly replaced the commander-in-chief in South Africa, Sir Redvers Buller, with Lord Roberts and by June 1900, when he occupied Pretoria, it appeared that Roberts had won the war. The government rushed to capitalize on his victory by holding a 'Khaki election' at which they won a handsome majority. But they rejoiced too soon. Although their main towns had been occupied by the British, the Boers did not capitulate. They waged a guerrilla war and did not finally surrender until May 1902.

In 1899 the British had expected a short, cheap and victorious conflict. What they got was a lengthy and expensive war which helped to increase the budget from £117,000,000 in 1899 to £205,000,000 in 1902. In 1903, a year after peace was declared, it had fallen to only £194,000,000. Initially the government resorted to the traditional means of war finance. The income tax and duties on tobacco and tea were increased, the Sinking Fund was suspended and borrowing increased the national debt by a quarter. When these steps proved to be insufficient they resorted to a controversial duty on imported grain and attempted, with scant success, to persuade the self-governing Dominions to meet some of the cost of the naval defence of the empire. These measures were acceptable in wartime but they offended too many of the canons of political economy to be continued in peacetime. Even before the war ended the question of controlling the growth in public spending was at the top of the political agenda. The need to reduce the rise in public expenditure by limiting the growth in defence spending was one of the major factors which encouraged both the Conservative and Liberal governments after 1900 to tackle some of the thornier problems of defence. It is impossible to understand British diplomacy and defence policy after 1900 without reference to the widespread fear that the country and the government lacked the means to pay for an adequate defence policy. These constraints and fears have underlain British defence policy for almost the whole of the twentieth century.

The problem of balancing needs and resources was made difficult by Britain's precarious international position. The Boers' prolonged resistance revealed disquieting facts about Britain's vulnerability as a world power. The great powers gloated at the early defeats which the army suffered and another invasion scare swept the country in 1900. The British remained wedded to a 'blue water' defence policy but the war showed that some major shifts of resources were necessary if that policy were to remain viable. Between 1901 and 1907 the British could not spend their way out of their difficulties, so they reduced their strategic overextension by coming to political arrangements with potential enemies, they attempted to draw more heavily upon the resources of their empire and they tried to make their armed forces more efficient.

In the 1890s Salisbury had intimated to the French and Russians his readiness to come to a settlement with them over their colonial differences based upon some mutual concessions. This was a conservative solution to Britain's difficulties. It implied no major break with his preference for remaining formally uncommitted to either of the alliance systems. A more radical solution was advocated by some Conservatives and Liberal Unionists such as Joseph Chamberlain. The Far Eastern crisis of 1897–8 encouraged Chamberlain to begin a private diplomatic quest for an alliance with Germany. His initiative appealed neither to Salisbury nor to the Germans. The latter preferred to see the Russians engaged in the Far East rather than free to menace their own eastern frontier. When a second round of discussions in 1901 revealed that the price for German support against Russian expansion in China was a British commitment to the defence of central Europe, the British abandoned their quest. They would gain little if they reduced their difficulties in the Far East only to see them multiplied in Europe. The only other country interested in checking Russia in the Far East was Japan. The Anglo-Japanese Alliance of 1902 was acceptable because it was a local pact and because the Japanese possessed a navy which was sufficiently powerful, if it operated in conjunction with British vessels in the Far East, to check the combined Franco-Russian fleet.

However, many politicians were disturbed at its implications, for it included a pledge that at some unspecified date Britain might be obliged to fight on behalf of her ally. That prospect loomed closer in February 1904 when the Russo-Japanese war began. Neither the French nor the British wanted to be dragged into war against each other at the behest of their eastern allies and the British welcomed a better relationship with France because it would reduce their dependence on Germany for diplomatic support. In April 1904 the two powers signed the Anglo-French Entente. Germany was so antagonized at the way in which they had settled their outstanding colonial differences without any reference to her that she tried to destroy the entente by provoking a crisis in Morocco in March 1905. The initiative backfired and helped to begin to give an anti-German tinge to what had been intended to be only a settlement of colonial disagreements. The process of reducing Britain's military liabilities to more manageable proportions was carried further in 1904 by the Balfour government's decision to withdraw almost all of its remaining forces from the Western hemisphere on the grounds that war with the United States was unlikely and unwinnable. It was completed when the Campbell-Bannerman Liberal administration, which came to power in 1905, signed an agreement with Russia in 1907. The accession of Sir Edward Grey to the Foreign Office did not significantly alter the direction of foreign policy. Grey supported France throughout the concluding stages of the Moroccan crisis, warning Germany that if she launched an unprovoked attack against France, Britain would not remain neutral. Grey's predecessors had been seeking an Anglo-Russian agreement since 1894. Russia's defeat by Japan in 1905 made the Russians willing, for the first time, to compromise with the British. Grey seized this opportunity because he wanted Russia to counterbalance German power in Europe and because a settlement with Russia represented the only viable solution to the Indian defence problem.

The British garrison in India numbered about 231,000 men but in an emergency only 74,000 could be deployed in Afghanistan. The remainder would have to be retained in India on internal security duties. In 1901 and 1905 the potential Russian threat grew in the minds of British planners as the Russians constructed a railway passing north of the Caspian and linking the cities of Orenburg and Tashkent. By 1905 the British estimated that when it was completed the Russians could deploy 400,000 troops within sixteen months of the start of a war. A 'blue water' defence policy offered no solution to the problem of how to wage a land war in Central Asia for, as the First Sea Lord said in 1904, 'Russia's geographical position is such that she is very un assailable [sic] to a sea power with a small army'.[2] Russia's defeat offered a breathing-space, but the military authorities in Simla were convinced that within a few years she would have recovered. The British delayed renewing the Anglo-Japanese treaty in 1905 until Japan agreed to extend it to cover India, but the British never saw reliance on the Japanese as anything other than a last resort. The army in India remained committed to meeting a Russian advance at Kabul and Kandahar in Afghanistan rather than along the Afghan–Indian frontier. The few sceptics who insisted that a Russian invasion from Afghanistan or a British defence along the Kabul–Kandahar line were logistically impossible, were ignored. But to carry out their preferred strategy, the War Office estimated that the British would have to send 463,000 troops to reinforce India in the first year of a war and that the Indian railway network would have to be extended towards Afghanistan. The Liberal governments shied away from that. It would have been ruinously expensive and it would have demanded a complete recasting of their military policy. Men in such numbers could only have been raised by conscription. That was anathema to them, not least because of its economic impact and the votes it would have cost them. The only solution was to reach a political accommodation with Russia.

The significance of the Anglo–Russian agreement of 1907 was that it removed the immediate possibility that the Russians would continue to exert pressure around the frontiers of India. The combined significance of the diplomatic arrangements Britain reached with Japan, France and Russia between 1902 and 1907 was that although they did not obviate the need for some remodelling of the services, they enabled the British to postpone a wholesale recasting of their military arrangements until 1915–16.

When the British tried to draw more upon imperial resources they were disappointed. Since the 1860s the Treasury had believed that the land defences of the colonies should be the responsibility of their local governments and that empire-wide expenses incurred by the navy ought to be shared. It was a policy which most colonies resisted and the stronger their own representative institutions, the more successful they were. In 1897 the Conservative chancellor, Sir William Hicks Beach, suggested to the self-governing Dominions that they ought to contribute more to the cost of the Royal Navy. In 1902 the Colonial Secretary, Joseph Chamberlain, repeated the suggestion. They made little headway, not least because the imperial government wanted colonial money but would not grant the colonies control of the ships their money bought.

The inability of the imperial government to tap colonial resources to any real extent became significant because of the widening estrangement between Britain and Germany. The emergence of German economic power in the late nineteenth century underpinned a growing Anglo-German antagonism in the 1880s and 1890s that expressed itself in Britain in growing resentment at German penetration of British domestic and overseas markets and in a series of colonial quarrels. But after 1900 the crux of their antagonism was the Germans' decision to build a fleet. In 1898 and 1900 they had passed two Navy Laws which envisaged the creation of a fleet of thirty-eight capital ships. By 1907 the German navy minister, Admiral Tirpitz, was privately talking of building a fleet of sixty capital ships. Tirpitz's 'risk fleet' was designed to exert such political pressure on the British that they would become amenable to Germany's world-power aspirations. They would not dare to attack it for fear that they would lose so many ships that the Royal Navy would be too weak to resist a Franco-Russian combination. The challenge posed by the German fleet was of a different order of magnitude compared to that posed by the Russian, Japanese or United States fleets. The latter might threaten Britain's colonial possessions but distance made it unlikely that they would ever menace Britain herself. The German fleet was intended to do just that.

Tirpitz relied on the continuation of bad relations between Britain and the Dual Alliance to enable Germany to maintain good relations with Britain whilst Germany passed through the 'danger zone' when her fleet was sufficiently large to alarm the British but too small to deter them. However, as early as 1902 the Admiralty recognized that the German fleet was being created to threaten Britain. Faced by tightening budgetary constraints and unable to squeeze significant extra resources from the empire, the Admiralty's response to the growth of the other European fleets was to concentrate its most modern warships in home waters and to scrap large numbers of smaller vessels scattered across the globe. Britain surrendered the worldwide naval supremacy she had enjoyed for much of the nineteenth century to protect the home islands. For some time, however, that fact was concealed from the public because the accepted way of measuring naval power, counting capital ships within the framework of the two-power standard, left Britain with a clear lead over her next major rivals. But by the late 1890s the Admiralty recognized that although the two-power standard might give the Royal Navy superiority in European waters against France and Russia, it was insufficient to maintain her superiority against the growing fleets of the USA and Japan. Britain could not spend enough to meet these peripheral threats, nor dare she detach sufficient forces from home waters or the Mediterranean to counter them. Political accommodations with the peripheral powers were her only option. It was for that reason that in 1901 the Admiralty advised that Britain should not oppose the construction of the Panama Canal, even though it would increase the power of the US fleet. It was also why they supported the Anglo-Japanese treaty. The Admiralty continued to talk in public as if the two-power standard meant command of the sea whilst simultaneously surrendering that command in the Western hemisphere and Far East. Henceforth the security of Britain's possessions in those parts of the world no longer rested upon the Royal Navy but upon a much more fragile edifice, the goodwill of Japan and the USA.

In October 1904 Sir John Fisher became First Sea Lord. He brought to the Admiralty a single-minded determination to improve the efficiency of the navy and to cut the estimates. He began by inaugurating a major redistribution of the fleet. The China, East Indies and Australia stations were amalgamated into a single Eastern fleet based on Singapore. The Pacific station was abandoned, the North Atlantic, South Atlantic and West Africa stations were combined and the number of vessels outside home waters was reduced by scrapping small vessels which might otherwise have been easy prey for a handful of fast enemy cruisers. One result of his scrapping policy was that in 1905 the naval estimates fell for the first time in a decade. The crews of the redundant vessels were redeployed into active squadrons or used to form nucleus crews for ships in reserve. Most significant of all, Fisher redistributed the navy's capital ships. When he first elaborated his plans in November 1904 in the middle of the Russo-Japanese War, his new dispositions were not directed against the German fleet but were designed to meet all probable contingencies, including a possible war with the Dual Alliance. But the destruction of the Russian fleet at Tsushima in May 1905 and the first Moroccan crisis caused him to redraft his original plan and to concentrate the navy's capital ships to counter the German fleet. Before his reforms, 16 battleships had been deployed as part of the Channel and Home fleets and 17 had been deployed in the Mediterranean and on the China station. After his redistribution, 24 battleships were deployed with the Channel and Atlantic fleets, 9 in the Mediterranean and none on the China station. Between 1904 and 1906 the Admiralty recognized that the era of the 'Pax Britannica' had ended.

Throughout the Boer War critics assailed the army for its poor staff work, its outdated weapons and its lack of tactical skill. The war demonstrated that the Cardwell system could not supply the manpower needed to wage a large colonial war. To make good its deficiencies the War Office was compelled to lift its bar on using some volunteers abroad and more might have been sent but for the fact that only a fraction of the volunteer force had received sufficient training. In March 1900 there was not a single regular battalion in Britain. Salisbury appointed a new Secretary of State for War, St John Brodrick, and in

1901 he proposed to make good the worst deficiencies of the Cardwell system by dividing the United Kingdom into six districts, in each of which he wanted to base an army corps. The first three would consist of 120,000 regulars and would constitute a new expeditionary force. The remaining three would be a mixture of regulars and auxiliaries and would perform home defence duties. His proposals required an additional 11,500 regulars, would raise the estimates to £30,000,000, or 50 per cent more than what they had been in 1898 and he was prepared to introduce conscription if sufficient volunteers did not enlist. The opposition, confident that the navy could safeguard the home islands, condemned the cost of his proposals and disparaged conscription as an infringement of political rights and as likely to strain the economy. The Conservatives, with varying degrees of enthusiasm, initially rallied to his side but as the war continued, they also became uneasy at the projected costs. Brodrick's ideas were undermined by the report of the Royal Commission on the War in South Africa published in July 1903. The majority report recited many of the army's known deficiencies, but did not outline a plan for remedying them. But one of the commissioners, Lord Esher, was more ambitious. Esher had been one of the joint secretaries of the Hartington Commission and was passionately interested in all aspects of imperial defence. His minority report recommended the abolition of the post of commander-in-chief, the establishment of a council at the War Office similar in constitution to the Board of Admiralty and the appointment of an inspector general, responsible to the secretary of state, to oversee the efficiency of the army.

Some steps to improve the co-ordination of defence policy had been taken even before the Royal Commission's report was published. In July 1902 Salisbury had resigned as Prime Minister and was replaced by Balfour. Balfour recognized that the lack of co-ordination between the services had created a strategic vacuum in which uncertainty flourished. In December 1902 he reorganized the Cabinet's Defence Committee into the Committee of Imperial Defence (CID) and set it to work to discuss questions of concern to both services such as home defence and the defence of the North-West Frontier. In September 1903 he replaced Brodrick with H. O. Arnold-Forster and establishhed a small Committee of Esher, Sir George Cllarke, a former seccretary of the Colonial Defence Committee and Sir John Fisher, to reorganize the War Office. The Esher Committee completed its work in July 1904. It recommended that the CID should be strengthened by the addition of a permanent secretariat and that it should be responsible for advising the Prime Minister and Cabinet on all broad aspects of imperial defence. It wanted to abolish the office of commander-in-chief, establish an army council presided over by the secretary of state and create a general staff whose members should be recruited from amongst Staff College graduates and who, after serving successfully on the staff, should be recommended for accelerated promotion. Balfour accepted some of the committee's proposals with alacrity, constituting the Army Council and establishing the CID on a permanent footing with a secretariat before he left office in December 1905. The establishment of the CID marked the real beginning of the development of defence policy 'by committee'. It was the first step towards finding a bureaucratic solution to the problem of civil–military communications which had been caused by the growing separation of the military and political elites. But the CID never quite succeeded in harmonizing the policies of the various departments responsible for defence policy, especially before 1914 when the service departments and the Foreign Office remained jealous of their independence. But by bringing together representatives of the departments concerned, its advice to the Cabinet did at least usually represent the highest possible level of consensus. Balfour instinctively recognized some of these problems and it was for that reason that he was much slower to establish the general staff.

Arnold-Forster was a tactless minister who was in a hurry to reduce the estimates and solve the recruiting crisis he had inherited. He proposed to abandon both the army corps scheme and Cardwell's linked battalions and to replace them with large depots which would supply drafts to groups of battalions. He wanted to introduce two terms of enlistment. Men enlisted for nine years would be used to garrison the empire and provide an expeditionary force whilst men enlisted for three years could be retained at home. His plans came to nothing because he offended too many powerful interests. A convinced exponent of the 'Blue Water' School, he saw no need to retain large auxiliary forces at home and proposed to cut the estimates by reducing the militia and volunteers. Brodrick and his predecessor, Lord Lansdowne, objected to the way in which their reforms would be swept away. Other ministers led the outcry from the militia and volunteers at the cavalier treatment they were to receive. Balfour was appalled because, unless the latter bodies were reduced, Arnold-Forster's scheme would increase the estimates. With diminishing support from his Cabinet colleagues, these proposals also fell by the wayside. It was a measure of the Conservatives' failure that when they left office the army estimates for 1905/6 were a third higher than they had been in 1898.

The reforms which the Liberal secretary of state R. B. Haldane enacted between 1906 and 1911 were not designed to create an expeditionary force capable of intervening decisively in a continental land war. If Haldane had a guiding light it was the need to reduce the annual estimates below £28,000,000. He succeeded and they fell from £29,800,000 in 1905/6 to £27,400,000 in 1909/10. Haldane knew more about military matters before he entered the War Office in 1906 than he subsequently admitted, but his only significant preconception was that the navy, rather than the army, must carry the major responsibility for home defence. In 1906 it seemed that the army might find itself fighting the Russians on the North-West Frontier, the Boers in South Africa, or it might have to operate in concert with the French against the Germans in north-west Europe. In addition there remained the likelihood that portions of it might be called upon to conduct any one of a number of minor colonial campaigns in Africa or

Asia. To meet these contingencies his predecessor had left him 90,000 regulars in Britain organized into one army corps and six divisions. The first Moroccan crisis demonstrated that it would take two months to mobilize this force.

It was because it was impossible to foresee the exact circumstances or destination of any expeditionary force that Haldane organized it into six 'great' divisions, each of about 18,000 to 20,000 men. Within the fiscal limits which had been set for him, Haldane determined to produce a field force of 150,000 men organized into six divisions and four cavalry brigades. To provide drafts in peacetime to garrison the empire, he retained the Cardwell system, abandoned the Conservative's experiments with differing lengths of service and restored the old terms, seven or eight years with the colours followed by four or five years with the reserve. He also reduced eleven overseas battalions to achieve parity between units at home and abroad. To support the regulars he organized a Territorial Force, drawing on the manpower of the existing auxiliary forces and administered on a county basis by the lords lieutenant. When the regulars were abroad the territorials would defend Britain against enemy raids which might elude the navy and they were to provide the basis for an expanded army in the event of a great war. He hoped that they would number 312,000 men, organized into fourteen divisions. To advise him on matters of policy, in 1906 he completed the formation of the general staff, determining that it would be a 'blue ribbon' organization, free of administrative duties so that it could concern itself with offering the Chief of the Imperial General Staff strategic advice.

When Haldane introduced the legislation to give effect to his reforms in March 1907 he was careful to hide from the eyes of his suspicious radical colleagues that he envisaged that one day the territorials might be used overseas. Instead he emphasized their role as a home defence force and outlined a scheme by which the County Associations would encourage cadet corps, physical training and miniature rifle clubs so that after the passage of a generation the new military structure would take root in the nation as a whole. But perhaps the radicals did not look at the fine print of his proposals in any case. They were only too pleased with a secretary of state who was able to reduce the estimates. Much more serious opposition came from the militia and volunteers. Their colonels loathed the idea that their regiments were to be placed under the supervision of the County Associations because it threatened their almost proprietary control over them. Many were reluctant to join the territorials if it meant that their battalions might be reduced to providing drafts for the regulars in wartime. A way around that problem was found by retaining the militia depots as special reserve battalions to produce drafts for the regulars, and the Territorial and Reserve Forces Bill became law in August 1907.

Recruiting for the territorials and special reserve began well, thanks in part to another invasion scare in 1909. However, as the scare subsided, so did recruiting and neither organization had reached their full establishment by 1914. However, with their higher degree of organization, including its own artillery, engineers, supply and medical services, the territorials were a considerable improvement on the old auxiliary forces and after a further period of training they could take the field in France in 1914-15 in divisional sized units, something the volunteers could not have done.

Haldane's reforms reduced the army estimates but his colleagues at the Admiralty were not so successful. After 1895 peacetime spending on the navy regularly exceeded spending on the army and by 1904 the cost of the navy had almost doubled as Britain attempted to maintain the two-power standard. Despite the fact that by 1905 many of the assumptions upon which Tirpitz had based his 'risk fleet' had already been falsified, the Germans showed no sign that they would slow down their building programme and further increases in the Admiralty's estimates were likely if they wished to retain their lead. Hitherto the application of industrial technology to naval construction had often worked against the British by indirectly causing the estimates to spiral but in 1905 Fisher tried to make technology work for the British. He ordered the construction of a new class of battleship, HMS *Dreadnought*, and the *Invincible* class of armoured cruisers, later to be known as battle-cruisers. They were faster and more heavily armed than any comparable warships and rendered them obsolete. Higher speeds were secured by employing turbines instead of reciprocating engines and new gunlaying techniques and improved gun-mountings were introduced to ensure greater accuracy at longer ranges. Fisher believed that victory at sea would go to the fleet whose capital ships were fast enough to force battle on a reluctant enemy and whose superior armament (both the *Dreadnought* and *Invincible* carried uniform main batteries of 12-inch guns) would ensure that it could engage the enemy beyond the range of hostile torpedoes. Fisher envisaged the *Dreadnought* as an interim design. He placed most of his faith in the faster, although more lightly armoured *Invincible*. He believed that these ships would give the British a technological lead over their rivals and that the navy could build them without incurring unacceptable financial costs.

Initially he was correct. The Germans could not lay down a turbine-powered, all-big-gun battleship until 1910. The disruption that Fisher's innovations caused to the German warship-building programme, when combined with the savings from his other reforms and better relations with France and Russia, permitted the Admiralty to cut its estimates between 1905/6 and 1908/9 from £33,400,000 to £32,300,000. But Fisher had not found a permanent solution to the problem posed by the limited financial resources available for warship construction because the British did not maintain their technological lead. They tried to do so by developing bigger guns able to fire larger shells at greater ranges, by installing more powerful engines and, in 1912, by deciding to replace coal with more efficient oil fuels. These innovations were meant to deter the Germans from trying to compete with the Royal Navy. They failed, in part because unlike the *Dreadnought* they did not represent another quantum leap which would have completely disrupted German building plans.

The British did have an opportunity to take such a leap. But Fisher's determination to brook no opposition meant that defective organization at the Admiralty, and especially the absence of a naval staff, meant that they missed it. Fisher left the Admiralty in 1910 and a naval war staff was not established until in 1912, after the Agadir crisis had revealed to the CID that the First Sea Lord's near-monopoly of strategic planning had left the navy without a viable operational plan. In the absence of a naval staff the Directorate of Naval Ordnance was able to block the adoption of a promising mechanized fire-control system devised by a civilian inventor, Arthur Pollen. They did so ostensibly because it was too fragile to survive under active service conditions, because they believed that they had developed an equally efficient, cheaper and more robust manual system and because they believed that accuracy at very long ranges was unnecessary because visibility in the North Sea was often poor and the Germans intended to fight at ranges under 10,000 yards. In reality the directorate's refusal to adopt the Pollen system may have reflected their fears that by mechanizing fire control, Pollen would deprive gunnery specialists of their elite status. Adoption of the Pollen system might have given the navy a monopoly on accurate long-range gunnery and the British might have been able to employ a smaller number of qualitatively superior capital ships to match a larger number of German *Dreadnought*s, and so achieve a welcome reduction in the estimates.

Instead the navy adopted a much less effective manual fire control system and engaged in a costly naval arms race with the Germans. The British met what they thought was an acceleration in the German naval programme in 1909 by announcing that they would lay down four *Dreadnought*s immediately and a further four if the German threat seemed to be about to materialize. The naval race saw the estimates rise from £32,300,000 in 1908/9 to £48,800,000 in 1913/14. The Liberals found the money to meet these burgeoning bills by bursting free of some of the confines of nineteenth-century classical political economy. They imposed radical new direct taxes on wealthy, and presumably Unionist voters in the 1909 budget whilst simultaneously granting their own middle-class supporters tax reductions. The British therefore enjoyed a greater access to the wealth of their country than did the Germans, whose government did not adopt a similar policy for fear it would have incurred unacceptable political costs. But there remained political limits even on the British government's ability to raise new revenues and spend money on defence without resort to borrowing. Some Liberals wanted to increase social expenditure, whilst there was a significant haemorrhage from the party of middle-class voters alarmed at what Lloyd George's proposals might portend for the future in the 1910 elections. Grey approached the Germans at the second Hague Conference in 1907 and twice in bilateral negotiations between 1909 and 1911 and in 1912 in an attempt to reach a naval arms limitation agreement. The most the Germans would offer was a slowing-down in the pace of their construction programme. The price they demanded for an agreement, British neutrality in the event of a major European war, was too high and convinced some policy-makers that Germany was planning to fix her hegemony over Europe.

The Admiralty therefore carried further their policy of concentrating capital ships in home waters.

In November 1908 H. H. Asquith, who had replaced Campbell-Bannerman as Prime Minister in April, announced that his government would maintain the two-power standard. But such a goal was fast becoming unrealistic. France and Russia had been displaced by Germany and the USA as the world's second and third naval powers but an alliance between the latter was inconceivable. A standard designed to counter the fleets of any possible combination of two powers might produce a false sense of security because it could leave the navy too weak to meet the German fleet. Britain's diplomatic arrangements with France and Russia permitted her to concentrate her fleet in home waters to counter the German navy. In late 1906 the Mediterranean fleet was reduced from 8 to 6 battleships and in the war plans which the Admiralty hatched between 1908 and 1911 the recall of the remainder was considered.

But until 1912 these suggestions were resisted. Fisher and the Foreign Office were reluctant to abandon a region which the navy had controlled since Nelson's time and withdrawal would throw Italy and Turkey into Germany's arms, endanger Britain's hold on Egypt and threaten her communications with India. However, Tirpitz's Supplementary Naval Law, the failure of naval arms limitation talks and the growth of the Italian and Austro-Hungarian navies, prompted the new First Lord, Winston Churchill, to grasp this nettle. In March 1912 Churchill announced that the two-power standard was obsolete and that henceforth the navy would maintain a 60 per cent superiority in capital ships over the Germans. When Tirpitz's programme was completed the Germans would have 25 battleships in the North Sea, and the Royal Navy would need 33 to match them. To keep pace with the German programme the Admiralty would require an extra £3,000,000 per annum. It would also cost an extra £15 to 20,000,000 to match the *Dreadnoughts* the Italians and Austro-Hungarians were building. The Treasury could not meet the cost of matching all three fleets. Churchill argued that the only alternative was a naval agreement with France which would allow Britain to concentrate her fleet in the North Sea whilst the French were left with the responsibility of protecting their joint interests in the Mediterranean. In November 1912 the two governments struck such a bargain and the British withdrew all but a few ships from Malta.

In October 1904 the Balfour government announced that it would begin to construct a new naval base on the Firth of Forth, a base which could be designed only to counter the German fleet. The Admiralty's perception that any threat from the fleets of the Dual Alliance was being overtaken by the threat from the German fleet was shared by a wider public. This tendency was encouraged by the appearance of works like Erskine Childers's *The Riddle of the Sands*, published in 1903, which foretold a surprise German descent on the east coast. In 1903 one of the first tasks of the CID was to assess the possibility of a German invasion. In the first of three prewar invasion inquiries, the CID supported the 'Blue Water' School and dismissed the possibility of a successful invasion. Such an operation would involve at least 70,000 men who would need 200 transports and require three days to embark and cross the North Sea. The navy would thus have ample opportunity to intercept them at sea. The CID's conclusions meant that it was no longer unreasonable for the general staff to contemplate dispatching an expeditionary force abroad in the event of a European war. However, an alliance of navalists and conscriptionists continued to exploit fears of invasion. The navalists did so to ensure that the Admiralty continued to receive the lion's share of defence spending and the conscriptionists led by Lord Roberts, who became president of the National Service League in 1905, used the fear of invasion to justify the introduction of national service. Ostensibly they wanted it because they believed that the auxiliary forces were too weak to defend the home islands. In private Roberts was convinced that one day the British would have to send a large army to fight on the continent and that only conscription would furnish enough men. No prewar government was ready to follow their recommendations. Two further CID invasion inquiries were held in 1907/8 and 1913/14. They also dismissed the probability of a full-scale invasion but did accept that a raiding force of less than 70,000 men might slip past the navy and suggested that it would be necessary to retain two of the army's six regular divisions at home to assist the territorials.

Britain's alliance with Japan in 1902 and her ententes with France and Russia in 1904 and 1907 were the product of her imperial and naval rivalries, first with France and Russia and ultimately with Germany. The Moroccan crisis of 1905–6 and the start of the Anglo-French military staff talks in December 1905 did not mark a sudden change in the direction of British defence policy from a concern to defend the empire to the adoption of a 'continental strategy' intended to lend assistance to the French in north-west Europe in the event of war with Germany. The shift in military policy before 1914 was more gradual and less complete. The first Moroccan crisis accelerated a trend in the service ministries and the Foreign Office to see Germany, rather than France and Russia, as the most immediate threat to British security. But it did not mean that the services harmonized their contingency plans for a war against her. From the spring of 1905 the general staff favoured dispatching an expeditionary force to north-west Europe even though it would only number at most 150,000 men and would be dwarfed by its allies and enemies. They argued that small as it was, if it operated in conjunction with the French army it would be large enough to tilt the military balance against the Germans and would lend much needed support to French morale, which had apparently collapsed in 1870 because the French had been bereft of allies. The navy would check the Germans at sea and the Russians would threaten them from the east. Balked of success on the oceans and on land, the Germans would be ready to make peace.

Fisher's understanding of naval technology was not matched by a comparable understanding of the likely impact of that technology on strategy. The Admiralty, confronted by the problem of how to fight a war against a major continental power, instinctively opted for a maritime strategy without considering its practicality. The lack of coherent strategic planning was one of the greatest failings of the prewar navy. The Admiralty deprecated the dispatch of the regular army to France. Their preferred strategy was to weaken the Germans by blockading their ports, sweeping their trade from the seas and forcing them to withdraw troops from the French front by using the British army to raid the German coast. Their plans were based on the dubious assumption that Germany was as dependent as was Britain upon overseas trade and they ignored the fact that in wartime the Germans would be able to use contiguous neutrals to supply themselves with many of their wants.

The general staff recognized that structural changes in the European economy in the late nineteenth century had reduced the efficacy and practicality of a maritime-amphibious strategy. The growth of the European railway system meant that coastal shipping was giving way to cheap land transport. That diminished the effectiveness of one of Britain's traditional weapons, naval blockade. Even in the eighteenth century Britain's ability to wage amphibious war around the European littoral had been circumscribed by the difficulty of transporting sufficient horses with every expedition. Unless they could be procured from a friendly indigenous population, amphibious expeditions tended to remain stranded near the coast and unable to move for lack of cavalry, artillery and transport. The growth of the European railway system made this problem worse. By enabling a land power to move troops rapidly to any part of its coastline, railways further widened the disparity in mobility between troops just landed on the coast and enemy forces with their proper complement of cavalry, artillery and transport sent to repulse them. Thus a blockade would work too slowly to help the French and a force landed on the German coast would soon be overwhelmed.

In theory the CID ought to have been able to ensure that the services harmonized their war plans and it might have acted as the agent through which the military resources of the empire could have been co-ordinated. In fact, because it never acquired the executive authority to overcome the autonomy of the service departments or the Dominions, it failed to perform either task. Although the Australians and New Zealanders agreed to fund part of the costs of squadrons in Far Eastern waters and the Federated Malay States presented a capital ship to the Royal Navy in 1912, in general the Dominions and colonies disgorged only a fraction of the money the Admiralty requested. At the Colonial Conferences of 1907, 1909 and 1911 the general staff asked the Dominions to organize and train their landforces on the same pattern as the British army to facilitate future co-operation. They only hinted that they envisaged such co-operation taking place in Europe, not on a colonial frontier, but even so they received a lukewarm reception. The great obstacles to closer co-operation remained the fact that when the imperial government envisaged utilizing Dominion resources it insisted that they should come under centralized control from London. That ran counter to the determination, shared to a varying degree by all the Dominion governments, that they should control the ships and troops they raised.

At home the Liberal government lacked the unified political will to use the CID to force the services to harmonize their plans. The Agadir crisis of 1911 showed that Asquith's cabinet was divided on the dispatch of an army to fight alongside the French in the event of a war with Germany. A small group of ministers, including Asquith and Grey, accepted the general staff's case, but believed that Britain's participation in the land war in western Europe could be confined to a handful of divisions. Another small group, who were representative of the extreme radical wing of the party, preferred to shut their eyes to the possibility of a European war. The largest group in the Cabinet formed a bridge between these two factions. They opposed the dispatch of troops to the continent but were willing to use British sea-power and economic strength to support the French and Russians. Their concept of Britain's proper strategy was rooted in a particular interpretation of how they believed their forefathers had acted in the eighteenth century. They rejoiced that the navy and Britain's island geography meant that she did not have to maintain a large standing army. They insisted that if Britain did go to war against Germany in concert with France and Russia, the British ought to blockade the German coast, refrain from raising a large army and husband her own economic resources so that she could outlast the enemy and supply her continental partners with the money and munitions they required to wage the land war.

This was the political background against which the general staff conducted intermittent staff talks with the French between 1905 and 1914. It meant that whatever the two staffs agreed, their decisions could constitute neither a binding alliance obliging Britain to fight in defence of France, nor even a moral obligation to do so. The staffs concerned themselves with technical military matters designed to facilitate the transportation of the British army across the Channel *if* the British Cabinet ever decided that they wished to send it. But Asquith left the final decision on whether or not to send the troops unresolved before 1914. His government already faced enough contentious issues and there was no need to add another to the list.

Britain entered the war in August 1914 because German attempts to build a fleet to rival the Royal Navy and her efforts to undermine Britain's friendship with France and Russia after 1905 had convinced some British policy-makers that Germany was determined to foist her hegemony on Europe in the same way that Napoleon had tried to do. British strategy between 1914 and 1916 rested on the assumptions that the defence of the empire and victory in Europe were interdependent and that the British not only had to guard against the ambitions of their enemies, Germany and Austria-Hungary, but also those of their friends, France and Russia. The agreements of 1904 and 1907 had muted Anglo-French and Anglo-Russian rivalries, but they had not silenced them. These misgivings meant that the British wanted a peace settlement which would weaken Germany but which would also ensure that neither of Britain's allies became so powerful that they in turn could menace British security in Europe, Africa, or Asia.

The British Expeditionary Force (BEF) which sailed for France in August 1914 may have had some defects, but it was the best-equipped and trained force which had ever left Britain's shores. But it was not intended to be the linchpin of British strategy. The Asquith government assumed that the French and Russian armies, with minimal direct British military assistance, were sufficiently powerful to check the armies of the Central Powers. Britain's main contribution to the allied war effort was to take the shape of the Royal Navy, which blockaded the enemy and the economic assistance she offered her allies. This was the strategy of 'business as usual'. In the meantime Lord Kitchener, who became Secretary of State for War in August 1914, began to raise a huge new army of volunteers. Kitchener foretold that by early 1917 the armies of the continental belligerents would have bled each other dry. But his 'New Armies' would be unbloodied and Britain would be able to intervene decisively on the continent, inflict a final defeat on the enemy and then be able to impose her peace terms on enemies and allies alike.

The success of 'business as usual' depended upon the ability and willingness of Russia and France to fight without significant British military help for two years. It was soon apparent that this was unrealistic. The Germans began the war hoping to defeat France quickly before turning against Russia. By December 1914, although they had occupied large tracts of allied territory, their plan had failed. Confronted by a two-front war, they began to inveigle France and Russia into making a separate peace. This news alarmed British policy-makers for they knew that there were politicians in both countries who had always believed that friendship with Britain was a mistake. In 1915/16 the British reluctantly accepted that they had to be seen to be doing whatever they could to assist their partners.

The Dardanelles campaign of 1915 was partially born out of this realization. Turkey joined the Central Powers in November 1914 and thus re-opened the Eastern question. The British landed troops at the head of the Persian Gulf, ostensibly to protect local oil-fields but in reality to re-establish their prestige. The Indian Mutiny and the Mahdist rising in the Sudan in the 1880s and 1890s had taught the British administrations in India and Egypt the danger which Muslim fundamentalism posed to their regimes. In February 1915 an Anglo-French fleet began to sail up the Dardanelles towards Constantinople. The operation was designed not only to knock Turkey out of the war but also to persuade Italy and the neutral states of the Balkans to join the entente. In March it seemed as if their efforts were about to succeed. British agents were conducting secret peace talks with dissident Turks. In fact the episode underlined the incompatibility of Russian and British objectives. The Russians had coveted Constantinople for most of the nineteenth century. Now, fearful that a Greek and not a Russian army might liberate it, they insisted that before they would agree to more states joining the entente, their allies had to promise them that Constantinople would become a Russian city at the end of the war. The British acquiesced for it would benefit them little if, in gaining Greece as an ally, they alienated Russia. But their promise made a separate peace with Turkey impossible. The Turks would never negotiate away their capital. The Italians drove a similarly hard bargain, this time at Austria's expense, before they joined the entente in May 1915. Thus negotiations intended to shorten the war only succeeded in making an early peace less likely. By then the naval attack at the Dardanelles had failed and whilst an army was landed on the Gallipoli peninsula in April it barely advanced beyond its beachheads. This failure encouraged the Bulgarians to join the Central Powers and in October they attacked Britain's Balkan ally, Serbia. An Anglo-French force which landed at the Greek port of Salonika failed to open an escape route for the Serbian army and by the end of 1915 the Germans had opened direct railway communications to Constantinople. After lengthy debate the British government (which had become a Coalition ministry in May 1915) agreed to evacuate the Dardanelles for fear that if they did not the Germans would arrive to drive them into the sea. The Salonika force remained in place until the end of the war, a source of considerable dissension between the Western Allies for the British suspected that French enthusiasm for the operation owed much to their postwar imperial ambitions in the Balkans. The British believed that the Dardanelles débâcle had badly dented their prestige in Muslim eyes and this led them to look for ways to restore it. The government of India tried to capture Baghdad but their attempt produced another humiliation when the expedition surrendered at Kut in April 1916. Simultaneously, the Egyptian administration tried to prevent a holy war by winning over to the Allied side the Sharif of Mecca by vague promises of postwar independence from the Turks.

The events of August 1915 marked a major turning-point for British strategy. A second landing failed to drive the Turks from the Gallipoli peninsula. Britain's bankers in New York warned them that they were running short of the dollars required to pay the bills they had amassed in the USA to pay for war materials for themselves and their allies. In the spring of 1915 the BEF had twice attacked the German line but their attacks had demonstrated that they did not have the necessary men, guns, or shells to break through. In the summer of 1915 Kitchener preferred to remain on the defensive in the hope that the Germans would dash themselves to pieces by attacking the Allied line in France. But they were not so obliging. The Germans captured Warsaw and rumours that France or Russia might make a separate peace unless they received more visible British military assistance intensified. In August Kitchener reluctantly informed the Cabinet that 'unfortunately we had to make war as we must, and not as we should like to'.[3] The Loos offensive of September–October 1915 was designed as much to reassure the Allies that Britain was committed to their cause as it was to inflict injury on the Germans.

Throughout 1915 entente strategy was handicapped by the absence of a common plan. Allied generals met in December 1915 to ensure that they were not similarly hindered in 1916. They recommended to their governments that the Allies should mount a series of concerted offensives on the eastern, western and Italian fronts in the summer of 1916 to negate the Central Powers' ability to use their interior lines of communication. Their plan was designed to force the Central Powers to sue for peace by Christmas 1916. The BEF's role was to attack north of the River Somme, in a joint operation with the French army to the south of the river. It has been suggested that British strategic policy during the First World War was vitiated because of a sharp division between 'easterners' and 'westerners'. Politicians like David Lloyd George (successively Chancellor of the Exchequer, Minister of Munitions and finally Prime Minister) were said to have preferred an 'eastern strategy' designed to defeat Germany by first overthrowing her weaker allies, Turkey, Austria-Hungary and Bulgaria. Their opponents, typified by Sir William Robertson (Chief of the Imperial General Staff from 1915 to 1918) and Sir Douglas Haig (Commander-in-Chief of the BEF 1915 to 1918) were said to have preferred to commit hundreds of thousands of troops to futile battles of attrition on the western front. But the way in which the Coalition government agonized until April 1916 before agreeing to launch the Somme offensive indicated that this interpretation was misleading. All responsible policy-makers were both 'easterners' and 'westerners'. They all recognized that unless the Russians could maintain an active eastern front and unless the French army could contain a large part of the German army in the west, the entente's chances of winning the war were small. The real division between British policy-makers lay elsewhere.

Before 1914 the government had planned to co-opt a small number of businessmen from the railway industry and the shipping insurance market to enact its plans to ensure that the economy did not collapse under the disruption caused by the impact of war. But in the summer of 1915 the apparent slowness with which business had responded to the army's burgeoning demands for munitions of all kinds persuaded the Asquith Coalition government to mobilize heavy industry to support the war effort under the auspices of the newly created Ministry of Munitions. But by August 1915 politicians like Reginald McKenna (the Chancellor of the Exchequer in 1915/16) thought that the growth of the army and the diversion of production from exports to war materials had gone far enough. They believed that the British could best assist their allies by limiting the size of their own army and giving France and Russia the money and munitions they needed to fight the Central Powers. By the end of the war Britain had advanced her allies £1,741,000,000 in assistance. It was a measure of her relative economic decline that in turn she received £1,365,000,000 from the USA, and her net expenditure on economic aid to her allies and Dominions was only about 9 per cent of her total spending on her own armed forces. McKenna's opponents, like Robertson and Lloyd George, championed the introduction of military conscription as being the only way Britain could raise a sufficiently large army to demonstrate to the Allies that Britain did not intend to fight to the last French or Russian soldier.

The debate on conscription reached a climax in the winter and spring of 1915/16. By December 1915 nearly one in four males of military age had already enlisted. But during the summer of 1915 voluntary recruiting began to decline and the general staff insisted that the only way to maintain the army in France during the summer and autumn of 1916 would be to introduce conscription. McKenna insisted that if more men were taken from the factories and put into uniform, Britain's balance of payments would collapse and she would be bankrupt before the Central Powers sued for peace. In past wars governments had taken care to conscript only the economically marginal. The Asquith Coalition had not abandoned the belief that Britain's real strength lay in her economic prowess, but by April 1916 the majority had reluctantly concluded that the war would end in an indecisive peace or even an enemy victory, if they did not abandon caution and gamble on the ability of the Allied armies to win the war before Britain faced financial ruin.

The consequences of the decision to raise a continental-scale army and to commit it to the western front in 1916 were that the ratio of spending on land and sea services (73:27) was weighted more heavily in favour of the army during the First World War than in any of Britain's great power wars between 1688 and 1945. Table 6.1 shows the distribution of the divisions the British raised during the war. In the first year of the war much of the army, consisting of partially prepared territorials and untrained Kitchener army divisions, was retained at home for training. But from 1916 onwards approximately two-thirds of the army's divisions were committed to the western front, whilst between 1915 and 1918 about a quarter were dispatched to overseas theatres, the Dardanelles, Salonika, Egypt, Mesopotamia, India, Africa and Italy. The small number of formed divisions in Britain after 1916 indicated that the government had not completely lost faith in a 'blue water' policy and continued to rely in the main on the navy as the first line of defence for the home islands. Under the actual stress of war the Dominions lost some of their prewar reluctance to commit their resources to the defence of the empire and about a fifth of the divisions

Table 6.1 Distribution of British and Imperial Divisions Annually on 1 October (Percentage)

	Britain %	Western Front %	Overseas[1] %
1914	72	14	14
1915	30	45	25
1916	14	62	24
1917	9	65	26
1918	4	66	30

Source: Committee of Imperial Defence, *Divisional Distribution Chart. Prepared by the Historical Section, Committee of Imperial Defence* (London: HMSO, nd).

Note: [1] Dardanelles, India, Salonika, Africa, Egypt.

the British raised consisted of Dominion or colonial troops and by 1917/18 they were bearing a considerable part of the burden of the land war outside Europe. But, in a break with precedent, imperial divisions performed the role which had been fulfilled by German mercenaries in the eighteenth century and fought in western Europe, providing nearly one-fifth of the British army on the western front in the final two years of the war.

The concerted Allied offensive in 1916 produced mixed results. The Russian offensive which began in June was a brilliant success and within weeks between a third and a half of the Austro-Hungarian army had been destroyed. The French contribution to the Somme had to be much reduced, for in February 1916 the Germans began to bleed the French army dry of manpower by launching their own offensive at Verdun. The British attack on the Somme, which began on 1 July, made little headway at great cost. The Russian advance and the spectacle of the Allies acting in concert persuaded Rumania to join the entente in August. But the Germans recovered quickly. They were not forced to sue for peace by Christmas and were able to mount a counter-attack on the eastern front and to occupy Bucharest in December.

The war at sea had been a disappointment to those who had hoped for the early defeat of the German High Seas Fleet. By 1912 the Admiralty had recognized that mines, torpedoes and submarines would make a close blockade of the German coast impossible, so in 1914 the Grand Fleet remained at Scapa Flow in the Orkneys, light craft blockaded the southern exit from the North Sea at the Dover Straits and a line of cruisers maintained a distant blockade across the North Sea. The High Seas Fleet, which was outnumbered by the British, prudently attempted to wear down Britain's numerical superiority with mines and torpedoes, and German heavy squadrons made forays into the North Sea in the hope of destroying isolated British squadrons before the remainder of the Grand Fleet could intercept them. There was only one great fleet action in the North Sea during the war, the Batttle of Jutland in May 1916. It ended indecisively. Poor visibility combined with faulty staff work at the Admiralty and the determination of both commanders not to risk their main fleets against what might be a superior force, meant that there was no second Trafalgar. But, although the British suffered heavier losses than the Germans, they retained their numerical superiority. The Germans did make other sorties into the North Sea after Jutland, but they never again sought a fleet action.

In 1914 the British had assumed that the Royal Navy would keep open the sea communications of the entente, Britain would act as the economic power-house of the alliance and the French and Russian armies would checkmate the armies of the Central Powers. Between the autumn of 1916 and the spring of 1917 these assumptions crumbled. The financial crisis which McKenna had feared materialized. By the autumn of 1916 two-fifths of the money Britain was spending on the war was being spent in the USA and most of her purchases there were made on credit. In November the United States Federal Reserve Board advised American bankers to stop lending to the belligerents. Even if cash could be found in the USA, the Germans' decision to launch unrestricted U-boat warfare against Allied shipping in February 1917 meant there was no guarantee that deliveries could be made. By the spring of 1917 one in four merchant ships leaving Britain was being sunk. The new German policy finally persuaded Woodrow Wilson to declare war on Germany in April 1917 but the Lloyd George government, which had come to power in December 1916, feared that American help would come too late for in March 1917 the tsarist regime was overthrown by a revolution which marked the beginning of the disintegration of the Russian army and two months later, after the failure of the Nivelle offensive in April, a large part of the French army went on strike. The British faced the prospect of waging a continental land war without active assistance from any major ally.

Faced by growing international competition in the 1880s and 1890s the British opted for a 'blue water' solution to the problem of how to defend their empire at reasonable cost. This was reflected by the fact that after 1895 peacetime spending on the navy regularly exceeded spending on the army. The Boer War demonstrated the unstable foundations of that policy. In the Edwardian period policy-makers decreased the disparity between their commitments and resources by making the armed forces more cost-effective and by using diplomacy to reduce the number of their potential enemies. They achieved a considerable degree of success in appeasing the USA, France and Russia. The estimates did rise but, thanks to the success of the Liberals' financial policies after 1909, the increases remained just within the bounds of what was politically acceptable. But they could not appease Germany because the price she demanded was too high. The British refused to isolate themselves from the continental balance of power. In 1914 the strategy of 'business as usual' was intended to prolong this success but the unwillingness of France and Russia to carry the burden of the land war without significant British military assistance undermined it. One element of a 'blue water' policy survived – the reliance on the fleet to defend the home islands assisted by only as many troops as were necessary to deal with raiding forces. But the commitment of the bulk of the army to the western front by 1916 was the death-knell of a 'blue water' defence policy and, together with the ratio of spending on land and sea services, it marked the clearest acceptance ever by the British of a continental commitment and rejection of the 'British way in warfare'.

7 Deterrence and Dependence, 1917–42

The history of British defence policy between 1917 and 1942 could be written around two assumptions. The first is that because in 1917 and 1918 Britain was only able to sustain her war effort at a level which made victory possible thanks to US financial and economic assistance, her status as a great power had disappeared and never returned. The second is that the men responsible for guiding British defence policy in the 1930s were so blind to the threats posed by the fascist dictators that they neglected to rearm in time and left Britain exposed to disaster. Both assumptions are misleading. In 1917/18 the balance of economic advantage did shift in favour of the USA but between the wars the USA failed to translate its economic potential into international political involvement. Britain's own international status was ambiguous after 1918. In November 1918 her empire reached its largest ever geographical extent and because so many of her rivals had collapsed her relative power was greater than it had been in 1914. Britain was the world's only global power throughout the interwar period. France, Japan, the USA, Soviet Russia, Italy and Germany were regional or hemispheric powers between the wars. But the Treaty of Versailles neither recreated the balance of power which had so benefited Britain between 1815 and 1870 nor did it establish the League of Nations as an effective instrument of collective security as a substitute for that balance.

In November 1918 Germany was in chaos but she still retained the demographic and economic potential to be a great power. The collapse of Austria-Hungary created a number of small states each too weak to resist German pressure when she recovered. Soviet Russia was a hostile force but her power was imponderable. The war had weakened France but left her in no mood to make the kinds of compromises necessary to appease Germany. Until the mid-1930s these shifts in the international system did not threaten Britain's security because her potential enemies were divided. But between 1934 and 1939 she was confronted by the insuperable problem of countering threats from Germany in Europe, Italy in the Mediterranean and Japan in the Far East simultaneously. When she had faced an analogous array at the end of the Boer War she had reduced the problem to manageable proportions by appeasing two of her three rivals. In attempting to appease the dictators in the 1930s Baldwin and Neville Chamberlain were only following a tried and successful course. But their predecessors had enjoyed two advantages. They had been able to maintain a credible level of armaments to deter their rivals and neither Russia nor France before 1914 had sought to recreate the existing international system on completely new principles. Compromises over secondary issues in North Africa and Central Asia were therefore possible. It was significant that the one power which Britain failed to appease before 1914, Germany, did want to restructure the world system on new principles and her ambitions could not be accommodated within a world order in which Britain remained a dominant power. But in the 1930s Britain's relative economic decline made it impossible for her to sustain a credible deterrent against three simultaneous threats and the Axis powers did want to establish a new world order in which compromise between their interests and Britain's would be impossible.

The second half of 1917 was a period of gloom for Lloyd George's War Cabinet but they rejected a peace without victory. The Germans were unwilling to evacuate Belgium so they permitted Sir Douglas Haig to attempt to expel them by mounting the third Battle of Ypres. It was an expensive failure. When it ended in November 1917 Haig was no nearer ejecting the Germans from Belgium and the entente's strategic situation had worsened. In October part of the Italian army collapsed at Caporetto. The euphoria occasioned by a successful British offensive at Cambrai which was spearheaded by the new Tank Corps, evaporated when the Germans successfully counter-attacked. Finally, in December the Bolsheviks, who had overthrown the Russian provisional government in March, signed an armistice with Germany.

At the end of 1917 three factors compelled the government to clarify Britain's war aims in public. When the USA entered the war in April, President Wilson distanced himself from the imperialist war aims of his new partners. The USA was an associated power, never an ally. Wilson pursued a policy which was similar to the one Britain had tried to follow in 1914. He wished to give the entente just enough assistance to enable them to defeat the Central Powers, on the assumption that at the end of the fighting they would be so dependent upon the USA that they would not be able to resist his attempt to impose American peace terms. These terms included a territorial settlement based on self-determination, no annexations or indemnities, free trade, an end to secret diplomacy, freedom of the seas and the establishment of a League of Nations to preserve peace. In the negotiations which followed the Russian armistice, Germany tried to encourage war weariness amongst the entente by claiming that she supported a similar peace settlement. In November Lord Lansdowne, who had left the government in December 1916, published a letter advocating peace before the war destroyed British society. Organized labour, angered by the high profits being made by many employers and forced by the government to surrender many of its prewar practices, was suspicious that the war was being needlessly prolonged. At the end of December the Labour Party told the government that they would only continue to support the war if they were assured that it was being fought to make the world safe for democracy. Some of these demands could be construed in such a way as to be acceptable to the British government. But others, notably Wilson's insistence on freedom of the seas, threatened Britain's maritime security and a peace without annexations ran counter to the determination of the Dominions to retain control of the German colonies which their troops had occupied. But Lloyd George could not afford to alienate Wilson or organized labour and in January he provided the necessary public reassurance. He paid lip service to Wilson's views about the postwar colonial and naval settlement, supported French and Italian claims only where they could be justified by the principle of self-determination and, whilst he called for the independence of Britain's smaller allies, was careful not to endorse their territorial ambitions.

The tsarist regime was no longer a serious rival in Asia but the collapse of the Russian army meant that the British faced the possibility that the Germans might penetrate the Caucasus, Transcaspia, Persia and Siberia and threaten the entire British Empire in Asia. In January 1918 Haig suggested that as the British had already gained much in Africa and Asia it was time to make peace by granting the Germans a free hand in Russia, for if the war continued the USA would emerge as the world's dominant power. Lloyd George shared his concern that the longer the war lasted the more likely it was that the USA would dominate the postwar settlement but he did not believe that the empire was yet sufficiently secure to warrant making peace. In October 1917 he had decided that, as Britain was virtually bereft of European allies, she ought to remain on the defensive in the west in 1918 and await the arrival of a powerful American army before delivering the final blow against the Germans in 1919. In 1918 he wanted to safeguard the security of the empire by defeating Turkey and creating a cordon of buffer states in the Middle East to block Germany's advance towards India. One crucial factor in impelling him towards this conclusion was Britain's growing shortage of manpower. Manpower policy in 1917–18 was a battle between the army's need for soldiers and the insistence of ministers responsible for the economic conduct of the war that if too many men were placed in uniform, the armies could not be adequately supplied and Britain would be bankrupt. In December 1917 a Cabinet committee on manpower produced a manpower budget designed to stretch Britain's ability to wage a long war. It gave a higher priority to shipbuilding, food production and the manufacture of tanks and aircraft than to supplying drafts to the army.

The success of Lloyd George's policy depended upon the Allies not losing control of the sea-lanes and on the Germans remaining inactive on land for almost a year. The introduction of convoys after April 1917, coupled with a rigorous system of rationing imports, ensured that although import tonnage dropped in 1917/18, enough cargoes reached Britain to sustain her economy. But on land the Germans did not oblige the Allies. In March 1918 they signed the Peace of Brest-Litovsk with the Bolsheviks and by May German troops had occupied Sebastopol and were threatening to advance into Transcaucasia. And in March the Germans began an offensive in the west which for a time threatened to divide the French and British armies and drive the latter into the Channel. The western front was not stabilized until July. In 1918 the War Cabinet did not believe that if they lost the war in France the British Empire could safely withdraw into imperial isolation. Like their Asquithian predecessors they recognized that the western and eastern fronts were interdependent. The only thing that had changed was that the eastern front was no longer in western Russia but was now in the Middle East. British divisions were withdrawn from Palestine and sent to France but the Palestine front was maintained by Indian troops. The War Cabinet ordered Haig to remain on the defensive until the Germans had been compelled once again to divert troops eastward. Sir Henry Wilson, who became the Chief of Imperial General Staff in February 1918, tried to create a new strategic frontier along the shores of the Caspian and Caucasus by offering support at various times to the Georgians, Armenians, the Mensheviks, the Shah of Persia, the Japanese and the Cossacks. The British also made a series of public commitments to the subject nationalities of the Austro-Hungarian Empire, hoping that the promise of national self-determination would undermine the Habsburg's ability to resist.

In the summer of 1918 Haig ignored his orders and in concert with the French and Americans mounted a series of limited counter-attacks. In March the German army had been promised that one final push would suffice to bring peace on German terms. The success of the allied counter-attacks and the knowledge that the arrival of US troops in France meant that the Allies were becoming stronger, ended the Germans' hopes of victory and their morale crumbled. When the German collapse came it was total and on all fronts. In September the Allied army at Salonika forced the Bulgarians to sue for peace. That success opened the road to Constantinople and in October the Turks sued for peace. Hitherto the Germans had been able to bolster their Allies. Now the German army was too short of men to do so and the morale of many of those that were in the field was collapsing. In October Germany asked Wilson for an armistice. During the resulting negotiations, the British were careful not only to insist on terms which safeguarded their precarious military superiority on the western front, but also ones which would not concede too much to the USA. Lloyd George accepted the armistice terms which were signed in November only after Wilson had conceded that final agreement about indemnities and freedom of the seas could wait until the peace conference and after he had threatened to make a separate peace if the European Allies did not fall into line.

The Peace of Versailles was signed in June 1919. Its terms were the product of several factors often pulling in opposite directions. War-weariness, the British government's fear that Bolshevism might spread to Britain and its knowledge that Britain had passed the peak of her military capabilities demanded an end to the war. Fear that a resurgent Germany might once again dominate eastern

Europe and threaten Britain's empire in Asia was matched by the belief that only a strong Germany could prevent the spread of Bolshevism westward. Tory imperialists supported the Dominions' insistence that they should retain the colonies their troops had acquired. The principle of self-determination seemed to be applied in favour of Germany's smaller neighbours and against the Germans themselves. To the east an independent Poland was established which physically separated Germany from East Prussia. The *Anschluss* between Germany and Austria was forbidden and a significant German minority was placed under Czech rule in the Sudetenland. Alsace-Lorraine was returned to France and the Rhineland was demilitarized and temporarily occupied by Allied troops. Germany was practically disarmed but even so the French continued to fear her resurgence. Subsequent treaties with Austria, Hungary and Bulgaria signalled the demise of the Austro-Hungarian Empire. The British kept control of Palestine and Mesopotamia under the guise of League of Nations mandates. The League of Nations was welcomed by Liberal and Labour opinion in Britain as a world body which would prevent future wars but it was shunned by imperialists as an international police-force which would diminish Britain's sovereignty. The settlement united Wilsonian idealists in Britain and German nationalists in the belief that it deviated too far from Wilson's ideals. It failed to settle the Franco-German antagonism. Its terms were too severe to be permanently acceptable to Germany, but were too lenient to prevent her recovery. It created a number of small states in eastern and Central Europe which would be too small to resist a resurgent Russia or Germany. Lloyd George recognized many of those defects and, like many of his contemporaries, looked to the League of Nations to provide the machinery to resolve them peacefully.

After November 1918 the demobilization of the largest army and navy Britain had ever produced was prompted as much by domestic political and economic considerations as it was by a decline in the threats facing the empire. In 1916/17 government spending, most of which was war-related, accounted for 57–8 per cent of gross national product as compared to only 7 per cent in 1913. Of the cost of war 30 per cent was paid for from taxation. The remainder came from loans which meant that most of the cost of the conflict fell upon postwar tax-payers who had to shoulder a vastly swollen national debt. Pressure to ease military burdens came from an electorate which had been almost tripled by the 1918 Reform Act, a burgeoning trade union movement and a Labour Party which replaced the Liberals as the official opposition in 1922. The days of the 'nightwatchman' state had begun to wither after 1909 as the Liberal government increased the percentage of the budget devoted to social services. That trend accelerated in the interwar period. Politicians of all parties now recognized that there were no longer votes to be won by promising to increase the estimates and that attempts to do so, in the absence of a careful campaign of public education, might be electorally damaging.

Opposition to higher estimates reflected public revulsion at the thought of another great war and a belief that the First World War had been caused in part by the prewar arms race. The League of Nations was held in high public esteem in the 1920s and for much of the 1930s. It appeared to offer the best hope for the peaceful adjustment of international differences. It also made it possible for the electorate to believe that since a future war would automatically involve all the signatories of the League's covenant, the weakness of Britain's own services mattered little. The human cost of the continental commitment of 1915/18 caused many policy-makers and the wider public to overlook the strategic reason why Britain had fought so hard on the western front. It also made them reluctant to do so again until every alternative had been exhausted. No attempt was made to construct defence policy anew from first principles. The structure of the policy-making elite in Whitehall changed remarkably little after 1918 except in two respects. The Cabinet, the service ministries, the Treasury and the Foreign Office remained the dominant institutional voices, but they were now joined by the Air Ministry, the Colonial Office and the chiefs of staff sub-committee of the Committee of Imperial Defence which was established in 1923. But, although the central machinery of policy-making did not always succeed in eliminating disagreements between departments, it was more successful in doing so than it had been before 1914. Defence policy again reflected the greatest possible level of consensus within the government, even if that level was not as high as it might have been in a more perfect world. There was one thing policy-makers were agreed upon after the war. There was no possibility that they would abandon Britain's wartime gains even though the need to devise a defence policy to secure them which was both cheap and politically acceptable to the nation at large, was more urgent and more difficult than before 1914.

The war seemed to have left the empire more powerful and cohesive than ever. India and the Dominions had contributed 2,500,000 men to the empire's armies. Imperial statesmen had sat in the Imperial War Cabinet in 1917 and 1918 and helped to make British strategy. Germany's collapse ended the threat which had dominated British strategic policy since the beginning of the century. Lloyd George's government was confident that it could establish a stable balance of power in Europe and the Pacific, foster British hegemony in the Middle East, maintain her maritime supremacy and perpetuate strategic co-operation between the victor powers. Defence spending fell from £568,000,000 in 1920 to £114,700,000 in 1925. But those figures concealed two factors. The British Empire did not immediately enter into an era of peace in November 1918. For the next three years British forces were engaged in a series of small wars in Ireland and throughout the Middle East. And the drop in the total estimates hid the fact that in the early 1920s both the navy and the Royal Air Force (RAF) embarked upon expensive rearmament programmes and it was only after 1925 that the Treasury succeeded in imposing reductions on all three services.

In the spring of 1919 the Treasury tried to compel the services to cut their total annual estimates to £110,000,000, a sum that was about 20 per cent less than it had been in 1913/14. It denied that Britain faced any serious external threats and insisted, echoing the eighteenth- and nineteenth-century orthodoxy, that reducing defence spending in peacetime would maximize Britain's war-making ability for 'instead of being bled white we should be safe to re-establish our reserve of wealth to be available if trouble thereafter occurs'.[1] However, the Treasury was only able to enforce this policy on the services in so far as the Cabinet supported it. The Lloyd George, Bonar Law, Baldwin and MacDonald Cabinets accepted that spending beyond the minimum necessary to ensure security would harm the long-term development of the economy and that excessively large armaments might alarm other powers and ignite a ruinously expensive arms race. But their perceptions of the threats facing Britain in the early 1920s were not static. The service estimates were determined by those perceptions, not by any standard fixed by the Treasury.

In August 1919 the Treasury persuaded the Cabinet that the services' strategic priorities should be imperial policing, not preparing to fight another great war. The Cabinet finance committee set the estimates at £135,000,000 which, allowing for inflation, was the same as they had been in 1913/14. The Cabinet also formulated what was subsequently called the 'Ten Year Rule'. It laid down that no great war in Europe was to be anticipated for ten years and no expeditionary force was required for that purpose. The War Office abandoned conscription in April 1920 and the army was reduced from 3,500,000 men in November 1918 to 370,000 men in November 1920. The services' principal responsibilities were the maintenance of order in Britain and the empire. Wherever possible air-power and other mechanical devices were to be used rather than manpower, on the grounds that 'substitution' would be cheaper. No alteration was made in the prewar standard governing the size of the navy, which was to be 60 per cent larger than the next largest navy, excluding the US navy.

The 'rule' was open to so many different interpretations that the Royal Navy and the RAF were able to bend it to suit their own purposes. It could be interpreted to mean either that they had to be ready for a great war in 1929 or that no such preparations need even begin until 1929. In 1919 it was impossible for the Treasury to control the services because the government seemed bent on governing the empire like a military fief. In both India and Ireland British troops acted vigorously, and sometimes brutally, to suppress agitators. But the resulting outcry in Britain and the cost of maintaining large garrisons to suppress hostile populations, made such a policy untenable. In 1921 political pressures mounted on the government to reduce spending and it capitulated and established a committee under Sir Eric Geddes to determine where cuts could be made. The service estimates were reduced after 1922 but this was done not because of the dictates of the committee but because of diminutions in the threats to the empire and reductions in operational requirements. In April 1921 the collapse of the triple alliance of dockers, railwaymen and miners meant that the number of troops committed to security duties in Britain could be cut. When support from the Dominions was not forthcoming the government abandoned the forward defence of India and withdrew from Afghanistan, southern Russia and Persia. Southern Ireland was granted Dominion status in 1921 because Sinn Fein's resistance demonstrated the impossibility of countering violent nationalism with nothing but military repression. In the Middle East the British secured their imperial communications in Egypt, Transjordan and Mesopotamia by reverting to their prewar policy of indirect rule, granting collaborationist regimes a large measure of self-government whilst retaining for themselves effective control over their foreign and defence policy. The forces committed to Turkey were withdrawn in 1923 when the Treaty of Lausanne was signed. The experiment of running the empire like a military fief was ended.

In the early 1920s the government recognized that the Treasury's image of a benign international order was also at odds with reality. Between 1919 and 1921 British hopes that a stable balance of power would emerge after the war were undermined by a combination of the Bolsheviks' victory in the Russian civil war, the Americans' withdrawal into isolation, the US and Japanese, governments' decision to continue ambitious naval building programmes, growing suspicions concerning Japanese ambitions in China, and continued French intransigence towards Germany. Britain was not willing to exist on French, Japanese or American goodwill and in these circumstances both the RAF and the Admiralty were able to justify expensive rearmament programmes. They were intended not as a prelude to war but to strengthen Britain's diplomatic bargaining position by preventing any of these powers developing such military strength that they could disregard vital British interests with impunity.

In 1919 British policy-makers had hoped to calm French fears of a resurgent Germany by jointly guaranteeing her security with the USA. That project collapsed when the USA rejected the Treaty of Versailles and the British withdrew their guarantee. But they did not follow the USA into isolation. In the next six years the British saw French intransigence as the main threat to European peace and they tried to pacify western Europe by a combination of diplomacy and deterrence. The former did not succeed until 1925 and in the meantime they were thrown back upon the latter. The RAF had been established as an independent service after a series of daylight air raids on London by German bombers in 1917 which the existing services seemed powerless to prevent. From 1919 and 1921 it justified its separate existence by developing the notion of 'control without occupation'. Sir Hugh Trenchard, the Chief of Air Staff, claimed that the revolt threatening British rule in Iraq could be cheaply contained if most of the expensive infantry garrisons were withdrawn and if the RAF were permitted to deploy a handful of squadrons to 'police' the region from the air. His confidence was justified. The cost of the Iraq garrison dropped and similar policies of control without occupation succeeded in Transjordan and Aden in the 1920s.

In 1922 the deterioration of Anglo-French relations presented Trenchard with a second argument to justify the existence of an independent RAF. He foretold that in a future war Britain's cities would face far worse devastation than they had done in 1917 unless something was done to prevent such attacks. In the spring of 1922 a subcommittee of the CID concluded that the French air-force could maintain a continuous series of air attacks on London for several weeks which would so demoralize the population that they would force the government to make peace. Defensive measures offered little chance of stopping the attackers and the solution the government accepted in August 1922 was to create an air strike force of twenty-three squadrons to deter the French from launching such an attack for fear of the destruction it could wreak on its own cities. In March 1923, following the French occupation of the Ruhr, the Conservative government established a committee under Lord Salisbury to examine the co-ordination of national and imperial defence and the relationship between the services and to determine the appropriate size of the air force for home and imperial defence. Salisbury recommended the creation of a Home Defence Air Force of 52 squadrons by 1929 and thanks to continuing concern about the French air menace the RAF's estimates rose by half between 1922/3 and 1925/6.

The fear of the bomber replaced the fear of invasion as the dominant concern of home defence planners. Although the Admiralty denied that air-power would have any significant impact on sea-power, the government had rejected the navy's claim to be Britain's first line of defence. In the 1920s and the 1930s governments accepted that no matter how wide was the Royal Navy's margin of superiority over other navies, Britain could still be subject to direct attack from the air. The exclusion of hostile powers from the Low Countries and the coast of France, long seen as vital to Britain's security against invasion, was now doubly important so as to ensure her safety from air attack. The way in which the home fronts of so many belligerents had collapsed in 1918, coupled with the social turmoil of the General Strike and the slump, led many policy-makers to doubt the durability of British society if it was subject to air bombardment. The Home Defence Air Force enabled the Air Staff to develop the theory of strategic interception and to postulate that by bombing the enemy's factories and civilian population the RAF would destroy his supplies, communications and national morale and so enable the army to defeat the enemy's ground forces at far less cost than had been incurred on the western front between 1914 and 1918.

The scuttling of the German High Seas Fleet at Scapa Flow in 1919 ended the German naval threat but it also shifted the naval centre of gravity of the British Empire to the Pacific where Britain was challenged by the Japanese and US navies. Lloyd George's government tried to counter the Americans by authorizing the Admiralty to build against the US navy in March 1920. It also considered whether it would be advantageous not to renew the Anglo-Japanese treaty for fear that its continuation would only encourage the Americans to build even more rapidly. Building a fleet to a two-power standard to match the Japanese and American fleets was politically impossible and financially undesirable. To deal with the Japanese they opted for a strategy of deterrence by announcing in June 1921 the creation of a major naval base at Singapore to which the fleet could be sent in an emergency. According to the Deputy Chief of Naval Staff it would 'cause Japan to hesitate before embarking on a course of action running counter to British interests'.[2] The Singapore strategy was cheaper than trying to maintain a two-power standard but the cost was still high. The British therefore accepted President Harding's invitation to a naval conference in Washington in December 1921 and his proposals that the world's five major naval powers, the USA, Britain, Japan, France and Italy, should maintain fleets of capital ships in the ratio 5:5:3:1.75:1.75 and end capital ship construction for a decade. Britain, whose merchant fleet was scattered across the world, insisted that no limits should be fixed for cruisers or destroyers because the French would accept no limit on submarine building. The Anglo-Japanese Alliance lapsed, the four Pacific powers agreed to respect each other's Pacific possessions, to maintain an 'open door' policy towards China, and Britain was permitted to continue work on Singapore.

The Cabinet accepted these terms because they recognized the lesson of 1917–18. An Anglo-American war was unthinkable and in the long term in another major great-power war, America's latent strength would mean that Britain's security lay in Anglo-American co-operation. At the 1921 Imperial Conference South Africa and Canada had insisted that the Anglo-Japanese Alliance would be worth little if it harmed relations between the empire and the USA. The Lloyd George government doubted whether renewal of the treaty would afford Britain much control over Japanese policy and they were certain that American resources meant that Britain could not win an Anglo-American naval race and that British tax-payers would not countenance it. The Sea Lords protested that the treaty meant that for the first time for over two hundred years Britain was content with naval parity rather than superiority, that suspension of new building would reduce the warship-building industry to decrepitude and that British interests in the Far East would no longer be safeguarded by the Japanese. But in the 1920s the Washington treaty permitted Britain to maintain a one-power standard measured against the USA and gave her superiority over the next two largest fleets, those of Japan and France. The naval balance of power in the western Pacific was not upset to Britain's disadvantage in the 1920s.

The army suffered the most severe cuts in the 1920s because it could not point to a unique threat which would justify increasing its estimates. In 1922 the Cabinet decided that the army's responsibilities were home and imperial defence, that it need not prepare to send an expeditionary force to Europe, and reduced its establishment to below the prewar level. But otherwise the postwar army was remarkably similar to the prewar army. The rank and file continued to be recruited from amongst the least skilled sections of the population, and its officers were recruited from the public schools. The special reserve was effectively abandoned in 1919. The Territorial Force was reconstructed in 1921 as the Territorial Army and organized into fourteen divisions. It differed from the prewar force in that its establishment was reduced and its members were obliged to take a general service commitment but as it was poorly equipped, undermanned and badly trained, its capabilities existed only on paper. By the late 1920s the regular army's strength had stabilized at 137 infantry battalions, 23 cavalry regiments and 4 tank battalions plus supporting arms. In theory the regular army in Britain should have been able to furnish 4 infantry divisions and 1 cavalry division for an expedition outside Europe. In practice, the basic shortcomings of the Cardwell system remained and home service units were often skeleton formations which had been milked dry of drafts for their sister units overseas.

In the 1920s the general staff failed to produce another Henry Wilson ready to argue for the need to prepare to dispatch an army to western Europe. Instead the growing strength of Bolshevik Russia caused the army's attention to revert to the defence of India. By 1928 about 60,000 British troops, including a third of the army's infantry, were stationed in India. Their policy, to keep trouble away from the North-West Frontier by preventing the Russians from undermining the existing regime in Afghanistan, bore a marked similarity to prewar policies. But carrying it out with Indian resources was impossible. India maintained about 190,000 troops of her own but as domestic unrest developed in the 1920s so many were deployed on internal security duties that few were available to guard against external attack. In 1927 the War Office, conceding that the government of India could not provide sufficient troops from its own assets, prepared a plan calling for the dispatch of eleven divisions from Britain. It was manifest nonsense, for such a force could only have been raised by conscription. India's role as a reservoir of manpower for imperial operations east of Suez was also under increasing pressure after 1919. Given the Dominions' reluctance to contribute to the general defence of the empire, the British were anxious that India should do more than she had done in the past. But Indian nationalists vehemently denounced the employment of Indian troops outside India and the government of India repeatedly insisted that in the event of an imperial crisis there would probably be such unrest in India that it would be impossible to detach significant numbers of troops overseas. Nor was the Indian army immune from the effects of the home rule movements. The British tried to contain their spread by a policy of 'Indianisation' and announced that their eventual aim was to grant complete control of the army to Indians. A token start was made by admitting ten Indian cadets to Sandhurst annually and by selecting a handful of units which were to be 'Indianised' over two decades. Until 1933 the cost of all troops stationed in India was met by the Indian tax-payer and nearly one-third of the Indian government's revenues was spent on defence. However, in 1933 in an attempt to quiet nationalist objectors, the British government began to subsidize the Indian defence budget. They also paid for the Indian troops they employed outside the subcontinent, a decision which in practice precluded raising large new Indian forces to defend the empire east of Suez.

It would be wrong to assume that the demands of the empire and financial stringency meant that the army turned its back completely on modern war or modern weapons in the 1920s. The mental horizons of many officers did not extend far beyond their regiments and the promotion system did block the rise of many able men. But a generation of officers emerged between the wars who were anxious to learn the lessons of the First World War. A tank corps survived the postwar cuts and throughout the 1920s, despite financial stringency, Britain remained the leading pioneer of mechanization. In 1927 an 'Experimental Mechanized Force' of tanks, armoured cars and artillery and infantry was established to develop techniques for armoured warfare. However, in 1928 it was disbanded because the money it absorbed was needed to mechanize infantry and cavalry units and because its continued existence could only be met by disbanding other units, an impossibility because of the manpower needed for imperial policing.

The Treasury's views did not determine service policies until between 1925 and 1928 and when they did so it was as a result of the stabilization of the international situation, not because they had usurped the function of the Cabinet as the ultimate arbiter of policy. By 1925 deterrence seemed to have worked. The position of comparative strength the naval and aerial rearmament programmes gave Britain enabled her to pursue a policy of international reconciliation by persuading France and Germany to accept the Locarno treaties guaranteeing the Franco-German and German-Belgian frontiers. By depriving Japan of any possible European ally, the agreement encouraged the Foreign Office to assume that there would be no war between Britain and Japan for a decade. The decline in tension with the French and Japanese persuaded the British to postpone completion of the Home Defence Air Force programme from 1929 to 1935 and to delay work on Singapore. The relaxation of international tension continued in 1926 when Germany joined the League of Nations and in 1928, when fifteen powers signed the Kellog-Briand Pact and renounced war. In 1928 the Foreign Office was so confident about the future that it raised no objections when the 'Ten Year Rule' was placed on a rolling basis. Only one problem remained. In the late 1920s the US government, balked by the Baldwin government's refusal to grant them formal parity in cruisers, threatened to embark on a major cruiser-building programme. The British responded by authorizing a construction programme of their own. But the Macdonald government elected in 1929 was committed to international disarmament and wanted to extend the Washington treaty to cover other classes of warship. At the London Naval Conference in 1930 they avoided a cruiser race with the USA but at the cost of surrendering the capital ship supremacy they had retained over Japan since 1922. The conference agreed on a moratorium on capital shipbuilding between 1931 and 1936 which meant that the ratio of British to Japanese capital ships would fall from 20:10 to 15:9 by the mid-1930s. If 6 British capital ships had to remain in home waters, the navy would be able to send only 9 to the Far East and they would have no margin of superiority over the Japanese.

Although the Locarno treaties demonstrated in theory that Britain accepted, in the words of a general staff memorandum of 1925 that 'The true strategic frontier of Great Britain is the Rhine', the British lacked the forces to uphold them and they could not draw on imperial resources because at the 1926 Imperial Conference the Dominions refused to accede to them.[3] Austen Chamberlain, the Foreign Secretary, rejected an examination of the strategic implications of the agreement because he assumed that the pact alone would pacify Europe for the foreseeable future. In practice Britain's actual strategic priorities in the late 1920s were much the same as they had been in the early 1890s: the security of the home islands, the protection of imperial communications and overseas bases and – a distant last – the provision of forces to act in concert with continental allies. The pattern of defence spending was also similar, except that the RAF now received a share of the budget. Between 1925 and 1935, when rearmament proper began, the ratio of spending on the army, navy and RAF was 36:49:15. The three services were in practice planning to fight three different wars, the navy against the Japanese in the Far East, the RAF against the French across the Channel and the army against the Russians on the North-West Frontier.

Between 1922 and 1932 the British had met threats from great powers by a combination of diplomacy and a modest degree of rearmament. That worked because their potential enemies remained divided and in the late 1920s the British felt able to embark upon a search for arms reduction, partly from fear that if they did not Germany might denounce the military clauses of the Treaty of Versailles. This quest culminated in the disarmament conference which met in Geneva in February 1932. The conference did not finally collapse until 1934 but within weeks of its convening the benign international environment which the British had shaped in the mid-1920s began to disintegrate. In September 1931 the Japanese had invaded Manchuria and in March 1932 they withdrew from the conference and the League of Nations. Embroiled in the slump, the National government created in August 1931 could only refer to the principles of the League of Nations and offer protests. But the chiefs of staff reacted swiftly to this more hostile world. In March 1932 they persuaded the government to abandon the 'Ten Year Rule' and in October to resume work on Singapore. In 1933 the international situation further worsened when Hitler gained power and withdrew Germany from the disarmament conference and the league. The chief of staff promptly told the Cabinet that Germany would soon be a formidable military power and that within three to five years her aggression might involve Britain in another continental war. The chiefs of staff's warning that Britain now confronted threats from not one but two great powers and at different ends of the globe persuaded the Cabinet in November 1933 to establish the Defence Requirements Committee (DRC). Its task was to recommend how to redress the worst deficiencies facing the services. Its chairman was Sir Maurice Hankey, the Cabinet secretary, and although its members included the chiefs of staff, its deliberations were dominated by the permanent under secretaries of the

Foreign Office, Sir Robert Vansittart, and of the Treasury, Sir Warren Fisher. They rejected Hankey's contention, which was supported by the First Sea Lord, that Japan was Britain's most dangerous enemy and insisted that Germany's geographic proximity to Britain and her economic potential made her the most dangerous long-term threat against whom the services should prepare. The DRC recommended a programme costing £170,000,000 over five years. Although it recommended the completion of the Singapore base, it insisted that the only real security for the Far Eastern empire lay in a political accommodation with Japan. It wanted to execute a modified version of the 1923 Home Defence Air Force programme and provide an expeditionary force of five divisions of regulars supported by fourteen territorial divisions. If this were sent to the Low Countries it would deprive Germany of airfields from which she could bomb Britain and 'would as a deterrent to an aggressor, exercise an influence for peace out of all proportion to its size' whilst encouraging allies for they would recognize that behind it 'is the whole might of the British Empire ready and determined to wage war'.[4]

By identifying Germany as the most serious threat to British security and by insisting that Britain could not hope to rearm successfully against more than one potential enemy, the DRC's report laid down two of the premises upon which British defence policy was based until 1939. It also demonstrated that left to themselves the services could not agree on a common, as opposed to an aggregate, programme. Their failure to do so was significant in the 1930s because any major rearmament programme was bound to be constrained by shortages of real resources. The National government had been created to engineer a recovery from the slump. Ministers, especially Neville Chamberlain, the Chancellor of the Exchequer between 1931 and 1937, believed that the economy could only recover if the budget were balanced at the lowest possible level and private industry were given the maximum scope to invest. However, after 1935 the pace of German rearmament persuaded the Treasury to abandon its adherence to a balanced budget. Rearmament was not retarded by the Treasury's reluctance to adopt deficit financing and to borrow to cover the cost of rearmament. Beginning in February 1937 the Treasury took powers to borrow money to finance rearmament and between 1937 and 1938 the proportion of the rearmament programme financed by borrowing rose from a quarter to a half. The Treasury did attempt to ration the money available to finance rearmament in 1937/8. But they did so not because they were afraid of an unbalanced budget but because too much spending on rearmament would place an insupportable burden on the nation's productive capacity.

The crucial factor retarding the rearmament programme was not the government's adherence to an outmoded economic philosophy but a shortage of real resources in the economy. After 1919 the defence industrial base had shrunk and when the government sought to expand it after 1934 they encountered shortages of factory space, skilled labour and machine-tools. More resources could only have been made available by diverting assets from domestic civilian production or from production for exports. The former would have threatened living standards and the latter would have endangered the balance of payments. The Treasury knew that Britain's financial position was not as favourable as it had been in 1914 and that she had fewer foreign reserves she could liquidate to buy the overseas supplies she would need in wartime. Help on the scale she had received from the USA after 1917 was problematic because in 1935 and 1937 Congress passed legislation compelling the President to bar the sale of arms to belligerents. Policy-makers were convinced that precarious as was the state of the British economy, the German economy was even less able to sustain a long war. It was therefore imperative that Britain should not, by excessive or premature rearmament, forfeit her ability to outlast Germany in a long war and only after the German occupation of Austria in March 1938 did the government ask industry to give priority to rearmament orders.

That is not to say that the government could not have made more efficient use of its resources. It could have ceased to rely upon the unregulated market and established a command economy. But civil servants lacked the expertise to run factories and any attempt to mobilize the economy depended upon the willing co-operation of capital and labour. That was a difficult political problem, especially for a Conservative-dominated government. For much of the 1930s trade unions in the engineering industry refused to accept the dilution of skilled labour, fearing that any boom caused by rearmament would be temporary and that when it collapsed their members would face competition for jobs from dilutees. Their employers were equally loath to accept state direction of industry for they knew that in return for dilution the unions would insist on tight controls over their profits. The government shied away from these dilemmas, the Chancellor of the Exchequer writing in 1938 that the adoption of either policy would mean that 'we turned ourselves into a different kind of nation'.[5]

In order to ensure that rearmament did not impose an insupportable strain on the economy or the existing social order, successive Cabinets permitted the Treasury considerable influence over the shape of the rearmament programme between 1934 and 1938. Chamberlain was especially critical of proposals to form an expeditionary force. It would be costly and he believed that the public, who still had painful memories of the western front, would be hostile to it. His opposition to a continental commitment was given intellectual underpinning by Liddell Hart who popularized his notion of a 'British way in warfare' in the 1930s. In June 1934 Chamberlain argued that the government should concentrate on measures for the direct defence of the United Kingdom which the public would support and that objective could be secured by creating an air-force of eighty squadrons. The force would be without the reserves necessary actually to fight a war but that would not matter because its bomber squadrons were intended to deter German aggression by threatening them with an aerial counter-offensive. Any decision on a major naval rearmament programme could be postponed until after the forthcoming London Naval Conference. Work on Singapore could continue but if the Far Eastern situation could be stabilized by a *rapprochement* with Japan, the plan to send a fleet could be dropped. Chamberlain's arguments, as far as they pertained to the services, were accepted by the Cabinet and the RAF was given priority over the other services in the quest for new funds. But his suggestion of a *rapprochement* with Japan was stoutly resisted by MacDonald and the Foreign Office on the grounds that it was certain to alienate the USA.

The first DRC programme promised to do little more than to repair the services' existing deficiencies. It was not until 1935/6 that rearmament proper began. Hitler denounced the limitations placed on Germany's forces by the Treaty of Versailles and claimed falsely that the *Luftwaffe* had achieved parity with the RAF. The short-lived Stresa Front of Britain, France and Italy engineered to contain Germany collapsed in October 1935 when the Italians invaded Abyssinia. The London Naval Conference of 1936 was a failure. Japan rejected British proposals for further naval arms limitations and abrogated the London treaty. British planners now had to confront three possible enemies. In July 1935 the DRC had been reconstituted and in the autumn presented a new programme. It called for the creation by 1939 of a two-power standard navy measured against Germany and Japan, an air force of 1,736 first-line aircraft and a field force of five divisions which could be dispatched to the Low Countries and could be reinforced by twelve territorial divisions. It also reiterated the unpalatable truth which had underpinned British defence policy since the Boer War. The armed forces alone could not preserve Britain's security in a three-front war and it was therefore vital for the Foreign Office to ensure that they never had to do so.

The Cabinet accepted the committee's report in February 1936 but with two important alterations. It agreed that the Admiralty should build beyond the one-power standard but it did not authorize the proposed 'New Standard' because there was insufficient industrial capacity to construct it. It did not challenge the military or political needs for the field force but insisted that public opinion would not accept such a large continental commitment. Only the five regular divisions were to be prepared for a continental land war. The cost of this programme, plus the fact that the services were still unable to agree on a common, as opposed to an aggregate, programme, persuaded Baldwin to appoint Sir Thomas Inskip as Minister for the Co-ordination of Defence. Like Chamberlain, who became Prime Minister in December 1937, Inskip believed that economic and social stability were themselves powerful deterrents to war. In December 1937 he wrote that 'Nothing operates more strongly to deter a potential aggressor from attacking this country than our stability, and the power which this nation has so often shown of overcoming its difficulties without violent change and without damage to its inherent strength'.[6]

Chamberlain did not invent appeasement. He pursued it because he was convinced that the public would not tolerate war over an obscure dispute in eastern Europe and that the best way to preserve the political dominance of the Conservative Party and his own leadership was to resolve peacefully the external threats facing Britain. He was encouraged in his belief by the Dominions at the Imperial Conference in 1937 and his years as chancellor meant that he listened carefully when Treasury officials wondered what Britain could do if she completed her rearmament programme in 1940 and then had to maintain her forces indefinitely at their new level. He was suspicious of Soviet Russia, and he had little faith in France. He believed that in a long war US economic assistance would be vital but that it was unlikely to be forthcoming. He feared that even if the Americans did proffer help, the price might compromise Britain's economic independence.

Chamberlain believed that stronger defences would deter war whilst diplomacy would remove its causes. He did not pursue a policy of piecemeal concessions to buy off the dictators but sought a binding and comprehensive settlement of their grievances. Between May 1937 and September 1938 he looked for a political agreement with at least one of the dictators whilst accelerating air and naval rearmament at the expense of the army's continental role. But even before he became Prime Minister inflation was increasing and the balance of payments was sinking into deficit. In December 1937 the Cabinet approved a paper by Inskip pointing to these dangers and describing economic stability as 'a fourth arm in defence... without which purely military efforts would be of no avail'.[7] They fixed a limit of £1,500,000,000 on defence spending between 1937 and 1941. That was more than the 1936 programme but less than the services wanted. Chamberlain and Inskip also persuaded the Cabinet to accept a new set of strategic priorities, placing the air defence of Britain first, the protection of seaborne trade and the defence of the empire second and the dispatch of an expeditionary force to an Eastern theatre a long way last. The territorials were to be trained to man anti-aircraft defences in Britain whilst the regulars were to be deployed in Egypt to counter further Italian aggression and in Palestine to keep the peace between Arabs and Jews. The army's case for a continental commitment went by default. Most senior officers were only too well aware that in its present state of unpreparedness it would meet with disaster on the continent. By the spring of 1938, on the eve of Hitler's invasion of Austria, Britain's policy was intended to give her the ability to withstand a knockout blow from the air and to deter Germany by confronting her with the prospect of a long war in which Britain's greater economic strength would be decisive. A policy of limited liability on the continent had become a policy of no liability at all.

The feasibility of these policies was destroyed in the next three years. After the *Anschluss* the chiefs of staff informed the Cabinet that the weaknesses of Britain's defences and the possibility that she might have to confront Japan (who had signed the Anti-Comintern Pact with Germany in November 1936), Italy and Germany simultaneously meant that there was no way in which she could save Czechoslovakia if Germany invaded her. The French had no plans to assist the Czechs by attacking in the west and the chiefs of staff, conscious of how little help they could give France, did nothing to persuade them to change their plans. In September 1938, when Chamberlain attempted at Munich to satisfy Hitler's demand that the Sudeten Germans must be returned to Germany, he had the broad support of the British public and the chiefs of staff. The latter insisted, probably correctly that the Germans could quickly overrun Czechoslovakia, that the possibility of Russian military help could be discounted and that Czech independence could only be restored after a prolonged war. They feared that such a conflict would soon develop into a world war as the Italians and Japanese took the opportunity offered them by Britain's preoccupations in Europe to attack her empire in the Middle and Far East. But the Air Staff's prediction which most alarmed the Cabinet, that the war would begin with a knockout blow from the air against Britain, was erroneous. The *Luftwaffe* did not possess large numbers of bombers capable of attacking Britain from bases in Germany and had abandoned the development of long-range strategic bombers in 1936. The Air Staff's delusion was a product of their belief that Germany would have to seek a quick victory because her economy could not withstand a prolonged war, their own commitment to strategic bombing and the inability of politicians and the public to understand the limitations of the rapidly changing technology of air-power. The fear of a German knockout blow from the air which played a major role in paralysing the Cabinet's will to resist Hitler at Munich, was made even greater by the RAF's inability to retaliate in kind. It was not until 1937 that the Air Staff undertook any serious study of how to conduct an air offensive against Germany and it revealed that they had little idea of what targets they could hit and of what losses they might incur. They recommended that the RAF's efforts should be devoted to counter-force operations designed to reduce Germany's own air striking power, rather than attacks against industrial targets. But in 1938 even that seemed hopelessly ambitious to the Commander-in-Chief of Bomber Command. Far from acting as an effective deterrent, the RAF had itself been deterred.

In the winter and spring of 1938/9 it became apparent that the Munich settlement had not pacified Europe and had left France without a reliable continental ally. In the autumn of 1938 the French started to insist that Britain had to replace the Czech divisions now lost to them. When the Chamberlain government had abandoned a continental role for the British army, it had been impervious to arguments that French morale would falter unless given visible British support. Now Lord Halifax, the Foreign Secretary, began to fear the spread of defeatism in France and in February 1939 the chiefs of staff told the Cabinet Britain would have to take a share in the land defence of France for unless the British supported France to the utmost, she might seek a *rapprochement* with Germany. It was easier for the Cabinet to accept the implications of these proposals in 1939 than it would have been before Munich. The public had greeted Munich with relief because it averted an immediate war but even in September 1938 some Cabinet ministers had followed Chamberlain with little enthusiasm and one had resigned in protest. Small groups of Conservative backbenchers led by Churchill and the former Foreign Secretary, Anthony

Eden, deplored the settlement. But the most significant changes of attitude occurred in the Liberal and Labour Parties where support for the ideals of the League of Nations had once been strongest. Faith in the league had been shaken by its failures during the Abyssinian crisis and during the Spanish Civil War some socialists had campaigned for the creation of a 'popular front' against fascism. Trade union leaders like Ernest Bevin were critical of Nazi domestic policies and rejected Labour's opposition to rearmament. Their revulsion at the implications of Munich was only intensified by reports of Nazi attacks on Jewish property in November 1938.

During the Munich crisis there were large-scale withdrawals of foreign currency from London. But despite this intimations of what the economic repercussions of more speedy rearmament might be, in the spring of 1939 the government accepted that it must have larger armaments. The Treasury predicted that if Germany continued to borrow to finance her rearmament programme she might soon face economic chaos. By January 1939 Halifax believed that within a year Hitler would be compelled to execute a spectacular coup to distract attention from his domestic economic failures. That coup seemed about to happen in February 1939 when rumours of a German attack on Holland reached London. The Cabinet responded by agreeing to prepare a field force of six divisions for dispatch to France, to equip some of the Territorials for the continent and to begin joint planning with the French. They did so not in the belief that war was inevitable but in the hope that by increasing the pace of British rearmament they could deter German aggression.

The Nazi occupation of Prague a month later dealt a heavy blow to their hopes. Before Prague Hitler was able to claim that he was only trying to right the wrongs done to Germany under the Treaty of Versailles. But the Czechs were not Germans and had no wish to be ruled by Germans. The British public greeted the occupation with dismay. Recruits, believing that Britain's national survival might soon be threatened by an aggressive power inspired by a nihilistic philosophy, poured into the Territorial Army whilst in the Dominions, with the exception of South Africa, public opinion also began to accept that war with Germany was inevitable and just.

In February 1939 the chiefs of staff had prepared plans for war against Germany and Italy and they were broadly accepted by the French in April. They planned for a long war falling into three stages. It would begin with a massive enemy offensive which the Allies would have to resist. The British would have to give all possible aid to France by dispatching the field force and would have to retain control of Egypt from whence a counter-attack could eventually be mounted against Italy. Peace in the Far East was vital because the fleet could not be sent from the Mediterranean to Singapore until after Italy's defeat. In the second stage the Allies would mobilize their own resources. That would be facilitated by the fact that the Royal Navy would command the seas and that would give the Allies access to worldwide supplies. The Allies would simultaneously weaken Germany and Italy by blockade and propaganda. The

British exaggerated the ease with which that could be done for their economic intelligence concerning Germany was defective. They incorrectly assumed that her greatest strategic weakness was her dependence upon imported raw materials, that the German economy was already fully stretched and that an air and sea blockade would materially reduce her war-making potential within twelve to eighteen months. In the final stage the Allies would mount their own counter-offensive.

Britain's fundamental assumption was that time was on the side of the Allies and that the French army would be sufficiently powerful to check the Germans in the west with, initially, minimal direct British military support. In reality time might not be on their side for, as the Treasury never tired of pointing out, the Royal Navy alone could not give Britain access to overseas supplies. Britain was heavily dependent upon imported food-stuffs and raw materials. In a long war in which men were mobilized for the armed forces and factories were switched from producing exports to producing weapons, her balance of payments might collapse. In 1935 the British had spent only 3 per cent of their gross national product on defence compared to the German figure of 8 per cent. In 1939 the British spent 18 per cent compared to the German figure of 23 per cent. By the start of the war Britain was producing more tanks and aircraft than was Germany. But it was problematic how long the British could maintain this level of spending. In April 1939 a Treasury representative told the chiefs of staff that 'If we were under the impression that we were as well able as in 1914 to conduct a long war, we were burying our heads in the sand'.[8] But, convinced that they could not win a short war, they had no option other than to plan to win a long one.

In March 1939 rumours of an imminent German attack on Poland persuaded Chamberlain to promise her support. Similar guarantees were given to Greece and Rumania in April. This was the first time the British had ever guaranteed frontiers in eastern Europe. Chamberlain did not issue these guarantees to create a military coalition to fight Germany and Italy but in the hope that 'The actual fact of the undertaking having been made, may indeed have the effect of deterring Germany from aggression, or at least forcing her to postpone it'.[9] In late March the Territorial Army was doubled as a public gesture of Britain's new resolve and in April conscription was introduced to encourage the French. It met almost no public opposition but the War Office foresaw that it would actually reduce the army's readiness by compelling them to break up existing units to provide training cadres. Unknown to Britain, three days after they issued the Polish guarantee, Hitler had ordered the *Wehrmacht* to be ready to attack Poland by 1 September.

The chiefs of staff welcomed the guarantees only in as much as they might compel the Germans to retain a number of divisions in the east and give Britain and France more time to prepare their own defences. They never believed that Poland and Rumania would be able to maintain a sustained resistance, they prepared no plans to give them direct military assistance and the Treasury vetoed any economic aid. The British realized that only the Soviet Union might be able to tilt the military balance in eastern Europe against Germany but British intelligence had a low estimation of Soviet military efficiency after the Great Purges of 1937–8 and the Poles were loath to permit the Soviets to deploy their forces on Polish soil. It was also hard for Conservative politicians who had spent their whole careers denouncing the evils of communism to court Russia and half-hearted attempts to reach an Anglo-Soviet accord collapsed in August.

Germany attacked Poland on 1 September. Deterrence had failed because it was not supported by plausible military sanctions but appeasement had not yet ended. Chamberlain hesitated for two days before pressure from all sides of the Commons forced him to accept that the German attack was a case of unprovoked aggression and he reluctantly declared war. The chiefs of staff's predictions about Poland's inability to withstand a German assault proved accurate, especially in view of the fact that the signing of the Nazi-Soviet Pact on 23 August exposed Poland to a two-front war, and by the end of September she had collapsed. Otherwise the strategic situation was better than the chiefs of staff had envisaged for Italy and Japan had not taken advantage of Britain's preoccupation with Germany to prey on her empire. Throughout the winter of 1939/40 Chamberlain remained convinced of the soundness of the plan the British and French staffs had agreed in April 1939. Reports of the unpopularity of the Nazi regime and the antipathy towards the war felt by many Germans convinced him that a satisfactory peace, which would include the removal of Hitler from power and the German evacuation of Poland and Czechoslovakia, could be secured by intensifying the policy of deterrence he had been pursuing since 1937. In October 1939 he wrote that 'My policy continues to be the same. Hold on tight. Keep up the economic pressure, push on with munitions production and military preparations with the utmost energy, take no offensive unless Hitler begins. I reckon that if we are allowed to carry on this policy we shall have won the war by the Spring'.[10] As part of this build-up of pressure the British accepted a continental commitment. The proportion of the army's divisions deployed in France increased from 12 per cent in October 1939 to 41 per cent in May 1940.

This Fabian strategy was challenged by Churchill, who entered the War Cabinet in September as First Lord of the Admiralty, and by two successive French premiers, Daladier and Reynaud. Their differences crystallized over three issues: the size of the British army, military intervention in Scandinavia and a plan to float mines down the Rhine. The *Luftwaffe*'s superiority during the Polish campaign further convinced Chamberlain of the necessity of creating a powerful RAF and he did not see how doing so could be reconciled with the creation of a fifty-five division army. Churchill recognized that limiting Britain's commitment to the land war would be unacceptable to the French for it would seem that the British remained intent on fighting to the last Frenchman. In this case Chamberlain acquiesced but he was harder to convince on the other two issues. Churchill wanted to intensify the economic pressure on Germany by disrupting traffic on the Rhine and the flow of Swedish iron-ore through the Norwegian port of Narvik. Troops sent to Scandinavia would also give assistance to Finland, which had been attacked by Hitler's ally, Russia, in November 1939. The British welcomed the Russo-Finnish War in the belief that it would reduce the quantities of supplies that the Russians could send to Germany and would preclude Russian pressure on Turkey which might threaten the approaches to India. The French deprecated mining the Rhine for fear of German reprisals against their own industries but favoured operations in Scandinavia because they promised to keep the war at a safe distance from France. Chamberlain eventually agreed to the French policy because of reports which reached him in the winter and spring of 1939/40. They indicated that there was a limit to French readiness to maintain general mobilization unaccompanied by military operations designed to hasten the end of the war. They also indicated that the French blamed the British for the inactivity. Fortunately for the Allies Finnish resistance collapsed before Allied troops landed in Norway in April 1940 and so they did not add Russia to their enemies, but otherwise the operation was a disaster. The Germans landed just ahead of the Allies who arrived too late to dislodge them and suffered considerable losses upon evacuation.

The Norwegian débâcle marked the beginning of a strategic and political revolution for the British. On 10 May 1940 Chamberlain resigned, Churchill became Prime Minister of a Coalition government and the Germans launched an offensive in the west which by the end of May had forced the British to begin to evacuate 338,000 British and French troops from Dunkirk. France accepted Hitler's armistice terms on 22 June and the fundamental assumption upon which British strategy had rested, that the French army was at least strong enough to hold the Germans in the west, was destroyed. In June 1940 Churchill and his government publicly insisted that there could be no peace short of total victory. In private the War Cabinet agreed that no satisfactory peace could be secured from Hitler until the British had demonstrated their ability to resist invasion but once they had done so they might be prepared to negotiate with a German government shorn of Hitler and to agree to terms which included the cession of some colonies and an acceptance of German domination of Central Europe, provided that Britain's own independence was assured. In the summer of 1940 RAF Fighter Command and the superiority enjoyed by the Royal Navy in home waters kept Britain safe from invasion but otherwise her strategic situation seemed to be a good deal worse than it had been in the First World War. From 1914 to 1918 it had taken four years of relentless attrition on two fronts to wear down Germany's war-making capacity. But in June 1940 Britain was without continental allies. The Churchill government did what earlier British governments had done when confronted with a similar situation: they resorted to economic warfare to weaken their enemies, they defended the empire and they sought new allies. They opted for the 'British way in warfare' from necessity, not choice.

From 1940 to 1941 British strategy rested on a combination of blockade, propaganda, the bomber and subversion. France's collapse marked a dangerous alteration in the balance of naval power for Italy joined Germany on 10 June and menaced the British Empire in the Middle East and Mediterranean. To protect their maritime security and to prevent the French fleet falling into German hands the Royal Navy sank part of it at Oran in July. British intelligence assumed that the Germans would not have dared to go to war until their economy was fully mobilized and that consequently they were highly vulnerable to aerial bombardment and blockade. In fact their economy was only partially mobilized in 1940 and German arms production did not peak until the middle of 1944. Their conquests meant that they could avoid the worst consequences of the blockade by drawing upon the resources of almost the whole of Europe. Churchill created the Special Operations Executive in July 1940 to organize guerrilla resistance in occupied Europe. Faith in strategic bombing expanded to fill the vacuum which had been created by the collapse of the French army. In September 1940 the chiefs of staff thought that together they could destabilize Hitler's Europe by 1942. The *Wehrmacht*, paralysed by lack of supplies and guerrilla attacks, would collapse under its own weight and the British army would be able to return to the continent not to fight a costly war of attrition, but to accept the Germans' surrender. These beliefs were slow to fade and help to explain Britain's opposition to US proposals to launch a cross-Channel offensive between 1942 and 1944.

American assistance came much more slowly than Churchill expected. In September 1939 the Cabinet's Land Forces Committee recommended that Britain should attempt to produce 2,250 planes per month and enough equipment for fifty-five divisions. The Treasury estimated that this programme would exhaust Britain's foreign exchange within two years and a senior Treasury official wrote that 'without direct US assistance we could not support a two year war'.[11] He was correct. After the fall of France economic mobilization took priority over fiscal prudence. British ordering in the USA increased so rapidly that by December 1940 the drain on Britain's dollar and gold reserves was such that she confronted the same choice she had faced in December 1916. She could either accept German peace terms or become dependent on the USA. The Roosevelt administration eased the situation in March 1941 by inaugurating the Lend-Lease Programme. It would be wrong to exaggerate its immediate significance for Britain paid cash for most of the American goods she obtained in 1941. But by 1945 Britain had received $27,000 million in lend lease assistance and the reciprocal assistance the British granted the USA accounted for less than a quarter of that. Between 1942 and 1945 US economic aid represented about 9 per cent of Britain's total war expenditure. The programme marked a dramatic shift in British strategy. In the eighteenth century Britain had paid others to fight for her. Now, as one

British journalist in Washington remarked, 'we shall be playing the role of the Hessians'.[12]

Italy's entry into the war in June 1940 threatened Britain's position in the Middle East and the government took considerable risks to defend the empire. In August they dispatched 150 tanks to Egypt and between December 1940 and February 1941 they drove the Italians from Cyrenaica. However, they did not advance into Tripolitania and eliminate Italy's North African empire because in March Hitler invaded the Balkans. The British believed that he had done so to undermine the blockade, to spread discontent amongst the Arab populations of the Middle East and to sever Britain's imperial communications in the eastern Mediterranean. They dispatched troops from North Africa to Greece in a vain attempt to support the Greeks but also in the hope that they might act as a catalyst for the formation of a coalition with Yugoslavia and Turkey. But in April the remnants of the force were evacuated and in the meantime the arrival of German reinforcements in North Africa enabled the Axis to reoccupy Cyrenaica.

The land war in the Middle East was an imperial, not a purely British undertaking. Between the wars the Dominions had added little to Britain's immediate war potential. They spent a smaller fraction of their gross national product on defence than had Britain and after the experiences of 1914–18 all except New Zealand had made it plain that they would never allow Britain to commit them to a war without prior consultation. But the insistence of successive governments in the 1930s that the defence of Britain must come before the defence of the empire meant that the British did not dissipate a large proportion of their defence effort overseas. The fleet was concentrated in the Mediterranean against Italy, not at Singapore against Japan. The RAF was built up to fight Germany, not to defend the empire. Only the army's manpower was diverted to a considerable extent to imperial defence. In 1938 just over half of the army was serving in the empire. But the Cabinet's decision in December 1937 to eschew a continental commitment was not the reason why the army was slow to acquire the kinds of armoured divisions which the Germans used so successfully between 1939 and 1941. Tank design and production problems antedated 1937. The army's failure to create modern armoured divisions reflected the government's decision to give priority in allocating industrial plant and skilled labour to the RAF and navy. The chiefs of staff were correct to calculate that in a long war the empire would make a significant contribution to the war effort, not because they could produce munitions in large quantities, but because they could provide military manpower. Between 1940 and 1942 the British concentrated the bulk of their own army at home where it prepared to meet the expected German invasion but they were able to use Indian and Dominion divisions as an imperial reserve in the Middle East. In October 1941 73 per cent of the divisions allocated to the Eighth Army in North Africa were from the empire and only 27 per cent were from Britain. Without imperial and Dominion forces Britain could not have secured her interests in the Middle East and Mediterranean during the Second World War.

But although operations in the Balkans and Middle East might protect the empire, they would not overthrow the Axis and by mid-1941 it was apparent that expectations of a German collapse caused by blockade and air attack had been optimistic. Between June and December 1941 Britain gained the allies she needed to defeat the Axis, not through any strategic coup of her own, but thanks to the fact that Germany attacked Russia and Japan attacked the USA. When Hitler invaded Russia in June 1941 the British were slow to recognize their good fortune for few policy-makers believed that Russia's resistance would be prolonged. They saw her entry into the war as an opportunity to pursue their own interests rather than as a chance to devise a new alliance strategy. They rejected Russian appeals for a landing or a large raid in France and in the west the British contented themselves with intensifying air attacks on Germany. In North Africa Churchill urged his commanders to take the opportunity of Germany's preoccupation with Russia to mount a counter-offensive in Libya, whilst in the Middle East the Foreign Secretary, Anthony Eden, worked with the Russians to eliminate German influence from Iraq and Persia. It was not until the Russians mounted a successful counter-attack in front of Moscow in December 1941 that the British accepted that their resistance would not rapidly collapse and that a new factor had entered the conflict, an army large enough to match the German army on the continent. For the rest of the war the Germans never deployed less than half of their ground forces on the eastern front.

By the time the Russians had launched their first major counter-attack Britain had acquired a second ally. In 1935 Chamberlain had hoped to appease Japan by negotiating a non-aggression pact but he failed because neither Britain nor the USA would grant Japan naval parity. He was thrown back on deterrence and at the Imperial Conference in May 1937 the Admiralty accepted that Singapore was the corner-stone of the defences of the Far Eastern empire. It told the Dominions that it planned to send eight to ten capital ships there in an emergency and in 1938 the Singapore dry-dock was completed. But the British government refused to say whether they would send a fleet if a war had already started in Europe. France's collapse and Italy's entry into the war in 1940 upset their calculations because even had the 'New Standard' fleet envisaged in 1936 been ready the British would still have relied upon the French navy to contain the Italians. But after June 1940 they were confronted by the Italians in the Mediterranean and the Germans in home waters and they had no capital ships to spare to send to Singapore.

Between 1940 and 1941 Churchill, who seriously underrated Japan's military capabilities, preferred to concentrate British and imperial resources in the Mediterranean and to postpone war with Japan for as long as possible. Staff talks with the Dominions, the Dutch and the USA began in October 1940 but served only to highlight the deficiencies in all their preparations. Above all they did not lead to the one thing which would have sustained Britain's Far Eastern strategy, a decision by the USA to send their fleet to Singapore. British troops which might have been sent to Singapore in 1941 went to the Middle East and aircraft which might have gone to support them went instead to Russia. When it seemed that the appeasement of Japan had failed, Churchill resorted to a pale imitation of the Singapore strategy and dispatched two capital ships in the hope that they might 'be a decisive deterrent'.[13] They arrived in December 1941, just in time to be sunk by Japanese aircraft, and Singapore fell in February 1942. Japan's entry into the war was a calamity and a blessing for Britain. It was a calamity because by May 1942 Japan had conquered Malaya and Burma and was at the frontier of India. It was a blessing for Britain because Japan began her bid to establish an autarkic empire by attacking Pearl Harbour which brought the USA into the war on Britain's side.

Between 1915 and 1918 the seriousness of the German threat and the exigencies of alliance politics compelled the British to make their largest ever continental commitment. The result appeared to be a triumph for the British, albeit one bought at great cost. By 1922 a more benign international environment and the abandonment of a brief attempt to run the empire as a military fief, meant that the government could reduce the service estimates. The British did not retreat into isolation in the 1920s. In the mid-1920s modest air and naval rearmament enabled them, from a position of rough parity, to pacify France, Japan and Germany. This policy worked until the mid-1930s. When the international environment then became less benign the British attempted to deter and to appease their rivals. But deterrence is a long-term policy. Its success rested on Britain's ability to enlarge and then to maintain her forces for just as long as it took for diplomacy to remove the source of the dictators' grievances. The policy failed for two reasons. The ambitions of the fascist dictators constituted such a challenge to the international system that they left no room for compromise. Domestic economic and political constraints made it impossible for the British to create defence forces of sufficient size with enough rapidity to pose a credible deterrent to three challengers simultaneously. Churchill was right when he told the Commons in January 1942 that the fundamental problem was insoluble for

> There has never been a moment, there never could have been a moment, when Great Britain or the British Empire, single handed, could fight Germany and Italy, could wage the Battle of Britain, the Battle of the Atlantic and the Battle of the Middle East – and at the same time stand thoroughly prepared in Burma, the Malay Peninsula, and generally in the Far East.[14]

The balance that the Chamberlain government struck between economic stability and defensive readiness did at least enable Britain to withstand the German and Italian onslaught of 1939–41.

British strategic policy between 1939 and 1942 approximated to the mixed paradigm. Between 1939 and 1940, although the British continued to place considerable reliance on economic blockade, assisted by the new weapon of air-power, the exigencies of alliance politics again compelled them to make a significant and growing commitment of landforces to the continent. That commitment was only terminated when the Germans drove the BEF into the sea at Dunkirk. After Dunkirk they opted for the 'British way in warfare' from necessity, not choice. The bulk of the British army was kept at home to counter the threatened German invasion and the British relied heavily on imperial forces to secure their interests in the Middle East. The Japanese conquest of Singapore, Malaya and Burma called into question the viability of this strategy. It shattered Britain's prestige – that is to say, the reputation for invincibility which she had enjoyed in the eyes of many of her colonial subjects and which was one of the most important pillars of her imperial power. And it posed such a direct threat to India and Australia that it cast doubt upon how much longer they would allow the British to use their forces for British ends.

8 The End of Empire, 1942–82

In retrospect it can be seen that in the forty years after the fall of Singapore Britain ceased to be a global power and reverted to what she had been before 1688, a power of the second rank, only intermittently able to play an independent role in the state system. Even the most obtuse policy-makers realized that in these changed circumstances the way in which they exercised British power would have to be remodelled, that it would not be prudent to clash with the USA and that in some regions of the world predominance would have to be yielded to Washington. But for a generation after 1942 most policy-makers did not believe that they were presiding over the wholesale abandonment of Britain's empire and great-power status. They believed that despite Britain's evident inferiority to the USA and Russia in economic and military resources, Britain could remain a great power. They thought that they were engaged in a selective shedding of commitments which would leave Britain that much stronger and more able to retain those overseas assets which really mattered. As late as the mid-1950s Russian and American dominance in Asia and Africa was far from complete and there still seemed to be room for the British to exercise a predominant influence in parts of both continents. It was not until the late 1960s that the British decided that the time had come to withdraw from east of Suez. The resilience of old habits of thought in the face of changing world circumstances can be measured by the fact that even after India, the core of Britain's Asiatic empire since the mid-eighteenth century, had been granted her independence, the British remained determined to acquire an independent nuclear deterrent because Britain was still a great power and great powers must possess the most powerful weapons. British defence policy, like her foreign policy, was designed to preserve as much as possible of Britain's world power in increasingly adverse circumstances.

Until December 1941 the Churchill government's main concern was to continue fighting. But from 1942 onwards they realized that the Allies' economic and human resources would eventually wear down the Axis powers. Consequently they saw no reason why they should engage the enemy unless they did so in overwhelming force. The USA had enormous latent power but it took time to transform it into military force. By contrast the British were already close to the peak of their strength in 1942 and until the middle of 1943 they were able to dominate the Anglo-American strategic discussions. But by mid-1943 the USA had achieved a rough parity of power with the British and soon began to overtake her. In the changed circumstances of the last two years of the war it was the Americans who dominated the strategic councils of the Western Allies.

The USA's entry into the war encouraged the British to revert to much the same policy of attrition they had agreed with France in 1939. In February 1941 the British and Americans had agreed that if the USA entered the conflict the Allies would give priority to the war against Germany and only sufficient forces to prevent further Japanese advances would be allotted to the Far East. When they met as Allies at the 'Arcadia' conference in December 1941 the two governments reaffirmed that decision. Anglo-American strategy rested upon their superior economic resources but that superiority could be nullified if the weapons, food-stuffs and raw materials they required were sunk by U-boats so they agreed that their first priority was to defeat the U-boat offensive. Britain's naval rearmament programme of the late 1930s had produced too few convoy escorts and between September 1939 and December 1941 the Allies lost nearly 8 million tons of merchant shipping, only one third of which was replaced by new launchings. Shipping shortages were to dictate Allied strategy for much of the war. Churchill and Roosevelt decided that the Germans were to be worn down by a combination of the Russian army, supplied with Western war material, and large-scale air raids and amphibious operations launched from Britain. They would isolate the European Axis powers from the outside world through 'tightening the ring' by occupying North Africa and Tripoli and by persuading Turkey to join the alliance. These operations would also reduce the strain on Allied shipping by reopening the Mediterranean. Churchill hoped that these operations would culminate in the surrender of Italy. Only then would a final assault be mounted against Germany by simultaneous land operations mounted by Russia from the east, the USA from the south and Britain from the west. To co-ordinate their strategy the two governments established the Combined Chiefs of Staff, consisting of the American and British Joint Chiefs of Staff. As the British chiefs were located in London, they were represented in Washington by a former CIGS, Sir John Dill. Despite the fact that the two Allies still clashed over strategic priorities, these arrangements marked the beginning of an intimate collaboration between the two powers which was unique in its closeness. Until the middle of 1943 the Combined Chiefs of Staff gave the British the opportunity to foist their strategic ideas on to their allies. In 1944 and 1945 it gave them the right to discuss their needs on equal terms with the Americans instead of being in the position of an importunate client grateful for whatever help their patron might offer.

The British prevailed at the 'Arcadia' conference because they had arrived more carefully briefed than had the Americans and because they had more forces already in contact with the enemy. But lack of American criticism left them with the impression that a greater degree of Allied unanimity existed than was the case. Some American policy-makers were reluctant to accept many British proposals at their face value because they suspected that the emphasis the British placed on the Mediterranean was an attempt to draw them into defending British imperial interests. The US navy questioned the policy of 'Europe first' and the army was sceptical of Churchill's preference for a peripheral strategy and his apparent belief that it would be possible to overcome the Germans without defeating their army in the field. Drawing upon a strategic tradition that stretched back to General Grant and the final stage of the Civil War, the Army Chief of Staff, General George Marshall, preferred a more direct approach. He believed that the best place to deploy the 200-division army he planned to raise was the plains of north-west Europe because they offered the shortest route to the heart of Germany. The British retorted that the Americans failed to recognize the formidable practical problems of fighting the Germans in north-west Europe. Their defeats between 1940 and 1942 and their experiences on the Western front in the First World War left them with great respect for German fighting power. The destruction of the amphibious expeditions dispatched to Norway and Greece and the sinking of the *Prince of Wales* and the *Repulse* by the Japanese testified to the fact that the strategic flexibility which possession of superior sea-power might once have conferred upon the British, had now disappeared. The benefits of superior sea-power could now only be garnered by amassing large fleets of vulnerable surface warships, transports and specialized landing-craft which could not operate in safety unless they were protected by friendly aircraft. Such operations were expensive and time-consuming to mount and meant that it was the defender, who could use roads and railways to mass his reserves, who now enjoyed strategic flexibility unless Allied air-power could disrupt his communications. The failure of the Dieppe raid in August 1942 pointed to the pitfalls of mounting an invasion without adequate preparations.

But there were still deeper reasons why the British were reluctant to suffer the expected heavy losses that would ensue if they embraced Marshall's plans. They knew that by 1943 they were reaching the end of their resources. British economic mobilization was probably more extensive than that of any other belligerent but by 1943 about 46 per cent of the labour force was deployed in the armed services, in civil defence, or in munitions industries and despite this enormous effort she could not keep pace with the Americans. American munitions production equalled Britain's in 1942 but by 1944 it was six times as great. Britain came to be heavily dependent upon lend-lease assistance. She received $27,000,000,000 in lend-lease assistance between 1941 and 1945, a figure which was in no way matched by the reciprocal assistance she granted to the USA or the $2,074,000,000 of assistance Britain sent to Russia. Britain's relative decline as a manufacturing nation had important strategic consequences. Her shipbuilding industry could not cope with the competing demands of the surface fleet and the merchant navy and the Americans built most of the thousands of landing-craft required for amphibious landings. That gave them an effective veto over British operations in the Mediterranean and the Far East and enabled them to steer Allied resources towards the second front in north-west Europe.

It was paradoxical that it was during the Second World War, when her grip on her empire was slipping away, that Britain relied more than ever before upon imperial manpower. Three times as many Indians enlisted in the Indian army in the Second World War than had done in the First World War. In the course of the war Britain and her empire and Dominions mobilized 103 divisions or their equivalents. Only 49 of them (47.6 per cent) were raised in Britain and 54 (52.4 per cent) were raised in India, West Africa and the Dominions. Some of these formations had only a brief existence or only existed on paper and so by 1945 Britain and her empire were maintaining forty-two divisions or their equivalents. But forty-three of the non-British formations did make a real contribution to the war by serving outside their country of origin. The empire also provided 39 per cent of the RAF's air-crews.

The opening of the Japanese war marked a major turning-point in how the British used their imperial manpower resources. Before 1942 they had been able to deploy Indian and Dominion divisions as an imperial reserve. After 1942, although some imperial forces continued to play a significant role in the Mediterranean and north-west Europe, the majority of Indian and Australian formations were recalled to defend their own countries. Tables 8.1, 8.2 and 8.3 show the composition of the combat divisions of selected formations at particular dates between 1943 and 1945. The only major British army in which British forces predominated by 1944–5 was Field Marshal Montgomery's 21 Army Group. When it was committed to the continent in June 1944 76 per cent of its

Table 8.1 Eighth Army, Italy, August 1944: Percentage of Combat Divisions by Nationality

	%
British	36
Imperial	45
Polish	18

Table 8.2 South-East Asia Command, November 1943: Percentage of Combat Divisions by Nationality

	%
British	15
West African	15
Indian	70

Table 8.3 South-East Asia Command, May 1945: Percentage of Combat Divisions by Nationality

	%
British	17
West African	25
Indian	58

Sources: W. Jackson, *The Mediterranean and Middle East* (London: HMSO, 1987), vol. 6, part 2, p. 225; L. F. Ellis, *Victory in the West* (London: HMSO, 1962), vol. 1, pp. 521–32; S. W. Kirby, *The War against Japan* (London: HMSO, 1965), vol. 4, p. 472.

combat divisions were British, 18 per cent were Canadian divisions and 6 per cent were Polish.

Tensions between the Western Allies concerning the strategic direction of the war first began to arise in April 1942 when the Americans attempted to cajole the British into agreeing to an invasion of north-west Europe in the spring of 1943. The British accepted the plan with the reservation that sufficient forces must be retained to protect the Middle East and Indian Ocean, which was then threatened by the appearance of Japanese warships in the Bay of Bengal. But closer inspection showed that the forces the Allies could muster for a cross-Channel invasion would be inadequate and as most of them would be British, Churchill vetoed the plan. But Roosevelt had already promised the hard-pressed Russians that he would launch a second front in 1942 and he also felt that it was necessary to get American public opinion involved in the European theatre at a time when Pearl Harbour had riveted its attention on the Pacific. In July 1942 he approved Churchill's suggestion for a landing in North Africa to hasten the tightening of the ring around Germany. The American chiefs of staff never wholly accepted Churchill's opportunistic strategy and correctly argued that mounting the operation would divert so many resources from the build-up of forces in Britain that a cross-Channel invasion in 1943 would be impossible. Despite their misgivings the North African landing took place in November 1942 and this, in conjunction with Montgomery's troops who had advanced westward along the North African coast from El Alamein, meant that by May 1943 the Axis armies in North Africa had been defeated.

Britain's war aims were shaped at least as much by the need to placate her allies as they were by her own security interests. Roosevelt shared many of the goals that Woodrow Wilson had sought in 1917 and 1918. He believed that the existing world order was unstable and unjust and ought to be replaced by one based upon collective security, disarmament, self-determination and the elimination of trade barriers and colonialism. These ideals were primarily directed against the Axis powers but some of them were applicable to Britain, who maintained her own imperial trading bloc and remained the world's largest imperial power. Anglo-American co-operation did not mean that the Allies shared the same goals, for as Churchill insisted in November 1942, he had not become Prime Minister to preside over the dissolution of the British Empire. To avoid highlighting these differences he refrained from making public statements about war aims. However, in August 1941 Roosevelt, anxious to compel the British to endorse his own goals, coaxed Churchill into accepting the Atlantic Charter. Churchill did so because it seemed to bring an American declaration of war on Germany nearer and because he believed that its references to self-determination applied only to those nations with whom Britain was at war. But colonial politicians in Britain's African and Indian possessions soon showed that they believed that the Charter should also apply to the British Empire and by 1942 Roosevelt agreed with them.

Britain also tried to placate the Russians. This was more difficult because in the opening stages of the war the British were unwilling to underwrite Russia's territorial war aims in eastern Europe and incapable of launching a second front in north-west Europe to relieve the pressure on the Soviet army. The Western Allies never forgot that Stalin and Hitler had once been allies and were assailed by doubts that unless they demonstrated their support for the Soviets, Stalin might make a separate peace with Hitler. The Foreign Office welcomed the Anglo-Russian treaty of May 1942 because it made no mention of future frontiers and included a pledge that neither party would make a separate peace with Germany. In Eden's words, 'This may not prevent him [Stalin] double-crossing us but it will at least remove pretexts'.[1] But the British and Americans were never certain that Stalin would abide by its terms. Some justification of their fears was provided by discussions, started on Soviet initiative, between Russian and German diplomats in Stockholm between December 1942 and July 1943. In the course of them the Soviets, who were painfully conscious of the cost of expelling the Germans from their territory, intimated their willingness to make a separate peace if the Germans evacuated Russian territory. It was fortunate for the alliance that the Germans refused to listen. At the Casablanca conference in January 1943 Roosevelt, with Churchill's acquiescence, tried to assuage some of Stalin's doubts by declaring that the Western Allies were fighting to impose unconditional surrender on the Axis powers. The declaration was intended as a sop to Stalin, who was not satisfied that the North African landing constituted a real second front. Roosevelt insisted that it did not imply that the Western Allies were seeking the destruction of the German and Japanese peoples, merely the complete overthrow of their existing governments. The declaration was subsequently criticized for needlessly prolonging the war by depriving resistance movements in the Axis countries of the hope of fair treatment if they revolted against their existing rulers. These claims were exaggerated. Mussolini was overthrown by an internal revolt only eight months after the declaration was announced and Hitler was almost killed by a bomb plot in July 1944.

At Casablanca the Western Allies also agreed on their future strategy. The defeat of the U-boats remained their first priority, followed by opening the

Mediterranean to Allied shipping and the mounting of a combined bomber offensive from bases in Britain to weaken Germany's war-making capacity to the point at which invasion became possible. They hoped that the invasion of Sicily, combined with air and sea action, would force Italy to surrender without the need to engage in a land campaign on the mainland. They did not see Italy as a 'soft underbelly' through which Europe could be invaded. Rather they believed that Italy's collapse would further contribute to the attrition of German resources by forcing them to assume heavy commitments not only in Italy but also in Italy's Balkan empire. This was an opportunistic strategy rather than a deliberate attempt to defeat Germany by chipping away at the periphery of her empire. The Western Allies had committed considerable landforces to the Mediterranean and lacked the shipping and landing-craft to mount a cross-Channel invasion in 1943. If they did not attack Sicily, these forces would remain idle in 1943 whilst the Russians continued to occupy the bulk of the *Wehrmacht*. This operation would assist the Russians and pave the way for a cross-Channel invasion in 1944.

Hitherto at every Anglo-American conference the Americans had, albeit often reluctantly, accepted Britain's views about Allied strategy because they had too few forces in the field to enable them to overrule their ally. But by the middle of 1943 the balance of power in the Western alliance was shifting towards Washington. That fact was underlined in the course of the 'Trident' conference in May 1943. The British succeeded in persuading the Americans to agree to a landing on the Italian mainland, an operation they justified by arguing that it would cause the diversion of considerable numbers of German troops from France and Russia, would give the Allied air-forces bases from which they could bomb targets in Central and south-eastern Europe and would encourage resistance movements in the Balkans. But in return the Americans insisted that henceforth the Mediterranean would be a subsidiary theatre, that a firm date, 1 May 1944, must be set for the cross-Channel invasion and that seven divisions would be withdrawn from the Mediterranean and sent to Britain in preparation for the cross-Channel invasion, now code-named Operation 'Overlord'.

The Anglo-American armies landed in Sicily in July 1943 and occupied the whole island in August. Mussolini was overthrown and in September Italy surrendered when Allied troops landed in the south. The Germans were not willing to give up Italy without a fight and by December 1943 they had deployed twenty-five divisions to hold it and dispatched another twenty divisions to retain control of the Balkans. The Mediterranean strategy therefore fulfilled its promise of diverting German forces from other fronts and also gave Allied troops the experience they needed before embarking upon the formidable task of mounting 'Overlord'. But 'Overlord' would have been impossible had it not been for the fact that in 1943 two-thirds of German ground forces remained on the Russian front.

The success of the British air offensive against Germany is more difficult to assess. In July 1941 the Chief of Air Staff still clung to the notion of strategic interception, believing that heavy bombing of Germany's cities would ensure the collapse of German war production. But Bomber Command was incapable of fulfilling that mission. Before 1939 too much effort had been devoted to creating a shop-window force in the hope that mere numbers would suffice to deter the Germans. Over-rapid expansion meant that too little attention had been paid to creating a force which was operationally effective. By the middle of 1941 the Command could only commit about 400 bombers to operations. In 1939 they had discovered that the strength of German fighter defences made daylight raids prohibitively expensive and so they switched to night attacks, only to discover in August 1941 that navigation errors meant that only one in five bombers was dropping its bombs within five miles of its target. The Air Ministry continued to exaggerate the vulnerability of the German economy to air attack. Although they understood the interdependent nature of a modern industrial economy, they were mistaken in thinking that interdependence would work to their advantage. They predicted that industrial societies were inherently fragile and tended towards self-destruction and that only a small tonnage of bombs would suffice to destroy German civilian morale and bring German society crashing down. In practice, although the German economy did have a number of economic bottle-necks, it also offered plentiful alternative sources of supplies and power.

In February 1942, now aware of the great difficulty of hitting small targets at night, the Air Ministry told Bomber Command that henceforth their primary mission was 'the morale of the enemy civil population and in particular of the industrial workers'.[2] The order was given in the expectation that by mid-1943 area bombing could destroy the morale of the German population. Opponents of the policy within the government condemned it on the grounds that the statistics used to support it were bogus and the aircraft involved would have been better employed in the Battle of the Atlantic. Had more long range aircraft been diverted from strategic bombing and given to Coastal Command, the war against the U-boats might have swung in the Allies' favour before the spring of 1943. The availability of more and heavier bombers enabled Bomber Command to increase the tonnage of bombs dropped on Germany but they could not wreck the German economy or win air superiority over western Europe. Between March 1943 and March 1944 Bomber Command mounted a series of campaigns against the Ruhr, Hamburg and Berlin. The introduction of new navigation and bombing aids enabled them to bomb with increasing accuracy and some raids caused massive destruction and heavy losses to the German civilian population. But by the winter of 1943/4 the Germans were imposing unacceptably heavy losses on Bomber Command and German war production was actually increasing. It was not until the US Eighth Air Force destroyed the *Luftwaffe*'s fighter arm in a series of daylight raids over Germany in the spring of 1944 that the Allies achieved air superiority in western Europe. Bomber Command was then able to assist in interdicting German communications in France before 'Overlord' and then resume the strategic air offensive against

Germany. Ironically, in the light of some of the claims which had been made for the bomber, the resumption of the strategic air offensive was made easier by the fact that in August 1944 Allied ground forces overran many of the Germans' early warning radar stations in France. Despite the dogmatic assertions of some air marshals strategic bombing alone did not defeat Germany. By 1945 she had been overcome by a combination of the air offensive, shattering losses on the eastern front, and the advance of Soviet and Western armies into Germany herself.

But when Churchill went to Quebec for the 'Quadrant' conference in August 1943, Germany's defeat lay in the future. He was intoxicated by Italy's rapid collapse, still haunted by memories of the western front and impressed by the ability the Germans had demonstrated in Sicily and Italy to wage a stubborn defensive war. His enthusiasm for 'Overlord' had disappeared and instead he advocated major amphibious operations against northern Italy so that in 1944 the Allies could advance either west into southern France or north-east towards Vienna. But the balance of power within the alliance had now passed away from the British. The Americans believed that Churchill's ideas were intended to postpone the cross-Channel invasion and at a three-power conference at Teheran in November the Russians sided with them and insisted that 'Overlord' had to be given priority.

The Royal Navy did not win the war for Britain but in the spring of 1943, in the course of the Battle of the Atlantic, it did contribute to a decisive victory over the U-boats. But it was a victory which demonstrated the limitations as much as the strengths of sea-power. It would not have been achieved without the provision of adequate air cover, radar and intelligence provided by intercepted signals. The number of U-boats sunk rose from 70 in 1942 to 237 in 1943 and to 263 in 1944. And the significance of this success was limited. This was a defensive victory in that it ensured that Britain would not be starved into submission and that the Allies could mass their armies in Britain for 'Overlord'. But in 1944 and 1945 sea-power could not have liberated western Europe up to the River Elbe any more than Nelson had been able to save Austria in 1805. The former task could only be done by Allied ground forces operating in conjunction with Allied naval and air forces.

The Anglo-American armies landed in Normandy in June 1944. Given America's growing preponderance there was never really any doubt that their supreme commander would be an American. The man chosen was General Eisenhower, who had previously been the Supreme Allied Commander in Italy. Britain's contribution to his ground forces consisted of Montgomery's 21 Army Group composed of sixteen British, Canadian and Polish divisions. For the British the invasion of north-west Europe in 1944/5 represented a definite return to a continental commitment. Between the fall of France and the start of 'Overlord' the British had deployed at least 60 per cent of the divisions they raised in Britain at home. After 'Overlord' that figure fell to only 23.5 per cent. By October 1944 43 per cent of British divisions were in north-west

Europe, 27 per cent were in the Mediterranean and 7 per cent were in the Far East. The opening weeks of the Normandy campaign marked the last occasion on which the British could claim anything like parity with the Americans in terms of forces in the field. Montgomery's divisions were Britain's last army. In December 1943, faced with the choice of either reducing the size of the army because of a shortage of men or running down munitions production to free men for the services, the government opted for the latter course on the assumption that the war against Germany would be over by the end of 1944. The gamble failed and between August and October 1944 Montgomery had to disband two of his divisions to provide drafts for the remainder. But while the British army became smaller, the US army grew in size until by January 1945 the USA had sixty divisions in France. Henceforth the British were the junior partners in the Western alliance.

After nearly two months of bitter fighting the Anglo-American forces broke out from their beachheads in late July and by the end of August had liberated Paris. Brussels fell in early September but the Allies, beset by logistical problems were unable to sustain the momentum of their advance. In mid-September Montgomery failed to secure a bridgehead over the Rhine at Arnhem and the chance of ending the war in Europe before the end of 1944 faded. In December Montgomery helped to repel a last German counter-attack in the Ardennes and in February 1945 he began to advance from the Nijmegan salient, crossing the Rhine in March. Once across the river his troops advanced westward until he received the surrender of all German forces in north Germany, Holland and Denmark on 4 May.

Compared to the Mediterranean and north west Europe the British gave a low priority to the war against Japan. From 1942 the Americans were responsible for the conduct of the Pacific war and Britain abdicated her responsibility for the defence of Australia and New Zealand in favour of the USA. The Americans were interested in the war in Burma only in so far as operations there might lead to the reopening of the Burma road which the Japanese had cut in April 1942. Once it was reopened the Americans hoped they would be able to equip a large Chinese army to tie down a considerable portion of the Japanese army in the interior of China. Churchill was anxious to postpone active operations in Burma until after the end of the war in Europe and to avoid a costly land campaign there. His preferred plan was to mount amphibious operations against northern Sumatra and Singapore. The British had suffered their most shattering imperial defeat at Singapore and Churchill, who did not accept that the days of the British Empire in Asia were numbered, was insistent that 'It is the only prize that will restore British prestige in the region'.[3] But the British lacked the shipping and landing-craft for such operations, the Americans would not provide them and so, in the words of one senior British staff officer, 'the hard fact is that the Americans have got us by the short hairs...We can't do anything in this theatre...without material support from them...So if they don't approve they don't provide, and that brings the whole project automatically to an end'.[4]

In August 1943, in an effort to impart some momentum to the campaign, a new South-East Asia Command (SEAC) was established by the Western Allies. The supreme commander was a British admiral, Lord Louis Mountbatten. But the Americans' insistence that steps be taken to reopen the land route to China, and their continuing suspicion that the British were only concerned to re-establish their imperial power in Asia, meant that his deputy was an American. That the Allies did succeed in reopening a land route to China and reconquering Burma owed at least as much to Japanese miscalculations as it did to their own foresight. The main British force engaged against the Japanese by early 1944 was General Slim's Fourteenth Army, composed mainly of Indian and African divisions. Campaigning in Burma presented tremendous logistical problems but fortunately in the spring of 1944 the Japanese played into Slim's hands by attacking his forces at Imphal and Kohima on the India-Burma frontier. It was the Japanese rather than the British who operated at the end of a lengthy and tenuous supply line whilst Slim's forces were fighting close to their base and he was able to resupply formations which had been surrounded from the air. By July the Japanese fifteenth Army had lost over half its strength and began to retreat and between September 1944 and May 1945 SEAC was able to liberate Burma overland. But in military terms the operation was futile. The American naval blockade and air offensive had crippled Japanese industrial output. Without consulting the British, President Truman, Roosevelt's successor, obviated the need for an invasion and forced Japan to surrender by dropping atomic bombs on Hiroshima and Nagasaki in August 1945.

By 1945 Britain retained many of the responsibilities of a world power but she lacked the material base to carry such a burden unaided. Between 1939 and 1945 her total foreign debts had risen from £500,000,000 to £3,250,000,000. Over 11 million tons of shipping had been sunk, bombing had damaged or destroyed a considerable amount of property, industrial investment had been postponed and the economy was ill-equipped to make good the yawning gap in her foreign trade. When the war against Japan ended the USA immediately terminated lend-lease assistance to Britain. The Treasury predicted that the outcome would be a financial Dunkirk. Between the wars Britain had spent an average of 3 per cent of her gross national product on defence. By 1946 she was spending 20 per cent of her gross national product on defence. The Labour government's first priority was to engineer an economic recovery which would enable Britain to pay her way in the world. A still huge overseas defence establishment only made that goal more difficult to achieve. For thirty years after 1945 both political parties agreed that they had an obligation to manage the economy and to allocate resources so as to preserve full employment and to provide a range of social services for the population. Defence had to compete for money with other government services and, especially after the mid-1950s, came off a poor second or third. Within these constraints the development of defence policy for most of the postwar era remained in the hands of much the same narrow policy-making elite who had controlled it before 1939. The crucial actors remained the Cabinet, and more particularly its specialized subcommittees which dealt with defence-related questions, the service ministries, the Foreign Office and the Treasury. Defence was rarely a major issue dividing the two major political parties. Until the mid-1970s both the parties and the electorate were in broad agreement that the government must maintain Britain's defences at a credible level.

The problems confronting policy-makers might have been fewer had it not been for the fact that the world in 1945 was a much more hostile place than it had been in 1935. The British had yet to assess the military significance of the A-bomb. But it seemed likely that it would still further reduce the security Britain had once been afforded by her island geography. The subject peoples of her empire were anxious for their own independence. She had to provide armies of occupation in Germany and Austria and garrisons in her own colonies and ensure the security of the United Kingdom and her maritime communications. But, above all, the European balance of power had been shattered. The Russians were in occupation of much of Eastern and Central Europe and they possessed an army which overshadowed anything the British could mobilize.

The Attlee Labour government did what its predecessors had habitually done over the previous 250 years when confronted by too many potential threats and too few resources, it looked for other powers with whom to share these burdens. In 1945 the USA was the world's leading naval, air and financial power. But at the Yalta conference in February 1945 Roosevelt had told Churchill that American forces would leave Europe within two years of the end of hostilities. That was not welcome news for the British. The Labour government, like their Conservative predecessors and their military and civil-service advisers, took it for granted that Britain could remain a great power. But as early as July 1940 the Foreign Office had recognized that 'the future of our widely scattered Empire is likely to depend on the evolution of an effective collaboration between ourselves and the United States'.[5] Even before the end of hostilities they had decided that Britain's postwar security needs could be met by creating a West-European security system working in close association with the USA and the commonwealth. Britain could sustain her position as a world leader by mediating between those three bodies. In this context, the Foreign Office decided 'It must be our purpose ... to make use of American power for the purposes which we regard as good ... If we go about our business in the right way we can help steer this great unwieldy barge, the United States of America, into the right harbour'.[6]

In 1945 the greatest danger to peace that British policy-makers foresaw was a resurgent Germany. To meet it Ernest Bevin, Labour's Foreign Secretary, signed the Treaty of Dunkirk with France in 1947. But after the Potsdam conference in August 1945 the lack of agreement between the Western powers and the Soviets over Germany, coupled with Soviet policies in Eastern Europe and the

Mediterranean, meant that fear of a resurgent Germany was gradually replaced by fear of an expansionist Russia. Britain was too weak to contain that threat on her own. In February 1947 Bevin warned the US government that if US aid was not granted, the British would have to terminate the military assistance they were giving Turkey and Greece to defeat the communist insurgents operating in their countries. President Truman replied by announcing the 'Truman doctrine' and Marshall, now Secretary of State, offered the European powers an aid programme to assist their economic recovery. It was rejected by the Russians and the East European states they had occupied. Bevin seized this offer with alacrity and organized the West-European states to receive it. But he wanted more than US economic assistance. He believed that to rebuild West-European confidence it was essential that the USA give a written assurance that they would become involved at the beginning of the next European war. He assumed that the mere presence of the USA in a regional defence agreement would encourage democratic forces in Western Europe to oppose the spread of communist influence. To achieve this end in March 1948 he signed the Brussels Pact with France, Holland, Belgium and Luxembourg. The leading role he played in creating the pact, plus the Soviet blockade of West Berlin in 1948-9, convinced the US government that the Western powers were prepared to defend themselves and enabled Bevin to act as a broker between the USA and the West-European governments. The outcome was the establishment of the North Atlantic Treaty Organization in April 1949. The signing of the NATO treaty marked the formal division of Europe into two antagonistic blocs each dominated by a single superpower. It also signalled the breakdown of the multipolar world within which Britain had operated as a great power since 1688 and created a bipolar world dominated by the USA and the Soviet Union within which Britain's scope for independent action was limited.

The British saw NATO as a way of preserving democracy in Western Europe and as a means to enable them to share the burden of their common defence needs with their allies. But there was a price they had to pay to persuade the USA to commit itself to Western Europe, although it only slowly became apparent. Neither the Brussels Pact nor the NATO treaty obliged Britain to commit particular force levels to Western Europe. Bevin could congratulate himself that with Western Europe made secure by the US guarantee, the British had resources to devote to their interests outside Europe. In May 1948, after much agonizing, the British chiefs of staff had accepted in theory that under the Brussels Pact Britain would have to fight alongside her allies on the continent in the event of war, but by 1950 she still had only two weak divisions in West Germany. But the explosion of the first Russian atomic bomb in 1949 and the beginning of the Korean War in 1950 convinced NATO planners that the alliance must increase its conventional forces. In Eastern Europe 14 NATO divisions faced some 210 divisions. It was not until 1954 that the actual peacetime level of Britain's commitment was settled. By 1950 the British had realized that West German ground forces would be essential if NATO was ever to deploy a credible army. But the French could not be expected to welcome a rearmed Germany. Their preferred solution was to establish a European Defence Community (EDC) which would integrate the various national armies into multinational units. NATO would be able to use West German manpower without the French feeling they were being threatened by a West German army. However, both the Attlee government and the Churchill government elected in October 1951 refused to integrate British forces into the EDC and it was still-born. The onus was upon the British to find a solution. The need to do so was made more urgent in February 1952 when the NATO council meeting at Lisbon decided that the alliance should be able to field an army of ninety-six divisions by 1960 and in December 1953 when the US Secretary of State, John Foster Dulles, hinted that his government might reassess their commitment to West-European security if the Europeans did not make some progress on West German rearmament. Churchill's Foreign Secretary, Anthony Eden, produced the eventual solution in the form of the Paris agreement of October 1954. The West Germans and Italians were admitted to the Brussels treaty. The West Germans were allowed to raise and commit to NATO an army of twelve divisions supported by a tactical air-force. In return, to reassure the French, the British promised to commit four divisions and a tactical air-force to Europe until 1994. Ironically, the level of British landforces committed to the British Army of the Rhine (BAOR) was determined by what was necessary to reassure one ally that it would be supported if it were attacked by another.

The treaty was the first time in over two hundred and fifty years that the British had agreed to station major ground forces on the continent of Europe in peacetime as part of a military alliance. The break with past precedents was recognized by Eden who announced when it was signed that 'what I have announced is for us a very formidable step to take. You all know that ours is above all an island story. We are still an island people in thought and tradition'.[7] But in another sense this was not a break with tradition. Meeting their security needs by co-operating with other powers had been the norm, not the exception, for the British in both peace and war since 1688. All that changed in 1954 was the nature of the price Britain had to pay to secure that co-operation. Nor did the treaty mark a decisive shift in British policy away from Africa and Asia and towards Europe. NATO enhanced Britain's security in Europe but she did not cease to function as an imperial power. The 1950 Defence White Paper asserted that her defence interests were not restricted to NATO because 'the Middle East is a vital strategic area and the maintenance of our position in the Far East is essential to the security and well being of the Commonwealth'.[8] The Labour and Conservative governments of the 1950s and the chiefs of staff believed that if Britain abandoned her imperial possessions she would sink to the status of a second-class power. They were therefore confronted with the task of trying to strike some kind of balance between Britain's diminished economic power on the one hand and her security needs in Europe and in the empire on the other.

The result was a piecemeal disengagement from the responsibilities of empire accompanied by a series of small colonial wars which extended over thirty years. Even in 1947 it was apparent that the British could not hope to retain the whole of their prewar possessions and decolonization began when India was granted her independence. But even though the British had abandoned formal political control they still hoped to retain some influence over Indian policy and in particular they wanted to be able to use Indian military manpower in any war involving commonwealth countries in the Middle East or Indian Ocean. It was to achieve this end that India was admitted to the commonwealth even though she was a republic. But their hopes were disappointed. The loss of India had a paradoxical impact on British defence policy. It meant that Britain no longer had to defend India with British soldiers. But it also meant that the British could no longer do what they had done for much of the nineteenth century and use Indian soldiers to defend some of their other interests east of Suez. Britain had first become involved in the Middle East to defend the route to India and the loss of India should have led to a thorough reappraisal of British interests in the region and a rapid withdrawal from Egypt. It did not because of a combination of old habits of thought, the pull exerted by Britain's investments in the region and her dependence on Middle Eastern oil. To make good the shortfall in manpower caused by the loss of the Indian army the British maintained national service until 1962 and looked to some of their other commonwealth partners. Again they looked in vain. Australia and New Zealand remembered that it had been the USA, not Britain, who had come to their aid in 1942. The signing of the ANZUS treaty in 1951 indicated that in future they intended to look to the USA rather than to Britain for defence co-operation. Despite this rebuff, until 1956 the British attempted to maintain most of the remainder of their overseas bases from their own resources. They agreed to withdraw from their base at Suez in October 1954 but established a new one in Libya to take its place and in April 1955, when they joined the Baghdad Pact, the RAF acquired the right to use Iraqi airfields so that they could interdict Soviet attempts to interrupt Western oil supplies from the Persian Gulf.

However, in the late 1940s and 1950s many of the factors which had once facilitated British military superiority beyond Europe were fast disappearing. Her NATO obligations meant that she had to retain a large proportion of her defence forces in Europe. International opinion was increasingly hostile to metropolitan governments who used armed force to support their colonial pretensions. Instead of inviting their own defeat by resorting to conventional warfare, the indigenous populations of India, Egypt, Palestine, Aden, Cyprus, Malaya, Borneo and Kenya refused to meet the British on their own terms and adopted a mixture of guerrilla warfare, urban terrorism and forms of non-violent opposition. Although the British did not suffer a series of conventional military defeats, for the insurgent nationalists were never in a position to invade Britain, their resistance was bitter and prolonged. That fact alone, implying as it did rising financial and human costs, was enough eventually to persuade policy-makers in London to negotiate a settlement which usually entailed the withdrawal of British forces and the granting of independence. They might have shown greater determination to remain in place for longer but for the fact that there was little public support to do so. Few national servicemen relished the prospect of fighting a series of bush wars and few tax-payers relished the prospect of paying them to do so. Although the right-wing press often reported these wars in a tone of strident jingoism, left-wing politicians and newspapers were uncomfortable with them. They believed that imperial rule and imperial military campaigns often involved the denial of the principles of justice and equality which were taken for granted at home. The commonwealth facilitated decolonization by satisfying both the internationalism of the left and the cravings of those on the right who still clung to the belief that Britain had a role to play as the leader of an influential world bloc. But the British did not surrender their predominance without a struggle. In November 1956 Anglo-French forces, operating in collusion with the Israelis, invaded Egypt in an attempt not only to regain control of the Suez Canal but also to topple the Egyptian leader, President Nasser. Eden, who had become Prime Minister in 1955, suspected that Nasser was determined to expel Britain from the Middle East by undermining governments in the region who were friendly to British interests. The invasion was a military success and a political disaster. It provoked a run on sterling and President Eisenhower vetoed its continuation by refusing to agree to a loan to Britain from the International Monetary Fund until a cease-fire had been declared and the Anglo-French forces had withdrawn.

Since 1945 the level of military manpower had been reduced but the armed forces were still recognizably the same as those which had emerged from the end of the war. But after Suez Eden resigned and in 1957 the new Prime Minister, Harold Macmillan, began a radical reshaping of the services. The débâcle had hurt national pride and damaged relations with the USA. Furthermore, Macmillan was convinced that Britain's economic growth was lagging behind that of her major economic competitors but she was spending a larger proportion of her gross national product on defence than they were. The government decided that if Britain's sluggish economy was to pick up, less resources must be devoted to defence. But Macmillan and his colleagues were no more ready than Attlee and his colleagues had been in 1945 to abandon their pretensions that Britain was still a great power. Macmillan's solution was to acquire an independent nuclear deterrent. This was not a revolutionary departure but represented the working out of a trend in British thinking which originated in the early 1950s. The British began research on an atomic bomb in 1940 but in 1942 the work was transferred to the USA. The passage through the US Congress of the McMahon Act in 1946 forbidding the disclosure of nuclear information to any other state may have delayed the production of a British A-bomb but it did not prevent it. In January 1947 Attlee decided to proceed with the programme because he instinctively believed that Britain was still a great power and therefore required the most powerful weapons that science could produce. This was a unilateral decision, taken for national political reasons and without close co-ordination with either the USA or Britain's European associates.

In June 1950 North Korean forces invaded South Korea. The Attlee government supported American intervention because they feared that if communist expansion remained unchecked it might spread to other parts of the Far East and threaten Britain's own interests in the region and because they feared that the invasion might be part of a larger plan by Stalin to distract the West's attention and clear the way for an attack on Western Europe. It was therefore vital for the British to demonstrate their support for US policy in the Far East in order to ensure continued US support for NATO in Europe. But the rearmament programme which Attlee inaugurated had placed a severe strain on the British economy and in 1952 the Churchill government wished to relieve it. The chiefs of staff believed that nuclear weapons were the answer to Britain's dilemma. They presented a memorandum to Churchill, Global Strategy Paper 1952, arguing that the development of nuclear weapons meant that total war had abolished itself. Britain should acquire a nuclear deterrent sufficiently powerful to persuade the Soviets to realize that aggression would be unprofitable because it would be met by a nuclear attack on Russia herself. British nuclear weapons would also allow Britain to reduce her defence costs because she could cut the size of her own expensive conventional forces, they would enhance NATO's nuclear deterrent, they would buy the British more influence over US policy-makers and they would maintain her status as a great power.

In October 1952 Britain became the world's third nuclear power when she exploded her own A-bomb. That persuaded the US Congress to ease the more onerous restrictions of the McMahon Act in 1954 and in 1955 the British government announced its adherence to a policy of 'massive retaliation' if the Soviets attacked Western Europe, adding that Britain had begun work on her own H-bomb. The Suez crisis hastened this trend towards increasing reliance on nuclear weapons at the expense of conventional forces. In the 1957 Defence White Paper Macmillan's defence secretary, Duncan Sandys, promulgated what became the 'Sandys doctrine'. He announced that Britain's security ultimately rested upon her economic strength and defence spending must be reduced. That part of his statement might have been made by any British defence minister after any great war in the preceding two hundred and fifty years. What was new was the way in which he wanted to achieve this objective. Sandys hoped that nuclear armed V-bombers would serve several purposes. They would enable him to abolish national service and reduce the armed forces manpower from 690,000 in 1957 to 375,000 by 1962, to cut the size of the fleet and to reduce the size of the ground forces in West Germany. The White Paper did not envisage that Britain would abandon her imperial commitments, merely that she would safeguard them more cheaply by retaining bases in Kenya, Singapore, Cyprus and Aden. Stores and heavy equipment would be stockpiled at each base in anticipation of an emergency and the arrival by air of troops drawn from a central reserve based in Britain. This combination of smaller garrisons and mobile reserves would be supported by a naval amphibious force stationed in the Indian Ocean.

By these means defence costs would be reduced and possession of a nuclear deterrent would enable Britain to remain a great military power. Although in private the government realized that Britain would not be able to use her deterrent unilaterally, Macmillan still hoped that it would increase Britain's bargaining position in Washington: 'The independent contribution gives us a better position in the world with respect to the United States. It puts us where we ought to be, in the position of a great power. The fact that we have it makes the United States pay a greater regard to our point of view'.[9] The American Dean Acheson once suggested that Britain had lost an empire but not found a role in the world. But perhaps British politicians did not look as hard as they could have done because they had found nuclear weapons instead and could retain the illusion that Britain remained a great power for a little longer.

Sandys's policy did have some successes. In 1958 an appeal by King Hussein of Jordan for assistance was met by troops airlifted from Cyprus and Kenya and in 1961 6,000 troops were sent to Kuwait when she was threatened by Iraq. But by 1962 it was apparent that Britain was incapable of creating her own cost-effective independent nuclear deterrent. The V-bomber force had been intended to be a stop-gap until the British could develop their own missile delivery system. However, escalating costs and the growing accuracy of Russian ballistic missiles persuaded the government to cancel *Blue Streak* in April 1960. In its place the USA agreed to sell the British 100 *Skybolt* stand-off missiles but then themselves abandoned the project. At the Nassau conference in 1962 Macmillan warned President Kennedy that there would be a serious rift in relations between the two countries if the USA did not offer him an acceptable substitute. Kennedy took the hint and sold the British the submarine-launched *Polaris* system. By 1970 the Royal Navy had four *Polaris* submarines in commission. Each vessel carried sixteen missiles with a range of 2,500 nautical miles. Each warhead, if it were to strike the centre of a Soviet city, was believed to be capable of killing approximately 250,000 people and injuring twice as many. In public the British still clung to the rhetoric of independence, refusing to integrate their missiles completely into NATO and reserving the right to withdraw them from the alliance 'where Her Majesty's Government may decide that supreme national interests are at stake'.[10] In reality a policy which was meant to demonstrate Britain's status as an independent power, only served to underline her dependence upon the USA.

Because the USA had paid the development costs of *Polaris*, Britain could remain a nuclear power into the 1970s at small cost. Its building costs accounted for only 5 per cent of the defence budget and its running costs for another 2 per cent. *Polaris* also gave the British more influence within the NATO alliance than they might otherwise have enjoyed for by 1964 total West German military manpower exceeded that of the United Kingdom. Moreover, a considerable proportion of Britain's armed forces was deployed outside the NATO area, whereas the whole of the West German armed forces were assigned to NATO's central front. Henceforth the West Germans were the main European pillar of the NATO alliance. But the deterrent did not fulfil Macmillan's hope that Britain would be able significantly to reduce her defence spending. In 1957 Britain was spending 6.9 per cent of her gross national product on defence. By 1965 that figure had only dropped to 5.9 per cent.

Nuclear weapons were a source of dissension within the Labour party in the late 1950s and early 1960s. The previous government's policy of 'massive retaliation' was regarded as being both morally dubious and strategically untenable. It meant that the nuclear threshold in Western Europe was very low. The growth of the Soviet nuclear arsenal made it likely that any attempt by the British to use their own nuclear deterrent would be met by a massive Soviet response. However, the Labour government of 1964–70 was impervious to public criticisms about the role of nuclear deterrence and the only gesture the Wilson administration made towards its left-wing critics was to cancel a fifth *Polaris* submarine. Otherwise it pursued much the same policy for much the same reasons as its Conservative predecessors. It also did little to increase Britain's conventional forces to give reality to the new strategy of 'flexible response' which NATO adopted in 1967. By the early 1960s US policy-makers knew that they might face nuclear annihilation if they were compelled to unleash their own nuclear arsenal because of the premature collapse of their European allies. They were therefore anxious to persuade the latter to increase their own conventional force levels so that in the event of a major Soviet attack they would be strong enough to buy enough time for diplomatic negotiations to defuse the crisis.

It was an economic crisis, not public opinion or US pressure, which compelled the Wilson government to reshape British defence policy and forsake almost all of Britain's remaining imperial commitments. Although by 1964 most of Britain's colonies had become independent, Britain had only marginally reduced her commitments outside the NATO area. About 100,000 service personnel were based east of Suez in the early 1960s. The Labour government believed that the commonwealth was still a viable instrument of British policy and that its survival depended upon the protection Britain could offer its members. Wilson also feared that any major withdrawal from east of Suez would compromise Britain's 'special relationship' with the USA. However between 1966 and 1968 a combination of inflation and balance of payments crises forced the government to face reality. In July 1967 the defence secretary, Dennis Healey, announced that Britain would abandon her mainland bases east of Suez by 1977, although she would retain some air-mobile ground forces which could be deployed in the region. A few months later there was a second economic crisis and in January 1968 Wilson announced that the timetable for withdrawal would be accelerated and forces would withdraw from Singapore, Malaysia and the Persian Gulf by the end of 1971.

This decision marked the end of Britain's role as a great imperial military power. In 1965–6 one member in four of the armed forces had been deployed outside Europe. The corresponding figure in 1973–4 was only one in ten. By 1981 forces raised outside Britain, which had once played such a large part in Britain's defence effort, had shrunk to only 3 per cent of total military manpower. Britain's forces had never been so nationally homogeneous. After 1968 British defence policy was firmly oriented towards Western Europe, NATO and the maintenance of a nuclear deterrent. The pull towards Europe was accelerated by several events. In 1968 the Soviet invasion of Czechoslovakia so alarmed the government that in 1970 they returned some units they had withdrawn from West Germany. The Czech crisis was followed by superpower discussions over strategic arms limitations which led to the SALT 1 agreement in May 1972. The start of that process alarmed the Wilson government because the US had proceeded with it after only minimal consultation with their European allies and Healey became a leading advocate of a ten-nation Euro-group within NATO to ensure that questions about European security were not settled by the superpowers over the heads of the Europeans. The trend towards closer co-operation with the states of Western Europe was intensified in 1972 when Britain joined the European Economic Community (EEC).

In 1970 the Heath government had accepted a European defence improvement programme as the price of extracting a promise from President Nixon that he would not withdraw US forces from Europe. But the Arab-Israeli War of October 1973 and the world oil crisis made impossible any significant increase in Britain's conventional force levels and, although the withdrawal from east of Suez had alleviated Britain's financial problems, it had not solved them. The proportion of the defence budget devoted to manpower costs was falling but the cost of sophisticated new equipment was spiralling upwards. The Labour government elected in 1974 tried to reconcile shrinking means with a still onerous range of commitments by concentrating resources in four areas: the defence of the home base; the maritime defence of the eastern Atlantic and the English Channel; the nuclear deterrent; and the defence of NATO's central front. These priorities remained in force until the late 1980s.

If post-1945 defence policy is seen as a reflection of a steady retreat from empire then the Falklands campaign of 1982 was an aberration. If, however, the conflict is viewed as the result of just another of a series of belated policy adjustments designed to preserve Britain's world power in increasingly adverse circumstances, it becomes more comprehensible. The Conservative government led by Mrs Thatcher which was elected in 1979 had to come to terms with a burdensome inheritance. The promise that nuclear weapons would reduce defence costs and enhance Britain's economic performance had proved to be an illusion. The economy was performing sluggishly. In 1979 the previous Labour government had assured its NATO partners that it would increase defence spending in real terms by 3 per cent per annum until 1986, a promise Thatcher intended to keep. During the election the Conservatives had promised to cut taxes and improve Britain's defences. But Mrs Thatcher's willingness to spend more on defence did not mean that she could avoid difficult choices. Equipment costs continued to rise, forces' pay had to be increased to improve sagging morale and money had to be found to modernize the strategic deterrent. The British *Polaris* submarines had been designed with an operational life of twenty years and, although that might be stretched by another decade, they could not continue indefinitely. Mrs Thatcher was convinced that nuclear weapons had kept the peace for forty years, she asserted that the British weapons enhanced NATO's deterrent capability because the existence of two nuclear decision-making centres in London and Washington would induce the Soviets to be cautious, and she believed that if the NATO alliance were ever to crumble, or if the USA were to withdraw its nuclear umbrella, the British deterrent would deter a Soviet nuclear strike on Britain. Some of these arguments were given added potency in the eyes of the Thatcher government by President Reagan's decision to develop the Strategic Defence Initiative in 1983, with its 'Fortress America' implications and by the superpower diplomacy which culminated in the Reykjavik summit in 1986.

After examining several alternatives the government announced in July 1980 that they would buy the American *Trident* system. But by 1980 public spending was already exceeding the government's self-imposed limits and in the eyes of the Treasury the Ministry of Defence was one of the worst offenders. *Trident* was expected to cost £5 billion over ten years and the defence secretary, Francis Pym, was reluctant to make the necessary cuts elsewhere so in May 1981 Mrs Thatcher replaced him with John Nott. Nott was responsible for the 1981 defence review, *The Way Forward*, a daring document, not least because it reawoke an argument between exponents of a continental commitment on the one hand and a maritime strategy on the other which had bedevilled the making of British defence policy since the end of the seventeenth century. Nott was determined not to reduce the defences of the home base. The government was bound by treaty obligations to maintain its existing commitments in West Germany. Nott believed that, 'the forward defence of the Federal Republic [of West Germany] is the forward defence of Britain itself' and that the political significance of Britain's commitment to the ground defence of Western Europe far outweighed its military value. The navy was chosen to be the unfortunate service and was destined to bear 57 per cent of the cuts in planned expenditure. Although its deployment in the eastern Atlantic afforded support to the US navy, it was of less military and political significance than maintaining forces in West Germany, for Nott thought that although the USA might withdraw ground forces from Western Europe, 'it is inconceivable that the US navy would ever withdraw from the Atlantic, which is the front line of the United States'.[11]

Had the Argentinean invasion of the Falklands in 1982 happened after the Nott review had been put into effect it is unlikely that the navy would have had sufficient surface craft to retake the islands. The economic value of the islands was so small that it did not justify the cost of retaking them. But the government decided that the political cost of not doing so would be too high. Its mishandling of the early stages of the crisis and the criticisms its failures provoked from all sides in Parliament meant that the government's political survival was at stake and it could not afford to accept the invasion as a *fait accompli*. The government was widely criticized for policies that permitted the Argentineans to invade the islands and a Gallup poll reported that the public believed that Mrs Thatcher was the worst Prime Minister since Neville Chamberlain. In the wider international arena, if the British had refused to try to retake the islands they would have cast doubt upon their willingness to defend the security of their allies in Europe. For the British the campaign was an almost textbook example of a limited war. The entire episode, beginning on 2 April 1982 with the Argentinean invasion and ending on 14 June with the surrender of Port Stanley, lasted for less than three months. Although much Argentinean military equipment was as good as, if not better than that deployed by the British, the British had some advantages. Their forces consisted of well-trained professionals but their opponents were frequently young, poorly trained and badly led conscripts. After some hesitation the US government and world opinion, in the form of the United Nations, supported Britain, not Argentina. The campaign to retake the islands was widely supported in Britain and there was never any possibility that it would have to be abandoned for lack of public support.

British strategy during the Second World War diverged from her policy during the First World War. She fought both wars in an effort to prevent Germany fixing her hegemony over Europe. On both occasions her enemies' strength compelled her to fight as a member of a coalition. But whereas in the First World War British policy closely approximated to the continental paradigm, her policy in the Second World War more closely approximated to the mixed paradigm. From 1939 to 1940 the exigencies of the Anglo-French alliance meant that the British did make a major commitment of their landforces to north-west Europe and there is reason to suppose that that commitment would have grown had the BEF not been expelled from France in 1940. Between 1940 and 1944 the British were compelled to adopt a peripheral strategy because of the formidable problems involved in securing a lodgement in Europe and because of the threats posed to their empire in the Middle East and Asia by the Axis powers. As in almost all of their previous imperial wars, the British again relied heavily on imperial, rather than on purely British forces to wage these campaigns. Between 1940 and 1944 the bulk of the British army remained at home, safeguarding Britain against invasion and training for the invasion of France. When alliance politics again made it imperative for the British to return to the continent in June 1944, nearly three-quarters of the divisions they committed to 'Overlord' consisted of British troops. After 1945 British defence policy was determined by the decision of successive governments that Britain ought to maintain as large a role as she could in the world. For more than twenty years after 1945 they believed that although Britain might have to shuffle off some of her more onerous defence responsibilities, she could still retain many of the trappings and responsibilities of her former status. It was not until the late 1960s that they finally decided that the costs of maintaining an imperial defence presence exceeded the benefits. In 1968 the Wilson administration renounced Britain's role as an imperial military power. By 1988 95 per cent of Britain's defence expenditure was concentrated within the NATO area. The Falklands War marked the last twitch of Britain's imperial reflexes.

Conclusion: From Thatcher to the Millennium

Throughout the period examined by this book British policy-makers did not *consistently* prefer isolation to engagement in Europe in peacetime nor in wartime did they *consistently* adopt either the 'British way in warfare' or the mixed paradigm outlined in the Introduction. In peacetime the great majority of policy-makers recognized that Britain could not afford to remain aloof from continental entanglements, however much they might have wished to do so. In the eighteenth century Britain was not engaged in a war against one or more of her great power neighbours for about forty-two years. But she was only without at least one peacetime treaty of alliance for about fourteen of those years. The Anglo-Dutch alliance of 1678 did not lapse until 1756 when the Dutch refused to supply Britain with troops. In 1716 it was supplemented by a treaty with the French which lasted until 1731. The French alliance was superseded by a treaty with Austria under which the British guaranteed the Pragmatic Sanction. Although co-operation between Britain and Austria was uncommon between 1733 and 1741, Britain fought to uphold the Pragmatic Sanction during the War of the Austrian Succession. The Anglo-Austrian alliance remained the basis of Britain's policy of forming an anti-Bourbon coalition until the 'Diplomatic Revolution' of 1756. Britain was only without continental allies in peacetime in the eighteenth century in the period preceding and following the American War of Independence. After the War of Independence it took the British some time to mend their diplomatic fences but they did so in 1788 when they signed a new triple alliance with Prussia and Holland guaranteeing Dutch independence against France. In the eighteenth century in peacetime, diplomatic engagement, not isolation, was the norm for the British.

Even at the height of the 'Pax Britannica' between 1815 and 1880 Britain was hardly less ready than the other great European powers to involve herself in the ententes and alliances of the European state system. Her security continued to rest upon the preservation of the balance of power in Europe and she safeguarded that balance by judicious interventions in the diplomatic system rather than by remaining aloof from it. The brief period of 'splendid isolation' which she experienced at the close of the nineteenth century was quickly brought to an end when policy-makers discovered that they literally could not afford to defend the empire with domestic and imperial resources. She experienced a brief period of isolation in the early 1920s until, by a blend of restricted aerial and naval rearmament and diplomatic initiatives which culminated in the Locarno Pact, she succeeded in at least temporarily pacifying Western Europe and the Pacific. In the period examined by this book Britain was neither sufficiently powerful compared to her continental neighbours, nor far enough away from them, for diplomatic isolation even in peacetime to be a realistic policy. Politicians exhibited their strategic preferences by the way in which they allocated defence expenditure between land and sea services. In the periods between Britain's great-power wars in the eighteenth century (1698–1701, 1714–17, 1721–25, 1730–38, 1749–55, 1764–74, and 1784–92) sea services absorbed a greater percentage of defence spending than did land services. Only in the period between 1713 and 1717 did spending in peacetime on the army come close to matching spending on the navy and the figures for this period were distorted by the need to augment the army to counter the Jacobite rebellion of 1715. At other times the average discrepancy in sums voted for sea services compared to land services was of the order of 20 per cent. There were several reasons why the navy was the favoured service in peacetime in the eighteenth century. A large peacetime standing army was unpopular with the political nation. They remembered Cromwell and James II and regarded it as a possible threat to their political liberties. The navy did not suffer from this stigma. The eighteenth-century British Empire was still a salt-water empire and it did not yet require large garrisons of troops. Until the development of the steamship and the railway after 1850 it was impossible for any power to threaten the home islands without first making lengthy preparations which were hard to conceal and gave the British ample time to prepare their defences. Before then the British did not have to spend lavishly on their defences in peacetime for fear that they might be the victims of a sudden attack which would cripple them before they were ready to fight. In peacetime in the eighteenth century governments habitually reduced the army to cadre strength and laid up most of the fleet. Cadre regiments were comparatively cheap to maintain and they believed, often with an excess of optimism, that they would be easy to fill-up on the outbreak of war. But they also recognized that the material, as opposed to the manpower of the fleet, could not be rapidly improvised in wartime. Ships of the line took several years to construct and dockyards took decades. British naval supremacy in wartime depended on the willingness of politicians to vote money to maintain dockyards and ships in ordinary in peacetime.

This pattern was reversed between 1815 and 1895 when Britain's maritime supremacy was at its height. At the end of the eighteenth century Britain began to acquire an Asiatic empire which grew in the nineteenth century. Each acquisition needed a garrison and so the army increased in size. By contrast the size of the fleet declined. That did not mean that British naval power compared to that of her potential rivals had also declined. It reflected the fact that during the French Revolutionary and Napoleonic Wars Britain had practically eliminated her eighteenth-century naval rivals and so after 1815 the British could maintain a higher level of naval predominance with less effort than had been necessary in the late eighteenth century. Between 1815 and 1895 the army absorbed about 16 per cent more of total defence spending than did the navy. But the peacetime ratio of defence spending reverted to the eighteenth-century pattern between 1896 and 1913 as the British tried to maintain a two-power standard against France and Russia, and then to keep their lead in the face of the German naval challenge. Spending patterns in the interwar period were complicated by the existence of a third service, the RAF. But between 1925, when the Geddes axe had been swung, and 1939, the navy regained the lead over the army it had re-established in 1896. Even so, the navy's lead was by no means overwhelming. Between 1896 and 1913 it had absorbed about 6 per cent more of the defence budget than had the army; between 1925 and 1939 the corresponding figure was about 10 per cent. In peacetime in the first half of the twentieth century British policy-makers opted for balanced defence forces.

The way in which policy-makers allocated defence spending between land and sea services (and the RAF in the Second World War) in wartime is shown in Table C.1. Wartime spending patterns reveal a similar refusal to adopt a single consistent strategy over the three hundred years discussed by this book. In the Nine Years' War, the French Revolutionary War and the Second World War policy-makers struck a rough balance between spending on land and sea services. In these wars they did not exhibit a strong preference for the 'British way in warfare' by devoting the bulk of wartime defence spending to sea services and subsidies. That was not true between 1702 and 1783 when spending was weighted, sometimes heavily, towards the navy. It was in this period, and more

Table C.1 Ratio of Spending on Land and Sea Services in Wartime

	Land	:	Sea	:	Air
Nine Years' War	46		54		
War of the Spanish Succession	40		60		
War of the Quadruple Alliance	35		65		
Anglo-Spanish War of 1726–9	40		60		
War of Jenkins's Ear/War of the Austrian Succession	38		62		
Seven Years' War	43		57		
American War of Independence	33		67		
French Revolutionary War	51		49		
Napoleonic War	57		43		
Crimean War	58		42		
First World War	73		27		
Second World War	38		36		26

Sources *Parliamentary Papers* 1868/9, xxxv, Public Income and Expenditure; *Parliamentary Papers* 1945–6 xv (Cmd 6856), Air Services, Detailed Statement of Expenditure and Receipts for the Years 1939–43; Air Appropriation Account for the Year ending 31 March 1945; Army Appropriation Account for the Year ending 31 March 1945; *Parliamentary Papers* 1945–6, xvi, Navy, Detailed Statement of Expenditure and Receipts for the Years 1939–43; Navy Appropriation Account for the Year ending 31 March 1945; War Office, *Statistics of the Military Effort of the British Empire during the Great War, 1914–20* (London: HMSO, 1922).

especially between 1714 and 1783, that Britain came as close as she ever did to pursuing consistently the 'British way in warfare'. By contrast in the Napoleonic War, the Crimean War and, most markedly in the First World War, spending patterns were weighted towards land services. What Table C.1 does not show, but what was undoubtedly true, was that over time the British did consistently spend a higher proportion of their defence expenditure on the fleet than any other great power.

It would be wrong to make too much of Britain's inclination to pay others to do her land fighting for her. The sums involved in hiring mercenaries and subsidizing European allies represented a comparatively small share of the defence budget. Britain's subsidy policy began during the Nine Years' War. The published accounts make it difficult to determine how much Parliament voted and how much was actually paid and suggest that about 2 per cent of the money the English spent on the war between 1689 and 1697 was used to purchase foreign military assistance. This is almost certainly a considerable underestimate for it takes no account of the pay due to the foreign troops on the British establishment. Between 1702 and 1712 Britain spent about 8 per cent of her defence budget on supporting her European allies and hiring mercenaries. She spent little on her allies during the War of the Quadruple Alliance and devoted less than 4 per cent of her defence spending to hiring mercenaries between 1726 and 1729. Britain's propensity to pay others to fight on her behalf reached a peak during the War of Jenkins's Ear/War of the Austrian Succession when the British devoted about 12 per cent of their defence budget to this end. But during the Seven Years' War the proportion of defence spending which went to hire mercenaries and to assist the allies fell to a more normal 7 per cent. During the War of Independence Britain had no European allies and so Parliament voted about 3 per cent of total defence spending to hire mercenaries. Even during the French Revolutionary and Napoleonic Wars, when Britain did have a series of great-power allies, subsidies absorbed only about 8 per cent of total defence spending. Governments might have wished to spend more but were inhibited from doing so by the frequent criticism voiced by opponents of Britain's involvement in continental land fighting that greedy foreigners demanded too much for their services and that their demands threatened to denude Britain of specie. In the twentieth century the boot was on the other foot. Between 1914 and 1918 Britain only just disbursed more in economic assistance to her allies than she received from the USA and during the Second World War she actually became a net recipient of foreign aid.

Except between 1702 and 1783 wartime spending patterns do not reveal that policy-makers had a clear and constant preference for the navy over the army. They never consistently preferred to spend large sums to pay others to fight for them. Similarly, the way in which they wished to deploy Britain's landforces in wartime does not reveal that they had a clear and consistent preference for a maritime/colonial strategy rather than a continental commitment. British policy-makers did not invariably avoid making a continental commitment, nor did they consistently retain the bulk of their army at home waiting for an invasion or dispatch it overseas to attack enemy colonies and to raid the enemy coast. They adopted one of these policies or a combination of them as opportunity and their political objectives dictated. During the wars of 1689–1713 which marked the emergence of Britain as a great European power, her existence as an independent Protestant state was at stake. It was therefore apposite that in both wars the great majority of the troops on the British establishment (including mercenaries) were committed to the continental land war, that a proportion were retained in England and only a handful of Royal forces were committed to the colonies.

Between 1714 and 1783, as befitted a state attempting to expand and then retain its overseas interests but unable to do so in safety by disengaging from the continent, Britain made no major continental commitment in the War of the Quadruple Alliance, the Anglo-Spanish War of 1726–9, or the American War of Independence. But the high proportion of troops retained at home during these wars was not just a reflection of the government's unwillingness to become engaged in extensive continental fighting. It also reflected the fact that before 1745 they were afraid for the stability of the Hanoverian regime if it were bereft of bayonets to support it. During the War of the Austrian Succession, the Seven Years' War and the War of Independence troops were retained at home because of the government's doubts about the navy's ability to safeguard Britain against invasion. The impossibility of disengaging from Europe when France was hostile to Britain caused them to commit a fifth and then a third of the troops on the British establishment to the continent during the War of the Austrian Succession and the Seven Years' War. However, on both occasions the majority of the troops Britain deployed on the continent were mercenaries.

But Britain did not conquer an empire by keeping troops at home or sending them to Europe. She had to fight for her new possessions in India and North America. Critics of Britain's propensity to send between a quarter and a third of the troops on her establishment to the colonies rather than to the continent during the War of the Austrian Succession and the Seven Years' War overlooked the fact that a large proportion of the troops who fought in North America, and the overwhelming majority of those who fought in India, were raised on the spot. Without the supplies and manpower the colonies provided the British could not have waged a successful war effort so far from home. The British were in no sense exercising a strategic 'option' when they raised men in North America or India for no one seriously believed that such forces could be sent to Europe. The difficulties the British had to overcome when they tried to fight a colonial war without raising substantial colonial forces became all too painfully apparent between 1775 and 1783. During the War of Independence Britain lacked continental allies and sent no troops to the continent and by 1777–8 she had concentrated nearly 42 per cent of her troops in North America. But thereafter the proportion fell to about 1 in 3 as France's entry into the war forced the British to dissipate their landforces to protect the remainder of their empire and the home islands. After 1778, nearly a half of the army (including the militia) remained in Britain. In these respects British policy accorded with the 'British way in warfare' but it is worth noting that the British relied on mercenaries far less in this war than they had done in any war since 1688. Mercenaries constituted about 15 per cent of the troops in British pay during the war and, whilst they averaged about 45 per cent of the troops in North America, that too was a smaller figure than for any major expeditionary force Britain had sent abroad since 1688.

The way in which the British deployed their landforces during the French Revolutionary and Napoleonic Wars exhibited some but not all of the features of the mixed paradigm. After 1793 their first priority was to form a coalition with at least two of the three eastern powers so that their armies could maintain an eastern front and contain the largest possible portion of the French army. When they succeeded in doing so they dispatched part of their own army to the continent. In 1793/4 the Commons voted that about 30 per cent of the troops on the British establishment should serve in Flanders. (That compared to the annual average of about 13 per cent they voted for the West Indies between 1794 and 1798.) But the majority of York's army (58 per cent) were German mercenaries. When the first three coalitions collapsed the army the British had sent to the continent was withdrawn before the French overwhelmed it. The British pursued a maritime war when they had no continental allies from necessity, not choice. They sought to strengthen their own defences and reduce the possibility of a French invasion by destroying enemy ships, securing overseas bases and capturing enemy colonies to expand their commerce and their ability to pay for the war. Until 1808 the navy shielded Britain from the worst consequences of the defeat of her continental allies. But the fleet alone could not safeguard Britain from invasion and it was for that reason that between 1793 and 1808 the British kept at least one in three of their troops at home. After 1808 they found in the Iberian Peninsula just the kind of theatre of operations which they had been seeking since 1795. Portugal offered them a secure bridgehead and the Spanish guerrillas made possible Wellington's survival by supplying him with intelligence and preventing the French from concentrating their superior numbers and crushing his field army. Between 1808 and 1814 the Commons voted annually to deploy about one-fifth of the troops on the British establishment in the Peninsula. Excluding the Portuguese troops who were under Wellington's command but not part of the British establishment, only 10 per cent of this force consisted of foreigners. Wellington's field army was the most 'British' expeditionary force the British had ever committed to the continent.

During the 'Pax Britannica' Britain engaged in a multitude of little wars but the wartime paradigms outlined in the Introduction were designed to analyse the way in which Britain conducted her great-power wars. Britain fought only one great-power war in this period, against Russia, and so the paradigms are of little value in analysing British policy for most of the nineteenth century. The First

World War marked Britain's clearest acceptance of a continental commitment and rejection of the 'British way in warfare'. In the first year of the First World War much of the army was too badly trained and equipped to be dispatched abroad. But from 1916 onwards approximately two-thirds of the army's divisions were committed to the western front, whilst between 1915 and 1918 about a quarter were dispatched to overseas theatres, the Dardanelles, Salonika, Egypt, Mesopotamia, India, Africa and Italy. The small number of formed divisions in Britain after 1916 indicated that the government relied largely, although never entirely, on the navy to repel an invasion. Imperial forces played a major role in defending the overseas empire and, for the first time, also constituted a major part of the forces Britain sent to Europe. The cost of the continental commitment was high but it was not only the fear of paying a similar price again which persuaded the British to pursue a strategy which approximated most closely to the mixed paradigm between 1939 and 1945. In 1939/40 the needs of the alliance with France compelled the British to makee a major commitment of their landforces to north-west Europe. There is reason to suppose that commitment would have increased had they not been driven from France in 1940. Between 1940 and 1941 they found themselves in much the same position they had occupied in 1795 or 1806 – expelled from the continent and bereft of allies. They had to adopt a peripheral strategy because of the formidable problems involved in securing a lodgement in Europe and because of the threats posed to their empire in the Middle East and Asia by the Axis powers. As in most of their earlier imperial wars, the British again relied heavily on imperial, rather than on purely British manpower, to conduct these operations. Between 1940 and 1944 the bulk of the British army remained at home, safeguarding Briitain against invasion and preparing for the cross-Channel invasion. When alliance politics again made it possible to return to north-west Europe in June 1944, nearly three-quuuarters of the divisions the British committed to 'Overlord' consisted of British troops and they accounted for over 40 per cent of the British army.

In summary, in eight of these wars, the British retained a considerable proportion of the army at home, suggesting that they were usually not content to rely upon the Royal Navy alone to prevent an invasion. But two caveats must be noted. Given the propensity of governments to reduce the army to cadre strength between wars, at the start of each conflict large numbers of recruits had to be assembled and trained before they were fit to be dispatched abroad and before the mid-nineteenth century troops were also kept at home to act as policemen. Operations outside Europe absorbed a large part of the army in the mid- and late eighteenth century. But critics of Britain's propensity to conquer enemy colonies rather than to send ground forces to the continent underestimated the part played by colonial forces in conquering the empire and mistakenly assumed that military resources were interchangeable between the continent and the empire. Only in the First World War, and to a lesser extent in 1944/5, did colonial ground forces play a significant role in Europe. Only a small proportion of the army was ever devoted to raids on the enemy coast. During the Nine Years' War, the War of the Spanish Succession, the War of the Austrian Succession, the Seven Years' War and the First World War, Britain did make a significant continental commitment. She made brief continental commitments during the French Revolutionary War between 1793 and 1795, the Napoleonic War between 1808 and 1814 and twice during the Second World War in 1939/40 and in 1944/5. The most favoured theatre for such a commitment was north-west Europe. Geographical proximity facilitated the dispatch of expeditionary forces to north-west Europe and British troops in the Low Countries could prevent an enemy from using their ports as the starting point for an invasion armada. After the Seven Years' War foreign mercenaries ceased to form a significant part of Britain's landforces, although to some extent their place was taken by imperial troops. But, as already noted, the exact role of these two groups was not analogous. Foreign mercenaries formed a disproportionately large part of the armies Britain sent to the continent between 1688 and 1763. Imperial forces formed a disproportionately large part of the armies Britain deployed outside Europe in the First and Second World Wars.

It is hard to argue that since 1688 policy-makers consistently pursued either the 'British way in warfare' or the mixed paradigm. The only generalization which is valid for the whole period is that British strategic policy was essentially adaptive. Policy-makers pursued policies which seemed to be best calculated to achieve their dominant policy aims at minimum cost. British defence policy was consistent only in its *apparent* inconsistency. It was shaped by the changing priorities of the policy-making elite. The appearance of inconsistency was a product of the fact that the elite was usually open to a considerable number of often competing interest groups. After 1688 defence policy was never the sole prerogative of one man or even of a small clique. That was true even when 'great' war ministers like Pitt the Elder, Lloyd George, or Churchill were at the helm. The constitutional arrangements created in the aftermath of the Glorious Revolution meant that a number of competing interest groups always had access to the corridors of power and had to be placated. In the eighteenth and nineteenth centuries Parliament was the arena within which their conflicting aims were mediated. In the twentieth century the dominance of the executive over Parliament was more pronounced but a system of governmental committees evolved around the Cabinet which enabled numerous interested parties to expound their frequently discordant strategic ideas in the corridors of power. It was not accidental that British defence policy since 1688 had been characterized by compromise and consensus. Critics have sometimes railed against this on the grounds that it reflected a dangerous penchant for relying on 'muddling through'. But before we accept the validity of their criticisms it is important to examine the result of 'muddling through'. Between 1688 and 1945 Britain lost only one of the great-power wars in which she was engaged: the American War of Independence. She drew three: the Nine Years' War, the War of the Austrian Succession and the French Revolutionary War. She won the remainder. 'Muddling through' brought Britain more victories than defeats.

It is now time to return to the question posed at the beginning of this book, and to determine if the development of defence policy over the past three centuries provides any guidance to contemporary policy-makers. History is an imprecise discipline and the attempt to use it to provide prescriptive formulae for future policies can be a dangerous exercise which a wise historian might avoid. This book is dotted with examples of policy-makers who were not historians and who constructed their own vision of a 'usable past' to justify their current policies. Their partial and defective understanding of what had happened in the past led them to repeat the mistakes of their predecessors rather than to learn from them. But if the reader believes that all military events have taken place within a unique environment and that social, political and economic changes are occurring so rapidly that no valid lessons can be drawn from the past, he or she should stop reading now. This book has been about the making of defence policy and, whilst it has paid some attention to the impact of changes in the technological environment within which policy-makers operated, its main focus has been on defence policy-making as a political process. My justification for believing that the past may have some lessons for the present is to be found in the fact that the fundamental nature of defence policy-making remains the same as it has always been. It consists of making difficult political choices. Nothing has happened to suggest that policy-makers will cease to be constrained, as they have been over the preceding three centuries, by the international political environment within which Britain finds herself, by the ability of the economy to produce the goods the defence forces need at acceptable cost and by the domestic political circumstances within which they work. Nor is it likely that there will be fundamental changes in the structure of government and that Britain will cease to be a parliamentary democracy, that equipment costs will do anything other than grow, or that policy-makers will no longer see their carefully calculated decisions nullified by unexpected crises.

Sometimes, although less often than harried policy-makers in search of easy solutions might hope, a serious study of history can produce obvious lessons. More often it can provide illumination and insight to thoughtful policy-makers who are prepared to spend time and effort on it. And always a knowledge of the past that goes beyond the merely superficial should prevent policy-makers from deceiving themselves and others with favourite, but usually distorted or partial images of the past. The British might not have rushed with such mistaken enthusiasm into war with Spain in 1739 if exaggerated stories of the achievements of Elizabethan buccaneers had not blinded them to the difficulties of amphibious warfare in the Caribbean. Lord North's government might not have underestimated the difficulties which would confront them in the thirteen colonies if they had possessed a more realistic vision of the military achievements of the colonial militia during the Seven Years' War.

Despite the fact that Britain is an island, isolation from Europe was not a viable option when she was a great power and even when, as between 1714 and 1783, her major ambitions were to acquire and then secure an extra-European empire. A stable and peaceful Europe was and remains a major British interest, both because so much of her trade was and is with Europe and because only from Europe can her physical security be endangered. Between 1688 and 1945 Britain fought twelve wars in which she was opposed by at least one other great power. In only two of those did she fight without at least one great power as an ally. The first was the war against Spain between 1726 and 1729 which the British won. The second was the American War of Independence. For the British the latter precedent at least was not a happy one. Meeting her security needs by co-operating with other powers was the norm for Britain, not the exception, both in peace and war before 1945. The only thing which membership of NATO changed was that to secure that co-operation, since 1954 Britain has been obliged by treaty to maintain forces on the continent in peacetime. Since 1949 her defence policy has been based upon membership of a peacetime coalition, NATO and her 'special relationship' with the USA. The division of Europe into two competing alliances after the Second World War served British security interests by ending the European civil war of 1914–45. BAOR (British Army of the Rhine) is the price the British have paid to help to maintain this division and to secure a peaceful Europe. It was cheap compared to the possible alternatives, a hopeless attempt to match the conventional and nuclear power of the superpowers by herself, or a third major war in Europe within the space of two generations. And it was also cheap compared to the price imposed on most of the states occupied by the Soviet army in Eastern Europe in 1945 and the price imposed upon the German people whose nation was split into two segments.

However, it is possible that both the American and the West-European pillars upon which British security has rested since the end of the Second World War may crumble in the 1990s. American policy-makers, concerned at what they perceive to be the USA's relative economic decline, may try to reduce their commitment to the defence of Western Europe in an attempt to compel their allies to carry a heavier share of the burden of their own defences. The issue of burden-sharing will not disappear as long as the USA has a serious trade and budget deficit. American disenchantment with, and partial military disengagement from Western Europe could be hastened if the completion of the Common Market in 1992 results in the creation of a 'Fortress Europe' which discriminates against American trade. Within Europe itself many West Germans are increasingly unwilling to live within the international structures imposed upon them after 1945. The perceptible thaw in the Cold War inaugurated by President Gorbachev's adoption of *perestroika* and *glasnost* was more warmly welcomed in West Germany than in almost any other Western country. It seemed to offer them the hope that the division of their country was not permanent and that the reunification of the two Germanies was possible. The subsequent collapse of communist rule in East Germany and throughout most of the Soviet

Union's Warsaw Pact allies in the second half of 1989 poses a delicate problem for the British. On the one hand a reunified Germany might be neutral and that would have serious repercussions for the cohesion of NATO. On the other hand the British cannot be seen to be advocating a larger degree of self-determination for the peoples of Eastern Europe whilst at the same time denying it to the Germans.

It should not occasion too much surprise that the stable European world created at the end of the Second World War may be collapsing. The international state system has always been a dynamic structure and change has always been endemic within it. The Utrecht settlement which marked Britain's emergence as a great power lasted until 1793, with some marginal changes. The Vienna settlement of 1814–15, which served British interests so well, lasted for an even shorter time and began to collapse in the 1860s. In the 1980s a new generation of political leaders emerged in Europe, some of whom are sceptical of the assumptions of their predecessors. Britain cannot afford to ignore any of these developments. Her policy ought to be directed towards preserving as much as possible of the political and military cohesion of NATO for there is no alternative collective security system on the international horizon which is likely in the immediate future to offer Britain a comparable measure of security. Isolation was rarely a realistic option when Britain was a great power and it is not one now when she is only a medium-sized power. In the 1990s, given her increasingly close economic ties to Western Europe and the range and destructive power of modern weapons, it is even less of an option than it was in the past. Mrs Thatcher was stating the obvious when she asserted at Bruges in September 1988 that 'Our links to the rest of Europe have been the dominant factor in our history'.[1]

Membership of NATO must remain the corner-stone of British defence policy for the foreseeable future. But that raises the question of what form Britain's involvement in NATO should take. The Defence White Paper published in May 1989 indicated the clear priority which the Thatcher administration gave to the defence of the central front. The British forces in West Germany received 39.1 per cent of the available funding, compared to 19.8 per cent allocated to the defence of the United Kingdom, 23.3 per cent to the maritime defence of the eastern Atlantic and the Channel, 10.4 per cent allocated to the strategic deterrent and 7.4 per cent allocated to miscellaneous commitments. Between 1979 and 1986 spending on defence increased by 26 per cent in line with the previous Labour government's promise to its NATO partners. That era has ended and the government's ability to fund defence will depend upon the overall performance of the economy. A pessimistic scenario suggests that the Thatcher government's policies have not reversed Britain's underlying economic decline. In the 1980s some of the more awkward consequences of that decline were hidden by the wealth generated by North Sea oil. But when the oil revenues decline in the 1990s, Britain will face a growing trade deficit. The government will find itself short of revenue to fund its activities and defence, being one of the largest-spending departments, might have to suffer a cut in resources. In 1988 Britain spent 4.3 per cent of her gross national product on defence, which was more than any other NATO country except Greece and the USA. How long she will be able to continue to do so in the future will depend upon whether the British government retains the political will to do so and on whether or not there is a fundamental improvement in the British economy. If no improvement occurs, the temptation to reduce the proportion of gross national product spent on defence will increase and a future government may have no option other than to conduct another major defence review.

Hitherto postwar governments have been able to reduce the mismatch between resources and defence commitments by selectively shedding Britain's more onerous extra-European commitments. That option is now virtually exhausted. A comprehensive defence review would inevitably lead to a recommendation to reduce one of Britain's major commitments within NATO. The Thatcher government has avoided confronting that obstacle by forcing the Ministry of Defence to reduce rising equipment costs by securing better value for money from its contractors. There is scope for securing greater cost-effectiveness in weapons procurement, but it is doubtful if this alone will suffice to eliminate the mismatch between commitments and resources. In the medium term the most positive way in which Britain can stretch her economic resources is by participating in more joint development programmes for new weapons with her European allies. In the longer term Britain's salvation may lie in the possibility that the establishment of a common European market in 1992 will produce sufficient economic growth to reduce some of the tighter economic constraints under which policy-makers now operate.

The Thatcher government's decision to maintain Britain's commitment to the central front and to modernize the strategic deterrent at the cost of reducing the navy's surface fleets soon provoked suggestions for alternative policies. The naval lobby suggested a return to 'limited liability': Britain's commitment to the central front should be reduced and resources should instead be concentrated on Britain's maritime defences. This may seem an attractive option in peacetime but it has little to recommend it. It would run counter to the increasing economic importance of Western Europe for Britain. It is not demonstrably apparent that a reduction in the size of the forces committed to the central front would free the resources to be spent on other defence requirements. But above all it smacks too much of a cost-accountant's concept of strategy. Historical experience suggests that when Britain has fought a European war in alliance with one or more great powers against a similarly constituted alliance, there has come a time when Britain's allies have demanded the presence of British troops on the continent as visible proof of her commitment to their common cause. States enter into alliances to share their defence burden with other powers who have similar security interests. Policy-makers are therefore bound to conduct some calculations of costs and benefits when considering their alliance policies. But it is dangerous to view alliances solely in the same way that an accountant might look at a balance-sheet. Alliances are also political relationships in which partners seek to establish a relationship of trust based upon mutual burden-sharing. The most secure alliances have been those in which each partner perceived that there was equality of sacrifice amongst the allies. The 'limited liability' strategies advocated by the country gentlemen in the eighteenth century, Liberal politicians like Reginald McKenna in the First World War, or Neville Chamberlain in the 1930s, had to be cast aside because they did not seem likely to produce mutual sacrifices. Their exponents believed that the options they were advocating were supremely rational. But from the point of view of Britain's allies it appeared that the British expected them to do most of the fighting and suffer most of the casualties whilst they stood back and, adding insult to injury, perhaps enriched themselves at their partners' expense. A unilateral decision to withdraw forces from West Germany would produce dangerous tensions within the NATO alliance and might make West German opinion still more ready to move towards neutralism. It would send the wrong signals to Britain's other European partners and would place considerable strains on the solidarity of the alliance at a time when many US policy-makers are determined that their European allies should carry a larger share of the defence of Western Europe.

Another option that was suggested in the early 1980s was that Britain might secure more resources for her conventional forces by pursuing a non-nuclear defence policy. Public opinion polls, and the results of the 1979, 1983 and 1987 general elections, indicated that the British public was ambivalent about nuclear weapons. The majority wished to retain a *British* deterrent for as long as the Soviet Union possessed nuclear weapons, but many people would welcome the removal of *American* nuclear weapons from Britain on the grounds that British governments have little or no control over their use. If the 1930s have any lessons for policy-makers in the 1990s it is that a defence policy designed to deter potential enemies is likely to fail unless it is supported by forces able to maintain a credible level of military effectiveness. Reliance on the navy to deter the Bourbons from pursuing a policy of revenge worked in the decade after 1763 because it took the French and Spanish some time to rebuild their own fleets. But once the British were embroiled in a war in North America the Royal Navy was too small to blockade the thirteen colonies successfully and maintain large enough forces in European waters to frighten the Bourbons into continued submission. For most of the 1930s Bomber Command consisted of units which were maintained without adequate reserves to give it a sustained war-fighting capability. This force was expensive to create, failed to frighten the potential adversary against whom it was directed and failed to give British policy-makers the confidence they required to confront them. Advocates of a non-nuclear defence policy must face the fact that nuclear weapons have provided the British with a relatively *cheap* deterrent and that to achieve anything like a comparable degree of security with non-nuclear forces would require the allocation of more, not fewer, resources to defence.

The creation of a credible non-nuclear defence policy may also be made more difficult by the shortage of manpower the armed forces may encounter in the 1990s. Between 1987 and 2000 the percentage of men aged 18–22 will decrease by about one-quarter and the number of active service personnel in the British forces could drop from 324,000 in 1987 to 242,000 in 2000. The British armed services are manned by volunteers and the cost of enlisting volunteers is high because service wages must compete with those in the civilian occupations. To compensate for this shrinkage service wages could be increased but, as pay consumes about one-fifth of the defence budget, that is unlikely to happen unless economies can be made elsewhere. The reintroduction of national service would decrease wage costs but it would do so in the face of extensive public opposition and any government anxious to be re-elected might hesitate before opting for it. It would require a campaign to persuade the public that they could no longer have a defence policy which was socially cheap at a time when developments in the Soviet Union and in many East-European countries seem to indicate that the threat from the Warsaw Pact is decreasing. The most practical option will be to make greater use of reserve forces even though to do so will produce some decline in training standards and diminish the overall readiness of the services for war. One choice policy-makers will do well to avoid is to follow the example of their eighteenth-century predecessors who opted at the end of each war to reduce their landforces to cadre strength in the mistaken expectation that they would be cheap to maintain in peacetime and could be rapidly expanded and made efficient in wartime. In the long run it is both cheaper and more effective to maintain a smaller number of units at a higher state of combat readiness.

The allocation of resources to the services is important but adequate resources do not by themselves produce a viable defence policy. The most difficult issues facing policy-makers in the next decade will be the challenge presented to NATO by the perceptible thawing of the Cold War inaugurated by President Gorbachev which may culminate in the disintegration of the Warsaw Pact as a military alliance. The demographic and economic constraints outlined above could become much less pressing if it is possible to negotiate large-scale conventional and nuclear arms reductions with the Warsaw Pact. President Gorbachev's policies of *perestroika* and *glasnost* may offer Britain and NATO great opportunities but only if he can remain in power and is able to implement them over a long period. Britain and her NATO partners must strike a delicate balance. They must be prepared to make sufficient concessions to encourage the Soviet government to continue down this path of mutual arms reductions and towards greater democratization of Soviet society. They must also recognize that it is probably not Gorbachev's aim to transform the Soviet Union into a Western-style capitalist state with a fully democratic political system. The Cold War in Europe will not be finished until the possibility of Soviet aggression against Western Europe has been removed by the ending of Soviet subjugation of Eastern Europe and the complete democratization of Soviet and East European political institutions. Until then prudence dictates that Britain and NATO must preserve credible defences which will persuade the Soviet government to continue to negotiate and provide the alliance with an adequate defence capability should Gorbachev fall from power or should his policies be halted or put into reverse. But Gorbachev is not bound to fail, and to think that improved relations between powers is impossible just because they have been antagonists in the past is to betray a serious failure of historical imagination. Britain's relations with Bourbon France between 1716 and 1731 or with the French republic after 1904 and tsarist Russia after 1907 demonstrate that old enemies can become new friends even if all their national interests are not in complete accord.

If the British government is to maintain this delicate balance it must be supported by public opinion. For most of the post-1945 era defence policy was not a salient political issue which divided the two major parties. That ceased to be the case in the mid-1970s as the post-1945 defence consensus between the two major political parties – a consensus which supported British membership of NATO and an independent British nuclear deterrent – began to crumble. The postwar consensus within the electorate eroded far less. Support for British membership of NATO remained high in the 1980s. By 1986 only 13 per cent of those questioned in a poll believed that Britain should withdraw from the alliance. But it would be a foolish government which took such support for granted, especially at a time of unprecedented political changes in the Soviet Union and Eastern Europe which are widely perceived in Britain as reducing the potential threat the Warsaw Pact might pose to the security of Brtiain and her NATO allies. Britain is a democracy and any government's ability to pursue a consistent defence policy will depend upon the degree of public support which it can muster. A limited degree of official secrecy is necessary in matters concerning defence policy. But the British system of government is prone to excessive secrecy in matters of defence and it is also resistant to advice from nongovernmental specialists. The regular interaction of ideas and personnel between the government bureaucracy, business and academe which is a feature of the American policy-making process, is almost unknown in Britain. The tendency of British policy-makers only to look inward for ideas, and their reluctance to provide more than the barest minimum of information concerning their activities to the wider public, may be counter-productive. If governments wish to mobilize and retain public support, they must be willing to trust the electorate with the information it needs to come to a reasoned judgement. If they do not, they may find themselves echoing William III's lament in 1698: 'I am so chagrined at what passes in the Lower House with regard to the troops, that I can scarce turn my thought to any other matter. I foresee that I shall be obliged to come to resolutions of extremity'.[2]

Notes

Introduction

1. Sir John Nott, 'British defence policy: wither now?', in D. Bolton (ed.), *Royal United Services Institute and Brassey's Defence Yearbook 1988* (London: Brassey's, 1988), p. 29.
2. Q. Wright, *A Study of War* (Chicago: University of Chicago Press, 1942), Vol. 1, p. 636.
3. D. Thomson, *England in the Nineteenth Century* (London: Penguin, 1950), p. 27.
4. C. von Clausewitz, *On War*. Translated and edited by M. Howard and P. Paret. (Princeton, NJ: Princeton University Press, 1976), p. 87.
5. ibid., p. 119.
6. ibid., p. 585.
7. A. T. Mahan, *The Influence of Sea Power upon the French Revolution and Empire* (London: Sampson, Low & Marston, 1893), Vol. 2, p. 118.
8. A. T. Mahan, *The Influence of Sea Power upon History 1660–1783* (London: Sampson, Low & Marston, 1890), pp. 64–5.
9. D. M. Schurman, *The Education of a Navy. The Development of British Naval Strategic Thought, 1867–1914* (Chicago: University of Chicago Press, 1965), p. 78.
10. Sir J. Corbett, *Some Principles of Maritime Strategy* (London: Longmans, Green & Co., 1911), p. 38.
11. ibid., p. 57.
12. B. H. Liddell Hart, 'Economic pressure or continental victories', *Journal of the Royal United Services Institute for Defence Studies*, vol. 76 (1931), p. 500.
13. C. Layne, 'British grand strategy, 1900–1939; theory and practice in international politics', *Journal of Strategic Studies*, vol. 2, no. 3 (1979), p. 310.
14. C. Barnett, *Britain and her Army, 1509–1970. A Military, Political and Social Survey* (London: Allen Lane, 1970), pp. xviii, xix, 149, 187–8.
15. G. S. Graham, *Tides of Empire. Discursions on the Expansion of Britain Overseas* (London/Montreal: McGill-Queen's University Press, 1972), p. 38.
16. ibid.
17. M. Howard, 'The British way in warfare: a reappraisal', in M. Howard, *The Causes of War and other Essays* (London: Temple Smith, 1983), p. 180.
18. B. R. Mitchell and P. Deane, *An Abstract of British Historical Statistics* (Cambridge: Cambridge University Press, 1962), pp. 397–8.

Chapter 1 The Emergence of a Great Power, 1688–1714

1 A. Lossky, 'International relations in Europe', in J. S. Bromley (ed.), *New Cambridge Modern History. Vol. VI: The Rise of Great Britain and Russia, 1688–1715/25* (Cambridge: Cambridge University Press, 1970), p. 157.
2 J. R. Western, *The English Militia in the Eighteenth Century. The Story of a Political Issue, 1660–1802* (London: Routledge & Kegan Paul, 1965), p. 207.
3 C. M. Clode, *The Military Forces of the Crown* (London: John Murray, 1896), p. 359.
4 A. N. Ryan, 'William III and the Brest fleet in the Nine Years War', in R. M. Hatton and J. S. Bromley (eds.), *William III and Louis XIV* (Liverpool: Liverpool University Press, 1967), p. 66.
5 G. Holmes (ed.), *Britain after the Glorious Revolution* (London: Macmillan, 1969), p. 137.
6 H. T. Dickinson, *Liberty and Property. Political Ideology in Eighteenth Century Britain* (London: Methuen, 1977), p. 185.
7 G. Holmes, *Politics in the Age of Anne* (London: Macmillan, 1969), p. 70.
8 Dickinson, *Liberty and Property*, p. 85.

Chapter 2 War for Empire, 1714–63

1 J. Black, *Natural and Necessary Enemies. Anglo-French Relations in the Eighteenth Century* (London: Duckworth, 1986), p. 35.
2 C. W. Eldon, *England's Subsidy Policy towards the Continent during the Seven Years War* (Philadelphia, Pa: Drexel Institute of Technology, 1938), p. 69.
3 Sir C. Whitworth, *A Collection of the Supplies and Ways and Means from the Revolution to the Present Time* (London: R. Davis, 1764), p. 43.
4 P. Woodfine, 'Naval power and the conflict with Spain, 1737–1743', in J. Black and P. Woodfine (eds.), *The British Navy and the use of Naval Power in the Eighteenth Century* (Leicester: Leicester University Press, 1988), p. 85.
5 H. Richmond, 'English strategy in the War of the Austrian Succession', *Journal of the Royal United Services Institute*, vol. 64 (1919), p. 250.
6 Black, *Natural and Necessary Enemies*, p. 39.
7 R. Middleton, *The Bells of Victory. The Pitt–Newcastle Ministry and the Conduct of the Seven Years War, 1757–62* (Cambridge: Cambridge University Press, 1985), p. 27.
8 Eldon, *England's Subsidy Policy*, p. 41.
9 W. K. Hackmann, 'William Pitt and the Generals: three case studies in the Seven Years War', *Albion*, vol. 3 (1971), p. 131.
10 Eldon, *England's Subsidy Policy*, p. 98.
11 J. M. Sosin, 'Louisburg and the Peace of Aix-la-Chapelle', *William and Mary Quarterly*, vol. 14, no. 4 (1957), p. 532.
12 R. Browning, *The Duke of Newcastle* (New Haven, Conn.: Yale University Press, 1975), p. 232.

Chapter 3 The American War of Independence, 1763–83

1. C. von Clausewitz, *On War*. Translated and edited by M. Howard and P. Paret (Princeton, NJ: Princeton University Press, 1976), p. 583.
2. J. P. Greene, 'The Seven Years War and the American Revolution: the causal relationship reconsidered', in P. J. Marshal and G. Williams (eds), *The British Atlantic Empire before the American Revolution* (London: Frank Cass, 1980), p. 85.
3. J. L. Bullion, 'Security and economy: the Bute administration's plan for the American army and revenue 1762–1763', *William and Mary Quarterly*, vol. 45, no. 3 (1988), p. 501.
4. J. Shy, *Towards Lexington. The Role of the British Army in the Coming of the American Revolution* (Princeton, NJ: Princeton University Press, 1965), p. 93.
5. S. Conway, 'To subdue America: British army officers and the conduct of the Revolutionary War', *William and Mary Quarterly*, vol. 43, no. 3 (1986), p. 381.
6. P. D. G. Thomas, *Lord North* (London: Allen Lane, 1976), p. 109.
7. S. R. Frey, *The British Soldier in America. A Social History of Military Life in the Revolutionary Period* (Austin, Texas: University of Texas Press, 1981), p. 5.
8. M. S. Anderson, *War and Society in Europe of the Old Regime, 1618–1789* (London: Fontana, 1988), p. 184.
9. P. Mackesy, *The War for America, 1775–1783* (Cambridge, Mass.: Harvard University Press, 1965), p. 186.
10. Linda Colley, 'Whose nation? Class and national consciousness in Britain 1750–1830', *Past and Present*, no. 113 (1986), p. 114.

Chapter 4 The French Revolution and Napoleonic Wars

1. W. H. McNeill, *The Pursuit of Power, Technology, Armed Force and Society since AD1000* (Oxford: Basil Blackwell, 1982), p. 192
2. J. Ehrman, *The Younger Pitt. The Reluctant Transition* (London: Constable, 1983), p. 269.
3. P. Mackesy, *The War in the Mediterranean, 1803–1810* (Cambridge. Mass.: Harvard University Press, 1957), p. 358.
4. P. Jupp, *Lord Grenville 1759–1834* (Oxford: Clarendon Press, 1985), p. 155.
5. P. Mackesy, *The War for America 1775–1783* (Cambridge Mass. Harvard University Press, 1964), pp. 35–6.
6. Ehrman, *The Younger Pitt*, p. 272.
7. M. Duffy, *Soldiers, Sugar and Seapower. The British Expeditions to the West Indies and the War against Revolutionary France* (Oxford: Clarendon Press, 1987), p. 377.
8. Ehrman, *The Younger Pitt*, p. 455.
9. G. E. Rothenberg, 'The origins, causes, and extension of the wars of the French Revolution and Napoleon', *Journal of Interdisciplinary History*, vol. 18, no. 4 (1988), p. 798.
10. C. Emsley, *British Society and the French Wars 1793–1815* (London: Macmillan, 1979), pp. 159–60.
11. Linda Colley, 'Whose nation? Class and national consciousness in Britain 1750–1830', *Past and Present*, no. 113 (1986), p. 115.
12. D. D. Howard, 'British seapower and its influence on the Peninsular War,' *Naval War College Review*, vol. 31 (1978), p. 60.
13. I. R. Christie, *Wars and Revolutions. Britain, 1760–1815* (London: Edward Arnold, 1982), p. 242.

Chapter 5 The Era of the 'Pax Britannica', c. 1815–80

1. C. J. Bartlett, *Great Britain and Seapower, 1815–53* (Oxford: Clarendon Press, 1963), pp. 13–14.
2. See C. Barnett, *The Collapse of British Power* (Gloucester: Allen Sutton, 1972/84).
3. K. Bourne, *The Foreign Policy of Victorian England 1830–1902* (Oxford: Clarendon Press, 1970), p. 252.
4. N. Gash, *Pillars of Government and Other Essays on State and Society, c. 1768–1880* (London: Edward Arnold, 1986), p. 49.
5. G. S. Graham, *Tides of Empire. Discursions on the Expansion of Britain Overseas* (London/Montreal: McGill-Queen's University Press, 1972), p. 85.
6. J. B. William, *British Commercial Policy and Trade Expansion, 1750–1850* (Oxford: Clarendon Press, 1972), p. 82.
7. M. Yapp, *Strategies of British India. Britain, Iran and Afghanistan 1798-1850* (Oxford: Clarendon Press, 1980), p. 303.
8. D. Steele, 'Gladstone and Palmerston, 1855–65', in P. J. Jagger (ed.), *Gladstone, Politics and Religion. A Collection of Founder's Day Lectures delivered at St. Deinol's Library, Hawarden, 1967–83* (London: Macmillan, 1985), p. 135.
9. ibid., pp. 128–9.
10. E. Spiers, *Army and Society, 1815–1914* (London: Longman, 1980),p. 164.
11. K. Jeffery, 'The eastern arc of Empire: a strategic view 1850–1950', *Journal of Strategic Studies*, vol. 5, no. 4 (1982), p. 538.

Chapter 6 The Rise and Fall of the 'Blue Water' Policy

1. D. M. Schurman, *The Education of a Navy. The Development of British Naval Strategic Thought, 1867–1914.* (Malbar, Fl.: Robert E. Keiger, 1984), p. 26.
2. K. Neilson, '"A dangerous game of American poker": The Russo-Japanese War and British Policy', *Journal of Strategic Studies*, vol. 12, no. 1 (1989), p. 68.
3. D. French, 'Allies, rivals and enemies: British strategy and war aims during the First World War', in J. Turner (ed.), *Britain and the First World War* (London: Unwin Hyman, 1988), p. 28.

Chapter 7 Deterrence and Dependence, 1917–42

1. J. Ferris, 'Treasury control, the Ten Year Rule and British service policies 1919–1924', *Historical Journal*, vol. 30, no. 4 (1987), p. 863.
2. J. Neidpath, *The Singapore Naval Base and the Defence of Britain's Eastern Empire, 1919–1941* (Oxford: Clarendon Press, 1981), p. 46.
3. B. Bond, *British Military Policy between the Wars* (Oxford: Clarendon Press, 1980), p. 77.
4. ibid., p. 108.
5. G. Peden, 'A matter of timing: the economic background to British foreign policy, 1937–1939', *History*, vol. 69 (1984), p. 22.
6. Bond, *British Military Policy*, p. 243.
7. Peden, 'A matter of timing:', p. 16.
8. R. P. Shay Jr., *Rearmament in the Thirties. Politics and Profits* (Princeton NJ: Princeton University Press, 1977), p. 279.

9   A. Prazmowska, 'The eastern front and the British guarantee to Poland of March 1939', *European History Quarterly*, vol. 14 (1984), p. 191.
10 R. A. C. Parker, 'Britain, France and Scandinavia, 1939–40', *History*, vol. 61 (1976), p. 370.
11 R. A. C. Parker, 'The pound sterling, the American Treasury and British preparations for war, 1938–39', *English Historical Review*, vol. 98 (1983), p. 264.
12 D. Reynolds, *The Creation of the Anglo-American Alliance, 1937–1941: A Study of Competitive Co-operation* (London: Europa, 1981), p. 167.
13 W. D. McIntyre, *The Rise and Fall of the Singapore Naval Base, 1919–1942* (London: Macmillan, 1979), p. 183.
14 Reynolds, *The Creation of the Anglo-American Alliance*, p. 250.

Chapter 8   The End of Empire, 1942–82

1   G. Ross, 'Operation Bracelet: Churchill in Moscow, 1942', in D. Dilks, (ed.), *Retreat from Power. Studies in British Foreign Policy of the Twentieth Century* (London: Macmillan, 1981), Vol. 2, p. 104.
2   J. Terraine, *The Right of the Line. The Royal Air Force in the European War, 1939–45* (London: Hodder & Stoughton, 1985) p. 474.
3   R. Callahan, *Burma, 1942–45* (London: Davis-Poynter, 1978)., p. 143.
4   C. Thorne, *The Far Eastern War. States and Societies 1941–45* (London: Allen & Unwin, 1985), p. 106.
5   D. Reynolds, *The Creation of the Anglo-American Alliance, 1937–1941: A Study of Competitive Co-operation.* (London: Europa, 1981), p. 122.
6   P. Weiler, 'British Labour and the Cold War: the foreign policy of the Labour governments, 1945–1951', *Journal of British Studies*, vol. 26 (1987), p. 57.
7   D. Kirby, 'Britain, NATO and European security', in J. Baylis (ed.), *British Defence Policy in a Changing World* (London: Croom Helm, 1977), p. 103.
8   M. Dockrill, *British Defence since 1945* (London: Basil Blackwell, 1989), p. 31.
9   J. W. Spanier, *Games Nations Play. Analysing International Politics* (London: Nelson, 1972), pp. 195–6.
10 T. C. Salmon, 'Britain's nuclear deterrent', in M. Edmonds (ed), *The Defence Equation. British Military Systems, Policy, Planning and Performance* (London: Brassey's, 1986), p. 52.
11 Sir John Nott, 'British defence policy: wither now?', in D. Bolton (ed.), *Royal United Services Institute and Brassey's Defence Yearbook 1988* (London: Brassey's, 1988), p.32.

Conclusion: From Thatcher to the Millenium

1   R. Owen, 'Will Europe see the join', *The Times*, 30 January 1989.
2   Louis G. Schwoerer, 'The role of King William III of England in the standing army controversy – 1697–1699', *Journal of British Studies*, vol. 5 (1965/6), p. 88.

Guide to Further Reading

The following does not purport to be a comprehensive bibliography, merely a guide to further reading. Students wishing to refer to a full bibliography should consult R. Higham (ed.), *A Guide to the Sources of British Military History* (Berkeley, Calif.: University of California Press, 1971) and G. Jordan (ed.), *British Military History. A Supplement to Robin Higham's Guide to the Sources* (New York: Garland, 1988).

Introduction

Barnett, C., *Britain and her Army, 1509–1970. A Military, Political and Social Survey* (London: Allen Lane, 1970).
Clausewitz, C. von, *On War*. Translated and edited by M. Howard and P. Paret. (Princeton, NJ: Princeton University Press, 1976).
Corbett, Sir J., *Some Principles of Maritime Strategy* (London: Longman, Green & Co., 1911).
Graham, G. S., *Tides of Empire. Discursions on the Expansion of Britain Overseas* (London/Montreal: McGill – Queen's University Press, 1972).
Howard, M., 'The British way in warfare: a reappraisal', in M. Howard, *The Causes of War and other Essays* (London: Temple Smith, 1983).
Kennedy, P. M., *The Rise and Fall of British Naval Mastery* (London: Macmillan, 1983).
Kennedy, P. M., *The Rise and Fall of the Great Powers. Economic Change and Military Conflict from 1500 to 2000* (London: Unwin Hyman, 1988).
Liddell Hart, B. H., 'Economic pressure or continental victories', *Journal of the Royal United Services Institute for Defence Studies*, vol. 76 (1931), pp. 486–503.
Mahan, A. T., *The Influence of Seapower upon History* (London: Sampson, Low & Marston, 1890).
Mahan, A. T., *The Influence of Seapower upon the French Revolution and Empire* (London: Sampson, Low & Marston, 1893).
Mitchell, B. R. and Deane, P., *An Abstract of British Historical Statistics* (Cambridge: Cambridge University Press, 1962).
Morgenthau, H. J., 'Alliances in theory and practice' in A. Wolfers (ed.), *Alliance Policy in the Cold War* (Baltimore, Md: Johns Hopkins University Press, 1959).
Nott, Sir J., 'British defence policy: wither now?', in D. Bolton (ed), *RUSI and Brassey's Defence Yearbook 1988* (London: Brassey's 1988), pp. 27–34.
Parliamentary Papers 1868–9, xxxv, Public Income and Expenditure.
Parliamentary Papers 1945–6, xv (Cmd 6856). Air services. Detailed Statement of Expenditure and Receipts for the Years 1939–1943; Air Appropriation Account for the Year ending 31 March 1945; Army Appropriation Account for the Year ending 31 March 1945.
Parliamentary Papers 1945–6, xvi. Navy. Detailed Statement of Expenditure and Receipts

for the Years 1939–1943; Navy Appropriation Account for the Year ending 31 March 1945.
War Office, *Statistics of the Military Effort of the British Empire during the Great War, 1914–1920* (London: HMSO, 1922).
Wright, Q., *A Study of War* (Chicago: University of Chicago Press, 1942).

Chapter 1 The Emergence of a Great Power, 1688–1714

Baugh, D. A., 'Great Britain's "Blue-water" policy, 1689–1815', *International History Review*, vol. 10, no. 1 (1988), pp. 33–58.
Baxter, S.B., *William III* (London: Longman, 1966).
Brewer, J., *The Sinews of Power. War, Money and the English State, 1688–1783* (New York: Alfred Knopf, 1989).
Bruce, A., *The Purchase System in the British Army 1660–1871* (London: Royal Historical Society, 1980).
Burton, I. F., *The Captain-General. The Career of John Churchill, Duke of Marlborough from 1702 to 1711* (London: Constable, 1968).
Childs, J., *The British Army of William III, 1689–1702* (Manchester: Manchester University Press, 1987).
Clark, G. N., *The Anglo-Dutch Alliance and the War against French Trade, 1689–1697* (Manchester: Manchester University Press, 1923).
Crowhurst, R. P., *The Defence of British Trade 1689–1815* (Folkestone: Dawson, 1977).
Dickinson, H. T., *Liberty and Property. Political Ideology in Eighteenth Century Britain* (London: Methuen, 1977).
Ehrman, J., *The Navy in the War of William III, 1689–1697* (Cambridge : Cambridge University Press, 1953).
Hattendorf, J. B., *England in the War of the Spanish Succession. A Study of the English View and Conduct of Grand Strategy, 1702–1712* (London/New York: Garland, 1987).
Holmes, G., *British Politics in the Age of Anne* (London: Macmillan, 1969).
Jones, D. W., *War and Economy in the Age of William III and Marlborough* (Oxford: Basil Blackwell, 1988).
Jones, J. R., *Britain and the World 1649–1815* (London: Fontana, 1980).
Langford, P., *Modern British Foreign Policy. The Eighteenth Century, 1688–1815* (London: A. & C., Black, 1976).
Marcus, G. J., *A Naval History of England. The Formative Centuries* (Boston, Mass.: Little Brown & Co., 1961).
Owen, J. H., *War at Sea under Queen Anne 1703–1708* (Cambridge : Cambridge University Press, 1938).
Scouller, R. E., *The Armies of Queen Anne* (Oxford: Clarendon Press, 1966).
Tomlinson, H. C., *Guns and Government. The Ordnance Office under the later Stuarts* (London: Royal Historical Society, 1979).
Viner, J., 'Power versus plenty as objectives of foreign policy in the seventeenth and eighteenth centuries', in D. C. Coleman (ed.), *Revisions in Mercantilism* (London: Methuen, 1969), pp. 61–91.

Chapter 2 War for Empire, 1714–63

Ayling, S., *The Elder Pitt, Earl of Chatham.* (London: Collins, 1976).
Baugh, D., *British Naval Administration in the Age of Walpole* (Princeton, NJ: Princeton University Press, 1965).

Black, J., *Natural and Necessary Enemies. Anglo-French Relations in the Eighteenth Century* (London: Duckworth, 1986).
Black J. and Woodfine, P., (eds), *The British Navy and the use of Naval Power in the Eighteenth Century* (Leicester: Leicester University Press, 1988).
Eldon, C. W., *England's Subsidy Policy towards the Continent during the Seven Years' War* (Philadelphia, Pa: Drexel Institute of Technology, 1938).
Guy, A. J., *Oeconomy and Discipline. Officership and Administration in the British Army 1714–1763* (Manchester: Manchester University Press, 1985).
Houlding, J. A., *Fit For Service. The Training of the British Army, 1715–1795* (Oxford: Clarendon Press, 1981).
Leach, D. E., *Arms for Empire. A Military History of the British Colonies in North America, 1607–1763* (New York: Macmillan, 1973).
Lenman, B. P., *The Jacobite Risings in Britain 1689–1746* (London: Eyre Methuen, 1980).
Mathias, P. and O'Brien, P., 'Taxation in Britain and France, 1715–1810. A comparison of the social and economic incidence of taxes collected from the central government', *Journal of European Economic History*, vol. 5 (1976), pp. 601–50.
Middleton, R., *The Bells of Victory. The Pitt-Newcastle Ministry and the Conduct of the Seven Years War, 1757–1762* (Cambridge: Cambridge University Press, 1985).
Pares, R., *War and Trade in the West Indies, 1739–1763* (London: Oxford University Press, 1963).
Pares, R., 'American versus Continental warfare, 1739–63', *English Historical Review*, vol. 51 (1936), pp. 429–65.
Parker, G., *The Military Revolution. Military Innovation and the Rise of the West, 1500–1800* (Cambridge: Cambridge University Press, 1988).
Richmond, Admiral Sir H., *Statesmen and Seapower* (Oxford: Clarendon Press, 1946).
Rodger, N. A. M., *The Wooden World. An Anatomy of the Georgian Navy* (London: Collins, 1986).
Savory, Sir R., *His Britannic Majesty's Army in Germany during the Seven Years' War* (Oxford: Clarendon Press, 1966).
Smelser, M., *The Campaign for the Sugar Islands, 1759. A Study of Amphibious Warfare* (Chapel Hill, NC: University of North Carolina Press, 1955).
Speck, W. A., *The Butcher. The Duke of Cumberland and the Suppression of the '45* (Oxford: Basil Blackwell, 1981).
Thomson, M. A., 'The War of the Austrian Succession' in J. O. Lindsay (ed.), *The New Cambridge Modern History*. Vol. VII: *The Old Regime 1713–1763* (Cambridge: Cambridge University Press, 1970), pp. 416–39.
Western, J. R., *The English Militia in the Eighteenth Century. The Story of a Political Issue, 1660–1802* (London: Routledge & Kegan Paul, 1965).
Whitworth, Sir R., *Field Marshal Lord Ligonier. A Story of the British Army 1702–1770* (Oxford: Clarendon Press, 1958).

Chapter 3   The American War of Independence, 1763–83

Billas, G. A.(ed.), *George Washington's Opponents. British Generals and Admirals in the American Revolution* (New York: William Morrow, 1969).
Bowler, R. A., *Logistics and the Failure of the British Army in America, 1775–1783* (Princeton, NJ: Princeton University Press, 1975).
Brewer, J., *Party Ideology and Popular Politics at the Accession of George III* (Cambridge: Cambridge University Press, 1976).
Christie, I. R., *The End of North's Ministry 1780–1782* (London: Macmillan, 1958).

Christie, I. R., *Crisis of Empire. Great Britain and the American Colonies, 1754–1783* (London: Edward Arnold, 1966).
Conway, S. R., 'To subdue America: British army officers and the conduct of the Revolutionary War', *William and Mary Quarterly*, vol. 43, no.3 (1986), pp. 381–407.
Curtis, E. E., *The Organization of the British Army in the American Revolution* (New Haven, Conn.: Yale University Press, 1926).
Dull, J. R., *A Diplomatic History of the American Revolution* (New Haven, Conn.: Yale University Press, 1985).
Higginbotham, D., *The War of American Independence. Military Attitudes, Policies and Practice, 1763–1789* (New York: Macmillan, 1971).
Higginbotham, D., (ed.), *Reconsideration on the Revolutionary War* (Westport, Conn.: Greenwood Press, 1978).
Mackesy, P., *The War for America 1775–1783* (Cambridge, Mass.: Harvard University Press, 1964).
Middelkauff, R., *The Glorious Cause. The American Revolution 1763–1789* (New York: Oxford University Press, 1982).
Robson, E., *The American Revolution in its Political and Military Aspects 1763–1783* (New York: Norton, 1966).
Shy, J., *Towards Lexington. The Role of the British Army in the Coming of the American Revolution* (Princeton, NJ: Princeton University Press, 1965).
Shy, J., *A People Numerous and Armed. Reflections on the Military Struggle for American Independence* (London: Oxford University Press, 1976).
Smith, P. H., *Loyalists and Redcoats. A Study in British Revolutionary Policy* (Chapel Hill, NC: University of North Carolina Press, 1964).
Syrett, D., *Shipping and the American War 1775–83. A Study of British Transport Organization* (London: Athlone Press, 1970).

Chapter 4 The French Revolutionary and Napoleonic Wars

Christie, I. R., *Wars and Revolutions. Britain, 1760–1815* (London: Edward Arnold, 1982).
Duffy, M., *Soldiers, Sugar and Seapower. The British Expeditions to the West Indies and the War against Revolutionary France* (Oxford: Clarendon Press, 1987).
Emsley, C., *British Society and the French Wars 1793–1815* (London: Macmillan, 1979).
Gates, D., *The Spanish Ulcer. A History of the Peninsular War* (New York: Norton, 1986).
Glover, M., *Wellington as Military Commander* (London: Batsford, 1968).
Glover, R., *Peninsular Preparation. The Reform of the British Army 1795–1809* (Cambridge: Cambridge University Press, 1963).
Horsman, R., *The War of 1812* (New York: Knopf, 1969).
Jones, C., (ed.), *Britain and Revolutionary France: Conflict, Subversion and Propaganda* (Exeter: Exeter Studies in History, 1983).
Jupp, P., *Lord Grenville 1759–1834* (Oxford: Clarendon Press, 1985).
Lewis, M. A., *A Social History of the Navy* (London: Oxford University Press, 1970).
Mackesy, P., *The War in the Mediterranean, 1803–1810* (Cambridge, Mass.: Harvard University Press, 1957).
Mackesy, P., *The Strategy of Overthrow, 1798–1799* (London: Longman, 1974).
Mackesy, P., *War without Victory. The Downfall of Pitt, 1799–1802* (Oxford: Clarendon Press, 1984).
Morriss, R. A., *The Royal Dockyards during the Revolutionary and Napoleonic Wars* (Leicester: Leicester University Press, 1983).

Sherwig, J. M., *Guineas and Gunpowder. British Foreign Aid in the Wars With France 1793–1815* (Cambridge, Mass.: Harvard University Press, 1969).
Yapp, M., *Strategies of British India. Britain, Iran and Afghanistan 1798–1850* (Oxford: Clarendon Press, 1980).

Chapter 5 The Era of the 'Pax Britannica', c. 1815–80

Anderson, O., *A Liberal State at War. English Politics and Economics during the Crimean War* (London: Macmillan, 1967).
Bailes, H., 'Technology and imperialism: a case study of the Victorian army in Africa', *Victorian Studies*, vol. 24 (1980), pp. 82–104.
Barnett, C., *The Collapse of British Power* (Gloucester: Allen Sutton, 1972/84).
Bartlett, C. J., *Great Britain and Seapower, 1815–1853* (Oxford: Clarendon Press, 1963).
Belich, J., *The New Zealand Wars and the Victorian Interpretation of Racial Conflict* (London: Penguin, 1988).
Bond, B., *Victorian Military Campaigns* (London: Hutchinson, 1967).
Bond, B., *The Victorian Army and the Staff College 1854–1914* (London: Eyre Methuen, 1972).
Bourne, K, *The Foreign Policy of Victorian England 1830–1902* (Oxford: Clarendon Press, 1970).
Cunningham, H., *The Volunteer Force. A Social and Political History 1859–1908* (Hamden, Conn.: Archon Books, 1975).
Davis, L. E. and Huttenback, R. A., *Mammon and the Pursuit of Empire. The Political Economy of British Imperialism, 1860–1912* (Cambridge: Cambridge University Press, 1986).
Gordon, D. C., *The Dominion Partnership in Imperial Defence, 1870–1914* (Baltimore, Md: Johns Hopkins University Press, 1965).
Harries-Jenkins, G., *The Army in Victorian Society* (London: Routledge & Kegan Paul, 1977).
Headrick, D. R., 'The tools of imperialism: technology and the expansion of European colonial empires in the nineteenth century', *Journal of Modern History*, vol. 51, no. 2 (1979), pp. 231–63.
Howard, C. H. D., *Britain and the Casus Belli, 1822–1902* (London: Athlone Press, 1974).
Jeffery, K., 'The eastern arch of Empire: a strategic view 1850–1950', *Journal of Strategic Studies*, vol. 5, no. 4 (1982), pp. 531–9.
Lambert, A., *Battleships in Transition. The Creation of the Steam Battlefleet 1815–1860* (London: Conway Maritime Press, 1984).
Platt, D. C. M., *Finance, Trade and Politics in British Foreign Policy, 1815–1914* (Oxford: Clarendon Press, 1968).
Preston, A. and Major, J., *Send a Gunboat. A Study of the Gunboat and its role in British policy, 1854–1904* (London: Longman, 1967).
Rasor, E. L., *Reform in the Royal Navy. A Social History of the Lower Deck 1850–1880* (Hamden, Conn.: Archon Books, 1976).
Rich, N., *Why the Crimean War? A Cautionary Tale* (London: University Press of New England, 1985).
Robinson, R. and Gallagher, J., *Africa and the Victorians. The Official Mind of Imperialism* (London: Macmillan, 1967).
Schroeder, P. W., 'The Nineteenth Century International System: Changes in the Structure', *World Politics*, vol. 39, no. 1 (1986), pp. 1–26.

Singer, J. D. and Small, M. D., 'Formal alliances, 1815–1939. A Quantitative description', *Journal of Peace Research*, vol. 3, no. 1 (1966), pp. 1–32.

Skelly, A. R., *The Victorian Army at Home. The Recruitment and Terms and Conditions of Service of the British Regular, 1859–1899* (London/Montreal: Croom Helm and McGill-Queen's University Press, 1977).

Spiers, E., *Army and Society, 1815–1914* (London: Longman, 1980).

Strachan, H., *Wellington's Legacy. The Reform of the British Army 1830–1854* (Manchester: Manchester University Press, 1984).

Yapp, M., *Strategies of British India. Britain, Iran and Afghanistan 1798–1850* (Oxford: Clarendon Press, 1980).

Chapter 6 The Rise and Fall of the 'Blue Water' Policy

Burk, K. M., *Britain, America and the Sinews of War* (London: Allen & Unwin, 1984).

French, D., *British Economic and Strategic Planning, 1905–1915* (London: Allen & Unwin, 1982).

French, D., *British Strategy and War Aims, 1914–1916* (London: Allen & Unwin, 1986).

Friedberg, A. L., *The Weary Titan. Britain and the Experience of Relative Decline, 1895–1905* (Princeton, NJ: Princeton University Press, 1988).

Gooch, J., *The Plans of War. The General Staff and British Military Strategy c. 1900–1916* (London: Routledge & Kegan Paul, 1974).

Gooch, J., *The Prospect of War. Studies in British Defence Policy 1847–1942* (London: Frank Cass, 1981).

Howard, M., *The Continental Commitment. The Dilemma of British Defence Policy in the Era of the Two World Wars* (London: Temple Smith, 1972).

Jordan, J. (ed.), *Naval Warfare in the Twentieth Century 1900–1945* (London: Croom Helm, 1977).

Kennedy, P. M., *The Realities behind Diplomacy: Background Influences on British External Policy, 1865–1980* (London: Fontana, 1981).

Lowe, C. J. and Dockrill, M., *The Mirage of Power. Vol. One. British Foreign Policy 1902–1914* (London: Routledge & Kegan Paul, 1972).

Marder, A. J., *The Anatomy of British Seapower. A History of British Naval Policy in the Pre-Dreadnought Era, 1880–1905* (New York: Knopf, 1940).

Marder, A. J., *From the Dreadnought to Scapa Flow. The Royal Navy in the Fisher Era*, 5 vols (London: Oxford University Press, 1961–78).

Neilson, K., *Strategy and Supply: The Anglo-Russian Alliance, 1914–1917* (London: Allen & Unwin, 1984).

Schurman, D. M., *The Education of a Navy. The Development of British Naval Strategic Thought, 1867–1914* (Malbar, Fl: Robert E. Keiger, 1984).

Steiner, Z. S., *Britain and the Origins of the First World War* (London: Macmillan, 1977).

Sumida, J.T., *In Defence of Naval Supremacy. Finance, Technology, and British Naval Policy 1889–1914* (London: Unwin Hyman, 1989).

Turner J. (ed), *Britain and the First World War* (London: Unwin Hyman, 1988).

Williamson, S. R., *The Politics of Grand Strategy: Britain and France prepare for War, 1904–1914* (Cambridge, Mass.: Harvard University Press, 1969).

Wilson, T., *The Myriad Faces of War* (London: Gower, 1986).

Woodward, D., *Lloyd George and the Generals* (Newark, NJ: University of Delaware Press, 1983).

Chapter 7   Deterrence and Dependence, 1917–42

Bond, B., *British Military Policy Between the Wars* (Oxford: Clarendon Press, 1980).
Ferris, J., *Men, Money and Diplomacy. The Evolution of British Strategic Policy, 1919–1926*. (Ithaca, NY: Cornell University Press, 1989).
Gibbs, N. H., *Grand Strategy. Vol. 1: Rearmament Policy* (London: Her Majesty's Stationery Office, 1976).
Grieves, K., *The Politics of Manpower, 1914–1918* (Manchester: Manchester University Press, 1988).
Howard, M., *The Continental Commitment. The Dilemma of British Defence Policy in the Era of the Two World Wars* (London: Temple Smith, 1972).
Jeffery, K., *The British Army and the Crisis of Empire, 1918–1922* (Manchester: Manchester University Press, 1984).
McIntyre, W. D., *The Rise and Fall of the Singapore Naval Base, 1919–1942* (London: Macmillan, 1979).
McKercher, B., 'Wealth, power and the new international order: Britain and the American challenge in the 1920s', *Diplomatic History*, vol. 12 (1988), pp. 411–41.
Murray, W., *The Change in the European Balance of Power, 1938–39* (Princeton, NJ: Princeton University Press, 1984).
Neidpath, J., *The Singapore Naval Base and the Defence of Britain's Eastern Empire, 1919–1941* (Oxford: Clarendon Press, 1981).
Peden, G. C., *British Rearmament and the Treasury, 1932–39* (Edinburgh: Scottish Academic Press, 1979).
Perry, F. W., *The Commonwealth Armies. Manpower and Organization in the Two World Wars* (Manchester: Manchester University Press, 1988).
Reynolds, D., *The Creation of the Anglo-American Alliance, 1937–1941: A Study of Competitive Co-operation* (London: Europa, 1981).
Roger Louis, W., *British Strategy in the Far East 1919–1939* (Oxford: Clarendon Press, 1971).
Roskill, S., *Naval Policy between the Wars. Vol. 1: The Period of Anglo-American Antagonism, 1919–1929* (London: Collins, 1968).
Roskill, S., *Naval Policy between the Wars. Vol. 2: The Period of Reluctant Rearmament, 1930–1939* (London: Collins, 1976).
Shay Jr. R. P., *Rearmament in the Thirties. Politics and Profits.* (Princeton, NJ: Princeton University Press, 1977).
Smith, M., *British Air Strategy between the Wars* (Oxford: Clarendon Press, 1984).
Wark, W., *The Ultimate Enemy: British Intelligence and Nazi Germany, 1933–39* (Ithaca, NY: Cornell University Press, 1985).

Chapter 8   The End of Empire, 1942–82

Bartlett, C. J., *The Long Retreat. A Short History of British Defence Policy, 1945–1970* (London: Macmillan, 1972).
Baylis, J. (ed), *British Defence Policy in a Changing World* (London: Croom Helm, 1977).
Bowie C. J. and Platt, A., *British Nuclear Policy Making* (Santa Monica, Calif.: Rand, 1984).
Callahan, R., *Burma, 1942–45* (London: Davis-Poynter, 1978).
Dockrill, M., *British Defence since 1945* (London: Basil Blackwell, 1988).
Douglas, R., *From War to Cold War, 1942–1948* (London: Macmillan, 1981).

Edmonds, M. (ed), *The Defence Equation. British Military Systems, Policy, Planning and Performance* (London: Brassey's, 1986).

Freedman, L., *Britain and Nuclear Weapons* (London: Macmillan and the Royal Institute for International Affairs, 1980).

Hastings M. and Jenkins, S., *The Battle for the Falklands* (London: Michael Joseph, 1983).

Howard, M., *The Mediterranean Strategy in the Second World War* (London: Temple Smith, 1968).

Jackson, W. G. F., *Overlord. Normandy 1944* (London: Davis-Poynter, 1979).

James, L., *Imperial Rearguard. Wars of Empire, 1919–1985* (London: Brassey's, 1988).

Jenkins, P., *Mrs Thatcher's Revolution. The Ending of the Socialist Era* (Cambridge, Mass.: Harvard University Press, 1988).

Mihiel, H., *The Second World War* (New York: Praeger, 1968/75), Vols. 1–2.

Northedge, F. S., *Descent from Power. British Foreign Policy, 1945–1973* (London: Allen & Unwin, 1974).

Pelling, H., *Britain and the Second World War* (London: Collins, 1970).

Sainsbury, K., *The North African Landing, 1942 : A Strategic Decision* (London: Davis-Poynter, 1976).

Terraine, J., *The Right of the Line. The Royal Air Force in the European War 1939–45* (London: Hodder & Stoughton, 1985).

Thorne, C., *The Far Eastern War. States and Societies 1941–45* (London: Allen & Unwin, 1985).

Index

Abercromby, Lord 52, 53
Abercromby, Sir Ralph 97
Aberdeen, Lord 132–3
Abyssinia 190, 193
Acheson, Dean 219
Acre 104, 131
Act of Settlement 23, 38
Act of Union xviii, 3
Addington, Lord 105–7
Aden 182, 216, 218
Adjutant–General 11
Admiralty 6–8, 15–16, 18–19, 33, 34, 47, 76, 80, 92, 130–1, 132, 138, 151–2, 158, 159, 160, 163–5, 166–7, 173, 182, 183, 190, 199
Afghanistan 105, 126, 157, 181, 185
  wars 120, 126–7, 147–8
Agadir crisis 164, 168
Air Ministry 180, 209
Air Staff 182, 183, 192
Aland islands 132
Albany 74
Alexander I, Tsar of Russia 104, 108, 110–111, 114
Alexandria 100, 104, 110
Alliance of Hanover (1725) 40
Almeida 113
Alps 27, 101
Alsace-Lorraine 179
American militia 66, 69, 70, 74, 80–1, 125, 229, 233
American War of Independence xii, xvi, 7, 29, 36, 91, 125, 225, 227, 228, 229, 230, 233
  origins 62–6
  conduct 66–87
  Saratoga campaign 73–4
  southern strategy 78–82, 86
  peacemaking 82–5
Amherst, Jeffrey 52–3, 58, 63–4, 67,
Amsterdam 88
Anschluss 179, 189, 191
Anglican Church 89, 96
Anglo-Austrian alliance 60, 225
Anglo-Austrian loan convention 100
Anglo-Dutch alliance 225
Anglo-Dutch fleet 15
Anglo-Dutch wars 1
Anglo-French alliance (1716) 39, 41, 225, 239
Anglo-French Entente (1904) 156, 157, 166
Anglo-French Staff talks 168

Anglo-German antagonism 158–9
  naval race 164–5
Anglo-Prussian alliance 55–6, 60
Anglo-Japanese alliance 156, 157, 159, 166, 184
Anglo-Russian agreement (1907) 156–7, 166, 239
Anglo-Russian treaty (1942) 207
Anglo-Spanish War xii, 59, 227, 229, 233
  origins and conduct 40–1
Anglo-Turkish Commercial Convention 125
Anson, Lord 43, 47, 50, 52, 53, 80
Anti-Comintern Pact 191
Antigua 35
Antwerp 88, 94, 112
Appalachian mts. 48, 63
appeasement 175–6, 177, 187, 190–5, 199–200
Arab-Israeli war 221
Aragon 26
'Arcadia' conference 203
Archduke Charles of Austria 22, 26, 28
Argentina 222
  and invasion of Falklands islands 222–3
aristocracy 5, 8
Armenia 178
Army Council 160
Army of Observation 51, 52
'Army of Reserve' 107
Arnold-Forster, H. O. 160–1
Asquith, H. H. 165, 168, 169
  Coalition 171–2
Association movement 83–4
Assiento 24, 29
Atlantic Charter 206–7
Attila the hun 93
Attlee, Clement 213–14, 217–18
attrition 2–3, 11–12, 16, 19, 25, 30, 70, 113, 193–4, 203, 208
Auckland, Lord 127
Aurangzebe 54
Australia 124, 125, 131, 167, 201, 211, 216
Austria xii, 1, 14, 20, 24, 27, 29, 33, 39–41, 43, 44–6, 48, 49–52, 55, 62–3, 88–118, 122, 124, 131, 132, 136, 148, 149, 154, 168, 175, 178, 179, 210
  Austrian Netherlands 45, 88, 90, 93–4, 101
Axis 176, 198, 199, 202–3, 206–7, 223

Badajoz 113
Baghdad 170
  Pact 216

balance of power xii, xiii, 3, 23–4, 31, 32–3, 40, 43–4, 108, 175, 180, 182, 213, 225
Baldwin, Stanley 176, 181, 186, 190
Balfour, A. J. 153, 156, 160–1, 165
Balkans 110, 132, 169–70, 198, 199
Baltic 7, 32, 39, 77, 111, 132–3
Baltimore 115
Bank of England 17, 98
Bantry Bay 98
Bantu 127
Barbados 42
Barcelona 26, 47
Barham, Lord 109
Barnett, Correlli xvi,
Barrington, Lord 36
battle,
   of Aboukir Bay (battle of the Nile) 100, 104, 117
   of the Alma 132–3
   of Almanza 10, 27
   of Arnhem 211
   of the Ardennes 211
   of the Atlantic 207, 209, 210
   of Aughrim 14
   of Austerlitz 109, 110
   of Balaclava 123
   of Barfleur 15
   of Bassignano 47
   of Bautzen 115
   of Beachy Head 15
   of Blenheim 11, 26
   of the Boyne 14, 18
   of Brandywine 74
   of Britain 196
   of Cambrai 176
   of Camperdown 99, 117
   of Cape Passaro 40
   of Cape St Vincent 99, 117
   of Copenhagen 111
   of Caporetto 1917
   of Cowpens 81
   of Culloden 47
   of Dettingen 45
   of El Alamein 206
   of Eylau 110
   of Fontenoy 46, 47
   of Friedland 110
   of Glenshiel 40
   'Glorious First of June' 94, 99, 117
   of Guilford Court House 81
   of Hastenbeck 51
   of Hohenlinden 103
   of Imphal 212
   of Inkerman 132
   of Jena 110
   of Jutland 173
   of Kohima 212
   of La Hogue 13, 15
   of Landen 18
   of Leipzig 116
   of Leuthen 52
   of Lexington 66
   of Long Island 69, 85
   of Loos 170
   of Lutzen 115
   of Malaga 25, 41
   of Malplaquet 28
   of Marengo 103
   of Mollowitz 43
   of Oran 197
   of Oudenarde 27
   of Plassey 55, 58
   of Princeton 72
   of Quiberon Bay 36, 53–4, 55, 56
   of Ramillies 27
   of Rossbach 52
   of the Saints 13, 85
   of Salamanca 113
   of Saratoga 74, 75, 78, 83
   of Sinope 132
   of the Somme 171, 173
   of Steenkerk 18
   of Tel-el-Kebir 147
   of Trafalgar, xvi, 108–9, 173
   of Trenton 72
   of Tsushima 159
   of Valmy 88
   of Verdun 173
   of Vigo Bay 26, 30
   of Wagram 112
   of Waterloo xvi, 14,
   of Ulm 109
   of Vimiero 112
   of Vittoria 115
   of Ypres (1917) 176
   of Yorktown 76, 77, 82–3, 84
Bavaria 1, 26, 43, 45, 93, 97, 103, 112
Bay of Bengal 206
Belgium 47, 97, 100, 116, 131, 176, 214
Belle Isle 54, 56
Bengal 54–5
Bentham, Jeremy 119
   Plan for a Universal and Perpetual Peace 119
Beresford, Sir William 113
Berlin 50, 100, 110, 209
   blockade 214
Berlin Decrees 110
Bevin, Ernest 193, 213–14
Bismarck, Count Otto von 131, 148
Black Sea 132, 147
'Black Week' 155
blockade 2, 13, 25–6, 40, 56, 70, 71, 74, 92, 131, 151–2, 167, 168, 169, 173–4, 193–4, 195, 196–7, 199, 201, 237
Blucher, Marshal 116
Blue Streak 219

INDEX

'blue water' school 150–2, 154, 155–7, 161, 166, 172, 174
Board of General Officers 11, 37
Board of Ordnance 6, 108
Boers 127, 161
Boer Wars 120, 154–5, 159–60, 174, 175, 190
Bohemia 45, 50, 51
Bolsheviks 176, 178, 182
Bomarsund 132
Bomber Command 192, 209, 237
Borneo 216
Boscawen, Admiral 49, 53
Bosphorus 147
Boston 35, 65–6, 67, 68–9, 72, 73
Boulogne 108
bounties 9, 92
Braddock, Major-General 49, 50
Brazil 111
Bremen 39
Brest 5, 18–19, 46, 47, 49, 52, 53, 79
Britain
   'British way in warfare' xv, xvi, 18–19, 23, 28, 29–31, 49–52, 58–9, 87–9, 96–7, 101–2, 106–7, 109, 110–11, 117–18, 145, 166–7, 169–70, 174, 189, 196–7, 200, 225, 227, 230, 232
   colonial wars after 1815 120–1, 123–8, 141–3, 230–1
   defence policy xi, xviii, 1, 4–5, 18, 32, 119, 123–8, 146, 150, 153, 166, 176–7, 180, 187, 191–3, 202, 212–13, 220–2, 223–4, 232–3, 233–9
   defence spending xviii, 46, 57, 59–60, 63–4, 68, 83, 91, 117, 119–20, 134, 136–7, 141–2, 149–50, 154, 157–8, 172, 173–4, 179–81, 185, 187, 191, 193, 194, 204, 212–13, 217–18, 219–20, 221–2, 224, 226–8, 235–6
   electorate and defence policy 32–3, 95–6, 106, 114, 119–20, 134, 149, 153, 179–80, 190, 192–3, 212–13, 237, 239
   great power wars xii, 120, 145, 226, 229, 234
   and the North Atlantic Treaty Organization (NATO) 213–15, 216, 219–22, 224, 234–9
   and nuclear weapons 202, 213, 217–20, 221, 222, 224, 236–7
   peacetime paradigms xii–xiii, 32, 38–40, 41–2, 60, 66–4, 88, 89, 121–3, 145, 146–9, 156–7, 180, 191, 200, 215, 222, 225–7, 236–7
   and *perestroika* and *glasnost* 238–9
   policy–making elite 4–5, 24–5, 32–3, 67, 84, 89–90, 121, 148–9, 152–4, 160–1, 180, 202, 213, 232–3
   subsidies to allies xiv, xv, xvi, 20, 23, 30, 39, 40, 45, 49, 52, 59, 93, 94, 99, 101, 103, 112, 113, 115–16, 118, 171, 194, 197–8, 204, 228
   taxation and public finance 4, 16–17, 22–4, 51, 53, 56–7, 60, 64–5, 71, 83, 98, 99, 106, 118, 119–20, 134, 136, 149–50, 164

   wartime paradigms xiii, xiv–xviii, 29–31, 58–60, 75–6, 87, 117–18, 166–7, 172–4, 195–200, 210–11, 223–4, 227–33
   withdrawal from east of Suez after 1945 202, 216–17, 220–1, 223–4
British army xv, xvi, 8–11, 33, 36–8, 46, 52, 69–70, 85–7, 91, 94–5, 101, 107, 112–13, 116–17, 123–30, 132–4, 151, 154, 159–63, 167–8, 184–6, 226
   administration 11, 92, 128, 133–4, 161–3
   deployment of land forces xviii, 10–11, 18, 19–20, 29–31, 46, 55, 58–60, 66, 68, 78, 81–2, 87, 93–4, 107, 112–13, 116, 117, 124–5, 137, 138, 141, 159, 162–3, 167–8, 172–3, 174, 181, 185, 192, 193, 195, 198–9, 200, 205–6, 210–11, 214, 218–19, 221, 223–4, 228–32
   establishment 9–10, 21, 37–8, 45, 58–9, 64, 67–8, 77–8, 91–2, 101, 107, 116, 160, 162–3, 181, 185, 195–6, 197, 205, 226
   estimates xvii–xviii, 59–60, 64, 160, 161–2, 181, 184, 227
   logistics 69, 72–3, 86, 133, 143, 167
   officer corps 8–9, 36–7, 64, 91, 92, 128–9, 184, 186
   mercenaries 10–11, 16, 30–1, 38, 45, 51, 59, 68, 82–3, 87, 92, 116, 118, 130, 221, 228, 229, 230
   recruiting rank and file 9–10, 64, 77–8, 86–7, 91, 92, 97, 107, 129–30, 135, 162, 171–2, 177, 181, 184, 194, 238
   standing army controversy 20–2, 226
   training 37–8, 64, 91, 172
British Army of the Rhine (BAOR) 215, 234
British Expeditionary Force 161–3, 166, 169–74, 188, 189, 190, 193, 201
Bruges declaration 235
Brunswick 40, 68,
Brussels 47, 94, 211
   Pact 214
Bucharest 173
Buenos Aires 110
Bukhara 147
Bulgaria 170, 171, 178, 179
Buller, Sir Redvers 155
burden sharing 234, 237
Burgoyne, Sir John 73–4
Burke, Edmund 95–6
   Reflections on the Revolution in France 95
Burma 200, 201, 211–12
   wars 120
'business as usual' 168–70, 173, 174
Bute, Lord 55–6, 63
Byng, Admiral 50

Cabinet 25, 49, 67, 90, 112, 116, 128, 151, 152, 160, 161, 168, 170, 180, 181, 184, 187, 189, 190, 191, 192, 213, 232
   committee on manpower 177
   Defence Committee 153, 160

Cabinet (cont.)
  finance committee 181
  Imperial War Cabinet 180
  Land Forces Committee 197
  War Cabinet 195, 196
Cadiz 19, 25, 47, 108–9, 112, 113
Cairo 147
Calcutta 54, 55, 104, 126
Camberley 133
Cambridge, Duke of 135, 152, 153
Campbell-Bannerman, Sir Henry 163, 165
Canada 28, 48, 49, 53, 56, 57, 63, 67, 74, 78, 79, 82, 115, 124, 125, 128, 184, 206
Canning, George 111, 112, 122
Canton 134
Cape Breton 42, 48
Cape Colony 122, 149
Cape Horn 43
Cape of Good Hope 97, 99, 104
captain-general 11, 25
Carlisle, Earl of 75
Carnarvon, Lord 151
Carnatic 54, 105
Caribbean 7, 19, 42–3, 53–4, 59, 64, 78, 86, 93–4, 97, 233
Cartagena 42, 43, 47, 53
Carteret, John (Earl Granville) 42, 45–6
Caspian sea 157, 178
Casablanca conference 207–8
Castile 26
Castlereagh, Lord 111, 112–13, 115–16, 117
Catalonia 19, 20
Catholic emancipation 105
Caucasus 178
Central Powers 169–73, 176
Ceylon 35, 76, 99, 105, 122
Chancellor of the Exchequer 93, 134, 135, 188, 189
Chandernagore 54
Childers, Erskine 165
  The Riddle of the Sands 165
Cardwell, Edward
  Cardwell system 107, 138–41, 154, 159–60, 161–2, 185
Caucasus 177
Chamberlain, Austen 187
Chamberlain, Neville, 176, 188, 189, 190–2, 194–6, 199, 200, 223, 237
Chamberlain, Joseph 156, 158
Charles II of Spain 22
Charles III of Spain 55
Charles IV of Spain 111
Charles XII of Sweden 39
Charleston 35, 69, 81, 82, 84
chartism 125, 134
Chatham 6, 35
Cherbourg 52, 94, 135
Chesapeake Bay 74, 82, 115
Chesterfield, Lord 57

Chief of Air Staff 182, 208–9
Chief of the Imperial General Staff 162, 171, 178, 203
China (see also Opium Wars) xii, 120, 121, 126, 131, 156, 182, 184, 211–12
Chisolm, H. W. xvii
Churchill, Lord Randolph 153
Churchill, Winston 165, 192–3, 195–200, 202–4, 206–7, 210–11, 213, 215, 218, 232
Cisalpine Republic 97
Ciudad Rodrigo 113
civil list 21
Clarke, Sir George 160
Clausewitz, Carl von xiii, 62
  On War xiii–xiv
Clinton, General 72, 73, 79, 80–1, 85
Clive, Sir Robert 55, 58
Coastal Command 209
Cobden, Richard 121, 124, 134
Coercive Acts 75
Cold War 213–14, 234–5, 238–9
Collingwood, Admiral 92
Colomb, Sir John 150–1
  The Protection of our Commerce and Distribution of Our Naval Forces Considered 150–1
Colomb, Admiral P. H 151
Colonial Conferences 167
Colonial Defence Committee 151, 160
colonial levies 58–9
Colonial Office 180
Colonial Secretary 158
Combined Army 11,
Combined Chiefs of Staff 203
commander-in-chief 11, 91, 128, 133, 135, 152, 153, 160
Commissary General 11, 128
Committee of Imperial Defence 160–1, 164, 165–8, 183
  chiefs of staff sub-committee of 180, 187, 192, 193, 194, 195, 197, 214, 215, 218
Commonwealth 213, 216, 217, 220
communications 14
Concert of Europe 121, 149
Concord 66
conduct of war 11–13, 26, 31, 67, 85–6, 89–90, 93, 121, 141–3, 152, 204
Congress of Berlin 147
Congress System 122
Connecticut 67
conscription (national service) 10, 95, 107, 154, 157, 160, 166, 171–2, 181, 185, 194, 216, 238
Constantinople 108, 110, 147, 169–70, 178
Continental Army 66, 69–71, 73, 74, 79, 81–2, 85–6
continental bills 72, 81, 87
Continental System 110–111, 114
Convention of Cintra 112
Convention of Klosterseven 51, 52

Convention of Westminster 49
convoys 177
Copenhagen 103, 111
Corbett, Sir Julian xiv–xv,
    Some Principles of Maritime Strategy xiv–xv,
Corfu 108, 109
Cornwallis, Lord 81–2
Corunna 112
Cossacks 178
Council of Trade 16
County Associations 162
Crimean War xii, 120, 122, 123, 128, 129, 130, 131, 134, 227, 230–1
    origins 132
    conduct 132–4
criminals 9
'crimps' 9, 92
Cromwell, Oliver 226
Crown Point 52
'Cruisers and Convoys' Act 25
Cuba 43
Cumberland, Duke of 36, 37–8, 46, 47, 51
Curragh 'mutiny' 153
customs 17
Cyprus 147, 216, 218, 219
Cyrenaica 198
Czechoslovakia 179, 191–2, 193, 195, 221

Dalhousie, Lord 127
Dalmatia 97
Dalrymple, Sir Hugh 112
Danube, river 26, 109, 132
Dardanelles 110, 147, 231
    campaign of 1915 169–70, 172
Davenant, Charles 24
    An Essay Upon Ways and Means of Supplying War 24
Deane, P. xvii
Declaration of Independence 69, 82
Declaration of Rights 66
defence industries 188–9
Defence Requirements Committee 187–8, 190
Defence White Paper
    (1950) 215
    (1957) 218–19
    (1989) 235
Defoe, Daniel 21
de Grasse, Admiral 82
Delaware, river 74, 115
Demerara 97, 107
Dender, river 12
Denmark 10, 16, 40, 103, 110–11, 211
Deptford 6, 35,
Derby 46
deterrence 176, 182, 184, 186, 188, 189, 190, 192, 194, 195, 199–200, 202, 217–20, 222, 237
Devon 80
Devonshire, Duke of 50

d'Estaing, Admiral 79–80
Dieppe raid 204
Dill, Sir John 203
dilution 189
'Diplomatic Revolution' 225
Directorate of Naval Ordnance 164
Director of Military Intelligence 151
Disraeli, Benjamin 123, 147–8
Dominica 56
Dominions 177, 179, 180, 182, 185, 187, 190–1, 193, 198–200, 205–6
Douai 12
Dyle, river 12,
Dual Alliance 148, 158, 165
Dulles, John Foster 215
Duncan, Admiral 99
Dundas, Henry (Lord Melville) 90, 93, 100, 103–5, 108, 116–17
Dunkirk 12, 19, 46, 196, 201, 212

East Anglia 108
'easterners' 171
East India Company 17, 54–5, 65, 104–5, 125, 126
    army 54–5, 58–9, 97, 104–5, 124, 127, 136–7, 229
    Eden, Anthony 192–3, 199, 207, 215, 217
    Edict of Nantes 4
    Egypt 100, 103, 104, 105, 123, 149, 165, 169, 172, 182, 193, 198, 216, 217, 231
        war of 1840–1 120, 123, 131
        invasion of in 1882 147–8
Eighth Air Force 209
Eighth Army 205
Eisenhower, General Dwight D. (later President) 210, 217
Elba 116
Elbe, river 210
Elector of Hanover 23, 38–9,
Elizabeth, Tsaritsa 55
Ellenborough, Lord 127
Emden 52
England
    see Britain
English Harbour 35
Enniskillen 14
Esher, Lord 160
    Committee 160
Euphrates, river 123
Euro-group 221
European Defence Community 215
European Economic Community (EEC) 221, 234, 236
excise 17, 57
'Experimental Mechanized Force' 186

Falkland Islands 63
    war 221–2, 224

Ferdinand of Brunswick 52, 55, 57
Ferrol 46, 108–9
Fighter Command 196
financial revolution 16–18, 23,
Finland 132,196
First Lord of the Admiralty 6, 50, 129, 130, 136, 138, 195
First Lord of the Treasury 32
First World War xii, xv, 179, 196, 223, 227, 228, 231, 232
  origins and British military planning 165–8
  British strategic policy 1914–17 168–74
  British strategic policy 1917–18 176–8
  war aims 176–7
Firth of Forth 27, 165
Fisher, Sir John 159, 160, 163–5, 166–7
Fisher, Sir Warren 188
Flanders 9, 14, 18, 19, 26–8, 30–1, 45, 48, 59, 91, 116, 230
Fletcher, Andrew 20
'flexible response' 220
Florida 42, 56, 63, 79, 82, 84, 85
Forbes, General 53, 58
Foreign Office 125, 157, 161, 165, 166, 180, 186, 190, 207, 213
Foreign Secretary 84, 90, 109, 111, 122, 187, 192, 199, 215
Fort Duquesne 49, 53, 58
fortresses 12–13, 113
Fort Ticonderoga 52, 53
Fort William Henry 52
Fourteenth Army 212
Fox, Charles James 84, 95, 109–10
France xii, xv, xvi, 1–31, 32–60, 62–3, 68, 71, 73–80, 82, 85, 88–118, 122, 123, 136, 147, 148, 161, 162, 166–71, 173–4, 175, 179, 182, 190, 191, 193, 195–6, 203, 214–15, 231
  air force 183, 192
  army 14, 18, 19, 26, 27, 28, 46, 79, 89–90, 98, 111–12, 124, 131, 154, 166, 174, 194, 197, 230
  Dauphin 22
  Directory 98, 100, 101
  famine 19, 27
  Grand Armee 89, 90, 109, 115
  Indian empire 54–5, 56, 105–6
  National Assembly 88
  navy 5–6, 13, 15–16, 25, 36, 47, 49, 50, 52, 53–4, 57, 62–3, 76–7, 80, 82, 98, 103, 108–9, 123, 130, 135–6, 148, 151, 152, 154, 158, 165, 199, 227
  tariff policies 3
  taxation and public finance 17, 57, 77, 82, 85
  West Indian islands 41–2, 53–4, 56, 78–9, 85, 93–4, 105–6
Frederick the Great xvi, 43, 45, 47, 49, 50, 51–2, 55–6, 57
free trade 125–6

French Revolution 62
French Revolutionary Wars xii, 88–105, 119, 226, 228, 230, 232
  origins 88–90
  War of the First Coalition 90–9
  War of the Second Coalition 100–5
Fructidor, *coup d'etat* 99

Gage, General 65–7, 72, 85
Gallipoli peninsular 170
Galway 14
Galway, Earl of 26, 27
Gambia 63
Gates, General 74
Geddes, Sir Eric 181
  axe 227
general staff 133, 152, 153, 160–2, 166–8, 185
General Strike 183
Geneva Disarmament Conference 187
Genoa 47, 97, 108
gentry 5, 8,
George I 32–3, 36–9, 120
George II 32–3, 36–8, 45, 50–1, 52
George III 55, 67, 75, 78, 79, 105, 110
Georgia 42, 48, 79, 81, 82, 178
Germain, Lord George 67, 69, 73–4, 79
Germany xv, xvi, 14, 26, 32, 45, 51, 52, 53, 55–6, 59, 103, 108, 148, 156–7, 161, 166, 168–74, 175–9, 186, 187–8, 190–201, 203–4, 207–12, 213
  army xv, 178
  Confederation 122
  navy 154, 158–9, 163–4, 168, 173, 183, 227
  rearmament in 1930 187–90, 192, 193–4, 197
Gibraltar 15, 35, 37, 40, 55, 76, 80, 81, 82, 85, 104, 128
Gladstone, William Ewart 134, 147–8, 152
Global Strategy Paper 1952 218
Glorious Revolution 1, 3, 4, 5, 88, 232
Godolphin, Sidney 25
Gorbachev, President 234–5, 237
Goree 53, 56
Graham G. S. xvi
Graham, Sir James 130, 132
Grand Alliance
  in Nine Years War 3, 14, 16, 19, 33, 60
  in War of the Spanish Succession 24, 26, 28–9, 33, 60
  after 1714 33, 48
Grand Banks 42
Grant, General U.S 204
Great Lakes 48, 50, 53, 85, 115
great powers xi–xii, 1, 147, 148, 176–7, 202, 214
Great Northern War 7, 39
Great Reform Act (1832) 119
Greece 131, 169–70, 194, 198, 204, 214, 236
Greene, Nathanael 81
Grenada 56, 80, 97

INDEX

Grenville, George 64
Grenville, Lord 90–1, 92, 93, 100–1, 103, 105, 109–10
Grey, Lord 124–5
Grey, Sir Charles, 93–4
Grey, Sir Edward 156, 164, 168
Grey, Sir George 126
Guadeloupe 54, 85, 94, 97
guerre de course 15–16, 25, 47, 56

Haddock, Admiral 42
Hague Peace Conference 164
Haig, Sir Douglas 153, 171, 176, 177, 178
Haiti 105
Haldane, R. B. (later Lord) 161–3
half-pay 33–4
Halifax 35, 69, 82
Halifax, Lord 192, 193
Hamburg 209
Hankey, Sir Maurice 187–8
Hanover 10, 23, 33, 38–9, 41, 45, 46, 49, 50–1, 52, 109–10
Hanoverian regime 229
Harding, President Warren 184
Hardinge, Lord 127
Hardwicke, Lord 45
Harley, Robert, Earl of Oxford 25, 28–9, 31
Hartington, Marquis of 152
Harwich 35
Hastings, Lord 105
Havana 42, 55, 56
Hawke, Admiral 36, 47, 53, 80
'head money' 36
Healey, Dennis 220–1
Heath, Edward 221
Heligoland 122
Herat 127
Herbert, Sidney 123
Hesse 40, 49, 68
Hicks Beach, Sir William 158
Hiroshima 212
Hitler, Adolf xvi, 187, 190, 191–2, 193, 194, 196, 198, 199, 207
HMS *Dreadnought* 163–5
HMS *Invincible* 163
HMS *Prince of Wales* 204
HMS *Repulse* 204
HMS *Warrior* 136, 154
Holderness, Earl of 32, 50, 51
Holland xii, 1, 3, 10, 14, 18, 23–9, 32, 39–40, 41, 46, 48, 49, 62, 71, 75, 85, 88–9, 94, 96–7, 100, 101, 106, 131, 193, 211, 214
Home Secretary 84, 90, 128
Honduras 63
Hong Kong 124, 126
Hood, Admiral 85
Horse Guards 125, 128, 135
House of Lords 5, 82

House of Commons 5, 16, 18, 21, 23, 36, 60, 67, 82–4, 87, 93, 95, 117, 119–20, 128, 134, 230
Howard, Michael xvi–xvii
Howe, Lord Richard 69–70, 79, 94, 99
Howe, Sir William 69–70, 73, 74, 79, 85
Howick, Viscount 110, 128
Hudson's Bay 29
Hudson, river 52, 67, 74
Huguenots 5, 8,
Hundred Years' War xiii
Hungary 179
Hussein, King of Jordan 219

Iberian Peninsula 26–31, 230
Imperial Conference 184, 187, 191
Imperial Federation League 151
Imperial Federation (Defence) Committee 151
income tax 57, 99, 119, 134, 135, 149–50, 155
India
  and the War of the Austrian Succession 54, 229
  and the Seven Years' War 54–5, 56, 229
  and the American War of Independence 75, 79, 229
  and the French Revolutionary and Napoleonic Wars 100, 104–5, 109
  British expansion in after 1815 123, 125, 126–7
  defence of, after 1880 147–8, 151, 157, 165, 169, 177–8, 180, 182, 185, 200, 201
  independence 202, 216
India Act 104
Indian Army (after 1858) 136–7, 144, 178, 185, 198, 205, 216, 231
'Indianization' 185
Indian mutiny 120, 133, 134, 169
industrial revolution xiii, 106, 117, 120, 149
Inskip, Sir Thomas 190
invasion panics ('bolt from the blue') 123, 134–5, 148, 151, 162, 165–6, 183, 191, 226
International Monetary Fund 217
Ionian Islands 100
Iraq 182, 199, 216
Ireland 9, 14–15, 64, 97–8, 99, 106, 128, 182
  army xviii, 21, 60, 64
  Exchequer xviii, 21, 29, 60
Israel 217
Istria 97
Italy xii, 14, 27, 29, 32, 45, 47, 97, 100, 101, 103, 106, 108, 148, 149, 152, 154, 165, 169–70, 172, 175, 176, 190, 192, 193, 197–9, 203, 231

Jacobites 4, 14–15, 19, 27, 37, 39, 40, 46–7, 51, 89, 226
Jamaica 35, 42, 128
James II 1, 4, 14–15, 20, 21, 24, 226
James III 24, 28
Japan xii, 154, 158, 175, 178, 182, 183–4, 186, 187–8, 190, 191, 192, 203

Jervis, Sir John (later Lord St Vincent) 99, 107–8
Johnson, Thomas 23
Joint Chiefs of Staff 203
Joint Naval and Military Committee 153
Joseph, Emperor of Austria 28
Journals of the House of Commons xviii

Kabul 127, 157
Kaiser Wilhelm II of Germany xvi
Kellog–Briand Pact 186
Kennedy, President John 218
Kennedy, Paul xvi
Kent 108
Kenya 216, 217, 219
'Khaki election' 155
Khandahar 157
Kinsale 35
Kitchener, Lord 169, 170, 172
Korean war 214, 218
Kut 170
Kuwait 219

labouring classes 10
labour market 10
La Gloire 136
Lagos 16, 53
Lake Champlain 115
Lake George 52
land tax 17, 40–1, 57, 83, 98, 99
Lansdowne, Lord 161, 176
Layne, Christopher xv
League of Armed Neutrality 75–6, 103
League of Frankfurt 45
League of Nations 175, 176, 179, 180, 186, 187, 193
League of the Three Emperors 148
Lend Lease Programme 196–7, 204, 212
Leopold of Austria 22, 24
Levant 29, 100, 108, 109
Levee en Mass Act 107
Libya 199, 216
Liddell Hart, Sir Basil xv, 189
Liege 48
Ligurian Republic 97
Lille 27
Limerick 14–15
limited war 62, 85–7, 89
Lisbon 55, 111, 113, 215
Liverpool, Lord 112–13, 119–20, 125
Lloyd George, David 153, 164, 171, 174, 176, 177, 178, 179, 180, 181, 183–4, 232
Lombardy 23
London 14, 46, 124, 126, 151, 167, 183, 193, 222
  Naval Conferences 186, 189, 190
Londonderry 14
Long Island 70
Lords of Committee 25
Lorraine 41

Louis XIV of France xvi, 1, 14–22, 28–9, 33, 41, 71, 89
Louis XV of France 55, 71,
Louis XVI 74–5
Louisburg 42, 47, 52, 53
Louisiana 48, 76
Louis Napoleon 134, 135
Louis Philippe 135
Low Countries 12–13, 14, 24, 27, 45, 63, 71, 93–4, 99, 100, 105, 112, 183, 188, 190, 232
loyalist associations (1790s) 95–6
loyalist militia (American War of Independence) 68, 69, 70, 73, 74, 78, 79–82, 84, 86
'loyalty loan' 99
Luddites 114
Luftwaffe 190, 192, 195
Luxembourg 214
Lys, river 12

MacDonald, Ramsay 181, 186, 190
Macmillan, Harold 217, 218, 219, 220
Madrid 22, 23, 26–7, 28, 112, 113
Madison, President 114
Madras 48, 54
Maestricht 48
Mahan, A. T. xiv–xv, xvi, 151, 152
  The Influence of Sea Power upon History xiv–xv,
  The Influence of Sea Power upon the French Revolution and Empire, 1793–1812 xiv–xv,
Mahdist rising 169
Maine 28
Malacca 97
Malaya 97, 167, 200, 201, 216, 220
Malta 100, 105, 109, 122, 128, 165
Manchester School 121, 125, 134
Manchuria 187
Manila 55
Maori wars 126, 127–8
Maratha Confederation and wars 104–5, 120, 126
Maria Theresa 41, 43, 45
Marlborough, Duke of xiv, xv, 8, 11, 25, 26–8, 153
Marshall, General George 204
  aid 214
Martello towers 108
Martinique 19, 53, 54, 56, 109
Massachusetts 28, 59, 66, 67
Massena, Marshal 111–12
Master-General of the Ordnance 11, 128
Mathews, Admiral 46
Mauritius 100, 122
McKenna, Reginald 171–2, 173, 237
McMahon Act 217, 218
Mediterranean 7, 19, 34, 35, 39–40, 47, 50, 53, 86, 100, 102, 132, 159

Mediterranean (cont.)
  Agreements of 1887 149
Medway, river 5
Mehemet Ali 120, 123, 131
Mensheviks 178
mercantilism 3–4, 16
mercenaries 10–11, 16, 20, 38, 45, 68, 92, 228, 230
Merv 147
Mesopotamia 172, 179, 182, 231
Metropolitan Police Act (1829) 123
Middle East, 177, 178, 180, 182
  war in, 1940–43 198–9, 205–6
Milan 22
militia 38, 53, 58, 87, 95, 101, 107, 117, 135–6, 161, 162, 230
Militia Act 51
Mill, James 119
Minister for the Co-ordination of Defence 190
'Ministry of All the Talents' 109–10
Ministry of Defence xi, 222, 236
Ministry of Munitions 171
Minorca 35, 40, 50, 53, 56, 76, 80, 81, 82, 84, 85
Mississippi, river 56, 76, 85
Mitchell, B. R. xvii
Moldavia 132
Monmouth, Duke of 15
Monongahela, river 50
Mons 18
Montgomery, Field Marshal Sir B. 205–6, 210–11
Montreal 52, 53
Moore, Sir John 112
Morea 108
Morocco 156, 159, 162, 166
Mountbatten, Lord Louis 212
Moyle, Walter 20
'muddling through' 232–3
Munich Agreement (1938) 191–2, 193
Municipal Corporation Act (1835) 123
Mutiny Act 128
Mussolini, Benito 207, 208
Mysore 100

Nagasaki 212
Namur 17, 18
Naples 22, 93, 100, 105, 108, 109
Napier, Sir Charles 132
Napoleon xvi, 89, 99–116
  Napoleonic Wars xii, xiii, xiv, 105–18, 119, 122, 132, 135, 226, 228, 230, 232
  origins 105–6
  War of the Third Coalition 108–10
  War of the Fourth Coalition 115–16
Nasser, President 217
national debt 16–18, 57, 83, 98, 119, 134
National government 187, 188
National Service League 166
Narvik 196
Naval Defence Act 152

naval war staff 164
naval stores 6–7, 39, 77
Navigation Acts 3, 92
Navy Board 6, 69, 76, 77, 130
Navy League 151
Nazi-Soviet Pact 195, 207
Nelson, Admiral Lord 99, 100, 108–9, 165, 210
Netherlands
  see Holland
'New Armies' 169, 172
Newcastle, Duke of 32, 33, 38, 46, 47, 48–50, 55, 60
New England 42, 47, 58, 66, 67–8, 74, 114–15
Newfoundland 29, 42, 56, 85
New Jersey 70, 72, 73, 74
New Orleans 115
'New Standard' fleet 190, 199
New York 35, 48, 52, 67, 69, 70, 71, 72, 73, 74, 79, 81, 82, 84, 170
New Zealand 124, 126, 127–8, 133, 167, 198, 211, 216
Niagara 53
Nice 88, 93
Nijmegan 211
Nile, river 149
Nine Years War xii, 10, 22, 227, 228, 232
  conduct 14–20
  origins 1–2
Nivelle offensive 174
Nizam of Hyderabad 105
Normandy 210–11
North Carolina 81, 82
North, Lord 65–6, 67, 68, 75, 77, 83–4, 233
North America (see also American War of Independence)
  and the War of the Spanish Succession 28–9, 229
  and the War of the Austrian Succession 47, 229
  and the Seven Years War 48–9, 50, 52–3, 229
North Sea oil 235
North-West Frontier 127, 133, 160, 161, 185, 187
Norway 196, 204
Nott, Sir John xi, 222
Nova Scotia 28, 35, 48, 69, 124

Ohio, river 48–9, 53
Opium Wars 120, 125, 126, 133
Orders-in-Council 110–11, 114
Orenburg 157
Orkney islands 173
Osborne, Admiral 53
Ottoman Empire xii, 32, 63, 100–1, 106, 110, 123, 125, 131, 132–3, 147–8, 165, 169–70, 177, 178, 182
Oudh 105
Oxus, river 147

Paine, Tom 89, 119
  The Rights of Man 89

Pall Mall Gazette 148
Palestine 178, 179, 191
Palmerston, Viscount 122, 125, 126, 131, 133, 134
Panama 40, 43
   Canal 159
Paris 88, 90, 101, 211
Parliament 4–5, 7, 9, 10, 17, 20–1, 23, 36, 38, 39, 51, 57, 64–6, 68, 75, 79, 83–4, 99, 128, 155, 228, 232
Parliamentary Reform Act
   of 1867 149
   of 1884 149
   of 1918 179
Parma 41, 106
Paul I, Tsar of Russia 100, 103
Paymaster General 11
Peace of
   Amiens 103, 105–6, 107
   Brest–Litovsk 178
   Campo Formio 97, 100
   Luneville 103, 105
   Paris 55–6, 63
   Pressburg 109, 112
   Ryswick 20
   Utrecht xiii, 28–9, 31, 39, 40, 41, 50, 235
   Westphalia 88
Pearl Harbor 200
Peel, Sir Robert 134
Pelham, Henry 46
Peninsula War 111–14, 115–16, 117–18, 230
Penjdh 147
Pennsylvania 70, 74
Pepys, Samuel 33
Perceval, Spencer 112
'perfidious Albion' 113
Permanent Fighting Instructions 13
Persia 126–7, 176, 182, 199
Persian Gulf 123, 169, 216, 220
Peterborough, Earl of 26–7
Philadelphia 35, 66, 74, 79
Philip of Anjou 22–4, 26, 28, 29
Philippines 126
Piacenza 41
Piedmont 20, 100, 103, 106, 131
Pitt, William (the Elder, later Earl of Chatham) xiv, 32, 42, 47, 50–3, 55, 56, 58, 79, 83, 232
Pitt, William (the Younger) xiv, 57, 88, 90–1, 93, 95–6, 98–9, 100, 103, 104, 106, 108, 109
Plate, river 29
Plymouth 6, 15, 35
Poland 88, 94, 97, 131, 179, 194, 195, 205–6
Polaris 219–20, 222
Pollen, Arthur 164
Pondicherry 54, 55, 85
Portland, Duke of 90, 110–11, 112
Port Mahon 35
Porto Bello 40, 43
Port Royal 28, 35

Portsmouth 6, 15, 35
Portugal 1, 26, 30, 39, 93, 104, 105, 110–13, 131, 230
Potsdam conference 213
Pragmatic Army 45, 47, 48
Pragmatic Sanction 41, 225
Prague 193
President of the Board of Control of India 90
press gang 7–8
Pretoria 155
Prince of Wales (later George IV) 95
Privy Council 25
prize money 36
Protestant succession 4
protectionism 17
Prussia (*see also* Germany) xii, 10, 40, 43, 45, 48, 50, 52, 55–6, 62, 88–118, 122, 124, 131, 132, 136, 151
purchase system 8–9, 36–7, 64, 92, 128–9, 133
Pym, Francis 222
Pyrenees, mts. 40

'Quadrant' conference 210
Quadruple Alliance (1718) 40–1
Quebec 28, 52, 53, 54, 58, 210
Queen Anne 23–5, 27, 30
Queen Mary 1, 4
Queen Victoria 153
Quota Acts 95

radicalism
   in American War of Independence 83–4
   in 1790s 89, 95–6, 98, 119
   after 1815 119–21, 133
   early twentieth century 168
Raffles, Sir Stamford 125
Reagan, President Ronald 222
rearmament policy in the 1930s 187–95
Recruiting Acts 9
Reichenbach treaty 115–16
Reykjavik summit 222
Rhine, river 52, 94, 101, 105, 116, 187, 195–6, 211
Rhineland 12, 88, 179
Rhode Island 72, 79, 82
Rhur 183, 209
Ricardo, David 119
Roberts, Sir Frederick (later Lord) 147, 153, 155, 166
Robertson, Sir William 153, 171
Rochefort 47, 49, 52
Rockingham, Lord 83–5
Rodney, Admiral 82, 85
Rome 100
Rooke, Admiral 13, 18
Roosevelt, President F. D. 197, 203, 206–7, 212, 213
Royal Air Force 180, 182, 189, 190, 196, 205, 216
   'control without occupation' 182

INDEX

Royal Air Force (**cont.**)
  estimates 183, 227
  Home Defence Air Force 183, 186, 188
  and strategic bombing 183, 192, 197, 208–10
Royal Commission
  on the Defence of the United Kingdom 136, 147
  on the Defence of British Possessions and Commerce Abroad 151
  on the War in South Africa (Elgin Commission) 160
  to inquire into the civil and professional administration of the Naval and Military Departments (Hartington Commission) 152–3, 160
Royal Navy xiii, xiv, xvi, 5–8, 15–16, 33–6, 39–40, 45–7, 56–7, 63, 68, 69, 70, 76, 79–2, 82, 85, 91, 99, 108–18, 123–8, 130–3, 134–5, 136, 147, 150–1, 158–9, 163–5, 167, 168, 173–4, 180, 181, 183–4, 193–4, 196–7, 198, 204, 210, 218, 219, 226–7, 230–1, 237
  construction and repairs of ships 6–7, 15, 35–6, 56, 68, 76–7, 91–2, 107–8, 134–5, 136–8, 163–5, 184, 186, 190
  dockyards 5–6, 15, 29, 35, 76, 91–2, 107–8, 165, 226
  estimates xvii–xviii, 6, 15, 29–30, 36, 57, 68, 91, 130, 135, 138, 154, 159, 163–5, 181, 222
  officer corps 33–4, 35–6, 132
  recruitment of seamen 7–8, 34–5, 91–2, 131–2, 138
  strategy of blockade of Brest 18–19, 46, 47, 50–1, 52, 53, 56–7, 79–80, 94, 108–9
Royal United Services Institute for Defence Studies xv
Rumania 173, 194
Russell, Admiral Earl 13, 15, 19
Russell, Lord John 135
Russell, W. H. 133
Russia xii, 32, 39, 40, 49, 50, 52, 55, 63, 75, 85, 89, 93–4, 100–1, 103, 108–11, 114–16, 122, 123, 125, 126–7, 130, 131, 132–3, 147–9, 151, 152, 154, 155–7, 163, 165, 166, 168–74, 175, 177, 182, 185, 191, 192, 195, 202, 227
  Revolution of 1917 174, 176
  civil war 182
  and Second World War 199, 207, 208
  since 1945 213–14, 218–22
Russo-Finnish War 196
Russo-Japanese War 156, 159
Russo-Turkish War 110

Salem 65
Salisbury, Lord 148, 149, 152, 153, 156, 160
  committee 183
Salonika 170, 172, 178, 231
Salzburg 97
Sainte Domingue 94

Sandhurst 129, 185
San Domingo 42, 97
Sandwich, Earl of 67, 68, 79, 80
Sandys, Duncan 218, 219
Sardinia 37, 40, 45, 47, 93
Savannah 80
Savoy, 1, 14, 16, 19–20, 27–8, 30, 88, 93, 100
  Victor Amadeus, Duke of Savoy 19, 25, 26, 29, 40
Saxe, Marshal 46–7, 48
Saxony 50
Scapa Flow 173
Scheldt, river 12, 88
Scheme of Trade 4
Schleswig-Holstein crisis 131
Scotland 3, 9, 27, 40, 46–7, 128
Sebastopol 128, 132–3, 178
Second World War xii, 86, 223, 227, 228, 232, 235
  origins and British war plans 188–95
  British strategy (1939–40) 195–6
  British strategy (1940–41) 196–9
  British strategy (1941–45) 202–12
  Italian campaign 208, 210
  Second front (Operation 'Overlord') 197, 199, 204, 206, 207, 208, 210–11, 223, 231
  war against Japan 205, 206, 211–12
Secretary at War 11, 36, 91, 92, 123, 128, 129, 133
secretaries of state 11, 32–3, 50, 84
Secretary of State for America 67
Secretary of State for Defence xi
Secretary of State for War 133, 152, 153, 159, 160, 169
Secretary of State for War and the Colonies 90, 111, 124–5, 128, 133
Senne, river 12
Serbia 170
Seven Years' War xii, 32, 36, 57, 58, 59, 62, 63, 70, 72, 75, 77, 80, 83, 227, 228, 229, 232
  origins 48–50
  conduct 50–60
Select Committee on finance (1818) 119–20
Select Committee on the state of the army before Sebastopol 133
Sharif of Mecca 170
Sheerness 6, 35
Shelburne, Earl of 84–5
Shrewsbury, Earl of 28
Siam 126
Siberia 177
Sicily 22, 29, 39–40, 100, 109, 208, 210
Sick and Wounded Board 6
Sikh Wars 120, 127
Silesia 48, 49
Simla 157
Sind 105, 127
Singapore 125, 211, 218, 220
  naval base and strategy 184, 186, 187–8, 189–90, 193, 198, 202, 199–200, 201

sinking fund 98, 150, 155
Sinn Fein 182
Skybolt 219
Slim, General Sir William 212
Smith, Adam 98, 119
   An Inquiry into the Nature and Causes of the Wealth of Nations 98
Smyrna 16
social Darwinism 147
South Africa 124, 125, 149, 155, 161, 184, 193
South Carolina 69, 79, 81, 82
South-East Asia Command 205, 212
South Sea Company 42
Spain xii, 1, 3, 4, 10, 14, 19, 20, 22–3, 24–30, 35, 39–41, 43–8, 55–6, 62, 74–6, 93, 97, 105–6, 111–13, 131
   navy 35, 40, 43, 47, 62–3, 76–7, 99, 108–9
   empire 42–3, 55, 85, 97
   guerrillas 111, 113, 230
Spanish Civil War 193
Special Operations Executive 197
'special relationship' 234
Spencer, Lord 152
'splendid isolation' 225–6
Staff College 151, 160
Stalin, 207, 218
Stamp Act 65
Stanhope, Edward 152
Stanhope, Viscount 39
States General 18
Stead, W. T. 148
St Eustatius 76
St John Brodrick, W. 159–60, 161
St Lawrence, river 50, 53
St Lucia 54, 56, 79–80, 85, 97, 107
St Malo 52
St Vincent 56, 80, 97
Strategic Arms Limitation Talks Treaty (SALT 1) 221
strategic bombing (*see also* Royal Air Force)
   fear of 182, 192, 208–10
Strategic Defence Initiative 222
Stockholm 207
Stressa front 190
'substitution' 181
Sudan 169
Sudetenland 179, 191
Suez 105, 147, 147, 149, 185
   invasion of in 1956 217, 218
Suffolk, Earl of 67
Sumatra 211
Surinam 97
Sussex 108
Sutlej, river 105
Sweden xii, 1, 4, 14, 16, 39, 40, 103, 110, 115, 132, 196
Swift, Jonathan 23
   Reflections on the Conduct of the Allies 23

Switzerland 101, 103, 105, 122

Tagus, river 111, 113
Tank Corps 176, 186
Tashkent 157
Teheran conference 210
telegraph 14, 124
Tennyson, Lord 136
'Ten Year Rule' 181, 186, 187
Territorial Army 185, 188, 190, 191, 193, 194
Territorial Force 162–3, 172, 184
Territorial and Reserve Forces Bill 162
Thames, river 5
Thatcher, Margaret 221–3, 235–6
The Times 106, 133, 135, 136
The Way Forward 222
Thomson, D. xiii
Thirty Years' War 4
Tipu Sultan 100, 104, 105
Tirpitz, Admiral 158, 163, 165
Tobago 56, 85, 105, 107
Torbay 80, 94
Torres Vedras, lines of 113
Tories 22–3, 28–9, 32, 47
Torrington, Earl of 15
Toulon 19, 25, 26, 27, 46, 93–4, 100, 108–9, 152
Townshend duties 65
Townshend, Viscount 40
Transcaspia 177
Transcaucasia 178
Transjordan 182
Transport Board 101
Treasurer of the Navy 6
Treasury 11, 69, 73, 128, 134, 149–50, 157–8, 165, 181–2, 186, 188–9, 191, 193, 194, 197, 212, 222
Treaty of
   Aix–la–Chapelle 48
   Chaumont 116
   Dunkirk 213
   Lausanne 182
   Locarno 186, 187, 226
   Nanking 126
   Paris 133
   Seville 41
   Tilsit 108, 109, 110
   Versailles (1756) 50
   Versailles (1919) 175, 178–9, 182, 187, 190, 193
   Vienna 41, 93, 121–3, 235
   Westminster 39
   Worms 45
Trenchard, Sir Hugh 182–3
Trenchard, John 20
   An Argument Showing that a Standing Army is Inconsistent with a Free government and Absolutely destructive to the Constitution 20
Trident 222
'Trident' conference 208

Triple Alliance 148
Tripolitania 198
Trincomalee 35, 76, 97
Trinidad 99, 105
Triple Alliance (1788) 89
Truman, President Harry S. 212, 214
   'doctrine' 214
Turin 27
Turkey 196, 198, 203, 214
   see also Ottoman empire
Turks Island 63
Tuscany 100
Twenty-one Army Group 205–6, 210–11
'two-power standard' 152, 154, 158–9, 165, 183–4, 190, 227

U-boat warfare 174, 177, 203, 207–8, 209, 210
unconditional surrender 207
United Irishmen 97–8
United Provinces
   see Holland
United Nations 223
United States of America xii, xiii, 114–15, 149, 156, 170, 171, 182, 191, 202, 212, 216, 236
   army 204, 211
   Congress 62, 66, 69, 70, 71–2, 75, 81, 189, 217, 218
   Federal Reserve Board 173
   navy 114–15, 130, 154, 158, 159, 165, 181, 183–4, 186, 200, 204, 222
   economic assistance to Britain 175, 197, 204, 228
   and First World War 176–7
   and Second World War 202–13
   and post-war West-European security 212–14
'usable past' 233
Ushant 79

Valencia 26
Vansittart, Sir Robert 188
V-bomber 218–19
Vendee 93
Venice 97
Verden 39
Vergennes, duke of 74–5
Vernon, Admiral 43, 46
Victualling Board 6, 130
Vienna 26, 28
Villeneuve, Admiral 109
Virginia 49, 82
Vistula, river 110
volunteer corps (1790s) 96, 116, 117
volunteer corps (1800s) 107, 110, 116, 117
volunteers (after 1859) 136, 147, 159, 161, 162

Waal, river 94
Walachia 132
Walcheren 112

Waldeck 68
Wales 98
Walpole, Sir Robert 40–3, 45
War Office 91–2, 112, 128, 136, 151, 152, 153, 154–5, 157, 159, 160, 161, 181, 185, 194
War of the Austrian Succession xii, 4, 57, 58, 59, 63, 225, 227, 228, 229, 232
   origins 43–4
   conduct 44–8
War of 1812
   origins 114
   conduct 114–15
War of Jenkins's Ear xii, 57, 227, 228, 233
   origins 41–2
   conduct 42–3
'war of posts' 71
War of the Polish Succession 41
War of the Quadruple Alliance xii, 58, 227, 228, 229
   origins 39
   conduct 39–40
War of the Spanish Succession xii, 39, 227, 228, 231
   conduct 24–31
   'no peace without Spain' 27–9
   origins 22–4
   peace negotiations 27–9
Warsaw 94, 170
   Pact 235, 238, 239
Washington DC 115, 202, 203, 219, 222
Washington, George 49, 69, 70–1, 72–4, 81–2
Washington Naval Treaty 182–3, 186
Wehrmacht 194, 197, 208
Wellesley, Marquis of 104–5
Wellington, Duke of xv, 111–13, 115–16, 125, 128, 135, 153
West Africa 128, 205
'westerners' 171
western front 171, 178, 183, 189, 204, 210, 231
West Germany 222, 234–5, 237
   rearmament and NATO 214–15, 219–20
West Indies xvi, 19, 34, 35, 40, 41–3, 46, 47, 56, 57, 76, 80, 84–5, 97, 107, 230
Westminster 4
Weymouth, Viscount 67
Whigs xvi, 22–3, 27, 28, 32–3, 41–2, 90–1, 95–6, 130, 147
Whitehall 4
Wilberforce, William 93
Wilkes, John 83
William III 1–24, 31, 153, 239
   and standing army controversy 20–2
   and strategy 14–24, 30
Wilson, Harold 220
Wilson, Sir Henry 178, 185
Wilson, President Woodrow 174, 176, 177, 178, 179, 206
Windham, William 91, 103, 105

Wolfe, James 37, 53, 54
Wolseley, Lord 147, 152, 153
Woolwich 35
Wright, Q. xiii
Wyvill, Reverend Christopher 83

Yalta conference 213
yeomanry 135

Young Pretender, Charles Edward Stuart 46–7
Younge, Sir George 92, 94
York, Duke of 91, 93–5, 96, 107, 230
Yugoslavia 198

Zaman Shah 105
Zulu War 120
Zurich 101